LOGOS
Proclaiming and Witnessing to God's Word

LOGOS
Proclaiming and Witnessing to God's Word

Biblical Essays in Honour of
Prof. Dr. Scaria Kuthirakattel, SVD

Editor
Thomas Karimundackal, SJ

Christian World Imprints

First Published in 2021 by

Christian World Imprints
Christian Publishing & Books from India
C-3, Wazirpur Industrial Area
Delhi-110052
cwidelhi2017@gmail.com
www.ChristianWorldImprints.com
Phone: +91 11 41526079

ISBN: 978-93-5148-513-1

Printed in India.

Contents

Foreword

Hearing the word of God with reverence and proclaiming it with faith is an imperative of every Christian believer. Fr. Scaria Kuthirakattel SVD, as Professor of Sacred Scripture for more than 35 years, has been proclaiming, teaching and witnessing to the word of God with great zeal and commitment. St. John made it clear in the beginning of his letter, "What we have seen and heard we announce to you, so that you may have fellowship with us and our common fellowship be with the Father and His Son Jesus Christ" (1 John 1:3). Fr. Scaria has tried his best to announce and communicate the Word so that our relationship with God and our fellowmen are deepened. This book, *LOGOS*: *Proclaiming and Witnessing to God's Word*, is a fitting tribute to his erudite biblical scholarship and passionate commitment to his teaching and preaching the Word of God.

As Fr. Scaria enters his golden jubilee year of priesthood, *LOGOS* is an apt compliment for his long years of service to the Word and its proclamation through teaching. Being his student, I can say from my experience that he has not only taught the Word but also walked in the light of the Word. His simple life and clear teaching are proof of a life touched by the Word. As a member of a Society which has the proclamation of the Word as its primary charism, he has lived that to the full.

As we know, the word of God is much broader than just the text itself, because its message is discerned in the faith-community and in its real-life situation. We realise that community and its *Sitz im Leben* form *loci theologici* for experiencing God in our midst. Therefore, the role of every minister of the word of God is to help the faith-community to discover where God is calling them in the hubbub of real life. I believe that, as a teacher and minister of the word of God, this was the mission of Fr. Scaria, i.e., enabling his students and hearers to discover God's calling and presence in the concrete flux of their life situation.

When there are problems, difficulties and failings associated with the interpretation of the Bible by the common people, it is the task of the biblical scholars to show right paths of interpreting the Bible which foster transforming action. Moreover, re-reading of the Bible today in the Indian context presents no easy task of interpretation, and indeed it is a challenge. It is in this context that I appreciate the long tenure of Scaria's commitment in teaching the word of God, giving directions and orientations for biblical interpretations and enabling to understand the biblical texts in the Indian context. He has showed and underlined the proper and necessary function of scientific exegesis for drawing inspiration from the word of God.

I am indeed happy to know that his colleagues and students came together to bring out this *Festschrift* to honour their mentor and *guru.* This book presents excellent biblical themes on proclaiming, witnessing and ministering the *LOGOS* - the word of God. Papers are well presented with sound exegesis, scholarly arguments, theological and hermeneutical application to the context. I am sure that this study volume will make an important contribution to the task of interpreting the Bible in the Indian context. I am glad to notice that scholars with national and international reputations contributed to this volume.

My sincere appreciation to the editor, Fr. Thomas Karimundackal, SJ, who brought together essays from a wide spectrum of biblical exegetes and theologians whose treatments of biblical texts and theological issues have hermeneutical significance for our context today.

May the *LOGOS* - the word of God transform the society and the lives of the people.

Bishop Chacko Thottumarickal, SVD
Bishop of Indore

Editorial

"Proclaim the Word (κήρυξον τὸν λόγον) and stand upon it no matter what! ….. Preach in the full expression of the Holy Spirit - with wisdom and patience as you instruct and teach the people" (2 Tim 4:2-3). These are the words that come to my mind when I think of Prof. Scaria Kuthirakattel, SVD. Prof. Scaria, through his lectures and writings, has highlighted ways of more effective proclaiming the Word of God (ὁ λόγος τοῦ θεοῦ) in today's world and have it inspire the lives of Christians.

St. Paul gives an urgent instruction to Timothy that he "preach the Word" (2 Tim 4:1), and this instruction carries extra weight as it should be done "in the presence of God and of Christ Jesus" and also "in view of his appearing and his kingdom" (2 Tim 4:1). Therefore, for Paul, as a preacher and teacher it is not a charge to be taken lightly! It is the God-designed means to bring people to faith that they may be saved (cf. Rom 10:14-15): someone is sent by God to preach the Word; when the preacher preaches, people hear and believe; when they believe, they call on the name of the Lord and are saved. No wonder Paul speaks about the "beautiful feet" of those who bring the good news (Rom 10:15), a reference to Isaiah 52:7![1] Prof. Scaria, as a preacher and teacher, preached and taught the Word of God as God-designed means to bring his students and people to faith. He did it with "wisdom and patience" (2 Tim 4:2) contemplating "the presence of God and of Christ Jesus" (2 Tim 4:1).

One of the most joyful experiences of being a disciple is to share one's experience of Jesus with others, and this is exemplified by "bearing witness" to Jesus. As Jesus has borne witness to his Father (cf. Jn 3:11.32-33; 5:31), the truth (cf. Jn 18:37) and to himself (cf. Jn 3:33; 5:31; 8:13.14.18), Jesus asks

---

1 The concept of "beautiful feet" in Isa 52:7 is a historic reference to the delight with which the exiles received the good news from messengers who told them they were about to be delivered from captivity and restored to Jerusalem.

his disciples to bear witness to him (cf. Jn 15:26-27). For Prof. Scaria 'bearing witness to Jesus' was one of the favourite topics for discussion in the class, and he was not speaking it as lofty ideas, but as a convinced disciple of Jesus. He used to say in the class that "our task is not to proselytize or judge others, or to witness the institutionalized Church, but to witness to the Good News of God's Kingdom." For him, Jesus of Nazareth alone was the hermeneutical key to understand the 'Christ of faith,' and the 'way' of Christianity.

Vatican Council II's Dogmatic Constitution on Divine Revelation, *Dei Verbum*, has proven to one of the most important and lasting actions of the Council, injecting new life and vigour into the biblical interpretation of the Catholic Church. Prof. Scaria courageously oriented the students and Indian Church with a bold pastoral vision of a liberated church, rooted in the Sacred Scriptures. He firmly believed that the Word of God would rekindle the spark of the Catholic faith in the third millennium, would breathe new life into the role of the Scriptures would play in the Catholic Church for generations to come.

Since Dei verbum appeared in 1965 there has been a flood of new methods for the study of Scripture. This has fostered lively debate among scholars about the utility of the many methods currently employed for interpretation of Scripture. Along with his mentor George Soares Prabhu, Prof. Scaria believed that one cannot simply interpret the Scripture literally without delving deeper into the larger questions of context, history, and the evolution of the biblical interpretation over the time. Confronted with the hard socio-cultural realities of Indian society, he has pursued a variety of liberative readings and analyses of the biblical texts in view of developing a contextual biblical hermeneutics for India. He has engaged creatively in the wider debate and discussion of various facets of the Bible and liberation. He has argued that it is far less possible for modern interpreters to reduce the scope and implications of biblical texts without considering the social, cultural, political and economic struggles portrayed in the Bible and the reader. To this respect he has distanced himself from the abstract, idealist, modern, western mentality and interpretation of the Bible. Rather, he has oriented to the concrete situation of the people, the socio-economic disparity discerning the class, caste, gender inequality and their struggles for liberation.

This special volume is a token of our gratitude to Prof. Scaria Kuthirakattel, SVD. Through this book, we acknowledge his contribution not only to the Indian biblical hermeneutics and Indian Church but also at the personal level. He has personally touched and inspired us. It is our tribute to his erudite biblical scholarship and personal accompaniment.

As seen above, the title of the book, *LOGOS: Proclaiming and Witnessing to God's Word,* is drawn inspiration from his own passion and commitment to the Word of God. As a teacher and preacher of the Word of God he was passionate in proclaiming and witnessing to God's Word (*LOGOS*). We have tasted the fruits of his teaching and sharing the *LOGOS*, and know they are good, and we desire that many may receive the same blessings.

The book is divided into four parts, reflecting Prof. Scaria's biblical vision and concerns: proclaiming the *LOGOS*, witnessing the *LOGOS*, ministering the *LOGOS* and relating the *LOGOS*. God's word, as *Dei Verbum* instructs, is a living reality: it contains messages old and new that apply to God's people in every age. It is our hope that the papers in this book will provide sufficient hermeneutical and theological clarity to understand 'God's Word' for our spiritual enrichment in our *Sitz im Leben.*

In the introductory article, Dr. Wilson D'souza makes an elaborate sketch of Prof. Scaria Kuthirakattel's life-roles and academic credentials. In his own words:

> What one notices in his writings and person is the innovativeness, newness, simple to the core and man with the vision. He is abreast not only with knowledge but also the realities of day-today life. His vision of the seminary, seminarians, professors and contextualized theology is praise-worthy. His intellect is coupled with deep nature-oriented spirituality. We dare to call him a 'man of personal convictions and St. Francis of Assisi of our times.'

The first part titled "Proclaiming the LOGOS" has five scholarly presentations which basically illustrate the faith and transformative aspect of God's Word. In the first article, Prof. Henry Pattarumadathil, SJ, the Dean of the Biblical Faculty at the Pontifical Biblical Institute, Rome, exegetically explores the narrative function of the story of the two disciples who walked to Emmaus with the risen Jesus (Lk 24:13-35), and its significance for today's believers. He argues that the two disciples' journey to Emmaus symbolizes the faith-journey of every believer of all times. In the second article, Rolphy Pinto, SJ, Professor of Ignatian spirituality at the Gregorian University, Rome reads the same story of the two disciples who walked to Emmaus with the risen Jesus (Lk 24:13-35) through an Ignatian lens. According to him "reading of this Lukan passage with the interpretative key of Ignatian Rules for Discernment of Spirits enlightens the spiritual journey of the disciples, and it sheds light on the spiritual experience underlying the codified Rules for the Discernment of Spirits" in the Spiritual Exercises of St. Ignatius.

In the next article, Simon Thomas, SJ studies exegetically the story of the woman with the hemorrhage in Mt 9:20-22, and shows that she becomes a unique model of faith in the gospel, the one who secretly expressed her faith but publicly praised by Jesus. Her faith in Jesus makes her dare to break all taboos of purity and impurity and Jesus in turn recognizing her courage and sincerity praises her faith and heals her. Errol Fernandes, SJ, the Vice-Principal (Commerce) of St. Xavier's College, Mumbai analyses the Markan pericope of the storm on the lake (Mk 4:35-41) in the context of the storm of the COVID-19 pandemic. He shows that although the disciples in Mark have been portrayed in much of the Gospel as a group who were slow to understand and believe, Jesus comes to their rescue when they found themselves caught in a storm. Having anlaysed the text, he asks exegetically, how much more will he accomplish in us if we put on the attitudes of serenity, fearlessness and faith. In his paper Bryan Lobo, SJ, the Dean of the Faculty of Missiology at the Gregorian University, Rome suggests a discursive methodology to profess Christian faith in the context of religious pluralism. He argues that with such a methodology issues of "religion" "Faith", "truth" and "experience" can be understood more comprehensively, and there would be more clarity especially for a Christian comprehension of itself among other religions.

The second part titled "Witnessing the LOGOS" has six excellent presentations which basically demonstrate the challenges of witnessing to the Word. In the first article of this section Prof. Thomas Malipurathu, SVD, the emeritus Professor of New Testament at Jnana-Deepa Vidyapeeth, Pune discusses the mission manifesto of Apostle Paul, as it is emphasised in 1 Cor 1:18-25. He shows that it is Paul's dynamic interpretation of Jesus' death on the cross functions as the veritable foundation of his theology. His paper concludes with a brief reflection on the implications of this crucial concept for the life and mission of today's Christian community. In the second article, Sunil Ranjar, SJ, Professor of New Testament Greek and Exegesis at the Pontifical Biblical Institute, Rome, employing the method of redaction criticism, studies Luke's portrayal of apostles and disciples in the Gospel and Acts. He shows that Luke presents the apostles and disciples in a positive light, and the Apostles are presented as the witness-bearers of the Christ event and as the ideal leaders of the early Christian community.

Isaac Padinjarekuttu, Professor of Church History and Patristics at Oriens Theological College, Shillong and former Dean of the Faculty of Theology, Jnana-Deepa Vidyapeeth, Pune suggests a missionary theory and praxis for our times in his paper. He argues that "if mission understood as the continuation of Christ's own mission of establishing God's Kingdom is paradigmatic for the Church, we have to speak about it, find ways and means to creatively engage in it and place it where it belongs, namely, at the centre of Christian existence." Thomas Manjaly, the emeritus Professor of New Testament at Oriens Theological College, Shillong, and former member of the Pontifical Biblical Commission, explores the inspiration of Lukan Writings. He shows that although traditional technical expressions around which we have developed the notion of inspiration – "inspired by God" (2 Tim 3:16-17) or "moved by the Holy Spirit" (2 Pet 1:19-21) - are not found in Lukan Writings,

Luke was deeply conscious that he was communicating not just history, but salvation history as a Spirit-guided movement or God's saving intervention in Jesus. In the last article of this section Thomas Karimundackal, SJ illustrates the imperatives of discipleship as they are illustrated in the Gospel traditions and their call for our wholehearted commitment to the demands of Jesus on discipleship in the present day. His analysis shows that Jesus calls everyone to his discipleship and to share in his mission and bring him known to the world around us.

The third part titled "Ministering the LOGOS" has two brilliant presentations which essentially present Jesus as the teacher par excellence in communicating the Kingdom message. In the first article, Jacob Parappally, MSFS, Professor of Systematic Theology and former Dean of the Faculty of Theology, Jnana-Deepa Vidyapeeth, Pune, and former President of the Indian Theological Association (2005-2011), analyses the pedagogical strategies Jesus used in teaching and communicating the way of God, and suggests the pedagogical methods that Jesus employed as best means for ministering the Word of God today. In the second article, Naveen Rebello, SVD, a research scholar at the Pontifical Biblical Institute, Rome, and former Faculty member of Scripture at Jnana-Deepa Vidyapeeth, Pune focuses on the narrative dynamics of the "teaching" of Jesus illustrated in Mk1:21-28. He shows that Jesus' "teaching" in Mk1:21-28 is "programmatic" in the Gospel of Mark, as it opens a window to Jesus' itinerary teaching mission in Galilee for announcing the reign of God.

The final part titled "Relating the LOGOS" has four excellent presentations which principally deal with the Logos' relationship with the 'other.' In the first article, Jacob Kavunkal, SVD, emeritus Professor of Missiology at Jnana-Deepa Vidyapeeth, Pune, and former Head of the Department of Theology and Mission at the Yarra Theological Union/University of Divinity, Melbourne, presents the *Logos* as the basis of biblical universalism. Analysing the different biblical presentations of the role of the *Logos* in the Bible, he shows that the *Logos* makes the Divine an ever-open horizon where believers of all religions can meet. In the next article, Dominic S. Irudayaraj, SJ, Professor of Old Testament Exegesis at Pontifical Biblical Institute, Rome, explores the interrelatedness of protagonist, place and proximate "other" in the Gospel of Mark. He brilliantly highlights "how in the contested Marcan (con)text, the cherished trope of Jerusalem persists and shares negotiated boundaries with the protagonist of the gospel—Jesus Christ." In the next article Dr. Wilson D'souza OFM, Cap reconnoiters the theological and hermeneutical significance of temple of Jerusalem in the Gospel of Mark. In this paper he shows the desired shift from human-made temple to God-made sanctuary based on spacio-temporal theology to the signs of the time. In the last article of this section Dr. Saji Joseph Kizhakkayil, an Old Testament exegete working as a pastor in the diocese of Innsbruck, Austria, exegetically analyses Isa 62:1-5 which portrays the intimate relationship of God to the renewed heavenly Jerusalem. While elucidating the theological meaning of the text, it brilliantly unravels Zion's marital bond to YHWH.

In the concluding article Prof. Francis X. D'Sa SJ, emeritus Professor of Systematic Theology and Indian Religions at Jnana-Deepa Vidyapeeth, Pune, and Director, Institute for the Study of Religions, Pune, makes plea to biblical scholars and Indologists in India to exercise a hermeneutic of suspicion about the world from which they practise their vocation, and become more aware of the world[view] of Gandhi's India. Thus, the intercultural challenges that he poses before the exegetes - biblical scholars and Indologists - in India brings a beautiful conclusion to this volume which we humbly offer to Prof. Scaria, a man who significantly contributed to develop a contextual Indian biblical hermeneutics.

My sincere gratitude goes to the Papal Seminary community, Pune especially to Rev. Fr. Bhausaheb Sansare, SJ, the Rector and Rev. Fr. Vincent Crasta, SJ, the Minister, for giving me ample opportunities for my academic and spiritual fulfillment. I am grateful to Prof. Dr. Francis Gonsalves, SJ, the President, Jnana-Deepa Vidyapeeth, Pune and Prof. Dr. Jose Thayil, SJ, the Registrar, Jnana-Deepa Vidyapeeth, Pune, for their encouragement and support.

My sincere thanks are due to Bishop Chacko Thottumarickal, SVD, the Bishop of Indore for writing a fitting foreword to this book and motivating us to lead a committed life to the *LOGOS*, and to impart its message for our future generations. This is also an opportunity for me to acknowledge the support and affection of Rev. Dr. Saji Joseph Kizhakkayil, during my stay in Innsbruck, and the financial assistance that he rendered for the publication of this book. Christian World imprints, Delhi deserves a special thanks and appreciation for the printing of this book with much interest and care.

May the *LOGOS* -Word of God- kindle our hearts and help bring peace to the earth!

Thomas Karimundackal, SJ
Jnana-Deepa Vidyapeeth
Pontifical Athenaeum of Philosophy and Religion, Pune

October 18. 2020
Feast of St. Luke, Evangelist

Introductory Article

1

Fr. Scaria Kuthirakattel, SVD Life and Mission

Wilson D'souza, OFM Cap

Introduction

As I walked into Ishvani Kendra to meet Fr. Scaria to know something more about him, he wholeheartedly welcomed me and with ease answered all the questions that I posed to him. Here, I make an attempt to describe his childhood, vocation to religious life, his ministerial priesthood, sacramental life and his personal convictions. Secondly, I will try to sum up some of his values and priorities inspired from Jesus, his real Teacher. Thirdly, we will see how he was inspired by the life and writings of George Soares Prabhu (hereafter we will use GSP), who later became his mentor and *Guru*.

1. Family Background and Childhood

On 29th January 1940 was born a little boy in a middle class farming family, the son of late Joseph and Elizabeth Kuthirakkattel. Fr. Scaria hailed from Kurumulloor of Kottayam District, in Kerala. Among seven children he is the youngest and much loved. His baptismal name was Scaria. At home, their day began with family prayers and ended by saying the Rosary by kneeling for "one who prays kneeling prays twice" was the strict understanding of his father. His high-school days were spent at Athirampura and every day he used to pray before and after the school, and God helped him to make a decision regarding his future after his Matriculation.

1.1. Options, Priorities and Values

The Palestinian situation in which Jesus lived and the situation we live in today is similar. Firstly, what we have in India is an ever-widening economic disparity between the rich and the poor. Secondly, a similar radical religious fundamentalism of Pharisees, Scribes, Zealots and Qumran is also found in India. Thirdly, there was a political pressure and systematic oppression and segregation of women, racial purity and despised trades that is rampant in India.[1] Such was also the situation of Fr. Scaria. He too made his priorities based on the teachings of Jesus taught by his parents. The Gospel was his guiding force. Fr. Scaria claims that his options came from the teachings of Christ and the church. As a growing child he had his priorities set and all the way he tried to achieve them. His values and priority were towards the oppressed, women, tax-collectors and sinners of our times, like his master Jesus Christ.

Jesus practiced compassion for the have-nots of the society as well as the powerless, but confronted the powerful.[2] Fr. Scaria too was no exception to it. He practiced the values of Jesus. Jesus had to face crucifixion and death. But, it was not the end; rather his *Abba* raised him to qualitatively new life as the Saviour of humankind. Similarly Fr. Scaria faced life challenges and criticisms and never ever compromised with the options, priorities and values he had chosen to preach, live, and practice.

2. Vocation to Religious Life

The prayers at home and school were the motivating factors for his vocation. One of his cousins who wanted to be a priest was his inspiration. He wanted to be a missionary priest and thus joined the Society of Divine Word. However, as a small child he suffered from giddiness and use to faint and fall. In a village set up there was no possibility to have a regular doctor but his parents used to sprinkle Holy water as a remedy. He was treated with country medicine. Believing to have been healed, he joined the above mentioned congregation but soon discovered the presence of the same disease. He was afraid of losing his vocation, thus requested his mother to pray to Our Lady by doing Novena at Kanakkary. He was thus totally healed by the miraculous intercession of our

1 Scaria Kuthirakkattel, "Formation of Christian Leaders: A New Testament Perspective", *Jnanadeepa Pune: Journal of Religious Studies,* Vol. 3, No. 2, (2000), 63-76, 63.

2 Ibid, 75-76.

Blessed Mother. 'Surrender your life to God and he will lead you to right path', was the little faith of little Scaria.

2.1. Call to Discipleship

As a Seminarian he believed that "the seminarian is not called to be mere priest but a disciple of Christ and the discipleship consists in following Christ and becoming the fishers of men". Later in his writings he says, call narratives presuppose the call to discipleship. It is an integral part of formation, then, of the apostles, and now, ours. We have a number of call stories in the NT: a call of the brothers namely Peter and Andrew, James and John (Mk 1:16-20). The initiative is from the one who calls, not from one who is called. The first two brothers were casting the net while; other two were mending their net. Every call has two dimensions:

a. To follow Jesus and
b. To become fishers of men.

Further Seminarian Scaria says, "Those who are called are to leave their possessions. It implies an 'authentic detachment' which is an essential feature of discipleship". The young Scaria was introduced to religious life by his cousin as the pattern followed by John in his gospel. It is John the Baptist who introduces his disciples to Jesus: Look, here is the Lamb of God (Jn 1:36). The disciples take initiative to follow Jesus (1:37). Then Jesus asked them: What are you looking for? (1:38). Here, we have an ensuing dialogue; Rabbi, where are you staying? "Come and See", was the response to them (1:39). The above dialogue is not an inquiry about Jesus' postal address but theological.[3] They came and saw where he was staying and then remained with him that day (1:39). Now, Andrew brings his brother to Jesus to become a disciple, so also Philip brings Nathanael, his townsman. Thus, for Scaria, vocation to religious life was a call to discipleship.

2.1.1. Decides to go to the Periphery

As pointed out by his cousin and convinced of his vocation Scaria wanted to serve the people at the periphery in North India, thus joined at Indore, MP and learned to read and write Hindi. He did his studies of Philosophy and Theology at the renowned institute of JDV, Pune. He was influenced by the life of Francis Pereira, SJ, and later took up the study of Sacred Scriptures. He studied at the well-known institute of Biblicum and Gregorian University at Rome thus obtaining his licentiate and doctorate.

Though he was excelled as a biblical scholar, his vision was clear: to be with Jesus in meeting the people of periphery. Again for him, to be with Jesus

3 *Ibid,* 63

means 'call for genuine personal relationship of faith and trust in him and opting for his values and priorities in life and ministry'.[4] And to be sent out, demands identification with humans in every respect, especially working for and sharing in the struggles of our suffering brothers and sisters.

2.1.2. As a Formator

Forming others to be Christ like was the mission, vision and passion of young Scaria. As we are aware, mission has to be communitarian. The main priority of the apostle is to proclaim, not so much to evangelize. We are to bear witness to the Good News. The apostles lived out their own mission by bearing witness to Jesus, who is sent by the Father. Mission needs empowerment in and through Christ, though there may be ups and downs. Failure in mission is temporary. The call is of the Master and failure of the apostles is bound to take place but it needs empowerment.[5] There is failure caused because of the hardness of heart (Mk 5:52, 8:14-21). Peter failed to understand Jesus, the Messiah (8:32-33, 9:32, 10:35, 41). Judas, betrayed him while other disciples flee away (Mk 14:20-21, 26-31, 43-50, 54, 66-72). Jesus empowers them with the necessary condition and its consequences for them (8:34-38, 933-37, 10:36-45). He knew failure to be part of it but still chose and appointed them with his own measuring rod, which is very different from the human criteria (Mt 28:20, Lk 24:49). Scaria says, formation does not mean success all the time but coupled with failure. 'Formee needs models in the form of a formator and a professor'. The apostles were to preach the gospel to those who open their hearts, to proclaim the forgiveness of Jesus (Mt 28:19). Thus, 'the crucial point of formation is to be empowered by the Risen Lord and the Holy Spirit,' says Scaria, the formator (Lk 24:47).

He believes that formees and formators must possess certain qualities like the apostles and Jesus. The main qualities of apostles are those lived out by Jesus in his life and ministry. They are not only called to preach, teach and proclaim but to serve. They served their Master and Lord by their self-sacrificing and self-emptying acts (Mk 10:45, Jn 13:1-11, Phil 2:5-11). It is a movement from the centre to the periphery, from upper to the lowest. It is a service to the poor, oppressed and the marginalized to the point of giving up one's own life. It is an option against oppressing, being greedy and against those who lord over others (Mt 6: 19-21, 24).

The second quality is suffering for Jesus. Indeed, oppression causes suffering. This suffering is a call and has inevitable consequences (Mk 8:34-38). The third quality is to be able to form human and spiritual communities, rather than build edifices. It demands interpersonal forgiveness (Mt 18:21-35).

4 *Ibid,* 64.

5 *Ibid,* 68.

The fourth quality is to have a wide horizon in thinking and broad-mindedness in praxis. This demands mature and seasoned spirituality and respect towards others. Other qualities are rendering listening ears to people, opening ones heart wide open to the oppressed and persecuted, giving helping hand to the underprivileged, standing for values of justice, freedom and love with genuine spiritual conviction and empowered by the Holy Spirit. We need to be people of willing acceptance and respect the differences (Mk 9:38-41).[6] The apostle is chosen from the people and for the people. What we need is our religious vocation should be situational of common people says Fr. Scaria. He further says, "The main hindrance to become a holy apostle is the worship of mammon. Let not our service be lips- service in contrast with heart-service. The apostles' heart should be filled with love, compassion, and concern and self-giving".[7]

2.1.3. A Progressive Thinker

Let our formation be open to the progressive ideas without compromising certain fundamental truths, says Scaria. Fundamentalism is not limited primarily to Christianity, it is found in a broader and wider sense in all religions. The Bible possesses the views on liberalism and fundamentalism, not in strict sense but in the broader sense.[8] Yahweh initiated the process of liberating Israel from a fundamentalism of a complex nature, namely economic and political. In this process, the Israelites experienced Yahweh as their Lord and liberator, and to form a community of sisters and brothers in intimacy and mutual sharing in contrast with the ancient Eastern exploitative, oppressive states.[9] Jesus undergoes a profound experience of God's unconditional love and humans as his sisters and brothers... thus he gives birth to a contrast community whose ultimate goal is accepting God as *Abba* and humans as sisters and brothers.[10] It was the foundational experience of God that enabled Jesus to identify himself with the oppressed ones and challenge the oppressive force. He was able to free himself from the ties of family, mammon, powers and position to live a life of an itinerant charismatic preacher, to lay his life and enjoy true freedom.

Fr. Scaria was a progressive and constructive thinker and believes that it should flow from our God experience. His views were not accepted to the organized church; however like his Lord and Master he remained firm and promoted progressive ideas.

---

6 *Ibid,* 72-73.

7 *Ibid,* 74-76.

8 Scaria Kuthirakkattel, "Fundamentalism: Biblical Perspective", *Jnanadeepa Pune: Journal of Religious Studies,* Vol. 6, No. 2, (2003), 24-47, 26-27.

9 *Ibid,* 27.

10 *Ibid,* 28.

3. A Committed Priesthood

Fr. Scaria believes that priesthood has a committed service to the people especially to the poor, the least and the last one of the society. It is not a job to get money but the vocation to priesthood is a full-time personal commitment to the person of Jesus and for this we require dedication, frequency to sacraments, especially the Eucharist and spend time in serving nature. He is the St. Francis of Assisi of our time who spends wonderful moments with nature and claims it to be time spent with God.

Looking at the priesthood of Jesus one begins to pose few questions. What sort of priest was he? What are the salient features and characteristics of his sacrifice? To find answers to these questions we now turn to S. Kuthirakkattel.[11] In the OT, we find different types of priesthood: a) the hereditary (Ex 28:1, 29:9, 44, Lev 8:2, Sir 45:15, 25), b) official event or sacerdotal consecration, (Ex 29:1-35, Lev 8:1-36), c) a sacrificial one (Lev 21:16-23) [12]. They identified themselves with the rich section of the society and became a separate and distinct class. The priesthood in the OT was hierarchical and of honour and offering sacrifice was the primary function of priests. The liturgical services were uniquely impressive and unimaginably breathe-taking, wholeheartedly appreciated and most dearly cherished by all. Sanctuaries and temple were the places of sacrifice where the individual Israelite entered into communion with his God. A priestly caste was set aside for this service (Lev 21:1-11).[13] Against this type of a Priest and priesthood Fr. Scaria promotes Jesus the priest as a model and example.

Jesus' priesthood was completely and totally different. It was radical in all the ways. He neither belonged to the hereditary, nor did he come from a priestly family (Lk 1:5, Heb 7:13-14). Jesus never underwent any ritual of sacerdotal consecration, nor did he ever wear such high priestly vestments. One of the outstanding features of Jesus' ministry was not of a separation from but one of solidarity and identification with humans; that too humans from all walks of life.[14] When it came to the sacrificial priesthood of Christ, he rejected the purity law (Mk 7:1-15); called the tax-collectors despised for their trade, to be his disciples (Mk 2:14-17). He healed the woman with a flow of blood (Mk 5:23-34), which considered to be ritually impure; but for him, a human being was greater than any ritual (Mk 3:35, Mt 6:9, 23:9). In doing so

11 Scaria Kuthirakkattel, "The Radicality of Jesus' Priesthood: The Problem, Procedure, Programme and Proposal", *Bible Bhashyam,* Vol. 25, No. 2, (1999), 85-103.

12 *Ibid*, 89-90.

13 Fernando Belo, A Materialist Reading of the Gospel of Mark, New York: Orbis Books, 1981, 42, 58.

14 Scaria Kuthirakkattel, "The Radicality of Jesus' Priesthood: The Problem, Procedure, Programme and Proposal", 89.

he internalized, radicalized and simplified the whole of rituals and morality (Mk 7:14-23, Mt 5:21-6:18).[15] Jesus' person, ministry and death did not fulfil the OT priesthood.

His anti-temple stance in his ministry is evident and continued in his trials and death (Mk 11:15-17, 14:58, 15:29-38). He was born in a no-man's home and had nothing to offer in the temple (Lk 2:7, 24). He was a wandering mendicant preacher (Lk 9:58). He was stripped of his own garments and died among the criminals on the cross (Mk 15:24-25). He authentically identified himself with the poor in every respect. Jesus did not cling to the honour and glory but emptied himself. He became a curse (Deut 21:22-23, Gal 3:13), a stumbling block to the Jews and folly to the Gentiles (1Cor 1:23). There is an incompatibility and contradiction in OT and Jesus' priesthood. Jesus did speak of sacrifice but by his blood of the covenant which is poured out for many[16] (Ex 24:6-8, Mk 14:24, Mt 26:28). Again, the blessing is connected with the sacrifice (Lev 9:22, Sir 50:20); Jesus, our paschal lamb has been sacrificed (1Cor 5:7, Rom 3:25, Gal 2:20, Eph 5:2, 1Pet 1:19).

Thus Fr. Scaria believed in the priesthood of Christ which was self-sacrificing, self-emptying and above all available to all in service. He promotes this radical priesthood of the Christians in the letter to the Hebrews.[17] The letter to the Hebrews could be divided into four expositions.[18] It gives a paradoxical association of exaltation and humiliation of the Son of God. Jesus assumed weak human nature, identified himself fully with humans, including suffering and death so that he might liberate them from the domain of death and thereby he is perfected and made suitable for the office of high priest. Jesus, the high priest offered prayers. He prayed with shouts of cries, tears and pleaded with God. This prayer and sacrifice was par-excellent not a covenantal liturgy with predetermined rites but an offering of human situation of intense agony accompanied with vehement cries and bitter tears.[19] The letter to the Hebrews deeply reflects the mystery of Jesus' person as Son of God and brother of humans. Thus, he became a perfect mediator between humans and God.

---

15 *Ibid,* 90.

16 *Ibid*, 95-96.

17 Scaria Kuthirakkattel, "The Radicality of Jesus' Priesthood", *Bible Bhashyam*, Vol. 26, No. 3, (1999), 200-243, 227-229.

18 *Ibid,* 204. 1. The prologue and first exposition (1:1-2:18), 2. The second exposition (3:1-5:10), 3. The third exposition (5:11-10:18), 4. The fourth and fifth exposition (10:19-13:25).

19 *Ibid,* 212.

Scaria enumerates in detail 'Christ priesthood' in Hebrew 5:1-10. He mentions the two-fold relation in 5:1-4:

a. Jesus' relation with sinful humans (5:2-3) and
b. His relation with God (5:4).[20]

Here, we see Christ's high priesthood authorized by God and realized in the self-emptying process of Jesus. High priesthood is a vocation from God to which no human has a claim. The God-made sanctuary refers to true tent not made by human hands but by the Lord (Acts 7:48-50, 17:24, Heb 8:2, 9:11). The 'tent' refers to the risen body of Jesus. Therefore, the saying of Jesus 'Destroy this sanctuary and in three days I will build it' (Jn 2:13-22) is clarified by the evangelist. The temple, Jesus meant was his own body. This is a God-made sanctuary. Thus, Scaria says, 'the risen body of Jesus is the new eschatological sanctuary, the locus where man authentically encounters God'.[21] It is the acceptance of Jesus' revelation animated by the spirit who lives in Christians in a dynamic principle of unity.

3.1.1. Priesthood for India

Answering a question about priesthood in India, he wishes that we contextualize our priesthood in the given circumstances and time. As far as Christianity is concerned, the religious experience of Jesus, his ministry, death and exaltation are prophetic and charismatic in nature and have to undergo transformation in terms of institutional structure in Indian context. Our Christian priesthood functions as a living sacrifice to God (Rom 12:1-3) and offers ourselves totally to him. Again, our priesthood is a call to self-abnegation and self-emptying.[22] In Indian context, the question arises: How do we live radically Jesus' priesthood? We must keep in mind our situation. It is characterized by massive poverty, pluri-form religiosity, oppressive dehumanized system, political instability, systematic corruption, in the name of God and religious violence and unwanted secularism above all religious fundamentalism and communal riots. To such problems, Scaria proposes new ideas.[23] As Israel was called by Yahweh to be a contrast community so we are called to be a

20 Scaria Kuthirakkattel, "Christ, the Self-Emptying High Priest: Meaning and Function of Heb 5:1-10", in *The Dharma of Jesus: Interdisciplinary Essays in Memory of George Soares- Prabhu,* Francis X D'sa (ed.), India: Gujarat, Gujarat Sahitya Prakash, 1997, 102-177, cf. 106.

21 Scaria Kuthirakkattel, "The Man-made Temple and the God-made Sanctuary: Some Aspects of the New Testament Theology of the Temple", *Jeevadhara,* Vol. 23, No. 134, (1993), 153-170, 166.

22 Scaria Kuthirakkattel, "Christ, the Self-Emptying High Priest: Meaning and Function of Heb 5:1-10", 146.

23 Scaria Kuthirakkattel, "The Radicality of Jesus' Priesthood", 241-243.

contrast community in our multi-religious context. As a priest of Christ, we need to manifest our identification and solidarity with people with whom and for whom we are working. In order to identify with the people we need to have a real personal experience of the plight of the people during our formation. For this, the real formation of the seminarians should take place in real life situation of the people. All that is dividing the church, such as rites, caste, languages are not the works of the Holy Spirit and are counter witness in the church. We need spirit-filled Christians to undergo any sort of persecution like the early church and bear witness to Christ and his message.

4. Symbols and Sacraments

Enquiring about his views on symbols and sacraments as a theologian as well as his practical life of sacrament he said the following: One of the ways to realize the symbol and sacrament is to relate them to one's own life. Speaking about the symbol, Scaria gives an example of taking bath which could be an external sign but that should become a symbol of internal cleansing. Further, enumerating his own sacramental life he says, they get priority and are celebrated meaningfully, with due preparation in private.

The various signs in the gospel of John have one specific purpose (2:1-11, 4:46-54, 5:1-18, 6:1-15, 16-21, 9:1.12, 11:1-45) and that purpose is self-disclosure of the Messianic status and the Messianic function of Jesus. Every sign renders as a symbol because a symbol participates in the reality itself. The symbolized reality in the seven signs; is the mystery of Jesus' person and of his mission. The symbol is not superficial, material and shallow, rather indicates spiritual insight.[24] The readers and listeners are invited to believe in Jesus more intensively and to commit themselves to fellow humans more radically in order that they may share in God's own life.

'The fourth gospel is 'non-sacramental' as proposed by German scholars, while, British advocated it as 'ultra-sacramental' says R. E. Brown.[25] One has to pose question: Does the gospel of John present Jesus as the primordial sacrament? Many claim that the fourth gospel has an allusion to the sacrament of Baptism and the Eucharist (3:1-15, 6:1-71). This is what Fr. Scaria is of the opinion. John speaks of Jesus' unique experience of his Father and his exclusive and intimate relation with him (5:26, 6:57, 10:30-38, 14:10-11, 16:15). Jesus could see his Father and could hear him (6:46, 8:40, and 11:41); he knew him (8:55, 17:25). Jesus experienced that his Father loved him (5:20, 10:17, 15:9); Father is the source of life (5:26, 6:57). Jesus came from the Father and

24 Scaria Kuthirakkattel, "The Beginning of the Symbols: The Meaning and Function of John 2:1-11", *Bible Bhashyam,* Vol. 24, No. 2, (1998), 79- 102, 101-102.

25 Raymond E. Brown, New Testament Essays, New York, Image Books, 2010, 51-53.

carried his mission (8:29, 38, 42, 13:3, 16:32).[26] The purpose of this revelation consists in enabling humans to participate in God's own life (Jn 1:12, 3:16-17, 12:44, 50, 20:31). In order to participate in the divine life humans must believe in Jesus who is sent by the Father (5:24, 38, 6:29, 44, 11:42, 17:3, 8, 21-23). Jesus, God's only Son manifests the transcendent and incomprehensible God, his Father, to humans and humans by believing in Jesus are enabled to participate in God's own life. Here, we begin to wonder if one is in Christ and has total experience of him: Does s/he need sacraments? Indeed, Jesus is the medium of message and messenger; he is communication and communion between God and humans (14:6). He is the primordial sacrament because all sacraments have their origin, significance and obtain their efficacy from Jesus.

In John 3:1-15, Nicodemus visits Jesus and has a dialogue with him. It enabled Christian believers to recall and relive the baptismal experience and commitment. It also calls for a reassessment of one's life and commitment and challenges one to reorient one's attitudes and values in tune with the baptismal experience and commitment.[27] The whole purpose of baptism is that one gets incorporated into the body of Christ which is the community. Secondly, it brings about unity and harmony and integrity and above all loving relationship and commitment. The sacrament of Eucharist, in John 6 seems to be having 'secondary and subordinate role'.[28] He does not deny it. Jesus' person and mission have a sacramental notion and John feels it is not necessary to narrate baptism and Eucharist. But the above two episodes give deeper meaning and true significance to both. Eucharist should enable us to abide in Jesus (6:56), and baptism assures participation in divine life, says Fr. Scaria.

4.1. Life of the Poor and Poverty in India Today

True sacramental life begins when we love the poor and share that sacramental life with others, says Fr. Scaria. During Jesus' time a few people in Palestine enjoyed resources and wealth while the vast majority lived in poverty and utter misery. The root cause for this was the unjust socio-economic structure. The poverty in Palestine was a structural evil contrary to the foundational and covenantal relationship, says Scaria.[29] In such a situation Jesus' mission-vision was founded on a profound God-experience. This experience is expressed in his ministry by his words and deeds. This experience liberated him from internal compulsion and from external pressure and enabled him to experience humans

26 Scaria Kuthirakkattel, "Johannine Perspective of Sacraments", *Bible Bhashyam,* Vol. 24, No. 3, (1998), 149-171, 152-153.

27 *Ibid,* 161.

28 *Ibid,* 167.

29 Scaria Kuthirakkattel, "Poverty in Palestine during Jesus' time, Poverty in India of our time", *Journal of Indian Theology*, Vol.7, No. 2, (2014), 7-29, 20.

from God's perspective and from His heart.[30] Looking at the poverty in India, he says, 'the causes seem to be same as that of Palestine and Jesus' time'. What is the role of the Christians and of the consecrated in such situations? Church has made a challenging and symbolic expression in her commitment to the poor. Even, she has lived an authentic and credible life.

The problems within the church based on caste, rites, and languages are counter witnesses to one's faith. Even, the vow of poverty and life style of the religious raise questions: How far is it credible and meaningful? Not forgetting the few exceptions to it. What is more saddening is the convenient interpretation and lame excuses given regarding poverty and poor by consecrated men and women! Scaria says, 'We need people with God-experience and a zeal for social justice'.[31] The symbols and sacraments that we celebrate need to be translated in our day today life in our Indian situation lest they become mere external signs and rituals. Jesus had an original experience of God and he translated it in humans as God's children in his mission and vision. 'Unfortunately, original experience of founders by the religious charism has been taken for granted or has been given a back seat', says Fr. Scaria.

5. The Dharma of Jesus

As a professor, Fr. Scaria followed George Soares Prabhu's (GSP) model especially relating with the student gently, followed punctuality and used simple ways and means of teaching. He believes that a good rapport with the student is the need of the hour. For, about 25 years he taught at the Orissa theologate of SVD and 35 years at JDV, Pune. He says, when students misbehave don't ignore, nor be aggressive rather meet him/her personally and talk to them. That is the real 'Dharma' we need to practice in the seminary. The Dharma of Jesus is the way of life. It is the concern for the poor, the marginalized and basic respect for the people.

I asked him what he liked most in GSP and he spontaneously said, "His views on Dharma". Along with GSP, Scaria enumerates the Dharma of Jesus as God experience, as *Abba,* the loving parent and Jesus as the unique Son. This experience of God as unconditional love ushers in freedom, fellowship and justice, symbolically expressed as the Kingdom of God.[32] It is characterized by Indian situation and context. To implement these convictions, we need personal God-experience as well as an active and an effective identification with the oppressed people in our country. God's self-revelation took place in the past through individuals, communities, institutions and above all in the

30 *Ibid,* 21-22.

31 *Ibid,* 27-28.

32 Scaria Kuthirakkattel, "Experience and Context: The Basis of Jesus' Dharma", *Jnanadeepa Pune: Journal of Religious Studies,* Vol. 18, No. 2, (2015), 57-75, 57.

person of Jesus Christ.[33] God made him known to Israel as 'liberator' and as 'inspirer',[34] and in the crisis of exile He made him known as 'remote and transcendent'.[35]

5.1. To be a Prophet

I met an elderly priest from the campus and said that I am writing something about Fr. Scaria and he out busted saying, 'he is a prophet and very constructively critical in his thinking and writings'. This is what Fr. Scaria manifested in his writings. He says prophetic literature is based on two major themes:

a. the denunciation of the idolatry and
b. passionate appeal for social justice.[36]

By virtue of the liberation of the people of Israel from bondage they accepted Yahweh as their Lord and God and they constituted as Yahweh's own possession (Ex 6:5-8, 34:10-16, Deut 7:6). In the course of time Israel too became the master of bonded labour and the tyrannical agent of oppression. At this critical stage Yahweh called prophets. They advocated authentic relation with Yahweh and genuine interpersonal relationship among fellow-Israelites. Their function and central concern was theology and morality. They were integral part of the Jewish society. The prophetic vocation and ministry were rooted in the covenantal relationship. They were free for the works of the Lord their God.[37]

But Scaria claims that Jesus is the prophet par-excellence. He has a new basis of his prophetic theologizing based on his God experience known as *Abba*. This foundational experience is expressed in terms of the reign of God. All humans are his children and brothers and sisters of Jesus. Further, his prophetic theologizing is enumerated from his symbolic deeds.[38] Jesus, the prophet read the scroll of Isaiah in the synagogue (61:1-2) and unveils the true meaning of text. The eyes of everyone were fixed on him and after reading he affirmed that 'today this scripture is fulfilled in your hearing' (Lk 4:20-21). It is a universal mission for all, especially the poor, oppressed, to release the captives, proclaim the year of the Lord and recover the sight of the blind.

33 *Ibid,* 60.

34 *Ibid,* 61, 64

35 *Ibid,* 72.

36 Scaria Kuthirakkattel, "The Role of Prophetic Theologizing in Jesus' Dharma", *Jnanadeepa Pune Journal for Religious Study,* Vol. 18, No. 2, (2015), 77-96, 78.

37 Gerhard Von Rad, The Message of the Prophets, Francisco: Harper-Collins Publisher, 1962, 50-59.

38 Scaria Kuthirakkattel, "The Role of Prophetic Theologizing in Jesus' Dharma", 86.

The religion which remains within the four walls and practices empty rituals loses its credibility and authenticity says, Fr. Scaria. To find its authenticity it has to be action oriented. To clear his ideas on the above statement we go to his article. Isaiah laments over the injustice in Israel (1:12-17), her producing bad fruits in the vineyard which symbolizes injustice and bloodshed (Isa 5:1-7) and again over the religious practices of fasting without genuine social concern (58: 1-12). Hosea condemns hypocritical worship (8:1-14) and depicts Israel as an unfaithful wife (1:2-3:5). Prophet Micah and Amos strongly censured the behaviour of Israel (Mich 2:1-5, Amos 3:15, 4:1-4).[39] The primary purpose of warning and censure was not condemnation but personal conversion and social transformation.

Finally, Scaria's writing about prophetic theologizing in 20th and 21st century gives an example of Pope Francis, Bishop George V Saupin and others. These men stood for social justice. Pope is 'Prophet of Mercy' and Bishop as 'Prophet of Simplicity'.[40] He gives the example of GSP. His death on the road was a prophetic fulfilment.[41] He lived and died like the poor of India. It was also radical following of Jesus even unto death.

5.2. In the Footsteps of the Guru

He was asked: What made you to take GSP the Jesuit to be your Guru? He answered saying, GSP was an exceptional Goan 'a Goan without liquor' to put it humorously. He was well-versed in his subjects especially 'the Resurrection of Jesus and Dharma of Jesus'. There wouldn't be place in the class-room so the students used to attend by standing out. His life was an inspiration, soft-spoken and had a special love for the poor and lived a life of poverty. He was asked by Biblicum to teach Scripture with a Roman-collar but he refused to do so least he would contradict his being poor, and do harm to his life of poverty. GSP would never speak ill and negative of the institution and individuals in the campus of JDV.

Fr. Scaria says, interpreting the Bible in the Indian context is the need of the hour. His Guru GSP was one of the champions of this method.[42] Scaria seems to be promoting his master's idea based on God experience, *Abba* as unconditional love of a parent and Dharma of Jesus. He is very much influenced by the thought pattern of GSP. GSP forth rightly disapproved western colonial mind-set and values for they manipulated and exploited the

39 *Ibid,* 84.

40 *Ibid,* 90-91

41 *Ibid,* 94.

42 Scaria Kuthirakkattel, "George M. Soares Prabhu: An Exegete and a Theologian", *Vidyajyoti Journal of Theological Reflection,* Vol. 73, No. 10, (2009), part I, 759-777 and part II, "An Exegete and a Theologian", *Vidyajyoti Journal of Theological Reflection,* Vol. 73, No. 10, (2009), 818-826.

third world economic front and there was no tangible transformation and he passionately advocated an exegesis and theology that address the aspirations and concern, the needs and struggles of the local communities.[43] Scaria personally believes that, GSP's interpretation of the Bible flowed from a deep spiritual experience and authenticity of his life. His entire academic were neither abstract, nor theoretical but experience based and action oriented. He touched practical topics with concerns and values which touched the hearts of humans and thereby transformed their lives. His writings were genuinely creative, profoundly insightful and thought-provoking.

Fr. Scaria not only promoted his Guru's teaching but also lived and practiced it in his personal life. He says, the teacher of Scriptures should impart content based on his/her personal reflection. They should live what they teach thus intellect should be seasoned with spirituality.

Conclusion

Having met him personally and gone through his writings, following are the some of the impressions I have about Fr. Scaria. Being born just before World War II, the man has experienced life through and through. His writings justify the formation and the discipline he enjoyed. He is directly responsible for the publication of the collected works of GSP which served wider and deeper interest in Biblical studies. It has thus done something to make JDV in general and GSP in particular better known. He served as a professor and the dean of theology in the institution. It is safe to say that professor Scaria himself considers his real life-work not in the things above mentioned, but in the classroom. His 35 years of meritorious service saw a great expansion of JDV. He had power to make his subject live for his students and to kindle their interest and enthusiasm. The article presented to him is a token of esteem and with the hope that he may long continue to share in the fellowship of the society of the Divine Word at the eve of his life.

43 *Ibid,* 763-764.

Proclaiming the LOGOS

2

Journey to Emmaus
A Journey of Faith

Henry Pattarumadathil, SJ

Introduction

Luke, who begins his gospel by promising Theophilus an orderly account of the life of Jesus "having followed all things closely", concludes the gospel by presenting three stories relating to the resurrection of Jesus and a final report on his ascension in the presence of his disciples. The story of the two disciples who journeyed from Jerusalem to Emmaus on the day of the resurrection is the second of these three resurrection accounts[1]. We can observe a narrative progression in the Lukan resurrection stories.[2] In the first episode, the women, the protagonists, find only the empty tomb and hear about the resurrection in a vision. But they do not see Jesus. They report it to the Eleven and others, but they are not believed (Lk 24:1-12). In the Emmaus story, the protagonists are two disciples who were with the Eleven. They do not recognize Jesus on their journey even though he joins them as their co-traveller. It is only later that they

1 Although a one-verse reference to Jesus' appearance to two disciples "as they were walking into the country" is found in the longer ending of Mark, it lacks detail (Mk 16:12).

2 In all three stories, the disciples' struggle to believe is highlighted. All three recall the divine purpose and necessity of Jesus' passion death and resurrection.

do recognize him, when he breaks bread and gives it to them (24:13-35). In the final episode, Jesus appears to a group of people composed of the Eleven and others. Surprisingly, they do not recognize him, even though he had already revealed himself to some of them. Moreover, they mistake him for a ghost. Jesus takes away their fear and opens their mind to understand the scriptures (24:36-49). Although the proclamation of the resurrection is the primary purpose of these stories, they also serve to help the reader realize how difficult it was for the Apostles and other disciples to believe in the resurrection and to recognize the risen Lord until they themselves had received a convincing experience of him. More importantly, they comfort readers in their own struggles to believe and live their Christian faith. They encourage them to move forward in their life journey with all its ups and downs, its consolations and desolations, by recognizing the presence of the risen Lord. In this article, we focus on the Emmaus story and reread it together with the "implied reader"[3] to explore its significance for the faith-journey of believers today.[4]

1. From Jerusalem to Emmaus: A Runaway Trip?

The Emmaus episode begins with a *kai idou* clause (and behold!) calling the attention of the reader to the departure of "two of them" (disciples?) from Jerusalem, going to Emmaus on the same day as they had heard the reports of the resurrection of Jesus.[5] This makes the reader curious: why do they leave Jerusalem on that "same day"?

The *kai idou* clause links the present episode with the previous one which describes the experience of the women who visited the sepulchre early in the morning. They had found the tomb empty and heard from "two men" in dazzling apparel that Jesus was risen from the dead. Although they went and reported what they had found and heard to the "Eleven and all the rest", they

3 As J. D. Kingsbury defines, "the term *implied reader* refers to an imaginary person who is to be envisaged … as responding to the text at every point with whatever emotion, understanding, or knowledge the text ideally calls for." Jack Dean Kingsbury, *Matthew as Story* (Philadelphia: Fortress Press, 1986), 38.

4 "What is the significance of this passage for the believer?" This was a question that we theology students often heard in the lectures of Fr. Scaria Kuthirakkattel SVD. In fact, he never left the explanation of a biblical passage without raising questions about its "significance" for its present audience. He not only taught us the gospels but also inspired us, through his life, to live the values of Jesus. I am deeply grateful to Fr. Scaria for initiating me into biblical exegesis and accompanying me in my academic and faith journey with his affectionate guidance.

5 Emmaus is located, according to the narrative, sixty stadia (seven miles) away from Jerusalem. Scholars observe that there were at least three places in Palestine called Emmaus (1 Macc 3:57; 4:3), and "the exact site of Luke's Emmaus is no longer known". See Craig S. Keener, *The IVP Bible Background Commentary: New Testament* (Lk 24:13) (Downers Grove, Il.: InterVarsity Press, 1993), 256.

were not believed by them. The narrator concludes the first announcement of the resurrection with a note on their unbelief: "And these words appeared to them as nonsense, and they would not believe them" (24:11). This comment reveals the disciples' initial resistance to believing in Jesus' resurrection. Maybe they needed more convincing evidence.

The narrative introduces the persons who travelled to Emmaus as "two of them". According to the narrative thread, the referent of the personal pronoun "them" is not the Apostles, but "all the rest" (24:9). Therefore, the first appearance of the risen Jesus was not to the Apostles (Eleven), but to "two from the rest". Who were they? The evangelist does not even call them disciples.[6] Later in the story, the name of one of them is given: Cleopas, a name that is not heard anywhere else in the gospel.[7] Their anonymity could be intentional; thus the narrator uses a larger canvas to portray the recipients of the first appearance of the risen Jesus.

It is quite evident that these two belonged to a close circle of people who were with Jesus. This must be why the women went and reported to them "all these things" (24:9). That said, how does the reader interpret their journey from Jerusalem to Emmaus "on that very day"? The reader might see these two characters representing some of Jesus' followers who were confused and even frightened by the news of "the empty tomb" and the resurrection of Jesus. Had they not been frightened, as close associates of Jesus, they would have remained in Jerusalem at least to verify the truth of what the women reported to them. However, on the contrary, they flee Jerusalem, perhaps fearing adverse consequences.[8] Although the text does not say anything specific about the intention of their journey, the reader might regard it as a runaway trip.[9]

---

6 In this article, we use the word disciples in a general sense to mean followers of Jesus.

7 Speculations about the identity of the companion of Cleopas include Peter, Nathanael, Simon, Cleopas's wife and, his son. For a summary of different proposals and their sources, see Joseph. A. Fitzmyer, *The Gospel according to Luke X-XXIV: Introduction, Translation, and Notes* (Garden City, NY: Doubleday, 1985), 1563; Darrell L. Bock, *Luke, Volume 2. 9:51–24:53,* BECNT (Grand Rapids, MI: Baker Academic 1996), 1911.

8 As Moloney opines, Jerusalem is presented in Luke's gospel as the centre of God's history, therefore the disciples' going away from Jerusalem clearly indicates that they made "the wrong choice". Francis J. Moloney, *The Resurrection of the Messiah: A Narrative Commentary on the Resurrection Accounts in the Four Gospels* (New York: Paulist Press, 2013), 81.

9 Some scholars are of the opinion that these two had their lodging in Emmaus, that is why they journeyed to that village. See Paul Beasley-Murray, *The Message of the Resurrection* (Nottingham: Inter-Varsity Press, 2000), 69. The text does not give us any specific information about it except the fact that they had some place to stay there. Even if it is true, what motivates them to leave Jerusalem "on the same day"?

2. On the Way

The narrative presents their discussion on the way in a summary form: "They were conversing with each other about all these things which had taken place" (24:14). Later in their exchange with the "stranger", they give an elaborate description of what they were conversing about (24:18-24). Most likely, it was pain and fear that accompanied them on their journey and pervaded their conversation.

The story takes a new turn as a new companion joins their journey. His identity is revealed to the reader, but it is hidden from the two. They do not recognize Jesus even though he joins them as their co-traveller. It is quite paradoxical. As his followers or his close associates, they must have shared several journeys with him. Now, after being away from him for three days, they cannot recognize him. However, it was not their fault. Their eyes "were prevented" from recognizing him (24:14). Two questions: who/what prevented them from seeing and why were they prevented? Since the agent of the passive is not specific, it can be considered a divine passive concluding that it was God who blocked their eyes. The reader could also assume that it was their fear and lack of faith, reflected in their flight from Jerusalem, that prevented them from recognizing him. Now, why were they prevented? The reader may presume that they were not yet ready or worthy to receive the revelation; they needed to be strengthened in their faith and conviction. Narratively, this delay in revealing Jesus' identity to the disciples and the ensuing conversation between the "stranger" and the disciples offers the reader an opportunity to recall again, albeit in summary form, the divine purpose of Jesus' life, death and resurrection.

These disciples had a good knowledge of Jesus and his life. All along the way they were discussing things that had happened to him. At one point in their conversation with the stranger, they even expressed their surprise at his ignorance of what had happened in Jerusalem during those days. Yet they were not able to recognize him even when he came as their co-traveller. They knew "only of the events, not their ultimate significance".[10] This offers an important insight to the reader about their journey of faith that knowing the events that happened in Jesus' life (the facts) alone is not enough to recognize him. If not knowledge, what else can help them recognize Jesus?

3. The Initiative

The disciples could not recognize Jesus, but he did not leave them blind. He took the initiative and asked them about what they were conversing with each other. Before presenting their response to Jesus, the narrator pauses for a moment to talk about their mental disposition: "they stood still, looking sad". The reader

10 Moloney, *The Resurrection of the Messiah*, 83.

can perceive an unspoken expression of surprise and disappointment in their desperate look. As D.L. Bock puts it, "they cannot believe that anyone coming out of Jerusalem does not know what has happened"[11].

Cleopas replies to him by expressing their surprise at his ignorance: "Are you the only visitor (*paroikein*)[12] in Jerusalem who does not know of the things which have happened there during these days"? Cleopas's rhetorical question betrays his thinking about the 'stranger'. He might have thought that the stranger was a visitor, perhaps a pilgrim, who had come to Jerusalem for the Passover. His reaction also shows his assumption that even a visitor to Jerusalem would have been aware of the things that had happened to Jesus during those days. Cleopas's question indirectly draws the reader's attention to the historicity of the "Christ-event" which will be briefly recalled in the next verses.

Jesus still behaves like an ignorant stranger. The narrative presents him as one who does not understand Cleopas's vague language. So, he asks for clarity, "what things"? And they explain to him everything that has happened, perhaps everything they have witnessed, in those days in Jerusalem.

4. Certitude, Expectation, Frustration, Confusion

The disciples told the stranger in detail what they were talking about. It concerned "Jesus the Nazarene". They explained to him who they thought he was, what they expected of him, what happened to him and finally what they had heard about him that morning. In their words, the reader can perceive some kind of inner conflict that they were going through. They seem to be tossed by rolling waves of memories and disturbing thoughts.

What the two were certain of was the prophetic identity of Jesus. They stated without hesitation that he was "a prophet mighty in deed and word before God and all the people" (24:19). Furthermore, they related to the stranger how their religious authorities had handed Jesus over to be sentenced to death and crucified. Through their description of Jesus, especially of his death, the disciples confess their conviction that Jesus was an authentic prophet.[13] Was he only a prophet? The reader may recall what the disciples said to Jesus when he asked them about people's understanding of his identity (Lk 9:18-19) and how he reacted to their response. "John the Baptist", "Elijah", "one of the ancient prophets" – the disciples immediately told him what they had heard from the people. He wanted to know if his disciples also held the same view

11 Bock, *Luke*, 1910.

12 "The verb *paroikein* often means to inhabit a place without citizenship, dwell as a resident alien; it can also be used of temporary visitors (which would suit the sojourn of a Passover pilgrim)", see Fitzmyer, *The Gospel according to Luke*, 1564.

13 Luke repeatedly emphasizes the prophetic identity of Jesus (see Lk 4:16-30; 7:16,39; 9:9, 18-19; 13,31-35, etc.).

or something more. He asked them further: "But who do you say that I am?" Peter's confession shows that at least at that moment the disciples rightly understood Jesus as "the Christ of God" rather than as a prophet.

They also related their expectation and frustration: "But we were hoping that he was the one to redeem Israel" (24:21a).[14] The pronoun "we" may refer to all those who followed Jesus. Their messianic expectation can be seen in the phrase "the one to redeem Israel". Their hope might have been that he would be a political messiah to free them from the yoke of Rome! However, it was only a hope and not a firm belief! The adversative conjunction *de* (but) and the imperfect of the verb *ēlpizomen* (we were hoping) accentuate their frustration rather than expectation. Their hopes were dashed. Having witnessed the type of death he had suffered, how could they still hope that he would redeem Israel? In short, was it possible that the one who could not even save himself be the Messiah (see Lk 23:35,39)?

They had been experiencing such frustration for three days. Although, they had lost all their hopes, they were sure at least of what had happened. But now they were disturbed by a confusion which began with the report of some women who went to the tomb that morning. They also shared that confusion with the stranger. What they described was not what they witnessed, but what they had heard and what had "amazed" them. Although the word "amazed" (*existayme*) is normally used to express positive feelings of wonder or surprise (see Lk 2:47; 8:56), its use here is rather negative. First, the report about "the empty tomb" came originally from "some women".[15] What the women said was not entirely convincing. They did not see him, but they claimed to have had an angelic vision through which they learned that Jesus was alive. Hearing their story, some of their companions went to the tomb and also found it empty. It is therefore likely that his body was not in the tomb. But what happened to it? The men who went to the tomb had no angelic vision, so they were not sure if what the women were saying about his status, that he was alive, was true. The two end their description with a sceptical note: "but they did not see him". Their words reveal that the women's report and the events that followed did not bring them any consolation or hope, but rather made them more confused.

5. The Illumination

The disciples were sad and were much affected by the events they were discussing. Jesus immediately recognized their problem: although they had expected him to be the Messiah, they had not really understood the nature of his messianic identity. Their fear, frustration, and confusion stemmed from

14 See Isa 41:14; 43:14; 44:22-24; Lk 1:68; 2:38.

15 Women's testimony was not commonly regarded as trustworthy in the first-century Palestinian society. See Keener, *IVP Background Commentary* (Lk 24:6-12), 256.

this lack of understanding, or in other words, from their misconception of his identity and mission. Jesus explains to them what kind of Messiah he is! He addresses them as "foolish (men)" because they had been slow to believe all that the prophets had said. The opening exclamation "O" expresses a tone of disappointment. Jesus does not accuse them of not believing what the prophets had said about the Messiah, but only says that they were slow of heart to believe "all" that they had said! They seemed to have believed some but not "all" of it. Slowness of heart occurs when someone is confused and unable to make a firm decision. Matthew's Jesus qualifies such slowness of heart as "little faith" (Mt 6:30; 8:26; 14:31; 16:8; 17:20; see also Lk 12:28). One has faith but is not fully convinced of it. As a result, the heart wavers and becomes slow to grasp and believe!

Jesus helped them clear up their misunderstanding and come to true faith. He began with a rhetorical question: "Was it not necessary that the Christ should suffer these things and enter into his glory"? The expected answer is, yes! Two issues that trouble their hearts and make them slow to believe are addressed here. They are perplexed by the suffering and death of the one who they had thought was the Christ, and now they are confused about the story of his resurrection. If they had believed that the suffering of Christ was necessary, they would not have been crushed by his death and would have awaited his resurrection. Luke often uses the impersonal verb *dei* (it is necessary) to underscore the divine will and the programme of salvation history (see Lk 2:49; 4:43; 9:22; 13:33; 17:25; 19:5; 21,9; 22:37; 24:7, 26, 44). Jesus instructs them that it was God's will for the Messiah to suffer and enter into his glory. No one can change that.

The narrator says that Jesus interpreted for them the things concerning himself in the whole of Scriptures beginning with Moses and with all the prophets. There is no explicit reference to a suffering Messiah in the scriptures.[16] Therefore his explanation cannot be seen as proof of his suffering and glory alone, but also of his distinct messianic identity. Referring to the Scriptures, Jesus was showing them that they were right in their expectation that he was the Christ. In fact, he himself had told them about the necessity of his suffering and death after they had confessed him as Christ! Perhaps they did not take his words seriously.

Listening to the risen Jesus explain to the disciples the necessity of his suffering, death and glory helps readers recognize and overcome challenges in their faith and continue their life-journey with the risen Lord. Likewise, it also makes them aware of their own mission: "just as Christ had to suffer all this in

---

16 Moreover, as Beasley-Murray observes, "[i]n Pre-Christian Judaism there was no notion of a suffering Messiah: Isaiah 53, for instance, was not at that stage interpreted as referring to the Messiah". Beasley-Murray, *The Resurrection*, 72.

order to enter his "glory," so "must" the Christian disciple suffer tribulations to enter the kingdom of God (Acts 14:22)".[17]

6. A Moment of "Acting"

The narrator draws the reader's attention to a dramatic act of Jesus. When they drew near to the village, where the two were going, Jesus pretended (*prosepoiēsato*) to go further.[18] In fact, this note about his "acting" is given only to the reader. The two disciples were unaware of what he was doing. This movement takes place after Jesus has finished clarifying their misunderstanding about his messianic identity and mission. He has given them enough clues to recognize him.[19] Jesus' 'acting' gives the reader the impression that he intends to stay with them, but also desires an invitation from them. Perhaps, he wants an appropriate response to his explanation of the Scriptures. It provides an opportunity for the disciples to express their kindness to him, a stranger.

7. Invitation

Yes, they ask Jesus to stay with them. Since the day was setting, they did not want him to continue his journey alone.[20] From their earlier conversation with him, they seemed to have learned that he was a stranger in that place. So if he were to travel alone, it would have been dangerous for him. Finding a place to stay could also have been difficult for him. They did not ask him anything about his onward journey or his destination but urged (*parebiasanto*) him to stay with them. They also gave the reason: "for it is toward evening and the day is now far spent". The reader can recognize something remarkably beautiful in their urging: their concern for a stranger. They did not want him to be exposed to possible dangers. If he stayed with them, they might be inconvenienced. But they did not seem to care about anything like that. Their compassion and concern for a fellow human being outweighed everything else. Without hesitation, Jesus accepted their invitation and remained with them. If they had not invited him to stay with them, he would have left them, and they would

---

17 Fitzmyer, *The Gospel according to Luke X-XXIV*, 1566. Gillman interprets the instruction of Jesus as a preparation for the disciples for their future mission "that will bring to them suffering and death". See John Gillman, "The Emmaus Story in Luke-Acts Revisited", in *Resurrection in the New Testament: Festschrift J. Lambrecht*, eds. R. Bieringer, V. Koperski & B. Lataire (Leuven–Paris: Leuven University Press, 2002), 175.

18 Many commentators are of the opinion that it was not just "play-acting"; Jesus would have left them if they had not asked him to stay. See, for example, Richard C. Blight, *An Exegetical Summary of Luke 12–24* (Dallas, TX: SIL International, 2008), 557.

19 In many ways, the Lord helps the believer to recognize him. But he never insists or imposes it.

20 "Night travel, particularly as one got farther from Jerusalem, would be dangerous due to robbers." Keener, *The IVP Bible Background Commentary* (Lk 24:29), 256.

have reached Emmaus and remained there! But their compelling invitation, motivated by their concern for the safety of a stranger, changes the whole story.[21]

8. The Revelation and Recognition

The disciples had taken the initiative to invite Jesus and show compassion towards him. Now, he also took the initiative to reveal himself by breaking bread. Normally, it is the host who blesses the bread before meals, but here Jesus, the stranger whom they invited to stay with them, took the bread, blessed it, broke it, and gave it to them. The language used here evokes the multiplication of the loaves (Lk 9:16) and the last supper with the disciples (Lk 22:19). It was an act that they must have been familiar with. Many times, when they were with Jesus, they would have witnessed the breaking of the bread.[22] As they witnessed this act of Jesus, their eyes were opened, and they recognized him. Then they realized that it was Jesus himself who was travelling with them. The narrator's comment "their eyes were opened" should be seen as a continuation of "their eyes were prevented from recognizing him" in verse 16. The passive "were opened" (*dianoichthesan*) can be interpreted as a theological passive, "their eyes were opened by God to see the significance of the action and thus to recognise Jesus".[23] When Jesus joined them on their journey they were confused and frustrated, and were not ready or prepared to recognize him, but once their confusion was removed they were made worthy of recognizing him.

The disciples recognized Jesus as he was breaking bread. But it was their compassion for the stranger that led to the breaking of the bread and the consequent revelation. When one shows kindness to one's fellow beings, the Lord reveals himself. As Gillman puts it, "[b]y the offer of hospitality the Emmaus companions were able to transcend their self-concern, sadness, foolishness and slowness of heart, thus preparing them for the revelatory experience around the table where they were nourished".[24] This event echoes the question of the righteous and the response of the King in the Last Judgement scene in the gospel of Matthew: "when did we see thee a stranger and welcome

21 Some scholars recognize a liturgical pattern in the Emmaus story qualifying Jesus' instruction as the "liturgy of the Word" and his breaking of bread as the "liturgy of the Eucharist". The compassion expressed by the disciples to a stranger is placed between these two (*liturgical*) acts of Jesus presenting it as a pivotal moment in the narrative.

22 "The memory of the many meals that Jesus has shared with them, and especially the meal he shared on the night before he died (22:14-38) opens their eyes and anticipates the many meals that will be celebrated in the future". Moloney, *The Resurrection of the Messiah*, 85.

23 I. Howard Marshall, *The Gospel of Luke: A Commentary on the Greek Text*, NIGTC (Grand Rapids, MI: Paternoster Press, 1978), 898.

24 Gillman, "The Emmaus Story", 185.

thee…?"; "truly, I say to you, as you did it to one of the least of these my brethren, you did it to me" (Mt 25: 38-40).

Jesus' vanishing from their sight after revealing himself is also highly significant. The Lord was no longer visible to them, but they could recognize his presence in acts of compassion and in the breaking of bread.

9. Burning of Hearts

When the disciples recognized Jesus, they also became aware of what was going on in themselves during their conversation with him along the way. With great wonder and joy, they exclaim: "Did not our hearts burn within us while he talked to us on the road, while he opened to us the scriptures?". Scholars interpret the metaphor of "burning hearts" using various terms that express human feelings: enthusiasm, expectation, joy, delight, energy, new faith, assurance, intense emotion of excitement and comfort, etc.[25] The disciples did not realize these feelings until Jesus revealed himself to them. The Scriptures do indeed kindle the heart, but only when one recognizes the Lord, does one realize that it is glowing.

10. The Return

The two disciples who left Jerusalem during the day returned to Jerusalem that same evening. The reader may recall how they had dissuaded Jesus from continuing his journey because the day was nearly over. Their return to Jerusalem at that very hour is deeply symbolic. As noted above, they might have left Jerusalem that morning out of fear, and possibly to avoid the adverse consequences resulting from the story of the empty tomb. They had been confused, scared, and frustrated, but now they were free from all such fears. They had met Jesus; they had recognized the risen Lord who journeyed with them from Jerusalem to Emmaus. All their fears were gone, and now they were a new people, and so they ran back to Jerusalem to share their joy with their companions and proclaim the risen Lord. The one who recognizes the Lord cannot but proclaim him!

The episode ends with them joining the Eleven and the other companions. So, they are back in the group of disciples. For a while they had left the group and gone away. Before they shared their experience, they heard from the Eleven the good news of Jesus' resurrection: "the Lord is risen indeed, and he has appeared to Simon" (24:34). His simultaneous appearance to Simon shows the omnipresence of the risen Jesus. He is present in different places at the same time. The two disciples also tell the others how they had encountered the risen Jesus. The phrase "in the breaking of the bread" is particularly significant in the narrator's summary of their proclamation. Readers may well hear an

25 See Blight, *An Exegetical Summary of Luke*, 561.

invitation to recognize the Lord "in the breaking of the bread" that was being practised in their community "in his memory".

Conclusion

The Emmaus story, placed at the end of the gospel, beautifully depicts the ebb and flow of the faith-journey of every disciple who believes in Jesus and in the divine life offered through his life, death and resurrection. The fear, frustration, and confusion that Cleopas and his companion go through until they recognize the risen Lord reflect the experience of disciples of all time – their desolations and consolations on the way. Throughout the story, readers are constantly reminded of the truth that the risen Lord is their co-traveller and they are invited to recognize him as such. However, it is only when God opens their eyes that they can see who he is. Just knowing about Jesus or the things that happened to him is not enough for someone to merit such recognition. If the disciples allow the Lord to travel with him and are willing to listen to him, he will lead them to a proper understanding of his messianic identity and mission. Moreover, following his model, if they show compassion to the needy, the Lord will surely take the initiative to reveal himself. The Emmaus story enlightens believers about the significance of "the breaking of bread" which Jesus gave his disciples as a parting gift at the Last Supper and asked them to repeat in memory of him. When Jesus celebrates it at Emmaus their eyes are opened, and they can recognize him. His vanishing from their sight after giving them the broken loaves symbolically invites readers to experience his invisible presence in the bread when they break it in memory of him. Not only are their eyes opened, but also their inner perception. Once they recognize the Lord, they review the whole journey with an illuminated heart. Recognizing the Lord as the co-traveller changes the course of life's journey. The faint-hearted disciples who flee Jerusalem run back to Jerusalem that same evening to spread the joy of their meeting with the risen Lord. With them the reader also shares the conviction that the Lord is risen; he is our co-traveller.

3

A Sapiential Reading of Lk 24:13-25 through an Ignatian Lens

Rolphy Pinto, SJ

Introduction

The Evangelist Luke is a storyteller at his best, perhaps with the exception of the parable of the Prodigal Son, in the passage of the "Walk to Emmaus".[1] The passage is heart-warming for most believers, as their own spiritual experiences find an echo in the narration.

The general goal of the Gospel narrative is that the reader may come to have Faith in the Risen Lord.[2] The goal is not to explain the movements of the

---

1 J. A. Fitzmyer, *The Gospel According to Luke X-XXIV: Introduction, Translation, and Notes* (New Haven; London: Yale University Press, 2008), 1558-9; "Luke's storytelling ability is beautifully displayed in this appearance story. He provides a sense of particularity by the rich use of detail: the name of the village and its distance from the city, the name of the disciple, the gestures of hospitality. The story is full of emotions subtly sketched: the men stopping in sorrow, their report that the women had 'stunned' them, their recollection of how their 'hearts had burned' while in conversation with Jesus". Luke Timothy Johnson, *The Gospel of Luke*, ed. Daniel J. Harrington, Sacra Pagina Series (Collegeville (MN): The Liturgical Press, 1991)., 398

2 "The divine purpose is to reveal the risen Jesus to them [the two disciples] gradually, through the Scriptures and the breaking of the bread". Pablo Turra Gadenz, *The Gospel of Luke*, Catholic Commentary on Sacred Scripture. (Grand Rapids (MI): Baker Academic,

spirit leading either to spiritual consolation or spiritual desolation. Likewise, Ignatius makes no mention of the Emmaus narrative while describing the Rules for Discernment of Spirits. Yet, when the passage is read with the experiential knowledge of the Rules, we come to an enriched understanding of both the Gospel text and the Rules for Discernment. This article is a substantiation of this point through a sapiential reading of the chosen Gospel passage.

Jules J. Toner in his *A Commentary on Saint Ignatius' Rules for the Discernment of Sprit*, gives, midway through the book, a summary of the First Week Rules in a chapter titled "A Synthesis through a Gospel Story, Rules I:1-14."[3] In this article I take a cue from his insights and wish to expand his work further. I also wish to amplify its scope by applying, when warranted, some Second Week Rules as well. I include some of my own reflections when appropriate. I will proceed by quoting a verse, a part it, or a group of versus from Lk 24: 13-25 and by providing a commentary after each quotation.[4]

1. The meeting (vv. 13-16)[5]

> [13] *Now on that same day two of them were going to a village called Emmaus, about seven miles from Jerusalem, ...*

Why are the two leaving? The fear of Jews (cf. Jn 20:19) who had crucified Jesus seems to be the principal reason. They were afraid because their faith in the promise of Jesus had dwindled. They yield to their fear. Ignatius advices against this (cf. *SpEx* [325]). Diminished faith or lack of it is a sign of spiritual desolation (cf. *SpEx* [313]).[6] Why do they go to Emmaus? Luke has a geographical concern. He sets Jerusalem as the location of Jesus' apparitions.

2018), 393; Cf. Luke Timothy Johnson, *The Gospel of Luke*, ed. Daniel J. Harrington, Sacra Pagina Series (Collegeville (MN): The Liturgical Press, 1991), 391.

3 Jules J. Toner, *A Commentary on Saint Ignatius' Rules for the Discernment of Spirits: A Guide to the Principles and Practice*, The Institute of Jesuit Sources: Series III. Original Studies, Composed in English (Anand (India): Gujarat Sahitya Prakash, 1982), 205-210.

4 Biblical quotations are from *The New Revised Standard Version Bible,* Catholic Edition (Bangalore: TPI, 1999).

5 The four-part structure is Fitzmyer's. *The Gospel According to Luke*, 1559.

6 *SpEx* = *Spiritual Exercises*. Text in Joseph A. Munitiz and Philip Endean, eds, *Saint Ignatius of Loyola, Personal Writings: Reminiscences, Spiritual Diary, Select Letters Including the Text of The Spiritual Exercises*, trans. Joseph A. Munitiz and Philip Endean, Penguin Classics (London [etc.]: Penguin, 1996). Ignatius calls spiritual desolation everything that is contrary to spiritual consolation (cf. *SpEx* [317]). He gives the following description of spiritual consolation:

On spiritual consolation. I use the word 'consolation' when any interior movement is produced in the soul that leads her to become inflamed with the love of her Creator and Lord, and when, as a consequence, there is no created thing on the face of the earth that we can love in itself, but we love it only in the Creator of all things.

That Emmaus is in the vicinity[7] of Jerusalem is what matters for Luke.[8] The mentioning of a concrete place could also indicate the real occurrence of the event.[9] Emmaus also has historical significance. The "plains near Emmaus" are mentioned in 1Macc 3: 40, 57; 4:3.[10] Judas the Maccabee and his men routed the forces of Antiochus in the battle of Emmaus in 166 BC. This was a victory that came after 500 years of foreign rule. It made possible the independence of Israel for a century[11]. Emmaus may thus be seen as a symbol of victory. Taking refuge in a place of past victory acts as a comfort zone.

With the crucifixion and death of Jesus, the dream of the fugitive disciples, that of participation in the reign of a political Messiah, was frustrated. Ignatius' dream of rising higher up on the ladder of political power was frustrated when his leg was shattered by the cannonball in the Battle of Pamplona, May 1520. Be it frustrated disciples, be it a wounded soldier, all retreat and retire into physical or metaphorical "secure places" (cf. *A* [1]).[12]

The disciples begin the journey "on the same day". It was meant to be a mere physical journey but ends up being a spiritual journey, a faith journey. That coming to faith and spiritual maturity is a process, a journey, is more than evident in this Gospel story. The fact that Ignatius provides two sets of Rules for Discernment, for the First Week and for the Second Week, necessarily presupposes spiritual life as a process. The Weeks are stages of spiritual growth. Different rules apply in different stages. In the initial phases of the journey, one discerns between things more easily perceived as good and evil (cf. *SpEx* [9]); while in the advanced phase of the journey, one needs to discern between the real good and the apparent good (cf. *SpEx* [10]).

The two *leave*. The suggestion in Acts 1: 4 implies that they should have stayed in Jerusalem. The two leave, abandoning the group of others who, in

---

Similarly, I use the word 'consolation' when one sheds tears that lead to love of one's Lord, whether these arise from grief over one's sins, or over the Passion of Christ Our Lord, or over other things expressly directed towards His service and praise.

Lastly, I give the name 'consolation' to every increase of hope, faith and charity, to all interior happiness that calls and attracts a person towards heavenly things and to the soul's salvation, leaving the soul quiet and at peace in her Creator and Lord. (*SpEx* [316]).

7 There is no agreement on the exact distance. Some estimate it to be 18.4 miles (160 *staida*) from Jerusalem. Cf. Fitzmyer, *The Gospel According to Luke*, 1561.

8 Cf. Fitzmyer. *The Gospel According to Luke*, 1562; D. L. Bock, *Luke Volume 2: 9:51-24:53*, Baker Exegetical Commentary on the New Testament (Grand Rapids, Mich.: Baker Books, 1996)., 1908-09; Johnson, *The Gospel of Luke*, 393.

9 Cf. Bock, *Luke*, 1909.

10 Cf. Fitzmyer, *The Gospel According to Luke*, 1561.

11 Cf. William Weir, *50 Battles That Changed the World. The Conflicts That Most Influenced the Course of History* (Franklin Lakes, NJ: Career Press, 2001), 113-116.

12 *A* = *Autobiography of St Ignatius*. Text in Munitiz and Endean, *Personal Writings*.

spite of the fear, continue to stay. It certainly was a time of desolation for all the disciples, ever since the moment of Jesus' agony in the garden. They were going from one desolation to another.[13] What should one do in the time of desolation? Ignatius' first advice is "In time of desolation one should never make any change", [14] as it is the evil spirit who counsels during this time (*SpEx* [318]). Not making a change in this case would have meant remaining in union with the rest of the disciples in Jerusalem. The disciples may have thought that going away from Jerusalem, i.e., making an external change, would change the way they felt. In *SpEx* [319], Ignatius advises the one in desolation "to make an intense effort to change oneself in a sense opposed to" the desolation (i.e., to make an internal change), by insisting on prayer and meditation. This would have meant the disciples' holding on to the promises of Jesus (cf. Lk 18: 33). It also would have meant their practicing the virtue that is to be practiced during desolation, which is patience, keeping in mind that consolation would soon return (cf. *SpEx* [321]).

The disciples will spend an entire day to cover the seven miles to Emmaus from Jerusalem. In the time of desolation, spiritual practices and everything else are difficult (cf. *SpEx* [13]). The disciples leave at daybreak. While there is light outside, there is darkness inside – lack of faith, hope and love (cf. *SpEx* [317]).

> **14** *... and talking with each other about all these things that had happened.* **15** *While they were talking and discussing, ...*

We know the content their talking, which is made more explicit in vv.19-24. They were talking about the things that had transpired mainly in the past three days. They were also "discussing". Discussion does not necessarily have a negative connotation, but at times can become argumentative over issues upon which the persons involved in the discussion do not agree. In the given circumstances, the probability of the discussion's having become discordant is likely. In the time of desolation, it is the evil spirit that is guiding[15]. The nature

---

13 This is an instance of "people who go from one mortal sin to another..." (*SpEx* [314]). "Sin" need not be interpreted here as an act of sinning but rather as something experienced as absence of grace, as is usually the case when people go through experiences of desolation. In general, though, this is characteristic not of a person in the very initial stages of spiritual journey but of a person going from good to better. Cf. Toner, *A Commentary on Saint Ignatius' Rules for the Discernment of Spirits*, 207.

14 In the decision taken in the preceding moment of consolation. Before the passion of Jesus, the disciples had confidently promised to stay with Jesus, affirming their readiness even to lay down their lives (cf. Jn 11: 16, Mc 14: 27-31)

15 There is no explicit mention of Satan in the episode (cf. Fitzmyer, *The Gospel According to Luke*, 1558). Yet, it would not be inappropriate to affirm that the actions of the two disciples were motivated by a spirit that is contrary to the spirit of God, or the good spirit.

of the evil one is to divide. He sows pessimism and makes one believe that all doors are closed. He presses a spiritual regression, leading persons to their old selves (cf. Col 3: 9-10; Eph 4: 21-22)[16]. The Emmaus journey here is symbolic of spiritual regression.[17]

> *[15] ... Jesus himself came near and went with them, [16] but their eyes were kept from recognizing him. [17] And he said to them, "What are you discussing with each other while you walk along?"*

Jesus enters softly, without making noise. "The good angel touches the soul *gently, lightly, and sweetly,* like a drop of water going into a sponge" (*SpEx* [335])[18]. Though the good angel enters softly, he is perceived as entering violently as a "drop of water falls on a stone" (*SpEx* [335]). The fearful disciples do not want to be discovered.[19] They detest a stranger's intrusion. Spiritually, they are going from one desolation to another. Hence they experience the soft, discreet coming of Jesus as disturbance.

Due to darkness in the soul "their eyes were closed".[20] The soul in desolation fails to perceive the presence of God, "the divine help [which] remains with them at all times, even though they may not clearly feel" it (*SpEx* [320]). When people are in desolation, even the most obvious seems obscure to them, as will be seen in a brief while in the case of the disciples.

Entering into a conversation with them, Jesus begins to walk with the disciples. Even though he knows that they should not have taken up the journey in the first place, he does not stop them. He walks in the "wrong direction" with them[21]. Ignatius advices Broët and Salmerón to employ the strategy of the enemy (cf. *SpEx* [332]) for the greater service of the Lord,

---

16 Cf. Toner, *A Commentary on Saint Ignatius' Rules for the Discernment of Spirits*, 205.

17 Cf. Toner., *A Commentary on Saint Ignatius' Rules for the Discernment of Spirits*, 207.

18 This is the manner in which the good spirit enters a soul in consolation. If a soul is experiencing desolation the movement of the good spirit is not readily embraced by the soul. The good spirit pricks the conscience in such instances (cf. *SpEx* [314]).

19 The enemy of the human nature induces the person to keep secret his evil intentions (cf. *SpEx* [326]).

20 Expressions speaking of the opening and closing of eyes appear also in the writing of Ignatius. Writing of when, in Loyola, he first became aware of the movement different spirits, he says, "his eyes were opened a little" (*A* [8]). Writing of when, in Manresa, the gift of discerning the spirits matured in him through the mystical illumination at the river Cardoner he says, "the eyes of his understanding began to be opened" (*A* [30]). V. 31 below will mention the opening of the eyes of the disciples.

21 Cf. Pope Francis, Post-Synodal Apostolic Exhortation *Christus Vivit* [292], Text available at http://www.vatican.va/content/francesco/en/apost_exhortations/documents/papa-francesco_esortazione-ap_20190325_christus-vivit.html. Access 08.07.2020.

> ...we should adopt the same procedure the enemy uses with a good soul – he always for evil and we always for good. The enemy enters through the other's door and comes out his own. He enters the other's door by praising rather than contradicting his ways [...] In the same way, we, [acting] for good, can praise a person or go along with him on some particular good point [...] Once we have won his love, we will better get what we want. Thus, we go in his door and come out our own.[22]

Jesus walks in the wrong direction with the disciples to win them over to himself.

2. The Conversation *en Route* (vv. 17-27)

> *... They stood still, looking sad.* [18] *Then one of them, whose name was Cleopas, answered him, "Are you the only stranger in Jerusalem who does not know the things that have taken place there in these days?"*

"Looking sad" is a clear sign of desolation (cf. *SpEx* [317]). The irritation in the tone of the reply to Jesus' question is evident. The reply is rude and does not answer Jesus' question in a simple and direct way. The response given does not invite a dialogue but, rather, cuts it short. People in desolation do not easily open up, and conversation with them is never easy. Sarcasm, cynicism, negativity, pessimism and anger are some more signs of spiritual desolation.

> [19] *He asked them, "What things?"*

Contrary to the attitude of the disciples, the openness of Jesus' question re-initiates a dialogue that seemed to have ended even before it began. In the way of the good spirit, there is neither anger nor irritation. His way is direct and simple. The good spirit opens up dialogue, but the evil one places obstacles.

> *... They replied, "The things about Jesus of Nazareth, who was a prophet mighty in deed and word before God and all the people,* [20] *and how our chief priests and leaders handed him over to be condemned to death and crucified him."*

This is all true.

> [21] *"But we had hoped that he was the one to redeem Israel. Yes, and besides all this, it is now the third day since these things took*

22 Letter to Alfonso Salmerón and Paschase Broët, Rome, early September 1541. In John W. Padberg and John L. McCarthy, eds, *Ignatius of Loyola: Letters and Instructions*, trans. Martin E. Palmer (Saint Louis (MO): Institute of Jesuit Sources, 2006), 66.

> *place. [22] Moreover, some women of our group astounded us. They were at the tomb early this morning, [23] and when they did not find his body there, they came back and told us that they had indeed seen a vision of angels who said that he was alive. [24] Some of those who were with us went to the tomb and found it just as the women had said; but they did not see him."*

A "but" leads into "we had hoped" – they feel deluded and deceived. "... it is typical of the bad spirit to harass, sadden and obstruct, and to disturb the soul with false reasoning, so as to impede..." (*SpEx* [315]). The disciples fail to see the obvious. They do not believe the testimony of the women nor the confirmation of their witness by those who were with them.[23] They keep insisting, with another "but", this leading into "they did *not see* him."[24] The evil spirit works in the intellect and obscures the reasoning. They reason, but speciously. Rather than practicing patience, they make a decision in a hurry, that of abandoning Jerusalem. They do not pause to ask, "What actually has taken place?" or "Why is there no body in the tomb?" The evil one is intelligent. His strategy is veiled and delusive. He does not tempt the disciples with the obvious or with an outright lie. He makes them say, "It is now the third day." This is a half-truth. The third day is not over yet. The disciples fall prey to half-truth (cf. *SpEx* [329]).

While the evil spirit induces one to make decisions hastily, the good spirit is patient. The good spirit listens, as does Jesus, to the entire story of the disciples and does not intervene until they have finished.[25] If need be, the good spirit may gently nudge the persons to speak up and to narrate the full story.

> *[25] Then he said to them, "Oh, how foolish you are, and how slow of heart to believe all that the prophets have declared! [26] Was it not necessary that the Messiah should suffer these things and then enter into his glory?"*

After listening patiently to the disciples, Jesus begins to "break the Word" for them. Unlike the evil spirit, who behaves irresponsibly by telling only what one may wish to hear, the good says what they should be hearing. The good spirit is fearless, even reprimanding, if need be. The language of the good

---

23 "The gradual revelation of Jesus contains irony: the empty tomb has not yet created an ecstatic change of view; in fact, the travellers lament that Jesus has not been seen even though the tomb is empty". Bock, *Luke.*, 1903.

24 Emphasis added.

25 Ignatius instructs Broët and Salmerón going to Ireland, to listen to the other for long and willingly and not to speak until the other has finished speaking and said everything. Cf. Padberg and McCarthy, *Ignatius of Loyola: Letters and Instructions*, 65.

spirit is clear and straightforward, at the same time not being harsh. The good spirit is not deceitful.

Often spiritual desolation is caused when one is unwilling to take up one's cross and runs away from it (the second cause of desolation cf. *SpEx* [322]). The disciples, who had always dreamt of a glorious messiah, were unable to understand the mystery of the cross and were unwilling to accept a suffering messiah.[26] The Evil one attacks the weakest point of the fortress (cf. *SpEx* [327]). Their difficulty in understanding and accepting that the messiah had to be a suffering messiah was their weak point.[27]

> [27] *Then beginning with Moses and all the prophets, he interpreted to them the things about himself in all the scriptures.*

The Word of God enlightens lives and illuminates spiritual journeys. The process of discernment, too, needs the mediation of the Word of God in order for it to be authentic.[28] In retrospect, the disciples will admit that it was when Jesus was explaining the Scriptures to them that the clouds of doubt were dispersed from their hearts. The Scriptures nourish the faith life of the believers. Jesus interprets the experience of the disciples in the light of the Scriptures. In the light of the Scriptures, life becomes more intelligible. One finds meaning in the midst of the trials of life. The light of the Scriptures reveals the snares set by the evil one along the path of a life's journey. This is the reason why one in desolation should be insistent on prayer and meditation (cf. *SpEx* [319]), which, invariably, should have the Scriptures as their source.

3. The Emmaus Meal (vv. 28-32)

> [28] *As they came near the village to which they were going, he walked ahead as if he were going on.*

Jesus desired intensely to remain with the disciples,[29] but the good spirit does not force its way and does not impose its will, but leaves one free at all times. It is the nature of the evil one, rather, to enslave persons (cf. *SpEx* [142, 146]). Under the influence of the good spirit, the exercise of one's freedom acquires its true purpose. It is then that one can make the right choices.

---

26 Cf. Fitzmyer, *The Gospel According to Luke.*, 1558; Bock, *Luke.*, 1916.

27 Cf. Toner, *A Commentary on Saint Ignatius' Rules for the Discernment of Spirits.*, 207.

28 Cf. Toner., 207, 209.

29 "He walked ahead as if he were going on" is simply a narrative device meant to bring liveliness and humanity to the story (cf. Johnson, *The Gospel of Luke.*, 396). Yet, it is characteristic of the behaviour of the good spirit, in being non-imposing.

> [29] *But they urged him strongly, saying, "Stay with us, because it is almost evening and the day is now nearly over." So he went in to stay with them.*

This is one of the most beautiful prayers in the Bible. It is also an example of the Spirit praying in us (cf. Rom 8: 26-27). In the time of desolation (especially), one should seek help. When one reveals one's embarrassing secrets to a confessor or a spiritual accompanier the evil one cannot succeed in his malicious purpose (cf. *SpEx* [326]).

> [30] *When he was at the table with them, he took bread, blessed and broke it, and gave it to them.* [31] *Then their eyes were opened, and they recognized him; and he vanished from their sight.*

After the completion of the "breaking of the Word", Jesus "breaks bread" for the disciples. The closed eyes of their soul are opened now. Lucidity returns to their souls. With the eyes of the soul open, they not only "see" but "recognise" Jesus. With their physical eyes they had only seen Jesus, but it is only with the eyes of the soul that they recognise Jesus.[30]

Jesus vanished from their sight, but the spiritual consolation they felt did not. It was not a momentary experience. This trait of durability is a sign that the consolation is authentic. This was the first difference that Ignatius had noticed when he became aware of the movements of spirits within his soul while he was convalescing in Loyola. Fantasy of worldly concerns gave him delight, but that delight left him as soon as the fantasy ended, whereas the consolation he felt when he thought about the ascetic and spiritual practices he would take up in the service of the Lord endured even after his setting those thoughts aside (cf. *A* [8]; *SpEx* [333]).

Jesus vanishing from their sights also teaches a valuable lesson in the art of spiritual accompaniment. Though Ignatius mentions a "spiritual person" who is versed in the discernment of spirits (cf. *SpEx* [326]), the Rules for Discernment do not explicitly mention the need for an accompanier in the process of discernment. This need, however, is clear in the Annotations (*SpEx* [1-20])[31]. The protagonists of the journey of the Spiritual Exercises are three, God, the exercitant and the accompanier, in this order of importance. The accompanier, "like the pointer of a balance, should leave the Creator to work directly with the creature, and the creature with the Creator and Lord"

30 Cf. Fitzmyer, *The Gospel According to Luke*, 1558.

31 More specifically, rules 8, 9 and 10 ([8-10]) presuppose the familiarity of the giver of the Exercises with the Rules for Discernment of Spirits and the giver's knowing when and how to give them to the exercitant.

(*SpEx* [15]). Jesus, himself the divine mystery, is also the mystagogue[32] who "vanishes" once the creature is placed in touch with the Creator. The role of the spiritual accompanier – be it in spiritual direction, in retreat direction, or in the accompaniment of a person in a process of discernment – is to help the one accompanied to find God and then to step back. It is never to take centre stage.

> *[32] They said to each other, "Were not our hearts burning within us while he was talking to us on the road, while he was opening the scriptures to us?"*

"Hearts burning": Timothy Johnson notes, "The notion of 'burning' (*kaiomenē*) is sometimes associated in Greek literature with emotions such as love".[33] In his description of spiritual consolation Ignatius writes, "… when any interior movement is produced in the soul that leads her to become inflamed with the love of her Creator and Lord…" (*SpEx* [316]). Another expression dear to Ignatius is "*abrazándola* [ánima] *en su amor y alabanza y disponiéndola*" (as He inflames her [soul] in His love and praise, disposing her. *SpEx* [15]). "*Abrazándo*" is also translated as embracing, and some early manuscripts of the *Spiritual Exercises* use the verb *abrazar* (embrace), while others *abrasar* (burn or inflame).[34] The burning of the hearts is spiritual consolation.

All along the way, the three have been conversing with each other. Such conversation can be fittingly called a spiritual conversation. After Jesus "vanishes", the disciples do a quick re-vision of what they had just experienced, i.e., an examination of consciousness. They exclaim, "Were not our hearts burning…". How did one know with certainty that the other's heart, too, was burning? A personal experience of God (consolation) enables one to perceive the experience of spiritual consolation in others. This is also a desired result of spiritual conversation: having an intuition of the movements of the spirit in the souls of the participants in the conversation. The discordant hearts of the disciples have now become concordant. Their hearts are harmonious.

4. The Return to Jerusalem (vv. 33-35)

> *[33] That same hour they got up and returned to Jerusalem; and they found the eleven and their companions gathered together. [34] They*

32 Cf. Pinto, Paul Rolphy, "The Mystagogical Dimension of Spiritual Conversation: An Ignatian Perspective", *Gregorianum* 101, no. 2 (2020): 391–403.; Toner, *A Commentary on Saint Ignatius' Rules for the Discernment of Spirits*., 208.

33 Johnson, *The Gospel of Luke*., 397.

34 Cf. Pietro Schiavone, ed, *Esercizi Spirituali: Ricerca Sulle Fonti*, Spiritualità/Maestri. Seconda Serie (Cinisello Balsamo (MI): San Paolo, 1995)., 85, 203; *Diario Espiritual* (18 de febrero) [43] in Santiago Thió de Pol, ed, *La Intimidad Del Peregrino: Diario Espiritual de San Ignacio de Loyola* (Bilbao: Mensajero, 1990).

were saying, "The Lord has risen indeed, and he has appeared to Simon!" [34] *Then they told what had happened on the road, and how he had been made known to them in the breaking of the bread.*

"That same hour": Spiritual consolation is other oriented. One gets out of oneself and reaches out to others because of increased faith, hope and charity. The two return to the other disciples, from whose company they had parted earlier. Their regenerated faith dispels all fear from their hearts. At this hour, it is dark outside, but there is light within their hearts. The inner movements in the soul may, at times, correspond with the external circumstances, but, as in this case, spiritual consolations and desolations are not determined by those external circumstances. Earlier in the day, when there was light outside, the disciples experienced darkness within. Now, with light in their souls, they walk back without fear in the dark of the night and seem to reach Jerusalem in no time, unlike the entire day they took to reach Emmaus. In the time of consolation, spiritual activity and all else seems effortless (cf. *SpEx* [13]).

In a time of spiritual desolation, the two disciples left the community. Encounter with the risen Lord, i.e., experience of spiritual consolation, builds community. They return to be with the disciples. The community of disciple will soon disperse, but this dispersion is not induced by fear. The new dispersion will be for mission.[35] Mission emerges out of the community united in the name of Lord. It will be the same risen Lord who will send them from the community united in his name.

Conclusion

The journey of the disciples on the road to Emmaus is a journey from deep and total spiritual desolation to sublime spiritual consolation. The experiences of the disciples are illustrative of the experiences underlying the Rules for Discernment codified by Ignatius. The Christian believer who walks with the disciples will understand the ups and downs, the consolations and desolations, involved in the spiritual journey of the disciples. The light of that understanding will, in turn, help one to understand one's own spiritual faith journey. Reading the Emmaus passage with the aid of the Ignatian Rules for Discernment sheds light upon the dynamics caused by the movements of different spirits – their origin, their direction and their end. Since the spiritual faith journeys of Christian believers are no different from those of the disciples on the road to Emmaus, to understand the dynamics of their journey is to understand the believer's own internal processes of spiritual consolation and desolation.

35 Persecution too will scatter the disciples from Jerusalem to other towns, but it becomes a means to spread the Word of God in other places (Cf. Acts 8:1-4; Mt 10: 23). What seemed like a hindrance to the proclamation of the Word, becomes a blessing in fulfilling the Jesus' mission. At no point fear will hold them back from proclaiming the Good News.

4

Secretly Expressed, Publicly Praised
The Faith Story of the Women with Hemorrhage in Matthew

Simon Thomas, SJ

Introduction

"Faith is the assurance of things hoped for, the conviction of things not seen" (Heb 11:1). The woman with the hemorrhage, whose story is presented in all three synoptic gospels, is a true example for such a profound faith with assurance, hope and conviction. The woman, who was considered impure and sinful due to her illness, had the courage to believe that even a touch of Jesus' clothes could make her well. She secretly expresses her courage and conviction, but publicly obtains healing and praise. Each synoptic writer presents her story with some particularities. In this essay, we read the expression of her faith as presented by the evangelist Matthew, who in his gospel narrates several such faith-stories of simple people, who were from the margins of the society (Mt 8:1-4; 9:2-8, 27-31, 32-34; 15:21-28), to help his readers learn from their unshakable faith-conviction.[1]

1 These stories tell the readers that it is not persons' ethnic identity, religion, colour, caste, creed, gender, or social status that makes them true followers of Jesus, but their unwavering

I choose the theme of faith for this paper as a note of gratitude to Fr. Scaria, who was my professor of *New Testament Theology* at JDV, Pune. Through his teaching and life, he has enriched my faith in Jesus, and he has motivated me to study the Word of God, and thus, go closer to Jesus and His people.

1. The Story in Matthew

It is assumed, following the two-source theory, that Matthew took this story from the gospel of Mark.[2] However, Matthew has made several changes in the story and placed it in the section of Miracles and Healings (Mt 8-9).[3] For example, Mark narrates the story in 10 verses (Mk 5:25-34), while Matthew in just 3 verses (Mt 9:20-22).[4] Though Matthew follows Mark by inserting the pericope between the story of the ruler who requests Jesus to restore his dead daughter (Mt 9:18-19, 23-26), he has done substantial redaction, however, by which he brings a turning point in the story of the woman as compared to Mark. Matthew focuses only on the faith expression of the woman and the power by which Jesus heals her, and he evades bringing the ruler, the disciples, and probably the crowd in the scene, though they are present with Jesus. Matthew also omits the lengthy introduction on the woman and her sickness which is depicted in Mk 5:25-27, before she touches the garment of Jesus. He only mentions that she had been suffering from bleeding for twelve years.[5] While Mark uses the Greek words ῥύσει αἵματος (flow of blood) or ἡ πηγὴ τοῦ αἵματος (the fountain of blood) for her sickness (which are mostly used in Lev

faith in him.

2 "The most widely held hypothesis about the relationship between the Synoptic Gospels is that the Gospel of Mark was a principal source for the Gospels of Matthew and Luke". See Everett R. Kalin, "Matthew 9:18-26: An Exercise in Redaction Criticism," *CTM* 15 (1988): 39-47.

3 These two chapters, according to France, are constructed to play a foundational role in the building up of Matthew's account of Jesus as the Messiah. See Richard T. France, *The Gospel of Matthew*, NICNT (Grand Rapids: Eerdmans, 2007), 299.

4 "Matthew needs a mere 48 words for the woman with the hemorrhage, compared to Mark's 154 words." See France, *The Gospel of Matthew*, 360. In fact, Mt 9:20-22 is the most abbreviated among all the pericopes taken from the gospel of Mark.

5 The duration of the sickness is given to indicate both the difficulty of the cure and the despair of the sufferer. It is vivid in Mk 9:21; Lk 13:11; Jn 5:5; 9:1; Acts 3:2; 4:22; 9:33; 14:8. See William D. Davies and Dale C. Allison, *The Gospel According to Saint Matthew: A Critical and Exegetical Commentary*, ICC 1 (Edinburgh: T & T Clark, 1988-97), 128. Matthew might have avoided giving a detailed explanation of the sickness as he presumed that his Jewish audience knew about the sickness. Donald A. Hagner, *Matthew 1-13,* WBC 33 (Dallas, TX: Word Books, 1993-95), 248.

15 and 20:18 in the LXX version), Matthew abbreviates the Greek words with the verb αἱμορροέω (haemorrhage) for the sickness.[6]

Matthew omits four verses of Mark, in which Jesus' ignorance of who touched him and the ensuing conversation between Jesus and the disciples are narrated.[7] As soon as the woman touched the fringe of Jesus's garment, he turned and saw her (cf. Mk 5:29-32). According to the first evangelist, there was no confusion; Jesus knew who touched her. He also omits the scene from Mark where the woman comes and tells Jesus why she touched him (Mk 5:33). In Matthew, Jesus knew why the woman touched him, and what was her disease. As soon as Jesus saw the woman, he told her, "Take heart, daughter; your faith has made you well". And the narrator ends the episode of the woman with a brief report on her healing: "And instantly the woman was made well". Thus, Matthew with minimum words portrays her great faith and Jesus' compassionate response to it.

The commonality that this healing story shares with other healing stories in Mt 8-9 is that most of the people who were healed by Jesus in this section were mainly from the periphery of Jewish society or were persons without any public status or power: a leper, the Roman centurion, a paralytic, daughter of the ruler, the woman with hemorrhage, the two blind men and a dumb demoniac. All of them expressed their faith in Jesus and he responded to them positively by healing them. The uniqueness of the story of the woman with a hemorrhage is that while all the other people went to Jesus and expressed their faith openly, she went behind Jesus and expressed her faith secretly. We will discuss this unique aspect of her faith-expression later in this essay.

2. A Sandwich Story

Scholars have various views concerning the insertion of Mt 9:20-22 between Mt 9:18-19 and 9:23-26. Some suggest that it is done to create suspense; others opine that it could be the result of author's carelessness or mistake. As Edwards (who studies Mk 5:25-34), rightly names it, Mt 9:20-22 is a "sandwich

6 "It is a NT hapax legomenon found in Hippocrates and occurring also in Lev 15,33 (for הַנִּדָּה). A uterine hemorrhage is undoubtedly meant". See Davies and Allison, *The Gospel According to Saint Matthew*, 128. Also, αἱμορροέω is to experience a loss of blood, bleed, suffer with hemorrhage. See BDAG, s.v. "αἱμορροέω." A similar abbreviation is also vivid in 8:28, where Matthew inserts δαιμονιζόμενοι instead of ἄνθρωπος ἐν πνεύματι ἀκαθάρτῳ of Mk 5:2.

7 In Mark 5:29, after she touched, the hemorrhage ceased; and she felt in her body that she was healed of her disease. Thus, she was healed because of her great faith. Then, Jesus turns (ἐπιστρέφω) in 5:30, because he realized power had gone out from him. He asks his disciples in 5:31 whether they know who touched, and they rebuke him. Then he looks around to see (περιεβλέπετο ἰδεῖν) who touched him in 5:32.

narrative" or an "intercalation"[8] with "an intentional and discernible theological purpose".[9] The faith of the woman forms the key to the interpretation of the faith of the ruler. It is an assurance to the ruler that if Jesus can heal a deadly sickness, he can surely heal his daughter and resuscitate her.

In accordance with the study in Mark by Guelich[10] and Garland[11], in Matthew too points of contrast and similarity between the two miracle stories could be detected.

- The points of contrast between the two stories are as follows: the man is a chief and reputed member of the society, while the woman is sick and isolated from the community; the chief comes before Jesus, while the woman comes behind Jesus; the chief comes to Jesus and intercedes him to come and touch his daughter and heal her, while the woman comes for her own healing, and she speaks to herself that she can get healed by touching the garment; and finally Jesus touches the daughter of the chief and heals her, while the woman herself touches Jesus and gets healed.
- Also, certain similarities are vivid between the two stories, such as: The stories are about two suffering females: one died around the age of twelve[12], and the other suffering due to her blood flow for twelve years. Also, the names of the chief and the woman are unknown.

8 Intercalation occurs when a story is intentionally imbedded between another story, thereby causing an interruption in the story. Intercalation frames the beginning and ending of a story in such a way that they both serve as a commentary on the imbedded. In other words, intercalation frames a story in an A-B-A' pattern, leaving the 'A' and 'A'' framework to function as a commentary upon 'B'. See James L. Resseguie, *Narrative Criticism of the New Testament: An Introduction* (Grand Rapids, MI: Baker Academic, 2005) 54-55.

9 The technique is, to be sure, a literary technique, but its purpose is theological; that is, the sandwiches emphasize the major motifs of the Gospel, especially the meaning of faith. The woman's faith forms the center of the sandwich and is the key to its interpretation. See James R. Edwards, "Markan Sandwiches: The Significance of Interpolations in Markan Narratives," *NT* 31 (1989): 193-216.

10 Robert A. Guelich and Craig A. Evans, *Mark 1-8:26*, WBC 34A (Dallas, TX : Word Books, 1989-2001) 293.

11 David E. Garland, *Mark*, NIV Application Commentary (Grand Rapids, MI: Zondervan, 1996) 224.

12 Though not specifically mentioned, Levine concludes based on the usage of Greek words such as θυγάτηρ and κοράσιον, that "she must be pubescent, but sexually inexperienced, a virgin more than likely, and she must be around twelve years old". See Stephenson Humphries-Brooks, "The Canaanite Women in Matthew," in *A Feminist Companion to Matthew*, ed. Amy-Jill Levine and Marianne Blickenstaff (Sheffield: Academic Press, 2001) 151. Also, the parallel pericopes in the gospels of Mark and Luke give us an indication that she must be 12 years old (Mk 5:42; Lk 8:42).

> Most importantly, both stories highlight the attitude of deep faith in Jesus, which provokes him to respond positively to both instances.

3. The Woman with her Illness

The woman is introduced in the scene with a short description of her illness. She had been suffering from a hemorrhage for twelve years. Her sickness recalls the purity laws in the Levitical Code.[13] According to Lev 15:19-33, a woman with discharge is unclean. Likewise, anything or anyone that she touches during her discharge also becomes unclean, and one must go through a ritual cleansing to become clean. If a woman is healed, she will be considered ritually clean only after seven days of her healing. On the eighth day, she must bring two turtledoves or two pigeons to the priest as a sin offering and burnt offering, and the priest will make an atonement for her before the Lord. Therefore, a woman with hemorrhage, in Jesus' time, suffered not only from her illness but also from the social and religious taboos which forbade her to go to any public place or meet any person.

The woman is alone with Jesus in the scene. This could indicate a lack of family network and/or community support for her.[14] Keener surmises possible physical, social, and psychological suffering this woman would have endured:

> The condition of the woman is desperate both for medical reasons and because of its social consequences; her partial ostracism would extend especially to her private life. Her ailment probably had kept her from marriage if it started at puberty, and almost surely would have led to her divorce if it began after she was married (which would have been within a few years after puberty), since intercourse was prohibited under such circumstances (Lev 18:19) and childlessness normally led to divorce. The stigma of childlessness, the pain of feeling "left over", the economic consequences of being unable to earn sufficient income, yet having neither husband nor children for

---

13 Some of the important verses of Leviticus 15 regarding this sickness is as follows: Lev 15:19: "When a woman has a discharge of blood, that is, her regular discharge from her body, she shall be in her impurity for seven days, and whoever touches her shall be unclean until the evening". Lev 15:25 is more serious. This verse is closer to our pericope. "If a woman has a discharge of blood for many days, not at the time of her impurity, or if she has a discharge beyond the time of her impurity, all the days of the discharge she shall continue in uncleanness; as in the days of her impurity, she shall be unclean".

14 Stuart L. Love, "Jesus Heals the Hemorrhaging Woman," in *The Social Setting of Jesus and the Gospels*, ed. Wolfgang Stegemann, Bruce J. Malina and Gerd Theissen (Minneapolis, MN: Fortress Press, 2002) 85-102.

long-term support, probably would have made her condition seem almost unbearable.[15]

4. Her Confidence

The woman expresses her confidence in Jesus firstly by going to him, and it is denoted by the Greek verb προσέρχομαι. This verb is largely used in the gospel of Matthew whenever a person goes to Jesus with unconditional faith.[16] Though she was an ostracized person, and was aware of her sickness and the social and religious stigma attached to it, she shows courage to go near to Jesus. She must have felt a strong sense of confidence in Jesus which can be considered as the first act of her faith.

The next expression of faith displayed by the woman is that she went and secretly touched the fringe of the garment of Jesus.[17] Usually, Jesus touches the people and heals them.[18] There is an instance in Mt 14:36 where people touch Jesus with permission and get healed. The woman with hemorrhage is the only character in the gospels who deliberately touches Jesus from behind without his permission and expresses her confidence in him secretly.

In Mark, the woman touches the garment of Jesus while in Matthew she touches the 'fringe' of his garment. The fringe of the garment indicates Jesus' Jewish identity.[19] According to M. Hutter, touching the garment and getting healed (in Mark and Luke) has a magical component; this is a typical Hellenistic belief. On the other hand, touching the 'fringe' of the garment has its roots in the OT and in the Mesopotamian literature. In the political parlance of the Mesopotamian world, touching the fringe of the garment of a ruler meant expressing one's dependency and fidelity to the ruler, and seeking his protection. In the religious realm, it was also a symbolic gesture of prayer and supplication.[20] There are at least two instances in the OT where touching the fringe of the garment symbolizes an invocation to implore help. In 1 Sam 15:27-28, Saul caught hold of the hem of the robe of the prophet,

15 See Craig S. Keener, *The Gospel of Matthew: A Socio-Rhetorical Commentary* (Grand Rapids: Eerdmans, 2009), 303.

16 Johannes Schneider, "ἔρχομαι," *TDNT* 2:666-84. Out of the total 202 occurrences in the Bible, 51 times it appears in Matthew.

17 "The fringe is the hem or border of a garment (in Heb. תְצִיצ). The Israelites were to make for themselves a fringe for each corner of their garments (Num 15:37-39). Attached to each fringe was to be a blue cord. This ornamentation was to remind the wearer of the Lord's commands and the requisite demand for holiness.". See Kevin D. Hall, "Fringe," *EDB* 472.

18 It is vivid in Mt 8:3, 15; 9:29; 14:36; 17:7; 20:34.

19 Donald A. Carson, *Matthew, Mark, Luke*, in EBC 8, ed. Frank E. Gaebelein (Grand Rapids: Zondervan 1984), 230.

20 Manfred Hutter, "Ein Altorientalischer Bittgestus in Mt 9:20-22," *Zeitschrift für die neutestamentliche Wissenschaft und die Kunde der älteren Kirche* 75 (1984): 133-135.

so that though he was rejected by YHWH, he might still be forgiven. But the hem of the robe tears off, symbolizing that YHWH has torn the kingship from Saul. In Zech 8:23, Zechariah prophesizes that ten foreigners shall take hold of the robe of a Jew in order to go to the holy land and entreat the favour of the Lord. In both the passages, 'taking hold of the fringe' is presented as a gesture of supplication through which help and salvation are implored.[21] Matthew's addition of the 'fringe' of the garment could be intentional and it adds an extra element in the faith-expression of the woman. By touching the fringe of his garment, she shows her dependence and fidelity to Jesus and silently asks for his help.

The report about her thought-process presented as an aside in the narrative also points to her great confidence in Jesus: for she said to herself, "if I only touch his garment, I shall be saved" (9:22). The imperfect tense of the verb λέγω shows that this desire or thought was going on in her for some time. So, even if her appearance on the scene is rather abrupt, her desire to go to Jesus and touch his garments and get healed has long been harboured. Her thinking resonates with that of the centurion who said to Jesus, "...but only say a word and my servant will be healed" (Mt 8:8). Although Jesus was ready to go to his house and heal his servant, the centurion just wanted a word from him. He was confident that with that word his servant would be healed. In both the cases the adverb μόνος serves to underline Jesus's power that 'only' a touch, 'only' a word will suffice.[22] An opportunity to touch his garments – that is all the woman wanted, and she knew that would make her well.

5. The Public Praise

The woman got a public praise from Jesus for her secret expression of faith in him. All those who accompanied Jesus on his way to the ruler's house must have witnessed it.

The narrator reports that Jesus turned towards the woman as soon as she touched the fringe of his garment. Jesus in the Markan story turns to know who touched him, but in Matthew he turns to recognize publicly the one who touched him. The turning of Jesus in the gospels often leads to an authoritative declaration.[23] It is also used to show Jesus' admiration for the persons who have

21 See Hutter, "Ein Altorientalischer Bittgestus in Matt 9:20-22," 134.

22 Davies-Allison, *The Gospel According to Saint Matthew*, 129.

23 It is seen in Mt 16:23 and Lk 9:55 when Jesus turns to rebuke; in Lk 10:23 he turns to declare the qualifications of a true disciple, in Lk 22:61 he turns to Peter after his prophecy of Peter's denial came true, in Lk 23:28, when he turned to console the women of Jerusalem on his way to Calvary.

faith in him.[24] It echoes the turning of God in the OT whenever the Israelites cried out for help in their distress.

Turning towards her, Jesus saw the woman. There was no further question. He understood everything, all that she was hiding: her sickness, her social stigma, her desire, and above all her great confidence in him. With paternal affection, he consoled and praised her: "Take heart daughter (θάρσει, θύγατερ), your faith has saved you"! The Greek verb θαρσέω means "to be of good courage," "to be confident," or "not to be afraid".[25] In the LXX[26], this verb is used as summons by men and prophets to individuals or people of Israel during their times of difficulties to give them assurance that God is with them and he is ready to help.[27] Similarly, in the gospels the summons is given by Jesus, indicating that in encounter with Jesus, God's action is accomplished as a liberating action, and thus it will give them joy and confidence, and it shall bring people into the goodness of the God whom they call Father.[28] In fact, when Jesus consoles the woman with the expression θάρσει, θύγατερ, it is an assurance to her that he is with her, and she is already liberated from her bondage.

Jesus further commends her faith saying, "Your faith has saved you".[29] Her motivation to come to Jesus, and her desire and action of secretly touching his garment is named 'faith' by Jesus. Evidently, faith is understood here as her confidence in Jesus. It is left to the reader to grasp the magnitude of her faith. If she was so confident that just touching the fringe of his garment can heal her, how great her faith in Jesus must have been! She had been carrying and nurturing that faith in her heart for a long time, and now she expressed it secretly amidst the crowd. Though she does not make any confession about Jesus' divine identity, she must have certainly believed in it and in his power. Her silence indeed proclaims more than any words and Jesus recognizes it as true faith.

---

24 In Lk 7:9, 44 and in our pericope he turns to admire the faith of the people after seeing their action.

25 In the NT, it is mainly used in the Gospels and Acts in Mt 9:2, 22; 14:27; Mk 6:50; 10:49; Jn 16:33; Acts 23:11.

26 The LXX uses θαρσέω frequently in Gen 35:17; Ex 14:13; 20:20, etc. Also, LXX translates the Hebrew expression לאָ ארי as θαρσέω in Gen 35:17; Ex 14:13; 20:20; 1 Kings 17:13, etc. together with other translations.

27 Walter Grundmann, "θαρρέω (θαρσέω)," *TDNT* 3:25-27.

28 *TDNT* 3:26.

29 The same phrase appears also in Mk 5:34; 10:52; Lk 7:50; 8:48; 17:19; 18:42. Matthew repeats the phrase from its synoptic parallel. Also in this section (Mt 8–9), Jesus admires various individuals who have expressed their faith in him in Mt 8:10, 13; 9:2, 22, 29; together with 15:28.

The Greek verb σῴζω[30] is used here for healing.[31] It appears three times in the episode. Twice it is used in passive which, in Greek, is termed as a 'divine passive', and it indicates that "the initiator of saving and helping action is God".[32] The connotation of σῴζω is not merely healing of the sickness, but the well-being of the whole person. It can also mean "salvation", the principal mission of Jesus: "for he will save his people from their sins" (Mt 1:21). By the usage of this verb Matthew demonstrates that the woman is not merely healed, but due to her faith, Jesus saves her from sins (as sickness was also considered a sin).

The narrator reports: "and at that hour the woman was made well (ἐσώθη). The unique healing that took place "in that hour" is a concrete expression of the salvation by faith that is always real.[33] By the phrase 'in that hour', Matthew tries to emphasize the correspondence between faith and fulfilment. Carson [34] and Nolland [35] understand 'in that hour' as the time at which the woman touched and was healed rather than after the words of Jesus. I, instead, agree with France [36] and Kalin [37] that healing was the direct result of Jesus' word [38] (unlike Mark and Luke), rather than of the previous touch, though her faith was instrumental in the healing that took place. Thus, the woman is no more an impure person, but a beloved 'daughter' saved by the Lord.

---

30 Usually in other parts of the gospel, σῴζω means 'to save' from sins or from any danger as in Mt 1:21; 8:25; 10:22; 14:30; 16:25; 19:25; 24:13, 22; 27:40, 42, 49.

31 The Greek words frequently used by Matthew for healing are θεραπεύω (in Mt 4:23, 24; 8:7, 16; 9:35; 10:1, 8; 12:10, 15, 22; 14:14; 15:30; 17:16, 18; 19:2; 21:14), ἰάομαι (in Mt 8:8, 13; 13:15; 15:28), and ὑγιής (in Mt 12:13; 15:31). This is the only pericope where he uses σῴζω for healing.

32 Walter Radl, "σῴζω," *EDNT* 3:319-321.

33 Ulrich Luz, *Matthew 8-20*, ed. Helmut Koester, trans. James E. Crouch, Hermeneia (Minneapolis, MN: Fortress Press, 2005), 42.

34 Carson, *Matthew, Mark, Luke*, 230.

35 John Nolland, *The Gospel of Matthew: A Commentary on the Greek Text*, NIGTC (Bletchley: Paternoster Press, 2005), 397.

36 Richard T. France, *The Gospel According to Matthew: An Introduction and Commentary*, TNTC (Leicester: Inter-Varsity Press, 1989), 175.

37 "In Matthew it is not the woman's touch, but Jesus' word that effects the cure, while in Mark, by contrast, it is the touch that heals, through a power that flows from Jesus, in apparent independence of his will and purpose and with a kind of life of its own". See Kalin, "Matthew 9:18-26," 45.

38 ἀπὸ τῆς ὥρας ἐκείνης (She was healed when these words were spoken). See Friedrich W. Blass and Albert Debrunner, *A Greek Grammar of the New Testament and Other Early Christian Literature*, trans. Robert W. Funk (Cambridge: University Press, 1961), 152. Similar instances are also seen in 8:13; 15:28; 17:18.

Conclusion

The story of the woman with the hemorrhage portrays the deep faith of a simple woman. Nothing is said in the narrative about her ethnic identity or religious background. She is only introduced on the scene with a reference to her illness, which would have made her an untouchable and impure within that society. Her faith in Jesus and in his divine power makes her courageous to break all taboos and goes to him and touches the fringe of his clothes secretly, even though he was amidst many other people. Jesus, recognizing her courage and sincerity, addresses her 'daughter', praises her faith and heals (saves) her. Thus, she becomes a unique model in the gospel story, the one who secretly expressed her faith but publicly praised by Jesus.

Her faith was "a supplicating faith that precedes miraculous healing and receives miracle itself."[39] She demonstrated her deep faith in Jesus while she was suffering, and even before the miracle occurred, she believed without doubt that just a touch of his garment would heal her. Her great faith stands in contrast with the little faith of the disciples who, although they were followers of Jesus, failed to trust him and in his divine power, especially when crisis situations arose.[40] Her faith is also in contrast to the lack of faith of the people of his hometown in Nazareth who doubted the source of his wisdom and deeds of power and took offense in him (13:54-58). It also stands against the hostile attitude of the religious leaders who attributed his divine power to the prince of demons (Mt 9:34; 12:24).

With her secret thought and gesture of touch the woman manifested her faith, thanks to which she was healed. The woman who was once considered impure, sinful and was ostracized from the society due to her sickness, is hailed in the gospel as a heroic and unique model of faith.

Through this brief pericope Matthew invites the readers to have the faith in Jesus as the woman manifested her faith. Thus, by faith "those who respond positively to Jesus and his message become members of his earthly family as his disciples and receive the grace of divine 'childship' [41].

---

39 Gerhard Barth, "πιστεύω," *EDNT* 3:91-97.

40 It is vivid in Mt 6:30; 8:26; 16:8; 17:20.

41 Henry Pattarumadathil, *Your Father in Heaven: Discipleship in Matthew as a Process of Becoming Children of God* (Roma: Pontificio Istituto Biblico, 2008), 203.

5

The Storm on the Lake
Two Contrasting Responses to the Same Stimulus and Our Response

Errol Fernandes, SJ

Introduction

One of the most striking features of the Gospel of Mark is the theme of the lack of understanding and even misunderstanding on the part of the disciples of Jesus. They misunderstand the teaching and parables of Jesus (Mk 4:13) his miracles (Mk 4:38; 6:52; 8:17-21) and even his mission (Mk 8:32; 9:32; 10:37, 41). On three occasions in his Gospel, Mark comments that the disciples fail to understand Jesus and his way of proceeding (Mk 6:52; 8:14; 9:32). This failure to understand who Jesus is, is also linked to their lack of faith (Mk 4:35-41; 9:28-29). From the time Jesus tells the first parable (Mk 4:3-9), he realizes that his disciples do not understand it (4:13) which is why he has to explain everything to his disciples in private (Mk 4:34).

Though the disciples have experienced apparent success in Mission after Jesus sent them out (Mk 6:30), their misunderstanding is obvious in their sarcastic response when Jesus asks them to give the people something to eat

(Mk 6:37).[1] Despite having been involved in the feeding of the five thousand[2], the disciples are still terrified when Jesus comes to them walking on the water (Mk 6:50). Jesus has to reveal himself to the disciples with the divine name[3] and ask them not to be afraid (Mk 6:50). Mark adds that the reason for the fear and misunderstanding of the disciples was because "they did not understand about the loaves, but their hearts were hardened" (Mk 6:52). These 'hardened hearts' are in plain view at the second feeding miracle for the four thousand when they ask Jesus how they are going to feed the large crowd in the desert (Mk 8:4).[4] Astonishingly this question is asked even after they experienced the earlier feeding and where they were involved in that feeding (Mk 6:41).

They had experienced success in Mission (Mk 6:30), but are unable to exorcise a demon (Mk 9:18) and the father of the possessed boy has to turn to Jesus who rebukes and labels his disciples here, as faithless (Mk 9:19) before he can exorcise the demon. It is also the disciples - who because they do not understand Jesus' saying on becoming like a child to enter the kingdom of God (Mk 10:15) - who try to prevent children from being brought to Jesus (Mk 10:13). Jesus is indignant with the disciples and makes clear that they are not to stop the children from coming to him. He has to respond in a similar manner when at the anointing at Bethany (Mk 12:3-9), they scold the woman who anoints Jesus' head with the costly ointment because they do not understand the context.[5]

1 France, R. T. (2002). The Gospel of Mark: a commentary on the Greek text (p. 265). Grand Rapids, MI; Carlisle: W.B. Eerdmans; Paternoster Press. Guelich, R. A. (1998). Mark 1–8:26 (Vol. 34A, p. 340). Dallas: Word, Incorporated, Dallas, Texas, thinks that their response is "more a rhetorical question than one expecting an answer".

2 In the Gospel of Mark, Jesus looks up to heaven, blesses and breaks the bread and gives it to the disciples to give to the people (Mk 6:41) so also Mt 14:19 and Luke 9:16; but not John who has Jesus give the bread to the people himself and not through the disciples (Jn 6:11).

3 Ex 3:14 See Garland, D. E. (1996). The NIV Application Commentary: Mark (p. 323). Grand Rapids, MI: Zondervan Publishing House. Guelich, R.A. (n 2 above p. 351); Edwards, J. R. (2002). The Gospel according to Mark (p. 198). Grand Rapids, MI; Leicester, England: Eerdmans; Apollos. Contra France (n 2 above p 262-264) who thinks that the identification here is merely self-identification and the disciples did not understand Jesus to have revealed himself as God. However, the point that Mark makes is the despite this identification of Jesus as divine, the disciples fail to understand who he is. This interpretation fits in with one of the overall plots of Mark which is to show the disciples as lacking understanding.

4 By contrast, though Matthew has taken this miracle from Mark he has changed the question of the disciples so that it does not set limits on Jesus' ability, but only seeks clarification.

5 By placing the text of the anointing (12:3-9) between the plot of the chief priests and scribes to kill Jesus (12:1-2) and decision of Judas Iscariot to betray Jesus (12:101-11), Mark has used a sandwich construction. Here it is to bring into sharp relief the misunderstanding of Jesus by the religious authorities {as represented by the chief priests and scribes} and

The reason why Mark has misunderstanding of the disciples as one of the prominent themes of his Gospel can be seen on two levels. On the level of the story, Mark wants to explicate that Jesus did not fit into the mould of the Messiah who was expected.[6] On the level of the theology of Mark, it seems that Mark's intention is to portray Jesus as the Messiah who would be misunderstood by all, crucified by the Romans through the religious authorities, die an abandoned death and only then rise again. This intention of Mark is realized through the technique of the command to silence.[7] In this technique, the Marcan Jesus silences demons whenever they identified him as "Son of God" (Mk 1:34; 3:11-12) tells some of those whom he healed not to tell anyone about the healing (Mk 1:44; 5:43; 7:36; 8:26) and commands even his disciples not to reveal that he is the Christ (Mk 8:30; 9:9).[8]

1. The Context of Mk 4:35-41

The scene in Mk 4:35-41 appears immediately after the Parable Discourse in the Gospel (4:1-34). At the beginning of Chapter 4, Mark states that Jesus began 'to teach beside the lake" (4:1). The first parable that Jesus tells (Mk 4:3-8)[9] is allegorized or explained (Mk 4:14-20) because the disciples give the impression that they have not understood the parable (4:13). The first parable states that despite the many challenges that might occur, success is certain.[10] In

---

the disciples {as represented by Judas} and compare it with the insight of the woman who Jesus says "has anointed my body beforehand for its burial" (Mk 12:8)

6 See Evans, C. A. (2002). Word Biblical Commentary: Mark 8:27-16:20 (Vol. 34B, p. 18). Dallas: Word, Incorporated.

7 For overviews of the numerous theories concerning the Messianic Secret, see Blevins, "The Messianic Secret in Markan Research", Washington, 1981; C.M. Tuckett, "The Problem of the Messianic Secret", in C.M. Tuckett (ed), The Messianic Secret (IRT 1), Philadelphia/London, 1983, pp 1-28. https://legacy.tyndalehouse.com/tynbul/Library/TynBull_1970_21_04_Dunn_MessianicSecretInMark.pdf

8 The only time a time limit is set on the command to silence is here, when they come down from the mountain after Jesus is transfigured. This time limit is "until after the Son of Man had risen from the dead" (Mk 9:9)

9 Though this parable was probably found by Mark in the tradition he received, most scholars would assign it to the ministry of Jesus. Guelich R.A. (n 2 above p 189)

"Originally, the number of these parables in which Jesus left his hearers to draw their own conclusions was considerably greater; this can be seen from the Gospel of Thomas, where all the parables, except the Burglar, the Great Supper, and the Pearl end without an interpretation. It is easy to understand that a tendency soon arose to provide an application for parables that had no interpretation. This is most clearly seen in the three parables to which a detailed interpretation has been secondarily supplied: Mark 4.13-20; Matt. 13.36--43, 49f.: Joachim Jeremias (1966), "Rediscovering the Parables" (p 82), New York: Charles Scribner's Sons.

10 The loss in three types of soil (the path, the rocky ground and the thorns) is matched by the three fold gain (thirty, sixty and a hundredfold).

the first three sowings, the outcome is loss of the seed. This loss is due to the seed being devoured, burned up and choked respectively. It is only in the fourth and final sowing that there is abundant gain. This three-fold gain corresponds to the three-fold loss. However, the enormity of the gain is indicative that the parable uses hyperbolic language to make its point. This is confirmed by the participles (growing up and increasing) which are used to emphasize growth.[11] The parable may therefore be termed as parable which stresses the contrast between the frustrations that result due to the first three unfruitful sowings and the enormity of the success after the fourth sowing.

The parable of the seed growing secretly (Mk 4:26-29) is prefaced with the phrase "The kingdom of God is as if..." (Mk 4:26). This parable is clearly about the kingdom. It describes a four step process, where the second follows the first and so on. The first step is that the person[12] scatters the seed after which he/she sleeps at night[13] and rises in the day. The seed (because it has been scattered) sprouts and grows. The point which the parable is making is connected intimately with the kingdom. Just as certainly as the seed sprouts and grows, just as certainly will the kingdom be established. An allied point that the parable makes is that there is no reason for agitation or attempting to hasten the process. The person has to ensure that he/she scatters and then and only then can the rest follow. Agitation or anxiety will not bring growth.

In the parable of the mustard seed (Mk 4:30-32), Mark stresses the smallness of the seed by using the phrase "smallest of all the seeds on earth", and describing the shrub that grows out of the mustard seed as "the greatest of all shrubs" In other words there is no other seed smaller than a mustard seed. What is contrasted therefore is the smallness of the seed with the expansiveness of the shrub.[14]

All three parables therefore might be seen as parables which contrast the negative/ everyday/ small beginnings to positive/extra-ordinary/large endings.[15] They are also a reflective summary of the ministry of Jesus. In his

---

11 Guelich R.A. (n 2 above p. 194)

12 The use of the "man" (which does not exclude women) is an indication that it not a farmer or sower or expert in agriculture that Jesus is talking about. In Mk 4:3, it is the "sower' who goes out to sow.

13 The placing of "sleep" after the seed is scattered and "rise" after sleep is an indication that it is a chronological process. Also the person sleeps at night and rises in the day which are common or regular activities at these times.

14 To emphasize the largeness even more than Mark, Matthew seems to have changed Mark's "greatest of all shrubs" to where the mustard seed becomes not only "the greatest of shrubs" but also "becomes a tree" (Mt 13:32). See Joachim Jeremias (n 10 above pp. 116-118)

15 The use of the term "negative" refers to the Parable of the Sower (Mk 4:3-9) where in the first three sowings, there is loss. The term "everyday" refers to the scattering of the seed by the person (Mk 4:26) and the term "small" refers to the size of the mustard which is

ministry, Jesus faced opposition right from the beginning (Mk 2:7, 16-17, 18, 24; 3:2, 6, 22)[16] because his way of proceeding did not fit in with what was expected of teachers at that time. This opposition grew as Jesus continued his ministry and would have had a negative impact on his disciples. They would have begun to wonder whether Jesus' way was the right way or whether he ought to change tracks and take another way.[17]

Mark summarises his Parable Discourse in 4:33-34 by stating that while for those who were not open to the teachings of Jesus, everything would be in parables.[18]However, though Jesus explains "everything in private to the disciples" (Mk 4:34), the disciples are unable to understand and behave like 'outsiders' in the scene that follows.[19]

---

also described as "the smallest of all seeds on earth" (Mk 4:31). These are matched by three antonyms namely, "positive" to refer to the soil which produces thirty, sixty and a hundredfold; "extra-ordinary" which refers to the growth of the seed because of the scattering and "large" to refer to the huge mustard shrub when compared with the small mustard seed.

16 Though the opposition to the ministry of Jesus continues after Chapter, I have restricted the references to only those which appear in the Gospel before the Parable can be told. Edwards, J. R. (n 4 above p. 129). See also Joachim Jeremias (n 10 above p. 118)

17 This desire for another way is seen in the misunderstanding of Jesus' way by the disciples (Mk 8:32; 9:33-34; 10:35-37) after each of the Passion and Resurrection predictions (Mk 8:31; 9:31; 10:32-34). It is a pointer that the disciples as individuals (represented by Peter and James and John) and as a group (represented by all the disciples) did not want Jesus to take the way of the cross. This is why after the first Passion and Resurrection prediction, Peter objects and "rebukes" Jesus. Jesus, however, is confident that like the seed sown in good soil which brings forth a plentiful harvest, like the seed that is scattered which will produce the stalk, the head and the full grain and like the insignificant mustard seed which will grow into the largest of shrubs, he too will be vindicated. He is confident that though it may seem on the surface level that the kingdom is nowhere in sight, God will see it through and the kingdom will indeed come. This is why he has to rebuke Peter and teach him that God's ways are different from human ways (8:33). He has also to teach the disciples about true greatness after they argue about it, even as he predicts for the second time in Mark his passion, death and resurrection (Mk 9:35-37) and he has to teach James and John (and the other ten who are indignant with James and John and so are of the same frame of mind as the brothers) that authority in the kingdom means service. He showed this to them in action and not only in words (Mk 10:42-45).

18 Mark makes a distinction between those outside and those inside. "Those outside" refers to those who were closed to the revelation that Jesus was making. This is indicated by their physical position (Mk 3:31) or their lack of openness (Mk 4:11-12, 24-25).

19 The points being made by the seed parables (4:3-9; 26-29; 30-32) is that even though it may seem at first glance that success is elusive and that God's presence is not real, the kingdom will indeed come. They also exhort the ones who hear to do what needs to be done and then with confidence and faith leave the rest to God and that from insignificant beginnings there will be great endings. They are thus parables which call for confidence and faith in God and the courage to do what one has to do without giving in to despair or losing hope.

2. Interpretation of Mk 4:35-41

Many details in the story of the storm on the lake in Mark indicate that the story is located in the very early traditions of the community.[20] The location of the story immediately after the parable discourse in Mark[21] indicates that Mark intends that this story be interpreted in the light of the Parable Discourse.[22] Also, the use of the pronouns "he" and "them" are indications that the story follows from what has gone on before and that "he" here refers to Jesus and "them" to the disciples who are referents in the previous verse (Mk 4:34). The double time reference, "On that day, when evening had come" (Mk 4:35) is another indication that Mark wants his readers to see this event as continuing what had happened earlier in that day namely the parable discourse. That Jesus and his disciples left the crowd behind can only refer to the crowd introduced in Mk 4:1 which is reintroduced in 4:33 and thus reinforces that this story which narrates Jesus' going across to the other side with his disciples is to be seen as a culmination of the Parable discourse.[23] That "other boats were with him" (Mk 4:36) is a detail mentioned only by Mark. Mark does not mention them again or tell what happened to these other boats and how they fared in the storm.[24] The boat in which Jesus was with his disciples could possibly

---

20 See Guelich R.A. (n 2 above p. 262)

21 Matthew places the story as part of his miracle cycle (Mt 8:23-27) whereas Luke has placed it as the first of the four miracles (Lk 8:22-56) found in Mk 4:35-5:43. Fitzmyer, J. A., S. J. (2008). The Gospel according to Luke I-IX: introduction, translation, and notes (p. 726). New Haven; London: Yale University Press. Marshall, I. H. (1978). The Gospel of Luke: a commentary on the Greek text (p. 332). Exeter: Paternoster Press. Talbert, C. H. (2002). Reading Luke: a literary and theological commentary on the third Gospel (Rev. ed., p. 104). Macon, GA: Smyth & Helwys Publishing.

22 Fitzmyer J.A.,S.J.(n 22 above p.726) for whom Lk 8:22 "One day he got into a boat with his disciples, and he said to them, "Let us go across to the other side of the lake") is clearly reactional which results in severing it from the previous episode (the true family of Jesus (Lk 8:19-21)). He also states that the reason why Luke has modified the text is because in Mark "the episode presupposes the beginning of the parable discourse".

23 Guelich R.A. (n 2 above p. 265) is of the opinion that shift in subjects from Jesus in Mk 4:35 to the disciples in Mk 4:36 along with the disciples taking Jesus "as he was" is used by Mark to tie everything together which began in Mk 4:1-2 where Jesus taught seated in a boat. See also R.T. France, (n 2 above p. 222).

24 Some think that Mark mentioned this detail because it was a genuine reminiscence of those who told the story. Others see it as pointing to a larger group of witnesses to the episode than merely the disciples as mentioned by Mark in 3:34 and 4:10. As a matter of fact, in Matthew, though it is the disciples who address Jesus as Lord and plead with him to save them (Mt 8:25), by the end of the episode it is the people and not the disciples who ask "What sort of man is this…? (Mt 8:27) Since the disciples recognize Jesus as "Lord", it means they know who Jesus is and so do not need to ask. While the mention of the people at the end of the episode could be Matthew's way of letting his readers react to the miracle (Luz 20) it could also be that though not mentioned at the start, other boats were present

accommodate about fifteen persons. It is therefore likely that all disciples were in the same boat with Jesus. The great gale that arises results in the waves from the sea beating into the boat.[25] That Jesus is asleep even as the waves enter the boat has led to the drawing of parallels with Jonah's sleep during his attempt to escape from the mission that God had entrusted to him (Jon 1:4-6). It has also been linked to the genre of rescue stories in which the saviour is present but unknown, to Jesus' faith in God's care, a sign of the security and sovereignty of Jesus and even of Jesus' humanity. Still others think that this detail is mentioned in order to contrast the calm attitude of Jesus with the disciples' panic.[26]The disciples react with fear and panic as is evident in the language they use to narrate their situation.[27]They also allege that Jesus does not care about their plight. They accuse Jesus of not caring about their survival.[28] Jesus' response is to rebuke the wind and ask the sea to be still. (Mk 4:39).[29]The effect on the wind and sea is immediate. The intervention of Jesus turns the situation

---

when Jesus and his disciples set out like Mark mentions at the beginning of his narrative. R.T.France (n 2 above p. 223); Guelich R.A. (n 2 above p. 265); Edwards J.R. (n 4 above p. 148).

Some amend the text to read "other boats were NOT with him". This fact that the boat in which Jesus and his disciples was the only boat heightens the danger since other boats could not come to their rescue. Marcus, J. (2008). Mark 1-8: a new translation with introduction and commentary (p. 332). New Haven; London: Yale University Press.

25 See the description of the fishing boats which would have been "26½ feet long, 7½ feet wide, and 4½ feet high" Edwards, J. R. (n 4 above p. 148). See also R.T. France (n 2 above p. 223), who translates "beat into the boat" as "falling into the boat". Collins, A. Y., & Attridge, H. W. (2007). Mark: A Commentary on the Gospel of Mark (p. 259). Minneapolis: Fortress Press, who interprets the boat being filled after being beaten by the waves as a "concrete variant of a widespread motif of danger of a storm or other adverse conditions at sea".

26 Guelich R.A. (n 2 above p. 266); Brooks, J. A. (1991). Mark (Vol. 23, p. 86). Nashville: Broadman & Holman Publishers; France R.T. (n 2 above p. 223); Edwards J.R. (n 4 above p. 149); Collins, A. Y., & Attridge, H. W. (n 26 above p.260).

27 It seems that Matthew has changed not only the address from "Teacher" to "Lord", but has also converted the allegation against Jesus into a prayer for salvation (Mt 8:25). Luke replaces "Teacher" with the twice repeated "Master" and here the disciples make no allegation but state what they think is happening (Lk 8:24). Edwards J.R. (n 4 above p. 149)

28 Some think that Mark has reworked the story to change what was originally a plea for help to an accusation. This would be in keeping with Mark's portrayal of the disciples as lacking in understanding. That this is plausible is confirmed by the question they ask after the calming of the storm (Mk 4:41). Guelich R.A. (n 2 above p.266)

29 "The use of the term sea for this relatively small lake is a sign of a Koine Greek influenced by Semitic languages and possibly of the locally limited world in which the story was told." Adela Yarbo Collins p 261

Unlike in Matthew where Jesus points to the "little faith" of the disciples BEFORE he can rebuke the winds and the sea (Mt 8:26), in Mark (and Luke 8:24-25) he first calms the storm before addressing the disciples about their fear and lack of faith (Mk 4:39-40).

from calamitous to serene. The "great windstorm" (Mk 4:37) is transformed to a "dead calm" (4:39) because of the words of Jesus. The use of terms like "great windstorm" and "dead clam" indicate that Mark wanted to draw a striking contrast between the two. The confusion, turmoil, disorder and fear of a moment ago has been transformed into serenity, calm and tranquility. The fear of the disciples is because they lack faith. Faith here must be interpreted as confidence and assurance that they would be protected even in the storm since Jesus was with them.[30]The disciples display a blatant lack of faith in their frightened reaction to the storm and in their allegations against Jesus. These allegations were indeed unfounded and were the result of their giving into panic, of their not having faith. This is why the questions of Jesus are about fear and faithlessness.[31] It is fear which overtakes the disciples and so does not allow faith to manifest itself. The fear acts as a block to faith and what it can accomplish. If the disciples were aware that they had the Lord with them (like they were in Matthew), they would not have given into fear. Consequently they would have realized that their response to the windstorm and waves ought to have been like that of the Lord who was secure, calm and tranquil even in the midst of the storm. It is clear that the disciples have not understood the parable of the sower and so cannot understand all the parables (Mk 4:13). Since the parables are connected with this episode[32], the disciples ought to have realized that there was no need to be afraid or be faithless. However, they focused too much on the seed sown along the path, rocky ground and thorns rather than on the seed sown in good soil. Also, they focused too much on the smallness of the mustard seed and not enough on the largeness of the shrub. Consequently they were unable to look beyond. They could not believe that the growth would be abundant, that the seed sown would indeed produce fruit and that the small mustard seed would grow into a great shrub.

The use of the terms "rebuked" and "Be still" point back to Mk 1:25 where the same verbs are used in the context of an exorcism. This indicates that Mark views the calming of the storm as an exorcism. Collins, A. Y., & Attridge, H. W. (n 26 above p. 261); Dowd S.E. (n 1 above p. 54); Edwards J.R. (n 4 above p. 150); Books, J.A. (n 27 above p. 87); Guelich, R.A. (n 2 above p. 267); contra France, R.T. (n 2 above p. 224) who thinks that to regard the calming of the storm as an exorcism is to conclude about too much from two verbs.

30 Guelich, R.A. (n 2 above pp. 268-269); France, R.T. (n 2 above p.225); Marcus, J. (n 25 above p. 334) sees faith not only as trust in God like Jesus had but also trust in Jesus. The movement is from seeing Jesus as a model of faith to becoming the object of faith.

31 Some think that the question of Jesus in 4:40a (He said to them, "Why are you afraid"?) was before Jesus' rebuke to the wind and words to the sea in 4:39. While this is plausible, it is clear that Mk 4:40b (Have you still no faith?") is placed by Mark after the calming of the storm to highlight yet again the theme of the misunderstanding of the disciples. Guelich, R.A. (n 2 above p.267); "The Collected Writings of George M Soares Prabhu S.J.," Volume II (Jnana-Deepa Vidyapeeth 2001), p. 251

32 See n 27 above.

The response of the disciples ("And they were filled with great awe") and the question they ask ("Who then is this, that even the wind and the sea obey him?") (Mk 4:41) is not a response to the questions of Jesus, but to the 'dead calm' that followed the 'great windstorm'. It indicates that the one who calms the waves and sea with a word cannot be comprehended with the external senses alone. The awe and question are both the result of being allowed a glimpse into the awesome power and majesty of the one who though he appears asleep, is aware of all that is going on. They are responses which know that they are before a majesty so incomprehensible that the only way to respond is through awe and wonder.[33] The questions reflect the amazement at the faith which Jesus displayed in the midst of the storm as well as his ability to calm the storm because of that faith.

3. The Reaction of the Disciples to and in the Storm

The disciples had been given the secret or mystery of the kingdom because they were insiders (Mk 4:11).[34] Yet, they were unable to understand the parable of the sower and seed (Mk 4:13). Because this was the case, they would find it difficult to understand all the parables (Mk 4:13). In the episode of the storm on the lake, not only do they not understand, but their reaction to their predicament is akin to 'outsiders' for whom "everything comes in parables" (Mk 4:11).

The disciples and Jesus leave the crowd and go in a boat.[35] The other boats disappear after the first mention of them. When the waves beat into the boat, the disciples panic and react rather than respond to the situation. While their address of Jesus as 'Teacher' may reflect their normal relationship with him[36] their allegation is that Jesus is unconcerned about their plight. They do

---

33 A novel insight into the rebuke by Jesus is that the disciples were rebuked not because they were not reassured of the presence of Jesus with them but because they were unwilling to perish with him. This perspective may have been convincing if the incident of the storm on the lake had been placed after the third passion and resurrection prediction (Mk 10:32-34) and the teaching that follows on what it means to be a disciple (Mk 10:41-45). This is because beginning from the first Passion and resurrection prediction (Mk 8:31), the Marcan Jesus explains what his way of life entails on three separate occasions (Mk 8:33-9:1; 9: 33-35; 10:41-45). In each of these teachings it is clear that the way to life is death on a cross and the way to save life is to be willing to lose it. However, the position of the episode immediately after the parable discourse and the connection with the parable discourse, points to the rebuke as a result of the inability of the disciples to have faith which was the result of their fear. George M Soares-Prabhu (n 32 above p. 252)

34 See n 22 above.

35 It is likely that all the twelve were in the boat with Jesus. The size of the boat (see n 29 above) makes such a scene very probable.

36 See Mk 9:38; 10:35; 13:1

not make any request of Jesus rather they accuse him even as they inform him of their plight. In this regard they display agitation, fear and faithlessness.

3.1. Agitation

The agitation of the disciples is evident in the manner in which they react. The fact that they had to wake Jesus up is already a sign of their consternation and disquiet. Though they have heard the parables of the sower and seed as well as that of the seed growing secretly and the mustard seed all of which have pointed out that despite appearances to the contrary God is still in control, the disciples have not understood the meaning and application of these parables. While it might seem that the reason for their waking Jesus up is to seek his help, it is unmistakable in their alleging question that this is not the case.[37] Instead they accuse him of insouciance and even lack of concern about their plight (Mk 4:38).

3.2. Fear

The response of Jesus to the disciples after he calms the storm points undoubtedly to the fear of the disciples (Mk 4:40). The fear arises in the hearts of the disciples because they have misread the situation. They have seen the storm as threatening and destructive. Their negative perception of the storm has led to their faulty and negative thoughts, namely that they were in grave danger. This in turn has led to their negative feeling, a feeling of fear. If they had perceived correctly that they would not be harmed in and by the storm because Jesus was with them, they would have responded rather than reacted.[38] The fear that they experienced led them to give in to despair instead of keeping hope. This was because they did not believe, they had no faith.

3.3. Faithlessness

The chiding questions of Jesus to the disciples after he calms the storm (Mk 4:40) have to do with their state of mind and heart in the midst of the storm. They are both afraid and faithless. Faithlessness here, is the result of their

37 In Matthew, where the disciples react by waking Jesus up and asking him to save them (Mt 8:25) and Luke where the disciples use the term "Master' (which is a term only disciples and followers use of Jesus) and who has them point instead to their perception of the situation (Lk 8:24) it is clearer that there is no allegation about Jesus' nonchalance or lack of concern about their situation. Fitzmyer, J.A., S.J.(N 25 above p. 270)

38 This Jesus was the one who in the three parables that were told before the storm (Mk 4:3-8; 26-29; 30-32) was preparing them for challenges they would face both in mission and in their lives. It was therefore not surprising to Jesus that there was a storm (and that is why he could continue to sleep even in the midst of the storm) because he knew that it would pass or that it could be overcome. If the disciples had understood the three parables, they too would have realised what Jesus did.

inability to understand the parables of Jesus and consequently to realise that even though it might seem at first glance that there is an insurmountable threat to life itself, the threat will pass and they will overcome. The faithlessness of the disciples stemming from their fear rendered them unable to believe that because Jesus was with them they would not be destroyed. The serenity of Jesus and the fact that he was sleeping in the midst of the storm ought to have prompted the disciples about their own response. However, because of their hardness of heart and because they had behaved like outsiders, they could not believe.

4. The Response of Jesus to and in the Storm

Jesus displays contrasting attitudes to that of the disciples. He had told the three seed parables (Mk 4:3-8; 26-29; 30-32) in which the message conveyed is that despite appearances that there is more loss than gain, and that the gain is definite and during the storm, he shows this in action. Accordingly, the qualities that Jesus displays are calmness and serenity, fearlessness and faith.

4.1. Calmness and Serenity

On one level it would seem that Jesus would have slept in the boat because he was tired. Since Mark narrates the story of the storm as following immediately after the Parable Discourse[39], it is likely that after such interaction with the crowds, Jesus would have wanted to rest. On another level it indicates that Jesus was unperturbed with what would happen in and around the boat because he knew that it could be responded to. It might have seemed that the boat which was inundated with waves from the sea was in danger of capsizing and yet, in contrast to the reaction of the disciples, the response of Jesus was serenity. This serenity came from the same conviction and confidence with which he told the parables. This was a parable in action. If the words of Jesus in the parables were an assurance of God's presence despite all evidence to the contrary, the action of Jesus in the storm matched his words.

4.2. Fearlessness

Jesus though asleep, is aware of the situation. As a matter of fact, one possible reason why he could sleep peacefully is because he was aware that the storm could not cause irreparable damage. He was also aware that the storm would pass. This fearlessness of Jesus is in stark contrast to the fear and panic of the disciples. The disciples are physically awake and doing nothing, Jesus is physically awake and doing everything. The sleep of Jesus enables him to respond serenely, whereas the bustle of the disciples results in the boat being

39 See n 27 above

rocked even more than by the storm. This fearlessness of Jesus is a result of his faith and confidence in God.

4.3. Faith

The faith that Jesus had alluded to in the parables was a faith that he now showed in action. This faith was in the omnipotence of God who would never let anything happen that was not according to God's will and plan. Though Jesus calms the storm with his words and thereby does what only God was capable of doing (Gen 8:1; Job 26:12; Pss 65:7; 74:13-14; 89:9; 93:3-4; 104:5-9; 106:9; 107:25-30; 114:3; Isa 50:2; Nah 1:4; 2 Macc 9:8), Mark does not so much intend here to portray Jesus as God as he wants to show the faith that Jesus had in God. It is with the intention that the faith of the disciples would increase that Jesus displays his own faith in action. Jesus could not have been expected to point to the disciples fear and ask about their faithlessness (Mk 4:40) if he was portrayed as God.[40]It is through his faith in God that Jesus was able to weather the storm and also calm it. It is in this context that the question of the disciples, "Who then is this, that even the wind and the sea obey him?" (Mk 4:41) must be read and interpreted. They have experienced the saving power of the faith of Jesus but are also unable to believe that anyone could have such depth of faith in so challenging a situation. Jesus stands on their side as a model of faith and on the side of God as God's ambassador of faith.

5. Our Response to the Storm of Covid-19[41]

This is possibly the first time in many centuries when the whole world is tested as it is now with the COVID-19 pandemic. At this point in the history of the world, the so-called rich nations and the so-called poor nations are all in the same storm (even if in different boats) trying to row to the shore. It is important to note that though the storm is the same, the boats are different. Some are in cruise ships, others in catamarans, others in dinghies and still others on rafts without even a paddle.[42] Even as we struggle to find our way forward, the contrasting reactions of the disciples and Jesus invite us to reflect on and choose what our reaction is and will be.

---

40 Contra Garland, D.E. (n 4 above p. 192); Guelich , R.A. (n 2 above p. 267); Edwards, J.R. (n 4 above p. 150) who all stress theophany.

41 COVID-19 here must be seen as a metaphor for the numerous challenges that keep coming up in the lives of everyone of us. To be sure, this pandemic is real at this moment, but it is also true that challenges that each of us face are not only with regard to COVID-19 or that they will end with the discovery of a vaccine for the disease.

42 The use of these four types of water transport vehicles is to typify the different classes of people within a country. Those in cruise ships would be the elite and super rich, those in catamarans the upper middle-class, those in dinghies would be the lower middle-class and those win rafts without a paddle would be the poor and marginalised.

5.1. Agitation versus Calmness/Serenity

We have prayed and petitioned God, we have implored and begged and we have realized that we are fragile, weak and mortal despite our numerous boasts of strength and of longevity of life. Therefore, like the disciples in the boat, we might choose to get agitated about the situation we find ourselves in. We too might think that God is asleep and does not care about our plight. How can God be a God of love if he will not save us from this danger? What kind of a God is it that does not come to the aid of his children? Because we are convinced that God is unconcerned, we might give in to despair and lose hope. Alternatively we might petition God and continue in our petitioning perseveringly without giving up, or we might alert the Lord about our situation.[43]

We might, however, decide to respond like Jesus and continue to stay serene and calm. In the parable of the seed growing secretly (Mk 4:26-29), we are given an insight into how we can respond like Jesus and how we must indeed respond if we are not to give in to frustration and lose hope. There is a depth in this parable that may not be visible at first reading. The parable speaks of a four step process which is also chronological. The first step is to scatter the seed. This would mean that we must take the initiative, the first step and do all that is required of us. It would mean that we leave no stone unturned or that we leave nothing undone. We put in every ounce of effort that we are capable of. The next two steps which speak of sleeping and rising night and day follow the scattering of the seed. They do not precede it. This means that because one has scattered the seed one can sleep and rise with no anxiety whatever. It also means that only after the seed has been scattered these activities take place. The fourth and final step is that the seed sprouts and grows. Though the one who scatters the seed might not have detailed knowledge of how the seed sprouts and grows ("he does not know how" Mk 4:27) what he/she does know is that the seed grows only after it has been scattered. In other words, if the scattering had not been done, there would be no growth.[44] Thus while certainty of the growth of the seed is certainly a lesson of the parable, an allied lesson is

---

43 These responses would be akin to the responses of the disciples in Matthew (8:25) where the disciples address Jesus as Lord and plead with him to save them or in Luke (8:24) where the disciples address Jesus as Master (which only disciples do in Luke) and point to their situation.

44 See Collins, A. Y., & Attridge, H. W. (n 26 above p. 254) where if the one who scatters the seed is likened to a disciple of Jesus, then the lesson is that they should not get impatient or get discouraged.

See France, R.T. (n 2 above p. 214) where it is suggested that because the parable could suggest a "quietistic theology" which advocates passive contemplation, because of which disciples might adopt a laid back attitude and not accept responsibility to do what they have to do. He also suggests that it was possibly this danger which cause Matthew not to include it in his Parable discourse.

that patience is not only required but also imperative. This is because after one has done all that one can do, the rest will be done by God. Jesus' response to the storm is therefore like the one who scatters the seed.

Because Jesus knows that he has done all that he is required to do, he can sleep and rise without agitation. He also knows that because one has to be patient and unhurried, it does not pay to give in to agitation. In the storm in which we find ourselves, we can take a cue from Jesus. Each of us must continue to live as best as we can in the circumstances. We must also realise that giving in to agitation, anxiety and needless worry will not help. Rather it will hinder. It will only result in rocking the boat further. To be sure, in all of this, the poor suffer more than others and unfortunately this is the reality of the situation. Despite this fact, however, whether poor or rich, old or young, male or female, we must respond like Jesus and not react like the disciples.

5.2. Fear versus Fearlessness

Fear is primarily the result of faulty perceptions. When we perceive something faultily, we think faultily and consequently feel faultily. In the famous example from Advaitic Vedanta of the rope and the snake, the rope is perceived as a snake which in turn leads to thinking that it is a threat and consequently feeling fear.[45] The point to be noted is that there is a real object. However, it is the manner in which it is perceived that causes the thoughts and feelings. In the above example, if the rope was perceived as rope, there would be no frightening thoughts and consequently no fear. It is because the rope is perceived as a snake that frightening thoughts arise and so the feeling of fear. In the case of the storm experienced by both the disciples and Jesus the storm was real, however, the manner in which they perceived it caused fear in the disciples. Since Jesus perceived correctly, he felt no fear, rather he was fearless. The fear of the disciples did not affect the storm. It continued unabated. On the other hand, the fearlessness of Jesus resulted in the calming of the storm.

Our perception of the COVID-19 pandemic will determine whether we will feel fear or be fearless. The point that we must keep in mind in the present context is that the pandemic is not an illusion but real. However, even as we realize this fact, we need to ask how we are going to perceive it. Are we going

---

See also Guelich, R. A. (n 2 above p. 240) where depending on where one focuses, one would interpret the parable in that light. If the focus is on the one who scatters then the lesson could be of patience or even on the reaping. If the focus is on the seed, then the lesson would be on the secret growth or the final harvest.

Garland, D.E. (n 4 above pp. 176-179) gives the variety of names for the parable from which he concludes that what the parable illustrates is open to several interpretations. He also gives six possible interpretations.

45 Andre V, June 12, 2019 – "Rope-Snake analogy Using Logic: How Falsehood becomes Truth", https://www.yesvedanta.com/rope-snake-logical-analysis-advaita-vedanta-analogy/

to let ourselves be overwhelmed by it? Are we going to let it affect how we go about life? Are we going to let the pandemic paralyze us?

The truth is that the pandemic will continue till a vaccine or other cure is found for it. What we can do now is respond to it courageously and fearlessly rather than with fear. Like in the case of the rope-snake analogy above, there will be times when we cannot but perceive the pandemic as a threat and so react rather than respond. However, these times must be few and far between. We must keep in mind that the more we respond[46] with equanimity, tranquility and serenity, the more we realise that we will not be overwhelmed by this storm. However, if we react to it, we are giving it more power than we ought to. Nature will continue to be what it is. It will offer no rewards or punishments, only consequences. If we realize this then our response will be a serene response like that of Jesus in the storm and who was surprised that his disciples could react so differently from the way he did.

5.3. Faith versus Faithlessness

If there is one sure thing that the COVID-19 pandemic has taught us it is that we are mortal and that life is fragile. We are here today but could be gone from this life in the next moment. In a word, we are here temporarily. To be sure, we knew this fact theoretically, but it has never been as real to us as it has become in the last three months. This ought to lead logically to another realization namely that we are not in control of anything including the present moment. All the technological and scientific advancements we have made so far cannot help in any practical way to deal with this pandemic. We realize that there is more to "heaven and earth than are dreamt of in our philosophies".[47] Consequently we must ask if we are willing to have faith and believe in the power of God. We must ask if we are willing to acknowledge that - even as we struggle with this challenge -God wants what is best for the world

There is no doubt that as a human community we have abused rather than used the world given to us in trust.[48] The measurement of success based

46 The words "Respond" and "React" are used in specific senses. When the word "respond" is used, it refers to a reply which is measured, unhurried and well thought out. The word "react" on the other hand is used in the sense of an impulsive reply which is hurried and not well thought out.

47 Adapted from Hamlet (1.5.167-8)

48 In Gen 1:28, God pronounces a blessing on humankind to be fruitful and multiply. A similar blessing is pronounced on sea creatures and birds (Gen 1:22), but whereas in this case a command is given, in the case of humans, attention is drawn to the personal relationship between God and humans by the addition of the phrase, "and God said to them" (Gen 1:28). Humans were meant to be God's representatives over the whole world and treat animals, birds, sea creatures, indeed the whole of nature as God treated them. Wenham, Gordon J WBC Vol I p 32. Humans are called to be shepherds of creation and not grasp, exploit and indulge the self alone. Walter Brueggemann Walter p 37. See Matthew Kenneth

on one's possessions has led so many to keep acquiring more with no end in sight. Often this has been done at the cost and expense of others and of nature. Many have been mercenary, ruthless and cold-blooded in their desire to acquire and have spared no thought for the other and for the environment.[49] This has resulted in wanton destruction of our world. It has also resulted in the rich becoming richer and the poor, poorer.[50]

The pandemic is calling us to a radical conversion. It is a conversion wherein we realise that we have not lived as we ought to. Our selfishness and self-centeredness has to be converted into a selflessness. We need a change of mind and heart and a change of vision. We need to reset our priorities and ask what it is that we value most and what it is that is most important in life. We need to become aware that though we have tried to be independent of each other and of God, we are not and we cannot be. We are interdependent. This interdependence is on each other, on nature and on God. This requires faith. It requires the faith that Jesus shows in the storm and encourages us to have. Faith is a necessary element for every one of us as we struggle with this incomprehensible pandemic. This faith is not merely intellectual assent, but an active faith which shows itself in deeds. This means that we never give up or give in. It means that we never lose hope. It means that we continue to believe that we will with the grace of God weather the storm just as the disciples did with Jesus. It means that even though we might at times accuse God of not caring about our plight, God does indeed care. If we believe that God created the world from love and continues to love the world, we must also believe that

---

p 174 who stresses that humans are meant to be "caretakers" not owners as is explicated in Gen 2:15.

49 James Conca, May 21, 2019 – "Nature On The Eve Of Destruction" - The UN Extinction Report, https://www.forbes.com/sites/jamesconca/2019/05/21/nature-on-the-eve-of-destruction-the-un-extinction-report/#4a76cdc762bd. See also Mike Gaworecki, "Audio: The links between COVID-19, wildlife trade, and destruction of nature with John Vidal", March 31, 2020 - https://news.mongabay.com/2020/03/audio-the-links-between-covid-19-wildlife-trade-and-destruction-of-nature-with-john-vidal/. Chris Baranuik, "We are wasting the beautiful earth we have been given", April 28, 2017 - http://www.bbc.com/earth/story/20170427-we-are-wasting-the-beautiful-world-we-have-been-given. Michael T Klare, April 3, 2020 – "Rethinking Our Relationship to the Natural World After Covid-19" , https://www.thenation.com/article/environment/coronavirus-nature-humans/.

50 See Ben Chu, January 21, 2019 – "World's richest get richer while planet's poorest get poorer, new Oxfam report shows", https://www.independent.co.uk/news/business/news/wealth-inequality-rich-poor-poverty-oxfam-forbes-davos-world-economic-forum-a8734951.html. OXFAM International Report, January 20, 2020, "World's billionaires have more wealth than 4.6 billion people", -https://www.oxfam.org/en/press-releases/worlds-billionaires-have-more-wealth-46-billion-people

with faith in God and doing what is required of us we will overcome any and all obstacles that keep coming our way.[51]

We need, however, to look beyond our noses and beyond the small cozy and comfortable worlds that we have created. We need to realize that while planning for the future may be necessary, obsession with and about the future can only cause harm. It causes us to forget to live in the present moment and enjoy that moment to the fullest.

Conclusion

The disciples in Mark have been portrayed in much of the Gospel as a group who were slow to understand and believe. They were accused of a lack of understanding (Mk 4:13), of hardness of heart (Mk 6:52), of not perceiving and understanding (Mk 8:17) of not being men of prayer (Mk 9:29) and of misunderstanding the way of Jesus (Mk 8:32; 9:33-34; 10:37,41). Despite this, Jesus came to their rescue when they found themselves caught in a storm and in spite of their agitation, accusation and lack of faith saw them through it. How much more will he accomplish in us if we put on the attitudes of serenity, fearlessness and faith.

---

51 "God's life-giving work is not extrinsic to creation as though it must always intrude. Rather, it characterizes the world. Creation is itself life-giving in the image of the God who gives all of life." Brueggemann, W. (1982). Genesis (p. 37). Atlanta: John Knox Press.

6

Religions and Christian Faith
A Discussion

Bryan Lobo, SJ

Introduction

The crucial questions that seem to be staring in the face of the Christian faith for quite some time now are the questions that Christianity started asking itself having entered into the study of other religions in its attempt at interreligious dialogue and research. Those religions which fundamentally originated with a non-theistic philosophy or spirituality like Buddhism and Jainism could be perspectives that challenge the theistic religions into at least asking themselves, do we need God for final liberation if by constant ascetically right practices the exercitant can reach a state of bliss or non-suffering that would be expected only in heaven; a state that could be understood as salvation by Christianity bearing some particular differences nonetheless? For *nirvaṇa* and salvation, is ethical living enough or is Divine intervention that includes revelation as understood by Christianity really necessary? Can *nirvaṇa* and salvation be equated at all? Does spiritual experience require the intermediation of God or not? How does one come to ascertain the question of truth in this situation? Are we condemned to subjectivity or does objectivity also form part of our truth paradigms? The questions can go on, and in the following article I may perhaps not be able to arrive at conclusive answers to these questions and other questions, neither will I be able to treat all the questions within the space allotted to me or enter into a discussion at length on the questions chosen; but I shall try to touch upon the problematic of the questions that confront us as we move on because the attempt will be to have a discussion where reflections are presented with some queries and temporary responses which would help to perhaps enlighten the matter at hand and not conclusively seal it.

1. "Religion", a Term used for all "Faiths"?

As we may know, "religion" as an overarching term used for all faith traditions may not be representative of a particular faith tradition especially with the semantic baggage that the word "religion" carries with it. Already, the *Oxford Advanced Learners Dictionary* shows how inadequate the definition or explanation of the term "religion" could appear when it states (as a countable noun), "belief in the existence of a god or gods, who has/have created the universe and given man a spiritual nature which continues to exist after death of the body". As an uncountable noun, religion is a "particular system of faith and worship based on such a belief (as stated above): *the Christian, Buddhist and Hindu religions*"[1]. The concept of god or gods would be problematic for the original teachings of religions like Buddhism or Jainism[2]. In any case, a dictionary cannot include the complexities of the reality of a faith tradition in a single word "religion". At the same time, while using the word "religion" or "religions" in interreligious encounters or Christian theology, there is perhaps the above dictionary meaning that lurks as a presupposition among members of different religions and especially among those that do not take the trouble to study other religions. However, the point that I would like to discuss here is simply that the word "religion" comes to be used as an umbrella term for all faith traditions today. Would it then be justifiable to use the term in such a way for the Christian faith seeking dialogue with Hinduism or Buddhism or Jainism especially in the Indian context?

Firstly, the word "religion" is not of Indian origin. As it is common knowledge, the word "religion" comes from the Latin *religio* which was first used quite frequently in Roman literature[3]. Although Cicero has been

1 Brackets mine. This edition was published by the Oxford University Press in 1993 "with corrections". In their site on the internet the similar meaning is given but with an addition "or in the teachings of a spiritual leader". In https://www.oxfordlearnersdictionaries.com/definition/english/religion (accessed 27/09/2020).

2 Today however, depending on the various schools and perspectives, god or gods could be considered as acceptable to certain denominations of these religions.

3 Before we go ahead, it would be useful to mention the comment here of Goetz, "The etymology of the Latin word *religio* is disputed. Some have tried to connect *religio* with other Latin terms (*relegere, religare, reeligere, relinquere*), but each scholar has been

considered as the initiator of the usage of *religio* distinctively in religious and theological discourse, words or qualities associated to the word *religio* like *religiosus* that referred to "diligent fulfilment of duties"; *religo est* that signified moral obligation and *religiones* that referred to "various cults" was prevalent in the Roman culture[4]. In such a context, Cicero's understanding of *religio* included "knowledge of the nature of gods"; "piety and holiness"; "justice", and "worship of gods" as contrasted with superstition[5]. Evidently then, *religio* appears to depend etymologically on the adjective *religiosus* "which is derived from the verb *relegere*, meaning to take up repeatedly" more as an attitude, behaviour or the virtue of diligence in matters dealing with the divine rather than "specific actions or ceremonies"[6]. The word was also known to be used generally in regard to duties towards one's own family, State or Emperor and even God. More than a doctrine or a Faith tradition, *religio*, commonly referred to a psychological state of conscientiousness towards one's own duties. Thanks to Lactantius, *religio* is also associated with the word *religari* ("bind oneself to something, to reconnect or join"). Augustine, deviating from Cicero as well, understood "*religere* from which "religion" could also be derived, to mean "re-elect" (and not "to read repeatedly" or "to take up diligently")"[7]. In this Christian re-interpretation of *religio* one who practises religion is understood as binding himself to God while making a fundamental choice for God and vice versa.

From the above well-known history of the etymology of the term "religion", the striking statement, which is normally not highlighted much in the discussion, is the understanding of *religio* as a state of conscientiousness towards one's own duties regardless of the cults and gods involved in the religious practice. It is no wonder then that Wilfred Cantwell Smith wanted to get rid of the term "religion" and phenomenologically accept the existence

influenced by his personal ideas, and no accord has been reached...But the problem becomes much more complicated when one wishes to examine the phenomenon of religion in cultures that do not use the Latin word". Goetz, "Religion", *New Catholic Encyclopedia*, Michigan: Gale & The Catholic University of America 2003, 56.

4 See Peter Henrici, "The Concept of Religion from Cicero to Schleiermacher", in Karl Becker and Ilaria Morali, *Catholic Engagement with World Religions: A Comprehensive Study*, Maryknoll: Orbis Books 2010, 2. For a survey of the concept of "religion" see also Mariasusai Dhavamony, "Religion", in René Latourelle & Rino Fisichella (eds.), *Dictionary of Fundamental Theology*, New York: Herder & Herder, 2000, 819-827.

5 Henrici, "The Concept of Religion from Cicero to Schleiermacher", 2-3.

6 *Ibid, 3*. In addition to Henrici we could also quote Dhavamony who explains that in Cicero's sense the word *religio* would mean "to ponder and observe," "to keep together," as opposed to negligere", ("to neglect, undermine"). Thus religion means the conscientious fulfilment of duty, awe of higher power". See Dhavamony, "Religion", 819.

7 Henrici, "The Concept of Religion...", 4-5.

of religiousness[8]. Although in today's terminology, religion cannot solely be understood as conscientiousness towards one's own duties but nevertheless, it remains as the fundamental, anthropological and existential fact that belongs to every human being. In this sense, every human being is a religious person (*homo religiosus*)[9] and this fact could be considered as a building block of religion but not religion in its fullest sense. To be called a religion in its fullest sense there need to be doctrines, God, knowledge of the divine, rites and rituals, in keeping with the comprehensive understanding of *religio*. But it is in this very sphere that differences are sometimes respected and sometimes refuted; similarities and differences are recognized but with opinions that could vary from group to group. It is because of the differences that conflicts between religions have existed from centuries and with all the progress made in different fields, these conflicts still continue. The hope of a solution could perhaps lie in going back to the very core of a human being where an apriori religiosity exists: a longing for God or liberation or an attitude of conscientiousness for one's duties from where all religions were finally born. This may be close to impossible because with such an apriori religiosity nonetheless, every human being is necessarily born within a belief system, whether it is religious or a-religious, or secular or call it what you may. A belief system and an adherence to the belief system will always exist because of the apriori "religious" fact understood in its most fundamental sense as stated above.

But the question one needs to ask here at least as a Christian and which is in effect the central problematic of this whole section is that was Christianity born from that innate religiosity in a human being or was it born because of

8 Smith asserts, "...the sustained inability to clarify what the word 'religion' signifies, in itself suggests that the term ought to be dropped; that it is a distorted concept not really corresponding to anything definite or distinctive in the objective world. The phenomena that we call religious undoubtedly exists". Wilfred Cantwell Smith, *The Meaning and End of Religion: A new approach to the religious traditions of mankind*, Minneapolis: Fortress Press 1991, 17.

9 "The phrase, homo religiosus, refers to the idea that human existence is inherently religious. There is a long lineage of scholars that have proposed this idea, including Georg Wilhelm Friedrich Hegel (1770–1831), Soren Kierkegaard (1813–1855), William James (1842–1910), Mircea Eliade (1907–1986), Rudolf Otto (1884–1939), Friedrich Schleiermacher (1768–1834), Gerardus van der Leeuw (1890–1950), Karl Jaspers (1883–1969), Paul Tillich (1886–1995), Erich Fromm (1900–1980), Abraham Maslow (1908–1970), Erik Erikson (1902–1994), Langdon Gilkey (1919–2004), and David Tracy (1939–). The inherent religiosity, these and other theorists refer to, is not a person's creedal beliefs or institutional commitments per se but refer to our existential drive toward transcendence, freedom, and meaning-making, no matter the differences of religious or a/religious backgrounds or convictions". Todd DuBose, "Homo Religiosus", in David A. Leeming (ed.), *Encyclopedia of Psychology and Religion,* Springer, Boston, MA 2014, https://doi.org/10.1007/978-1-4614-6086-2_308 (accessed: 18/10/20).

a unique, personal and transcendental God who breaks into the immanental, innate, religious core of a human being or a community of human beings? The polytheism that arose in the Greco-Roman period or in other cultures and religions of Latin America, Africa or in Asian religions like Hinduism, Daoism and some other Asian cultures testify to the élan of the *homo religiosus*. But the Judeo-Christian tradition stands testimony to a transcendental God who enters into the finite world of human beings interacting with them for their liberation or salvation: a testimony that does not defy or go contrary to the creativity of the *homo religiosus* but rather gives it a particular orientation that reveals the non-human origin of that tradition. Is it because of this fact that Karl Barth called Christianity the true religion?[10] We must not get Karl Barth wrong here. He is not against non-Christian religions, rather he is against all religions, even Christianity, because religion in itself is "unbelief"[11]. Barth was witness to the influence of science, comparative studies of oriental religions and the phenomenological and anthropological approaches to religions which was hermeneutically challenging the dogmatic Faith of Christianity. It was not even proving helpful in pastoral circumstances. Barth had to therefore assert that Jesus is the Truth ("the objective reality of revelation"[12]) in whom God's revelation has really happened and which is known in Scripture alone especially in the New Testament. We are therefore saved only by faith in Christ and by his grace. All the other additions by the Christian religion down the centuries are expressions of human idolatry. However, since Jesus Christ is the truth in the sense that only in him we receive justification from our sins, and if this truth is upheld by Christianity then Christianity must be considered as the true religion[13].

---

10 Even Lactantius and Augustine upheld Christianity to be the true religion. For a very brief presentation of this aspect, see Henrici, "The Concept of Religion from Cicero to Schleiermacher", 4-5.

11 Karl Barth dedicates a whole chapter to "Religion as unbelief". See his *Church Dogmatics: The Doctrine of the Word of God*, Edinburgh: Clark 1970, vol. 1/2, 297-325. Barth states "...religion is unbelief. It is a concern, indeed, we must say that it is the one great concern, of godless man... Above all it affects ourselves also as adherents of the Christian religion... It can be explained and expounded, but it cannot be derived from any higher principle than revelation, nor can it be proved by any phenomenology or history of religion... From the standpoint of revelation religion is clearly seen to be a human attempt to anticipate what God in His revelation wills to do and does do. It is the attempted replacement of the divine work by a human manufacture. The divine reality offered and manifested to us in revelation is replaced by a concept of God arbitrarily and wilfully evolved by man", 299-300,302.

12 *Ibid.*, 1.

13 Barth explains: "In the relationship between the name of Jesus Christ and the Christian religion we have to do with an act of divine justification or forgiveness of sins. We already stated that the Christian religion as such has no worthiness of its own, to equip it specially

We may see some openness towards other religions in the later Barth but no compromise in the centrality of salvation in Jesus Christ. Even though Barth's theology had a great impact on a large number of Christians and even gave a great impulse to missionary activity, it raised many questions: Does it mean that other religions have no truth at all and their members are eternally damned if they do not accept Christ – the Truth? Can we speak of divine revelation in other religions, if not in the historical Christic sense, at least in the transcendental and immanental sense where morality, prayer, worship, ethics, righteousness and other religious attitudes exist that could make us presuppose that they are not just human creations originating from an apriori reality of the *homo religiosus* but as God active in those religions in different ways? If the original perspectives of Buddhism and Jainism did not even presuppose God and still contained the religious attitudes mentioned above, do we need God to become holy, moral and righteous? In the context of these questions and many others, the exclusivism of Barth has not gone unchallenged by authors like John Hick, Paul knitter and others. The complex issues that these questions raise, make it clear that Jesus Christ cannot be used as a "tool" to negate and condemn religions. Jesus himself belonged to a religion and supported it. Thanks to the Jewish religion and the Greco-Roman philosophy, we have the fundamentals of Christian faith.

The Jewish religion, in a way, becomes the historical platform for the revelation of Jesus Christ. But later reflections on the life and sayings of Jesus and his Apostles which did not agree with many Jewish religious ideas or even Greco-Roman philosophy had to be dogmatised to avoid confusing and contrasting opinions. The Christian faith or the Christ event was then seen as a fulfilment of the Jewish religion. This was precisely the paradigm used to see the other religions as preparations for the Gospel[14]. Later on they

---

to be the true religion. We must now aver even more clearly that in itself and as such it is absolutely unworthy to be the true religion. If it is so, it is so by election, we said. And now we must be more precise: it is so in virtue of the divine justification of sinners, of the divine forgiveness of sins". *Ibid.*, 352.

14 Among the early writers who followed the fulfilment model in India, mention could be made of John N. Farquhar, *The Crown of Hinduism*, London: Oxford University Press, 1915; Pierre Johann, *Vers le Christ par le Vedanta*, Louvain: Museum Lessianum, 1932-1933. For Western authors, mention could be made of Jean Daniélou, *Les saints "païens" de l'Ancien Testament*, Paris: Seuil 1956; Henri de Lubac, *Catholicisme: Les aspects sociaux du dogme*, Paris: Cerf 1952; Id., *La rencontre du Bouddhisme et de l'Occident*, Paris: Aubier 1952. For a short survey of these authors and also of Hans Urs von Balthasar who is considered another Western author who shared a similar perspective like the one of Daniélou and de Lubac see, Jacques Dupuis, *Toward a Christian Theology of Religious Pluralism*, Gujarat: Gujarat Sahitya Prakash 2001, 134-143. See also Paul Knitter for a survey of the fulfilment model in his *Introducing Theologies of Religions*, New York: Orbis books 2002, 63-106. The fulfilment model is also evident in the "inclusivist paradigm".

were also seen as realities already containing Christ in a hidden way[15]. The document Nostra Aetate of the Second Vatican Council, in its openness, asserts that non-Christian religions contain rays of that truth (of Christ) and not the full truth in itself[16]. Such Christian interpretations of other religions may not seem fair because they smack of a superiority complex[17]. But how can that "superiority" be avoided if the resurrection of Jesus, that goes beyond all human understanding and that cannot be accepted in its true existential sense whether by religions in general or by philosophies in particular, is really experienced and proclaimed not only with confidence but miraculous results? Here lies the crux of the problem with the Christian faith and other religions. Differences and similarities are seen among various religions at the phenomenological and hermeneutical levels, but when it comes to the real and factual reality and not merely an understanding or an interpretation of the resurrection of Jesus, it surpasses all tangible experiences of other religions. The other religions, apparently find it unacceptable and those who do give it a hermeneutical twist call it a belief and not a historical fact. If the resurrection is not a historical fact and for that matter even a meta-historical fact, then Christianity could not exist or continue. All the theories of the resurrection as deep experiences[18] of

---

For the inclusivist paradigm, see Alan Race, *Christians and Religious Pluralism: Patterns in the Christian Theology of Religions*, London: SCM Press 1983, 38-69; Gavin D'Costa, *Theology and Religious Pluralism*, Oxford: Basil Blackwell 1986, 80-116.

15 Among a number of authors who held this theory two could be mentioned: Karl Rahner, "Anonymous Christians", in *Theological Investigations* VI, London: Darton, Longman and Todd 1969, 390-398. Connected to this topic other works of Rahner could also be mentioned but we shall limit ourselves only to one. See also Raimundo Panikkar, *The Unknown of Christ of Hinduism: Toward an Ecumenical Christophany* (revised edition), Bangalore: Asian Trading Corporation 1982.

16 "The Catholic Church rejects nothing that is true and holy in these religions. She regards with sincere reverence those ways of conduct and of life, those precepts and teachings which, though differing in many aspects from the ones she holds and sets forth, nonetheless often reflect a ray of that Truth which enlightens all men. Indeed, she proclaims, and ever must proclaim Christ "the way, the truth, and the life" (John 14:6), in whom men may find the fullness of religious life, in whom God has reconciled all things to Himself" (Nostra Aetate 2).

17 In fact, authors of the Theology of Religions are coming to realize that every religion and not only Christianity has superiority claims that Knitter thinks could be "understood and reformulated" for better communion among religions. See Paul Knitter (ed.), *The Myth of Religious Superiority: A Multifaith Exploration*, New York: Orbis 2005, viii.

18 According to Knitter, the resurrection narratives are "conversion experiences rather than photographic statements… they are offered as illustrations, stories, not as proofs of what had happened. The experience of the living Jesus was already there. Such stories, therefore, need not be taken literally, but they should be taken seriously". Paul Knitter, *No Other Name?: A Critical Survey of Christian Attitudes Toward the World Religions, London*: SCM Press 1985, 199.

the risen Lord and not the fact of the risen Lord fall short of the real Apostolic experience and proclamation. The truth of the resurrection of Jesus then, is the uniqueness of the Christian Faith that sets it apart from other religions. Rather than the resurrection leading Christianity to superiority, it leads it to wonder and awe and desires likewise that the others share in this wonder and awe even at the risk of being considered lunatics and inferior rather than superior.

2. Experience in Religions and Christian Faith

Most if not all religions have begun with an overwhelming experience either of human beings meeting God in varied ways especially in the Semitic culture (Judaism, Christianity and Islam), or of human beings beginning with the fear of the unknown: natural calamities that led not only to the personification of natural elements but also to a ritualistic placation of them namely of those personifications followed by constant personal meditation and asceticism leading to an experience of inner bliss and liberation (Vedantic Hinduism). To the experience of liberation, belong Buddhism and Jainism as well. If the initiator of the experience is God, like in the Semitic culture, then the initiator of the spiritual experience in the Indic cultures appears to be the human being. The question that we may ask here, probably at the risk of creating conflict, is that do we depend more on God's initiative or human beings' initiative? At the outset, this question would understand God's initiative in a very simplistic way. How can one really presume that the deep desire within the Upanishadic Hindus, the Buddha and the Mahavira for liberation from *karmic* suffering was not an initiative from God? How are we also so sure that Judaism, Christianity and Islam in their original experience of meeting a God were not actually hallucinating?

To address the first question, if there is an option between choosing initiative by God or by humans, then the choice would be surely initiative by God at least among theists. But by which God? Each God appears to be taking a different initiative. The God of the Israelites enters the lives of Abraham and Moses to begin with and then in the lives of all the prophets talking to them in the language that they understood demanding righteous living according to his laws. Precisely because God spoke to them, he was called a living God. Allah communicates with Mohammed, but one notices differences in that communication when compared to the God of the Israelites. The Christian God appears to be continuing the legacy of the Israelite's God but with the human form: Jesus who understands himself as the Son of the Jewish God, who after his resurrection sent the Holy Spirit who again speaks to the Apostles (Acts 10:19-20; 13:2). Why is God using different ways to approach man for his "salvation"? Does God regard each way equally effective for "salvation" or prefers one way to another? These questions are very difficult to answer, but by posing such questions we could launch into perspectives that we may not have been aware of before.

All three Semitic religions are monotheistic (Christianity is Trinitarianly monotheistic), but being monotheistic, there can be only one God. The one God is making contrasting revelations in each religion. The Christian God seems to appear heretical to Judaism and Islam. In the Semitic culture, presuming that God had taken the initiative, it could be that the human beings living in that culture understood God in different ways. If this is the case, then the Divine truth in these three Semitic religions are human interpretations and their divine validity could be questioned. The crux of the problem is then that in this God-human interaction the veracity of the human belief which is apparently an interpretation of the experience of God cannot be maintained because the instrument that is interpreting the God experience is finite and prone to making mistakes or as Richard Dawkins says "the human mind is extremely susceptible to hallucinations"[19]. The problem becomes more acute especially in Vedantic Hinduism where divinity is arrived at presumably without divinity itself, or rather without a personal divinity accosting human beings and inviting them to follow its. For especially the theistic religions, "information" coming from God would be more acceptable as truth than that coming from human beings about divine matters. Since the contrast in the "information" in the Semitic religions exist, we could temporarily conclude that either there are different Gods and monotheism is not a divine reality, or that there are different Gods and one of the Gods is the most powerful (something similar to monolatry in the OT), or that there is only one God and that God is pluralistic in his revelations. For Christianity, the Trinitarian God is a pluralistic God (unity in plurality), but Christianity cannot accept that God's pluralism leads to contradictions in the revelations of that one God to different religions Semitic or non-Semitic. Could these contradictions evince that there is a difference between God-experience or religious experience in general and God's revelation?

Religious experience as highly subjective is a general affirmation at least in philosophy after Immanuel Kant. But after Schleiermacher, Sabatier and others, experience is favourably identified with revelation[20]. Such a strict

---

19 See the short video on youtube of Richard Dawkins: https://www.youtube.com/watch?v=WmHDiJHxEic (accessed 04/10/2020).

20 For a brief presentation of this argument see René Latourelle, "Revelation", in René Latourelle & Rino Fischella (eds.), *Dictionary of Fundamental Theology*, New York: Herder & Herder 2000, 943-945. Here Latourelle, in disagreement with this thinking quotes Sabatier, "Revelation is 'a religious experience' that 'must be able to be repeated and continued as a present revelation and individual experience'" (944). Talking about Christianity, Sabatier states (as quoted by Latourelle), that "the essence of Christianity is to be found 'in a religious experience, an interior revelation of God that occurred first in the

identification of revelation with general experience in the Christian context is not acceptable to some theologians like Latourelle because it does not fully manifest the actual difference that Christianity maintains between the two concepts even though they go together in the original Apostolic experience. But it does not seem clear when Latourelle places the "self-consciousness of Jesus" under the "original, foundational experience" by which God's revelation of his self-gift is received, whether Jesus' self-consciousness itself is an experience. If so, then Latourelle would be in line with what Sabatier said as stated in ft.nt., 20 seeing religious experience as an interior revelation of God that occurred first in the soul (consciousness) of Jesus. In any case, the experience of Jesus' divine self-consciousness as the Son of God is not equivalent to the mystical experience of divine communion of a saint or a human being. Jesus' self-consciousness as the Son of God is an existential reality (because *it is so*) that is ratified by his words and deeds happening in history. His disciples who are part of this history are experiencing rather knowing Jesus' divinity as an external reality and not something internal as stated by Sabatier. Furthermore, the Apostles are internally experiencing a deep transformation in the Holy Spirit. One therefore sees an extrinsic-intrinsic movement happening in the revelation-experience dynamic of the Christ event. Christian revelation cannot therefore be simplistically identified with general religious experience. Furthermore, it cannot be considered as an "hallucination" because the experience of the revelation and most particularly the resurrection is happening to a group and not to any individual. A group having a similar hallucination all at one time is highly improbable. It is this Apostolic experience and testimony that is shared by the Christians down the centuries right up to this day. The Christian experience presupposes the Christian Faith and therefore cannot be considered as similar to other religious experiences.

Because of the above details, "experience" or "religious experience" in general has not been looked at favourably by Christianity. "Religious experience" could lead to an anti-dogmatic trend that was subtly evident in the work of William James (1842-1910): *The Varieties of Religious Experience*. If any religious experience is given priority over dogma which was in its primal form received in the Christ event through scripture, then the existence of that dogma is threatened by a human reality that is not always stable and therefore many a times erratic and requires oftentimes special investigation to ascertain its truth. Today, however, the Church is not fearful of using the word "experience" in its religious discourse. The word "experience" was often used by Pope John Paul II especially in his second encyclical, *Dives in Misericordia* (1980) where

soul of Jesus of Nazareth but occurs again, less luminously no doubt, but unmistakably, in the souls of all his true disciples" (944).

the noun is used thirteen times and the verb six times to refer both to individual and common experiences[21]. Religious experience, therefore, cannot and should not be considered as an enemy of Christian Faith. The moment it is considered as an enemy, Christianity will lose respect for other religions and that may prove detrimental not only to interreligious dialogue, fraternal respect for other religions and to interreligious activity to safeguard the world[22], but also to Christian theology itself. However, Christian theology would need to carefully analyse the authenticity of human and religious experience[23]. But even when we analyse human and religious experience, on what basis do we analyse these varied experiences that have already developed into belief systems? How do we even confirm the truthfulness of those experiences?

3. Truth and Religious Experience

We cannot get into a detailed history of truth here in Western and Eastern philosophy and theology to then see how it can be applied to religious experience. Our interest would be to try and understand, perhaps in an interdisciplinary way, certain elements of truth philosophically in connection to religious experience and most importantly to Christian faith that would in effect involve Christian theology as well.

Religious experience is one of the most complex phenomenon in human history. When one goes to rationally or philosophically come to grips with this phenomenon, there always seem levels that escape the mind of the philosopher. There have been mystics, saints, gurus, founders of religions and others down the centuries who have claimed to have had special experiences that could be considered divine or supernatural. Even though there existed other

---

21 Cf. Gerald O'Collins, "Experience", René Latourelle & Rino Fisichella (eds.), *Dictionary of Fundamental Theology*, New York: Herder & Herder 2000, 307. O'Collins, however, notes that the language of "experience" was not freely used in the Vatican II documents (307).

22 In this context the first paragraph of Pope Francis' document on *Human Fraternity* could be quoted here: "Faith leads a believer to see in the other a brother or sister to be supported and loved. Through faith in God, who has created the universe, creatures and all human beings (equal on account of his mercy), believers are called to express this human fraternity by safeguarding creation and the entire universe and supporting all persons, especially the poorest and those most in need". See http://www.vatican.va/content/francesco/en/travels/2019/outside/documents/papa-francesco_20190204_documento-fratellanza-umana.html (accessed: 18/19/20).

23 O'Collins writes, "Granted that the theme of experience constantly touches the central issues of the revelation of God in Jesus Christ, its credibility and its transmission, fundamental theology needs to analyse carefully what human and religious experience entails. Otherwise this complex notion and reality will not prove very productive in developing the discipline". *Ibid.*, 308.

religious phenomena that sought the personification of natural elements over which human beings were unable to have control leading to polytheism or the deification of natural elements (as stated before), ritualism and other religious activities performed by people, there existed those who were living within an experiential sphere that was considered above the normal everyday life-experiences of the common person. These persons tended to have had a special supernatural experience that led some of them to change the course of their lives or to challenge the existing religious structures and beliefs and in most if not all cases to found a new belief system. We cannot be exhaustive in giving names here but mention could be made of the most popular ones like Abraham, Moses, Buddha, Mahavira, Confucius, Lao Tzu, Jesus[24], Mohammed and others. The belief system begun by these religious figures, was it the "truth" or not the "truth"? It is here that many philosophers and theologians are at a loss to come to a unanimous decision. But is it really necessary to come to a unanimous decision in this case? It may seem necessary for some but not for others.

Firstly, those who are satisfied and happy within a belief system, do not find it necessary to seek the truth because whatever they believe is the truth for them and that belief functions perfectly for satisfaction and happiness. But if at all a grave calamity befalls the person or his family; a grave illness or financial crisis which the family is not able to deal with, then secular and religious means are sought to find a solution. In the search for a solution if at all a religious figure or a saint or a guru of another belief system which was sought perhaps due to some friend's persuasion or advise or for whatever reason, and that religious figure miraculously solves the problem, then changes happen within a previously held belief system. New beliefs enter in and old beliefs are discarded; new "truths" are embraced and old ones are rejected. Secondly, those who are not satisfied and happy within a belief system and find it meaningless, come about to find meaning in another belief system due to some religious figure or merely by acquiring knowledge about that belief system through literature, friends or others, make a sudden change of their belief system because it gives them new confidence, a spirit that was not experienced before and that changes their lives and their perspectives. It is within this scenario that we will try to reflect systematically but not exhaustively upon "truth" intrinsically connected with belief.

The theory of truth that could be applied for the above context is the pragmatic theory where, simply put, a belief is true if it is useful. As long as a belief system gives me happiness, meaningfulness and helps in alleviating my

24 Here we do not intend to reduce the full divine status of Jesus by placing him among historical personages. Our intention to mention Jesus in this list is to show that as a historical person he too was someone who initiated a special religious experience.

suffering it is true for me. Even the correspondence theory can be applied here where an individual joins a belief system because it promises happiness and freedom from suffering and that individual really acquires what is promised through the belief system and practices. To some extent even the coherence theory could be applied here where the belief is considered to be true because it coheres with other beliefs that are in favour of human happiness, welfare etc. In short a belief or a belief system is considered true if it leads to human wellbeing in all its aspects. Within this perspective, truth cannot but be subjectively understood in regard to a belief. A belief is true not in itself but only because it is useful. So if God is useful to me then God is true, or if ritual practices are useful to me, they are true otherwise they are not. Most belief systems function on such a paradigm. With all the arguments in favour or against such a paradigm, the fundamental objection would be that if one belief can be true to one and false to another depending on its usefulness, then truth is emptied of its universal validity. It is made dependent on vacillating human emotions and thereby extremely unstable. The Buddha would have functioned on this paradigm especially when he remained silent on metaphysical questions about the universe, soul, God etc. to focus more on the way to end suffering[25]. The justification of the Buddhist paradigm, is the liberating experience (Nirvāṇa) of Buddha himself. It is no wonder then that Buddha did not speak about God. Buddha was not a philosopher but a man who had attained wisdom or enlightenment (Bodhi), a state which philosophers seek rationally perhaps but which the Buddha attained spiritually. If philosophy offers us truth rationally, Buddha offers it spiritually in attaining nirvāṇa and not "knowledge" about metaphysical realities. Even if Aristotle and the philosophers used logic to arrive at the truth about metaphysical questions it was only a rational exercise because their conclusions made rational sense but lacked spiritual experience. In the case of Jesus however, there is a categorical declaration that "I am the Truth" (Jn 14:6). Even in Jesus' case there is no rational argumentation about how he is the Truth, but there is experience of his divinity through the verification of his miracles, most importantly the raising of dead individuals and finally the resurrection of himself that validates not only the divinity of Jesus but also the declaration that he is the Truth. In this case, we are not

25 Buddha, in responding to Māluṇkyaputta's metaphysical question with the following words shows how *useful* his way is in eliminating suffering: "It is not on the view that the world is eternal, Māluṇkyaputta, that a religious life depends: it is not on the view that the world is not eternal that a religious life depends. Whether the view is held that the world is eternal, or that the world is not eternal, there is still rebirth, there is old age, there is death, and grief, lamentation, suffering, sorrow and despair, the destruction of which even in this life I announce". Clarence H. Hamilton, *Buddhism*, Indianapolis: The Library of Liberal Arts 1952, 55. In Bina Gupta, *An Introduction to Indian Philosophy: Perspectives on Reality, Knowledge and Freedom*, New York & London: Routledge 2012, 87.

arriving at the truth about something but at the truth of Truth itself. A short reflection on this aspect would be helpful here.

To ask the question like Pilate, "what is Truth" is invalid because truth is not or cannot be an object of investigation and it is always secondary to a given reality. Namely, I can get the truth of a person or a matter or anything which is the primary reality to be verified to attain the truth of that reality. By itself therefore truth does not exist as a separate thing because it is dependent on being. Even when truth was considered as a "transcendental" right from the time of Aristotle down to the Scholastics, it depended on being. Being was one, good and true whereas truth was not being. Even the popular traditional theories of truth as stated above which apparently developed as an answer to the question "what is truth", define truth always in connection with another reality. To narrowly define truth as correspondence to a fact and present it as an answer to the question "what is truth", would not be to consider truth primarily in itself but secondarily as the end result of a process dependent on the fact. It is something similar to love. Love can be seen as existing or verified only through activity. The same can be said about truth. But when love and truth are applied to God, then in God's simplicity God does not *have* love and truth but *is* love and truth. It is in this context that truth, not as a human activity, but as a divine reality exists in a way which allows us to come up with an answer to the question "what is truth" (even though invalid) or better still, who is truth, as truth is God. Jesus' affirmation that "I am the truth" would causally amount to "because I am God".

When relating religious experience to truth, it is the former explanation (activity) that generally comes to play and not the latter (truth is God) as we saw earlier in the pragmatic sense of religious experience. At the former level relativism does exist; but at the latter level, relativism cannot exist because truth is not the result of a process and is not dependent on being. These two levels are at times confused by Christian thinkers especially those dealing with the theology of religions. Jesus Christ is the Truth but this statement (as a statement) does not necessarily lead to any religious experience. No doubt that the Apostles were experiencing the powers of Jesus externally leading to an internal experience of transformation, while the Buddhist exercises suggested by the Buddha were practices that brought about internal transformation. Buddha was presenting a way to attain nirvana while Jesus, among other considerations, worked miracles to reveal his identity as the Truth and therefore God. Revelation in Jesus Christ doubtlessly involves experience but the intention is not primarily a matter of religious experience which tends towards pragmatism but first a matter of Truth that requires ascent even to rational "impossibilities" followed by experience. The classical case is of Lazarus lying in the tomb for four days and Jesus tells the mourning Martha, "I am the resurrection and the life. Those who believe in me, even though they die will live, and everyone who lives and believes in me will never die. Do you believe this?" (John 11:25-27). Martha gives her ascent to what appeared as an impossibility and Jesus goes ahead and raises Lazarus and the people around experience something supernatural revealed in and through Jesus Christ. The revelation that is happening in Jesus Christ is true but is not under the control of rationality even though reason is used to understand that revelation. Therefore "non-rational"[26] faith is required in the person of Jesus Christ and the various aspects revealed through his life. The Christian Faith, the way it believes in the incarnation, the resurrection and the Trinity may appear unreasonable and also untruthful because merely believing in these dogmas apparently does not lead to the experience of self-transformation if self-transformation is presumed as the test of truthfulness. Nevertheless, they are truthful precisely because they go beyond and are not controlled by human experience and rationality and therefore are uniquely divine. As for transformative experience, it does exist depending on how the Christian collaborates with the Trinitarian God in doing God's will and receiving God's grace.

Conclusion

In conclusion we could say that our discussion could continue on the above aspects and on other aspects related to our fundamental theme that have not been considered in this discussion. As said in the introduction, we have not tried to be conclusive in our discussion but still the questions asked and the responses given may have led the reader to add aspects to his or her perspectives on the above issues that may appear conclusive in some respects and in-conclusive or rather open-ended in others. The complexity that exists in this exercise, namely interreligious theological interaction and the necessity of neutrality in it that appears existentially impossible but rationally possible even though reason can be controlled by our existential situation, background, emotions etc., makes the exercise difficult but also fascinating. In the encounter with other religions, the encounter that a Christian is capable of having with one's own faith could be more ratifying and also enlightening.

---

26 A "non-rational" faith need not necessarily be blind faith. It could be rational in a different sense. We could invoke the well-known phrase of Blaise Pascal here: "The heart has its reasons which reason knows nothing of... We know the truth not only by the reason, but by the heart". See https://www.goodreads.com/quotes/559339-the-heart-has-its-reasons-which-reason-knows-nothing-of (accessed: 20/10/20).

Witnessing the LOGOS

7

'We Proclaim Christ and Him Crucified' The Mission Manifesto of Apostle Paul

Thomas Malipurathu, SVD

Introduction

Plumbing the depths of the seminal ideas that the Pauline writings contain is a perennially challenging enterprise. One of those seminal ideas is what he proposes as the essence of Christian mission. When the Apostle declares with fierce conviction "we proclaim Christ and him crucified", what we can immediately conclude is that the crucified Lord is the irreducible kernel of the Christian gospel. It is, in fact, Paul's dynamic interpretation of Jesus' death on the cross which functions as the veritable foundation of his theology. Hence Pauline gospel is built on the theology of the cross (*theologia crucis*). This paper tries to explore in some depth the basic tenets of the *theologia crucis* as presented particularly in a significant passage such as 1 Cor 1:18-25. The study concludes with a brief reflection on the implications of this crucial concept for the life and mission of today's Christian community.

1. The Timeless Message of Paul the Apostle

Arguably no one else's faith assertions have been subjected to such relentless and extensive scrutiny and elaboration as those of the Apostle Paul. Pauline writings are a veritable treasure trove of stirring spiritual insights. In his times he was undeniably a thinker of genius proportions. Through the message he has left behind in his writings he has proved his exceptional prowess to reach out across generations. He speaks at times with exceptional clarity and at other times his pronouncements are disturbingly enigmatic. Surely no spiritually inclined person will remain unmoved, for instance, when hearing an exhortation such as "Only, live your life in a manner worthy of the gospel of Christ, so that, whether I come and see you or a, absent and hear about you, I will know that you are standing firm in one spirit, striving side by side with one mind for the faith of the gospel, and are in no way intimidated by your opponents" (Phil 1:27-28). Neither will such a person be able to ignore the profound significance of a statement like "I want to know Christ and the power of his resurrection and the sharing of his sufferings by becoming like him in his death, if somehow I may attain the resurrection from the dead" (Phil 3:10-11). Similarly, any genuine spiritual seeker will find his pulse quickening while reading the lines "My little children, for whom I am again in the pain of childbirth until Christ is formed in you" (Gal 4:19). Again, with the penetrating observation "Who will separate us from the love of Christ? Will hardship, or distress, or persecution, or famine, or nakedness, or peril or sword? ... No, in all these things we are more than conquerors through him who loved us" (Rom 8:35-37). So too, will any convinced believer not feel reaffirmed in his faith by the declaration "We know that all things work together for good for those who love God, who are called according to his purpose. For those whom he foreknew he also predestined to be confirmed to the image of his Son, in order that he might be the firstborn within a large family. And those whom he predestined he also called; and those whom he called he also justified; and those whom he justified he also glorified" (Rom 8:28-30).

Nonetheless, we feel baffled by many a statement of the Apostle. For instance, when he insists "Therefore I am content with weaknesses, insults, hardships, persecutions, and calamities for the sake of Christ, for whenever I am weak, then I am strong" (2 Cor 12:10). So too with a submission like "I do not understand my own actions. For I do not do what I want, but do the very thing I hate. Now If I do what I do not want, I agree that the law is good. But in fact, it is no longer I that do it, but sin that dwells within me... For I do not do the good I want, but the evil I do not want is what I do" (Rom 7:15-20). Equally enigmatic is Paul's affirmation "May I never boast of anything except the cross of our Lord Jesus Christ, by which the world has been crucified to me, and I to the world" (Gal 6:14). Or indeed, many might feel disturbed by the implications of an instruction such as "When you are assembled, and my spirit is present with the power of our Lord Jesus, you are to hand this man over to Satan for the destruction of the flesh, so that his spirit may be saved in the day of the Lord" (1 Cor 5:4-5).

Few such minor hiccups apart, Paul's assertions on most aspects of the Christian doctrine have always remained in pole position. In my early years of theological formation, it was scholars such as Scaria Kuthirakkattel who introduced me to the study of scripture, particularly the intricacies of Pauline thought through his course on the Letters of Paul.[1] It is indeed a privilege to get a chance to write a paper which will form part of the volume that is meant to pay tribute to him and his long years of service as a teacher of the word of God.

One of the highlights of Pauline literature is its emphasis on the theology of the cross. There is no doubt that Christian theology is heavily indebted to Pauline theology, more precisely on his dynamic interpretation of Jesus' death on the cross. Although all four gospels provide us with their own moving versions of the passion of the Lord, culminating in the chilling act of the crucifixion, they do not seem to propose a special theology of the cross. Their narratives are built on the kerygmatic and the cultic foundation of the passion story. Looming in the background is certainly the idea that Jesus meets his death as the sacrificial lamb of the New Testament.[2] The early Church's concern to depict the events of Jesus' life in line with the prophesies of the Old Testament will have surely influenced the shaping of some of the details of the passion narrative.

But Paul, on the other hand, out of the particulars he had gathered in the years following the experience on the road to Damascus, put together an elaborate theology of the cross. Just as he pays little attention to the vicissitudes of the life of historical Jesus, when it comes to the crucifixion too, his focus is trained almost exclusively on the saving significance of it rather than on its factual build-up.[3] In the *kenosis* hymn (Phil 2:6-11) his insistence is that in obedience to God's will and for accomplishing human salvation, Jesus (who already had set aside his divine status to become a human being) willingly embraced death, and for death he chose the most humiliating kind: death on the cross. That is how the cross assumes critical significance in the salvation history. In the various metaphors that he uses to describe the saving intervention of Jesus such as reconciliation, redemption and sacrifice, the cross is presumed as the decisive reference point.[4]

---

1 A couple of articles which he published in the immediately succeeding years I found them as containing stimulating insights into Pauline thought; (1) "Eucharistic Celebration in the Early Church," *Biblebhashyam* 4 (1978) 49-64; (2) "Law and Freedom in St. Paul," *Biblebhashyam* 6 (1980) 265-288.

2 Cf. J. Schneider, "*stauros*, etc." in *Theological Dictionary of the New Testament*, Vol. VII, 574.

3 Ibid, 575.

4 For a detailed consideration of these and other metaphors used by Paul to elaborate the saving significance of the cross, cf. James D.G. Dunn, *The Theology of Paul the Apostle* (London: T & T Clark, 2003) 218-231.

2. The Background of the Cross

The cross (*stauros* in Greek) literally means a stake or pole in vertical position, used for fencing or as a foundation. When referring to an instrument of torture for serious offences, *stauros* could take three forms: (1) a vertical pointed stake, (2) an upright stake with a horizontal beam above it resembling the letter "T" (*crux commissa*) and (3) two intersecting beams of equal length (*crux immissa*), the form that is most familiar to us.[5]

It is believed that the Persians were the first to employ crucifixion as a means of capital punishment. It was taken over by the Greeks and the Carthaginians from whom the Romans. The Romans, however, mostly used it as a mode of execution for slaves, foreigners and inhabitants of foreign provinces. In the Roman Empire especially, citizens were protected from crucifixion by law, although some autocratic governors at times ignored this protection. Rebellious citizens, who were perceived as a threat to the Empire or to those in power, those accused of treason that was potentially dangerous to security were from time to time put to death on the cross. In New Testament times crucifixion was regarded the cruelest form of execution, most painful and most disgraceful. Punishment by crucifixion was further considered as a disciplinary measure for the maintenance of the existing authority, more as a deterrent than as a means of retribution. The reason behind crucifying someone in a public place was precisely this.[6] In Roman provinces it continued until the time of the Emperor Constantine, who abolished it during his reign.

The Jews did not approve of crucifixion as a method of punishment. "In Judea, at the time of Jesus, sentencing to crucifixion and execution was entirely in the hands of the Roman authorities."[7] There was, however, the practice of hanging on a tree the body of hardened criminals such as idolaters and blasphemers after being stoned to death. The purpose was to serve a warning to potential criminals in their midst. To the traditional Jews crucifixion was the most humiliating form of death and they saw it as a stumbling block or scandal (cf. Gal 5:11). Against this background, when the early Christians claimed that the long-expected Messiah had come in the person of Jesus of Nazareth and he was put to death on the cross, it became a cause for their persecution. The Jews would refer to Dt 21:23 ("Any man who hangs on a tree is accursed by God") to justify their terrible sense of outrage when the Messiah, the great symbol of their long-cherished hope, was depicted by the Christians as having

5 Schneider, "*stauros*", 572.

6 E. Brandenburger, "*Stauros*" in The New International Dictionary of New Testament Theology, Vol. 1, 392.

7 Ibid, 390.

been crucified.[8] Paul's own early stance of uncompromising opposition to the Christian claim about the Messiahship of Jesus—to root out which he was ready to resort to even shockingly violent ways—has to be located somewhere along the line of this ideological continuum.

3. Theology of the Cross as the Quintessence of the Pauline Gospel

It is when seen against this background that Paul's spirited avowal "We proclaim Christ and him crucified" (1 Cor 1:22) appears absolutely stunning. His encounter with the risen Lord on the road to Damascus, and the drama that accompanied it, brought about this miraculous turnaround in him. The process of interpreting this crucial assertion will unveil for us the basic outline of the Pauline theology of the cross.

The foundational fact that Paul establishes through it is that the cross-resurrection dyad inaugurated a new age in which the glory of God became the destiny of creation.[9] This implies that if the cross of Jesus stands at the centre of Paul's theology, so does the resurrection of Jesus. Christ crucified is the one whom God raised to life. In fact, the significance of the one cannot be grasped in isolation from that of the other. "Without the resurrection, the cross would be a cause for despair. Without the cross, the resurrection would be an escape from reality."[10]

That the apostle's effort is to make the event of the resurrection the irreplaceable corner stone of Christian faith is beyond any shadow of doubt (cf. 1 Cor 15:14-17). He saw the resurrection as the act of God placing God's irrevocable stamp of approval on the saving work of Jesus. Paul's emphasis on the centrality of the cross is to demonstrate to believers that salvation is accomplished through the suffering and death of the Lord Jesus. He did not bring salvation by coming to earth as a powerful monarch or ruler but by taking upon himself the degradation of the gibbet of the cross. Thus, Jesus' atoning sacrifice at the cross is the means by which salvation is accomplished for all humankind. In this way the cross becomes the ultimate ground for the eternal blessings God bestows on believers. For Paul the crucifixion of Jesus is the saving event which radically transforms the world, providing humans with a new impulse for thought and action.[11] Paul's central assertion, therefore, is

8 Ibid, 573-574; cf. also Pierson Parker, "Cross" in *The Interpreter's Dictionary of the Bible*," Vol. 1, 745.

9 In simple words it can be formulated as follows: "Saint Paul's theology is basically a theology of salvation and its core is the death and resurrection of Jesus. Jesus through his death and resurrection has bridged the gap between the alienated man and God; in other words, he reconciled man to God"; Scaria K.J. (Kuthirakkattel), "Law and Freedom in St. Paul" *Bible Bhashyam* 6 (1980)265.

10 Dunn, *Theology of Paul*, 235.

11 Cf. Brandenburger, "*Stauros,*" 397.

that God the Father has triumphed over the forces of darkness (Satan, sin and death) through his Son's redemptive work on the cross.

Paul uses a whole range of metaphors to spell out the significance of the death of Jesus on the cross. But in fact, no single metaphor nor all the metaphors put together can exhaust the enormously rich significance of Jesus' death. That is why he at times employs different metaphors together: redemption and sacrifice in Rom 3:25, representation, reconciliation and sacrifice in 2 Cor 5:14-21, redemption and curse in Gal 3:13 and a series of them in Col 2:11-15. "Presumably", as Dunn points out, "the point is that no one metaphor is adequate to unfold the full significance of Christ's death".[12] One of the things that the Apostle insists through the use of these metaphors is that what is crucial in the saving work of Jesus is God's initiative. Jesus did not act in a manner independent of God, or much less, in opposition to God.

What the use of the varied metaphors underscores is the irrefutable centrality of the death of Jesus in Paul's gospel. In fact, Paul's soteriological vision cannot be expressed in terms of any other concept such as Jesus' teaching constituting the source of saving knowledge or wisdom or his taking of flesh in the incarnation healing the sinfulness of the flesh.[13] The scant evidence of theologizing from those early days suggests to us that it may have been Paul who gave the gospel its focus on the death of Jesus and it was he who stamped the image of the cross so distinctively on the gospel.[14]

3.1. The Presentation of the Theologia Crucis in 1 Cor 1:18-25

The word *stauros* occurs 10 times in Paul's letters (1 Cor 1:17, 18; Gal 5:11; 6:12, 14; Eph 2!6; Phil 2:8; 3:18; Col 1:20; 2:14). In addition, the verb form, *stauroō* has about eight occurrences. From the point of view of sheer number, it may not be too impressive in comparison to the frequency of some of the typical Pauline words and phrases. But somehow, what Paul articulates with the use of these words is of central significance for his theology. The passage that is considered as the key text for the elaboration of the Pauline *theologia crucis* is certainly 1 Cor 1:18-25. [15]

12 Dunn, *Theology of Paul*, 231.

13 Dunn, *Theology of Paul*, 232, quotes L. Cerfaux in this context who says that the Fathers juxtaposed the two theories on salvation (that is, salvation through the incarnation and through the resurrection), but Paul's position never varies: the starting point of his soteriology, which is the death and resurrection, and his conception of Christ according to the flesh, always prevent him from attributing to the incarnation a positive and efficacious action in the order of salvation.

14 Ibid, 231-232.

15 Although v.17 (the just preceding verse) can be considered as very significant to the interpretation of the cluster of verses that follows, it is best considered as a transitory verse. In so far as it speaks of the danger of cleverly formulated words of wisdom (rhetoric)

3.1.1. The Corinthian Problematics in Its Historical Setting

The application of sociological analysis to the situation described in 1 Corinthians has given new insights into the problems hinted in it and to accept the fact that it is impossible to understand the dynamics of the early development of the Church in Corinth purely in doctrinal terms, as older scholarship tended to do. There is clearly a socio-economic dimension to the tensions in Corinth, from the way in which the Eucharist was conducted (cf. 11:22), to the tendency to seek justice in secular litigation (only the rich could afford to go to court), and even over food offered to idols. It points to the existence of a very status-conscious society.

Having said all this, social factors do not explain everything in the Corinthian church. There were still some real ideological issues which led to menacing factionalism and the presence of divisive influences. Most of the literature on 1 Corinthians concludes that it was not so much a case of four separate parties slogging it out, following Paul, Apollos, Cephas or Christ (as 1:12 might suggest), as a matter of two sides being involved. Some scholars hold the view that an axis lies between Paul and Cephas, perhaps reflecting a Gentile–Jewish divide in the Church. Others have tended to see Paul and Apollos as the major foci of loyalty in the congregation. Recently, perhaps, the pendulum has swung more towards the Apollos theory, and the idea that the disputes in Corinth caused division, less between Jewish and Gentile Christians than among different groups of Gentile believers in the Church. This conclusion is normally arrived at on the basis of, among other things, the absence from the letter of the normal contentious issues in Jewish–Gentile Christian relations, such as law, promise, circumcision and the like.

Paul arrived in Corinth around the year 50/51-52 and according to Acts 18:1-3 Aquila and Priscilla (believed to be Jewish Christians earlier expelled from Rome following the edict of Emperor Claudius) were already there at that time. Paul's earlier experience in Philippi and Thessalonica had been marked by hostility and rejection and so it was with fear and trembling that he landed in Corinth (1 Cor 2:3). He stayed there for a year and half and perhaps it is because of this fact that he could claim that he planted and laid the foundation for the Church there and fathered the Christian community (1 Cor 3:6, 10; 4:15).[16] Sociological analysis has also shown how most of the people named in the letter were probably of high social status, and most probably supporters of Paul. There is also evidence to suggest that some within the Church were

robbing the cross of its enormous power, it belongs to the essence of what is proposed as the theology of the cross. Yet based on literary indices, it is better to be taken as a transitory verse.

16 Cf. Raymond E. Brown, *An Introduction to the New Testament* (New York: Doubleday, 1996) 514.

disdainful towards Paul, perhaps because of his lack of rhetorical ability (as opposed to Apollos) and his artisan status (he was a tent-maker by profession). It is arguable that this same group claimed that "there is no resurrection from the dead", that "there are no idols in the world" (1 Cor 8:4), argued for the right to eat in pagan temples, possibly joining in the cultic meals in honour of idols (1 Cor 8:1-13; 10:7-33), and displayed a strange mixture of sexual licence (1 Cor 5:1) and asceticism (7:1). It is possible to suggest ideological settings in first-century Corinth which would explain the origin of some of these ideas and practices. For example, local Epicureans, who held that knowledge of the essential principles of matter gave them power and superiority over others who lacked it, would have held a number of beliefs and practices which bear striking resemblance to some Corinthian positions. They believed, for example, that at death people simply cease to be, and that resurrection of any kind is nonsensical. They had a reputation for keeping themselves separate from the rest of society, in a way similar to those who ate apart at the Eucharist, and perhaps they felt that they had no need of those less gifted than themselves (1 Cor 12:21). Although not actually atheist, they held the gods to be of no account, distant and uninterested, and thus held that one could engage in pagan worship without its necessarily meaning anything, much like some Corinthian Christians seem to have done (1 Cor 8:10). And, of course, like all good first-century upwardly-mobile Greco-Romans, they were interested in wisdom and rhetoric.

In any case, it is a fair guess that the Church in Corinth was experiencing a power-struggle between two groups of wealthy Christians. One, perhaps converted by Apollos's rhetorical style and charismatic ability, may have been still influenced by close association with ideas and practices most evident in the Epicurean group in the city, and uncritically brought these ideas into their new Christian faith to justify their behaviour. In reaction, a number of those who had been in the Church longer, originally converted by Paul, may have stoutly opposed the distortions they introduced. Subsequent dispute had quickly degenerated into an argument about names and loyalties, one side disparaging the ministry and abilities of the other's "leader". The poor in the congregation, for example Chloe's slaves (1:11), saw the prevailing situation as just an argument over names. The rich took sides, some even staying aloof from the quarrel by claiming to follow the distant Peter. Paul, it seems, had to address two quite separate problems, namely boasting by those who followed Apollos and valued rhetoric, knowledge, wealth, status and charismatic gifting, so disparaging both the poor and Paul himself, and quarrelling between these and Christians who thought they were remaining loyal to Paul.

3.1.2. The Unpacking of the Theologia Crucis

It is into this poignant context that Paul introduces the redoubtable *ho logos tou staurou* ("the word/message of the cross" v. 18). In Paul's considered opinion, all the many claims of superiority of one view over the other, all expert considerations built on cleverly constructed arguments would pale into insignificance before the sublime message of the cross. For him the message of the cross is indeed the quintessence of the gospel, the irreducible kernel of the saving message. The gospel is simply the presentation of the crucified Christ (cf. Gal 3:1). It has two basic effects: it will appear as foolishness to those who are on the way to destruction, while for those who are on the path of salvation, it is the manifestation of the power of God.

The two groups (those who are perishing and those who are being saved—NRSV)—described by present participles (*appolumenois* and *sōzomenois)*—and the distinction between them are eschatological as destruction and salvation are consummated at the last day (cf. Rom 9:22; 13:11).[17] This division of humanity into two groups is not the result of God's predestination of some to salvation and others to condemnation. It happens on the basis of acceptance or rejection of the word of the gospel.[18] Those who are perishing reject the gospel because in their assessment it is absurd to look for God on the scene of the crucifixion. For them it is utter foolishness and a laughable pursuit. But for Paul in it is manifested the indomitable power of God. Interestingly in this context the counterpart of "foolishness" is not "true wisdom" or "God's wisdom", but "God's power". Whereas to the human eyes what the crucifixion scene reveals is abject weakness, what God reveals through it is God's supreme wisdom. Paul is eminently in line with the biblical tradition here which has consistently held that from weakness is born an enormous strength!

What v.19 presents as supporting argument from the scriptures is a quotation from Is 29:14 (LXX version). The "wisdom" that is mentioned here is clearly wisdom of this world (cf. v.20), which is humanly fashioned and which leaves God out of its purview. The point is that if you approach the great mystery of the crucifixion and the gospel that is built on it with this kind of wisdom, it will appear as nothing but foolishness. Paul is trying to show that the quotation supports what he had been trying to establish in that the Old Testament not only mentions the wisdom of this world, but it predicts that such worldly wisdom is destined to be overthrown. To that effect he brings in further scriptural evidence, this time through allusions to texts such as Is

17 Cf. C.K. Barret, *A Commentary on the First Epistle to the Corinthians* (London: A & C Black, 1971) 51, quoting W.G. Kuemmel.

18 Cf. Jerome Murphy-O'Connor, "The First Letter to the Corinthians," in Raymond E. Brown, et alii (eds.), *New Jerome Biblical Commentary* (London: Geoffrey Chapman, 1991) 801.

19:11-12; 33:18; 44:25 and Job12:17. Barret convincingly shows that "As the next verse (v.21) will make clear, God has now acted so as to expose what the world considers wisdom as the folly that it truly is, and so to put to flight arrogant and self-assertive wise men, scholars, and disputants."[19]

The irony of the situation is that while God made the world's wisdom folly by achieving what it failed to do and by doing it in a way which the wise ones of the world dismissed as foolish (v.21). Since the world's wisdom failed in reaching God, God's wonderful design,[20] now through the proclamation of the gospel, is making that goal within the reach of humans. Rational speculation on the part of the humans, which the world passes for wisdom, however, failed to recognize that God acted through the suffering saviour. And so unfortunately, the so-called wise have been rejecting this overture from God. It is to be presumed that by world's wisdom Paul is referring to the kind of wisdom the Gnostics tried to promote. But such wisdom is inherently corrupt as because of human self-seeking it recoils on itself. That is the failure of human wisdom. Paul refused to use words of worldly wisdom because these cannot grasp or expound the saving significance of the cross of Christ. Philosophical propositions which puts human wisdom in place of God's wisdom robs the cross of its saving content.[21] Salvation is attained not by the acquiring of *gnosis,* but by the acceptance of faith which Paul and others present as the kerygma.

In the following verses (vv. 22-24) Paul succinctly articulates the situation in which the gospel is preached and the content of that gospel itself. The Jews ask for signs because they are unwilling to take God on trust. They want God to present God's credentials in the form of visible and identifiable acts in which God's claim on humans and God's ability to meet their needs are validated. This attitude, although at times clothed in a religious garb, is essentially skeptical and egoistical. Similarly, the wisdom demanded by the Greeks is of the Gnostic variety, which represented a pretended revelation of God which in reality was a human speculative construction. Hence, as Barret concludes "In fact, in the Jewish demand for signs and the Greek quest for wisdom, we have the two expressions, religious and unreligious respectively, of man-in-the-world, man alienated from God and manifesting his rebellion in anthropocentric existence."[22] In the seeking after signs and wisdom what is essentially manifested is the self-centred ego that rejects with ingratitude

19 Barret, *A Commentary*, 53.

20 Murphy-O'Connor, "The First Letter," 801, rightly maintains that here the "wisdom of God" cannot be construed as "divine plan" as that would rob the argument of all its force. It is to be understood as the organization and beauty of creation.

21 Cf. Schneider, "*Stauros,*" 575.

22 Ibid, 54.

and disobedience God's claim on humans which would liberate them.[23] This in turn works out as a discounting of the cross and its proclamation for human salvation. The pursuit of wisdom no less than legalistic piety discounts the cross. Both deprive it of its significance.[24] In this situation of human inadequacy God takes the initiative by offering salvation through the gospel which has as its essential content the crucified Christ, God's power and God's wisdom.

This magnanimous offer of God which the icon of the crucified Lord represents, is not an act of coercion, similar to an organized system of philosophy, metaphysics or ethics. The biting irony of the cross is the core of God's offer of salvation. What God proffers to us humans in the form of Christ crucified stands in direct opposition to human ideas of wisdom and power, yet it achieved what human power and wisdom failed to achieve. "God's foolishness is a crucified Christ, who is refused by the Jews because of their messianic expectations and by the Gentiles because of their rationalism".[25] That is how God's foolishness turns out to be wiser than human wisdom and God's weakness becomes stronger than human strength!

4. Pauline Manifesto's Relevance for the Present-day Church and Its Mission

The foregoing analysis has shown how the Apostle Paul puts together an agenda for mission using the icon of the crucified Christ its frontispiece. In other words, for Paul his entire missionary outreach was an expansion of the rich content of his *theologia crucis*. Every move that he made in his missionary career was guided and motivated by the shining portrait of the crucified saviour which was indelibly etched in the innermost recesses of his heart and mind. It is this reality which he expresses when he declares with steely conviction: "We proclaim Christ and him crucified".

But for all we know, Paul was not merely giving us an indication of the motivating force of his life or of his preferred approach to mission when he wrote in this manner. There is hidden in his words an ardent invitation that all Christians of the succeeding generations adopt this as a model for their day-to-day life and mission. By expounding his theology of the cross using powerful words and imageries, Paul wants to remind the believing community of the paradigmatic nature of the cross; it is not solely a soteriological event which remains locked in the past, but is a paradigm of the way in which God always works. Because the *theologia crucis* depicts the God who does not abdicate power, but uses it for the healing and salvation of God's creation, exercising

23 Murphy-O'Connor, "The First Letter," 801: "The demand for miracles is a refusal to trust God and camouflages contentment with the status quo."

24 Cf. Brandenburger, "*Staturos*", 399.

25 Murphy-O'Connor, "The First Letter," 801.

God's own power in the foolish, powerless vulnerability of the cross, it can therefore offer an alternative model of power for the Christian community. The truth revealed in the *theologia crucis* is not oppressive, but liberating, because it is inseparably connected to self-giving love as its mode of expression. It tells us of a God who places the very self at the service of God's people and invites those people to follow suit.

The implications of the Pauline agenda of mission conveyed through his *theologia crucis* can be seen as falling into two broad categories depending on the subjects attempting to translate it into action: personal and communitarian.

4.1. Implications of Cruciform Existence for Individuals

In Phil 3:18 Paul describes certain individuals as the enemies of the cross. He appears to be quite disturbed that some have turned out to be of this kind in a community he always held in high regard.[26] He is speaking of Christians who do not deny the saving significance of the cross but who spurn the cross of Christ by their manner of life. In effect they are seen as not willing to accept the implications of the cross for the shaping of practical everyday life. In the passion predictions which we find occurring frequently in the synoptic gospels (Mk 8:31; 9:30-31; 10:33-34; Mt 16:21-23; 17:22-23; 20:17-9; Lk 9:21-22; 9:43-45; 18:31-34) Jesus saw his approaching death as offering a model for the life journey of his disciples, those in his company at that time and for all future ones. He thus demanded of the disciples a readiness for suffering and even crucifixion.[27]

Most Christians are used to marking themselves with the sign of the cross, perhaps several times during the course of the day.[28] To make the sign of the cross is to profess a commitment to live a "cruciform existence," that is, to let one's life be moulded by the pattern of the cross of Christ (cf. Phil 3:10). That idea will sound distasteful to a mind shaped by the values that our present-day culture considers as the only fulfilling ones and sees the cross solely as an emblem of pain and suffering. But the cross, as Paul himself discovers, is also the place of victory. On closer look, Paul realized that what looked like abandonment and defeat was paradoxically the most profound moment of God's loving and vulnerable faithfulness to humanity. Thus, to commit oneself to a cruciform existence is to participate in the victory of Christ. Participation

26 Commentators say that the Letter to the Philippians is the most personal of Paul's letters. This they attribute to the fact that he retained a special fondness for the members of the Philippian community. The community being buffeted by internal and external dangers was particularly disturbing to him.

27 Cf. Schneider, "*Stauros*," 578.

28 Some of the ideas that follow I found while browsing the internet in a short write-up by Bernardita Dianzon containing excerpts from her recent book *Glimpses of Paul and His Message*.

in that victory does not mean that pains and sufferings are totally done away with. Not at all. Rather, they are accepted as necessary ingredients of victory. The paradox of the cross is that weakness is turned into an immense source of power. The cross, when embraced by Christ, became God's means of subverting the world's values and thwarting its expectations.

Paul, the Pharisee and persecutor of the followers of 'the Way', thought that Jesus was a counterfeit Messiah, whose false claims brought him to the kind of humiliating and scandalous death that he deserved. But when he met the risen Christ on the road to Damascus, Paul realized how misguided had been his zeal to stamp out this small but highly motivated group. He understood that God had raised Jesus the Nazarene from the dead. For a Pharisee, who firmly believed in the resurrection of the dead, this was a sign that the eschatological age-to-come had dawned upon his generation. Paul immediately recognized the Christ-event as the awaited apocalyptic intervention of God in human history. He would subsequently realize that the cross which looked like a symbol of shame and defeat was, in fact, the place of unqualified victory.

It is a mistake to think that every kind of pain and suffering equals the cross. Actually, many of the sufferings that people endure are the result of deliberate wrong choices and human sinfulness. In Pauline vocabulary, this is referred to as the "wrath of God," (cf. Rom 1:18; 4:15; 9:22, etc.) which does not imply a capricious activity or vindictive emotion on the part of God. Rather, Paul uses this standard apocalyptic term to explain how God allows sin to work its course because of God's respect for human freedom. Human sinfulness thus brings about its own punishment, which is experienced as a form of pain and suffering. This is not a "cross," in the Christian sense, since, being a result of sin, it is not conformed to the cross of Christ. Where there is effort to remain faithful to one's commitment and fundamental option in life, where there is suffering endured for the sake of another, there one becomes a participant in the victory of the cross and reflects in one's life the paradox of "power in weakness".

4.2. Implications of Cruciform Existence for the Community

The most striking aspect of the message of crucifixion is that God's power is manifested in weakness, not in strength. This is in fact something that the biblical tradition has consistently showcased as a fundamental principle. Paul's vision remains constantly focused on the cross of Christ as the elevated place where God has revealed God's "wisdom", or God's "characteristic way of working". As he begins a carefully argued reply in 1 Cor 1:18, he shows that the unity of the Corinthian community, so easily fractured, is found in the fact that Christ has died for them. Paul was not crucified for them, Christ was. They were baptized not into Paul's or Apollos's death, but into Christ's.

Their dispute over who baptized whom would "empty the cross of its power" because it denied the reality of the unity which the cross achieved. The cross stands as the bedrock of the teaching which gave the church its original identity and unity (1 Cor 15:3). The contributions of individual leaders and pastors in Corinth and everywhere else, however substantial, is simply a drop in the ocean in comparison to the foundational saving work of Christ.

Beyond this, the cross acts as a model for the use of power, or more specifically, the cross as exemplified in the life of Paul the apostle. Paul appeals to the Corinthians to imitate him (1 Cor 4:16) in his role as servant/slave (1 Cor 3:5; 4:1). Leaning on the imagery of the crucifixion Paul portrays the apostolic life as one of shame, suffering and degradation. Paul's boast is that he "made himself a slave to all, that I might win the more" (1 Cor 9:19); that by choosing the life of a common artisan he became socially "weak, in order to win the weak" (1 Cor 9:22). Paul's own life has taken on a cruciform shape, sacrificing his own social power and status for the sake of others. The true content of Christian wisdom is not "knowledge" but "love": in other words, self-giving towards one's fellow-believers, and especially the poor. It is this pattern of life he recommends to all Christians, namely the way of servanthood, the way of the cross. A theology which begins at the cross is, for Paul, the radical antidote to any religion which is only a thinly veiled copy of a power-seeking superstructure.

The "word of the cross" assumes urgency as it knocks on the door of the Church of our times. The Church must seek to live ever more fully the *theologia crucis* in terms of personal piety, worship, pastoral care, administration of the sacraments and stewardship. Weakness in strength should be the focal point of the Church's identity. However, a celebration of the weakness is in complete opposition to the way influential sections within the Church have understood it to be.

Paul's idea of making the crucified Lord the defining symbol of Christian mission stands in direct contrast to the triumphalist stand which Christendom has adopted for a long time, the vestiges of which are still in evidence in many parts. There is still considerable resistance to the missionary Church's need to adopt the image of the "little flock" which Jesus had conferred on it (cf. Lk 12:32). A good part of the Church leadership still finds it more ego-boosting to presume that they are guiding the destinies of a Church seen as the replica of the kingdom of God. It is mainly this lethal desire in a large number of leaders "to be greeted obsequiously" (cf. Mt 23:7) as the functionaries of a towering organization and their reluctance to project the Church as a symbol and servant of the kingdom rather than as its replica which has led to the lamentable state of the Church's diminished image, which in turn has prompted believers to move away in droves from the institutional Church. When assessed along these lines, those who are loyal to the Church and concerned about its future will readily admit that Paul's theology of the cross and the conviction that the texts in his letters that speak so powerfully of the crucified Christ still have a cutting edge, and if anything, even sharper edge than 20 centuries ago!

8

"You are My Witnesses" Discipleship as Witness-Bearing in Luke-Acts

C. Sunil Ranjar, SJ

Introduction

One of the groups that stands out in the entire New Testament literature is the "apostles". These individuals belonged to the inner circle of the historical Jesus and they were the most prominent leaders of the early Church. The apostles were the earliest witnesses to the teaching and healing ministry of Jesus, and, after the Resurrection, they themselves continued the same ministry. Even though all the New Testament writers give prominence to the apostles, it is Luke who shows a further interest in this group. The importance of the term "apostle" (ἀπόστολος) for Luke is evident from the fact that among the evangelists, he is the only author who uses it more than others.[1] Among the eighty appearances of this word in the New Testament, six are in the Gospel of Luke and 28 are in Acts.

What is more interesting is that in the Gospel, Luke often redacts his source in order to insert the term "apostles". While the other evangelists tend to use the terms, "apostles" and "disciples", interchangeably, Luke is the only

1 For a comprehensive presentation of the "apostles" and "disciples", see P.S. Minear, "Jesus' Audiences, according to Luke", *NovT* 16 (1974) 81-100.

evangelist who seems to make a clear distinction between the two. This article aims to do a redaction critical study of the terms "apostles" and "disciples" in defining discipleship in Luke-Acts.

1. The Disciples (οἱ μαθηταί)

To understand the prominence Luke attests to "apostles" it is essential first to examine his use of the term "disciples". The "disciples" (οἱ μαθηταί) is noticeably a distinct group in Luke.[2] While in other synoptics, especially in Matthew, the disciples and apostles are used interchangeably,[3] in Luke they are two different groups. In Luke, the number of disciples is generally unlimited (Lk 6:17; 19:37), while in Matthew and Mark, most of the times that number is restricted to twelve. Only Luke mentions that Jesus chose the apostles from among the disciples (Lk 6:13).

Along with the apostles, the disciples form the audience for much of Jesus' teaching (Lk 6:20a; 8:9; 9:43; 10:23; 12:1, 22; 16:1; 17:1, 22). Luke makes a clear distinction between the disciples and others when it comes to Jesus' teaching (Lk 12:1, 22; 17:20, 22). Jesus speaks in parables to the people but explains their meaning to the disciples (Lk 8:4-14). He teaches them to pray (Lk 11:1-4). They are present at the miracle of the multiplication of loaves (Lk 9:11-17).They praise him when he enters Jerusalem (Lk19:37) and follow him to Gethsemane (Lk 22:39).

In the Acts of the Apostles, the post-Easter context gives a different meaning to the term "disciples". They are not the disciples of Jesus, as in the Gospel, but "believers" who respond to the Gospel preached by the apostles. Their number increases greatly (Acts 6:1,7; 14:21). Saul persecutes the disciples (Acts 9:1), and, after his conversion he associates with the same disciples (Acts 9:26). Further on in the narrative of Acts, Paul exhorts and strengthens the disciples (Acts 14:22; 18:23; 20:1). While there is a clear distinction between the apostles and disciples (Acts 6:2), the former dominate in the first half of the narrative, and, in the second half, especially in Paul's ministry, the latter take the center stage.

An important feature in Luke's presentation of disciples is that he includes women in the group (Lk 8:2-3; see also Lk 24:6,22). In the Acts of the Apostles there are a few prominent women who followed the teachings of the apostles and, thus, became disciples: Tabitha/Dorcas (Acts 9:36,40), Rhoda (Acts 12:13), Lydia (Acts 16:14,40), Priscilla (Acts 18:2,18,26).

For Luke, therefore, everyone who believes and follows Jesus is a disciple. The only requirement to be a disciple is total renunciation (Lk 14:26-

2 The term μαθητής occurs only in the Gospels and Acts. It has a total of 261 occurrences of which 72 are in Matthew, 46 in Mark, 78 in John, 37 in Luke and 28 in Acts.

3 See Mt 10:1; 11:1; 20:17; 26:20.

33; cf. Lk 5:11,28). Unlike in Mark and Matthew, where the term μαθηταί is almost always limited to the Twelve who had a specific role to play, in Luke, the group is very large. For him, the "apostles" is an exclusive group and "disciples" is more inclusive.

2. The Apostles (οἱ ἀπόστολοι)

As already mentioned above, no other evangelist gives so much prominence to the apostles as does Luke. In the episode of the choosing the twelve (Luke 6:12-13), though Luke follows Mark's content (Mk 3:13-14), he makes some significant redactional changes. Mark reports, "And he (Jesus) appointed twelve, to be with him, and to be sent out to preach and have authority to cast out demons" (Mk 3:14), and Matthew follows Mark almost verbatim (Mt 10:1). Nonetheless, Luke emphasizes their being chosen from the among the disciples, their being named as apostles and their identity by name (Lk 6:13-16).[4] Luke omits the detail of "being with him and being sent out to preach and have authority to cast out demons". The apostles will be sent on mission at a much later stage (Lk 9:1-6), after they have been with Jesus for quite a while, being present for his teachings (Lk 6:20-49; 7:24-35; 8:4-18) and after witnessing more healings (Lk 7:2-17; 8:26-56).

In the episode of the "return of the Twelve" (Lk 9:10a // Mk 6:30-31), Luke retains the term "apostles" from his Marcan source. They return from their mission and recount to Jesus "what they had done".[5] Further, in the Q-text[6] that deals with the "woes against the Pharisees", Luke mentions the "prophets and apostles" whom the Pharisees will kill and persecute (Lk 11:49), while the parallel text in Matthew (Mt 23:34) has "prophets, wise men and scribes". Noteworthy in Luke is the placing of the "apostles" (etymologically, those who are sent) alongside the "prophets" (who were sent by God).

In the teaching on faith (Lk 17:5-6), it is the apostles who ask Jesus to increase their faith; Matthew and Mark not only lack this request but they also place the teaching on faith in a different context (See Mt 17,19-21; Mk 9:28-29). In the narrative of the Last Supper, only Luke mentions that Jesus sat with the apostles (Lk 22:19), while Mark mentions "the twelve" (Mk 14,17) and Matthew "twelve disciples" (Mt 26,20). In the Resurrection narrative (Lk 24:10), the women who hear from the angels about the resurrection of Jesus report it first to the apostles.

---

4 Even though the parallel text in Mk 4:14 has "apostles", this has been regarded as an interpolation from Luke 6:13; see B.M. Metzger, *A Textual Commentary on the Greek New Testament* (Stuttgart ^{2}1994), 69.

5 Some manuscripts add ἀποστόλους, and others, μαθητὰς αὐτοῦ in Luke 9:1 after "twelve". This appears to be a later addition by the copyists to harmonize the text with that of Luke 9:10 which is an imitation of Mk 6:30; see Metzger, *Textual Commentary*, 122.

6 A Q-text is the text that is common to Matthew and Luke.

In Acts, the term "apostles" is exclusively used to designate the Twelve whom Jesus chose during his earthly ministry, with the exception of Judas, who is replaced by Matthias (Acts 1:26). It may be noted that Paul calls himself "apostle of Jesus Christ" in his letters to different communities (e.g., Rom 1:1; 1 Cor 1:1; 2 Cor 1:1; Gal 1:1). However, in the book of Acts, he along with Barnabas is called "apostle" only once (Acts 14,14).

3. The Distinction between the Disciples and the Apostles

For Luke, the apostles and disciples are two distinct groups (see Acts 6:2). It is only Luke who reports that Jesus chose apostles from among the disciples (Lk 6:13). The distinction between the "twelve" and the "disciples" is highlighted in Acts 6:2: "...the twelve summoned the multitude of the disciples (τὸ πλῆθος τῶν μαθητῶν)..." Furthermore, for Luke, the terms "the twelve" and "the apostles" are synonymous. He uses either "the twelve" or "the apostles" but never "the twelve apostles".[7] Note that in Acts 1:26, Luke mentions that Matthias was enrolled with the "eleven apostles". He qualifies the term "apostles" with the "eleven" since there was no twelfth apostle after the death of Judas. Once their number is complete with the addition of Matthias, he goes back to the familiar "twelve" or "apostles" (see Acts 6,2; 2:42,43; 5,12,18,29 etc.).

Luke also makes a clear distinction between the disciples and the others. When Jesus enters the city of Nain, "his disciples and a great crowd went with him" (Lk 7:11). Sometimes, some teaching intended for the disciples is imparted in the presence of the people. Hence, Lk 12:1 reads thus: "when myriads of the crowd had gathered, so that they trod upon one another, he began to say to his disciples first". Similarly in Lk 20:45: "and in the hearing of all the people he said to his disciples". When Jesus speaks to all, Luke makes it explicit (Lk 9:23; 11:29). The distinction between the disciples (also apostles) and the others is further brought out in the discourse of Jesus on discipleship in Lk 12:1–13:9, where the teaching is first addressed to the disciples, then to the crowds, and then again to the disciples. The disciples are addressed in 12:1, in the presence of the crowd. In 12:4, the disciples are addressed as friends. There is a change of audience in 12:13, because one from the crowd intervenes. The disciples are addressed again in 12:22 and they remain as the audience till 12:40. The ambiguity in the identification of the audience becomes explicit in 12:41, where Peter mentions that he is unsure to whom Jesus has directed the previous parable (Lk 12:35-40). The crowd appears again as the addressees in 12:54 and 13:1.

7 Luke 6:13; 8:1; 9:1,12; 18:12; 22:3; 22:47. There are textual variations in Luke 9:1 and Luke 22:14; cf. Mt 10:1; 11:1; 20:7; 26:20 (twelve disciples); 10:2 (twelve apostles); 10:5; 26:47 (twelve); Mk 3:14,16; 4:10; 6:7; 9:35; 10:32; 11:11; 14:10; 14:17,20:43 (twelve).

4. The "Favouritism" of Luke

Another distinct feature of Luke in presenting the apostles and disciples is that both groups are always presented favorably. Luke makes important redactional changes to the Marcan text in order to avoid portraying the apostles in a negative light. In the first passion prediction of Jesus (Mk 8:31-33 // Mt 16:21-23 // Lk 9:22), Mark reports Peter's rebuke soon after Jesus predicts his passion and the consequent reproach of Peter by Jesus. While Matthew retains the Marcan text as it is, Luke retains only the passion prediction but omits both the rebuke by Peter and the resultant reprimand of Peter by Jesus.

Also significant is the Lucan redaction in the portrayal of the restricted group of the Twelve whom Mark and Matthew often call disciples. In Mark, the disciples (i.e., the Twelve) are very often portrayed as incapable of understanding (Mk 6:52; 9:32), and Jesus frequently rebukes them (Mk 4:13; 7:18; 8:17:21; cf. Mt 15:16). Luke carefully avoids such embarrassing depictions. In the second Passion prediction (Mk 9:30-32//Lk 9:44-45), Luke follows Mark where he retains "but they did not understand this saying" (Lk 9:45//Mk 9:32), but immediately adds "for it was concealed from them that they should not perceive it". Through this redactional insertion, Luke shows that the disciples' inability to understand the necessity of Jesus' Passion is part of the larger plan of God (see also Lk 18:34). Jesus in Mark rebukes the disciples when they seek clarification about the parable of the sower: "Do you not understand this parable? How then will you understand all the parables?" (Mk 4:13). Only after this rebuke does Jesus explain them the parable. Luke omits this reproach (see Lk 8:9-10). At Gethsemane, while all the Synoptics mention the sleeping of Peter, James and John, only Luke adds "they were sleeping *because of* sorrow" (Mt 26:40 // Mk 14:37 // Lk 22:45).

Similarly, Luke also omits such a negative depiction of the disciples (i.e., the Twelve), as is found in Matthew, who often derides them for their lack of faith. In the episode of the stilling of the storm (Mt 8:23-27 // Mk 4:35-41 // Lk 8:22-25), when the disciples are afraid that they will sink, Jesus, in Matthew first rebukes them for their lack of faith and calls them "men of little faith" (ὀλιγόπιστοι)[8] and only then does he still the storm. In Luke (and also Mark), on the other hand, Jesus calms the storm first. The rebuke is also softened with a question, "where is your faith?" In the episode of Jesus walking on the water (Mt 14:22-33 // Mk 6:45-52), Matthew adds Peter's walking on the water and Jesus' reproach of Peter when he begins to doubt. Luke omits this entire episode. Again in the pericope of "the leaven of the Pharisees" (Mt 16:5-12 // Mk 8:14-21 // Lk 12:1), Matthew follows Mark rather faithfully, but

---

8 The adjective "men of little faith" (ὀλιγόπιστοι) is Matthew's preferred term; it appears three times in his Matthew and once in Luke. While Luke generally avoids using this term, he retains it once (cf. Mt 6:30 // Luke 12:28).

adds the phrase "men of little faith" when the disciples think that he refers to bread which they had forgotten to carry. Luke has a softened statement, "beware of the leaven of the Pharisees, which is hypocrisy" (Lk 12:1), which he places immediately after the denunciation of the Pharisees (Lk 11:37-54). Also noteworthy is Luke's omission of the episode of the request of the sons of Zebedee (cf. Mt 20:20-23 // Mk 10:35-40).[9]

5. Models of Perseverance

Luke also presents the apostles as models of perseverance in the ministry of Jesus. At the Last supper (Lk 22:24-30), Jesus commends his apostles as those who persisted with him (οἱ διαμεμενηκότες μετ' ἐμοῦ) in his trials and assigns them the Kingdom (Lk 22:29), recalling the promise made in the beatitudes (Lk 6:20). The use of the perfect participle of the verb διαμένω is significant here as it implies that the apostles have been faithful during the entire earthly ministry of Jesus and that this faithful included a willing response to his ethical demands.[10]

The faithfulness of the apostles is further demonstrated in the scene of the arrest of Jesus. Mark reports, "and they all forsook him and fled" (Mk 14:50 // Mt 26:56). However, Luke omits the flight of the disciples. It is also significant that during the Last Supper, Luke omits Jesus' foretelling of the apostles' running away during his arrest (cf. Mt 26:31 // Mk 14:27). Even though Luke mentions Jesus' prediction of Peter's denial, the entire episode is softened with the promise of prayer: "Simon, Simon, behold, Satan has demanded to have you, that he might sift you like wheat, but I have prayed for you that your faith may not fail. And when you have turned again, strengthen your brothers" (Lk 22:31-32). Noteworthy also is the scene of the denial where Jesus casts a merciful look at Peter (Lk 22:61).

The constancy of the apostles is further rewarded by the appearance of the Risen Lord (Lk 24:36-53). This scene, which is unique to Luke among the Synoptics (cf. Jn 20:19-23), ends with Jesus commissioning them to preach repentance (μετάνοια; cf. Lk 3:3,8; 15,7) and the forgiveness of sins (ἄφεσις ἁμαρτιῶν; cf. Lk 3:3; 4,18; Acts 2:38) to all nations (Lk 24:47). This recalls the Messianic program of Jesus at Nazareth (Lk 4:18-19), which the apostles continue to preach in the early Church (Acts 2:38; 5:31; 10:43; 26:18).

6. Apostles as Witnesses

The above survey reveals that Luke deviates from the other two synoptic evangelists when it comes to the presentation of the Apostles. While Luke is

9 In Matthew it is the mother of the sons of Zebedee who makes the request.

10 Cf. D. L. Bock, *Luke*. II. 9:51–24:53 (BECNT; Grand Rapids 1996) 1739; E.E. Ellis, *The Gospel of Luke* (London 1974) 256.

rather faithful in following his source, his redactional modifications in favor of the apostles and disciples raises questions. Why does Luke differ from the other evangelists? What were the guiding principles?

The answers to these questions can be found only when one considers the entire Lucan work. Luke definitely had in the mind the second volume, i.e., the Acts of the Apostles, when he redacted the Gospel narrative. In the second volume, it is the apostles who are the protagonists and they continue the ministry that Jesus inaugurated. Luke does not want to exaggerate the limitations of the apostles, who were the leaders of the early Church. It is for this reason that Luke modifies and redacts his source and presents the apostles in a very positive light.

There is abundant textual evidence to demonstrate this point. In the choosing of the substitute for Judas (Acts 1:15-23), Peter spells out the criteria to be an apostle of Jesus: "So one of the men who have accompanied us during all the time that the Lord Jesus went in and out among us, *beginning from the baptism of John until the day when he was taken up from us* - one of these men must become with us a witness to his resurrection (Acts 1:21-22)." An apostle, therefore, has to be an eyewitness from the beginning of Jesus' ministry.

In fact it is only Luke who presents elaborately the ascension scene both in the Gospel as well as in the Acts of the Apostles. It is noteworthy that among the Gospels, it is only in Luke that Jesus emphasizes the role of the apostles as witnesses: "You are witnesses (μάρτυρες) of these things" (Lk 24:48). The role of the apostles as witnesses is further confirmed in Acts 1:8: "you shall receive power when the Holy Spirit has come upon you; and you shall be my witnesses in Jerusalem and in all Judea and Samaria and to the end of the earth." As Fitzmyer rightly notes, "Luke introduces here for the first time the important role that Christ's disciples are to play in the third phase of salvation-history, in the Period of the Church."[11] While the great commission in Matthew consists of preaching, teaching and making disciples by baptism (Mt 28:19-20; cf. Mk 16:15-16), in Luke, it is bearing witness.[12]

The witnessing role of the apostles is narratively fulfilled in the second volume of Luke's work. Luke reports that the apostles, with great power, were continuously giving witness to the Resurrection of the Lord (Acts 4:33). Peter, filled with the Holy Spirit on the day of Pentecost, declares himself and other apostles as the witnesses of the Resurrection of Jesus (Acts 2:32). The initial discourses of Peter in Acts reveal the kerygma of the early Church, i.e., Passion, Death and Resurrection of Jesus to which the entire body of the Apostles is

11 J.A. Fitzmyer, *The Gospel According to Luke X-XXIV*. Introduction, translation, and notes (AB 28A; New Haven) 1584.

12 In Acts, Luke uses the noun "witness" (μάρτυς) and the related terms 14 times to describe the witness-bearing of the Apostles and the early Church (Acts 1:8,22; 2:32,40; 3:15; 4:33; 13:31; 14:3,17; 22:5,15,20; 26:16,22,26.

a witness: at the Temple after healing the lame man (Acts 3:12-15); before the council of the high priest (Acts 5:30-32); at the house of Cornelius (Acts 10:34-43). Paul also speaks about the witness-bearing role of the apostles in his discourse to the Jews at the synagogue of Pisidian Antioch (Acts 13:31). Further, Paul is not only commended for bearing witness in Jerusalem but is called to bear witness to the Risen Lord in Rome (Act 23:11; cf. 26:16).

Hence, in the Gospel of Luke, the apostles are "men chosen from the larger number of disciples to whom Jesus gives special authority to preach and to heal, and whom he sends out to minister to the crowds and to the people (cf. Lk 9:1-6)."[13] In Acts, they are directed to witness because they have experienced and are in position to testify not only about the earthly Jesus but also the Risen Christ.[14] In order to underscore this important role of the apostles, Luke redacts their portrait in the Gospel and minimizes their limitations. By always portraying the apostles (and disciples) in a positive light, Luke presents them as the ideal leaders of the early Christian community and as witness-bearers of the Christ event.

13 Minear, "Jesus' Audiences," 89.

14 Cf. J. Nolland, *Luke 18,35-24:53* (WBC 35C, Dallas 1993).

9

Towards a Missionary Theory and Praxis for Our Times

Isaac Padinjarekuttu

Introduction

There had been several initiatives of the Papacy in this decade, aimed at revitalizing missionary activity in the Church. It began with the constitution of the Pontifical Council for Promoting the New Evangelization in 2010, followed by the Synod of Bishops on the "New Evangelization for the Transmission of the Christian Faith" in 2012, Synod of Bishops for the Pan-Amazon Region in 2019, the designation of the month of October 2019 as Missionary Month, and the most recent instruction of the Congregation of the Clergy, "The Pastoral Conversion of the Parish Community in the Service of the Evangelizing Mission of the Church,"[1] to mention some of them. The reason is not far to seek. According to Pope Francis, the "missionary outreach is paradigmatic for all the Church's activity"[2] and so, all efforts must be made to focus the attention of all the baptized on this fundamental task. What has been the outcome of all these initiatives? It is difficult to answer this question

1 Instruction of 20.07.2020 calling for a "pastoral conversion that is essentially missionary" (No. 2).

2 *Evangelii Gaudium*, 15.

since there are no official statistics available. But one thing that can be said with certainty is that the Church has been on the defensive on many fronts in this decade, under threat from a violent secular and post-secular society, Islamic terrorism, right- and left-wing ideologies, the immensely destructive potential of science and technology with no regulation or institution that can say what to do and what not to do and the many self-goals scored by the Church herself. And to conclude the decade, there is the Corona pandemic which has shaken the foundations of the world order as we know it today. And yet, if mission, understood as the continuation of Christ's own mission of establishing God's Kingdom is paradigmatic for the Church, we have to speak about it, find ways and means to creatively engage in it and place it where it belongs, namely, at the centre of Christian existence.

1. A Short Historical Overview

Mission *ad gentes*, mission to the nations, a phrase that has become popular after the Second Vatican Council, belonged to one of the core activities of the Church from the beginning, as a sign of faithfulness to Christ's command to go out to the nations (Mathew 28:19-20). In fact, the earliest Christians believed that the apostles themselves had preached the Gospel in the whole world, as the Thomas Tradition of India attests. It took different shapes and forms in the first thousand years. During this period, the Christianization of Europe took place with the collaboration of emperors, Popes, bishops, monks, nuns and committed Christians, and outside Europe, the Nestorian missionaries reached as far as China and India, although there were long periods when there was little or no concerted and organized missionary activity. Even in the second millennium, in the first four hundred years we see very little organized missionary activity. The situation changes only in the wake of the navigational explorations of the Iberian powers, Spain and Portugal, towards the end of the fourteenth century. In fact, the efforts at conversion of non-Christians to Christianity come to be called "mission" only in the fifteenth century. It was the Portuguese who used the word "missions" to refer to groups sent out by the king for military, trade and religious activities.[3] Up to that time *missio* (sending) had referred to the "sending" of the Son and the Holy Spirit by the Father into the world. So it is roughly from the second half of the second millennium that the Church began to make more coordinated and concerted efforts at "going out to the nations" "*ad gentes*" as we have come know it today. For the Protestants, the story begins much later, at the end of the eighteenth century, and for the Orthodox

3 Paul Kollman, "At the Origins of Mission and Missiology: A Study of Religious Language," *Journal of the American Academy of Religion* 79 (2011) 425-58.

Churches it has become important only in the twentieth century. We shall first trace the history of these last five hundred years in a very brief way.[4]

What was it about the past five hundred years that suddenly prompted the rise of mission *ad gentes*? It is "globalization." Globalization became a catchword in the last quarter of the twentieth century, referring to the creation of an inter-connected world through the modern communications technology and liberal capitalism. But globalization, understood broadly as any qualitative leap in the possibility of commercial trade or other forms of exchange that opens up a social group to the wider world[5] occurred much earlier. The first real wave of globalization began in the fifteenth century, enabled through improved means of long-distance sea travel. This facility existed even in the Arabian Peninsula and China at that time, but it was only Europe that ventured to go out, which had far reaching consequences for Christianity and the history of the world.

This first wave of globalization marked by the Portuguese and Spanish explorations of the rest of the world, and followed by other European powers, like England, Holland, Denmark, France and others peaked from the late fifteenth into the late seventeenth century. It is during this period that the great mission outward from Europe took place, with heroic figures such as Francis Xavier. Mission accompanied the traders and the agents of mission were primarily the Mendicant Orders and the Jesuits. The founding of the *Propaganda Fide* in 1622 by Pope Gregory XV and the *Missions Etrangeres de Paris* in 1660 were other major steps that boosted this activity. Much has been written about the collaboration or even collusion between Christian mission and colonialism. Whatever may be the reality, it is undeniable that this first wave of globalization made both the various colonial empires and the world mission of Christianity possible.

The second wave of colonisation and globalization began at the turn of the nineteenth century and continued up to the outbreak of the First World War, according to Charles Taylor, up to 1960, which he calls the "age of mobilization".[6] The 19th century saw dramatic changes that altered the face of Europe. There were political and social upheavals of great consequences, like the collapse of the great imperial powers Germany, Austria and Russia, the nationalist fervour that accompanied the rise of liberal democracies and the rise of political parties, emergence of trade unions, anarchist movements, etc. The Catholic Church experienced these as a threat to its long standing

4 See for this historical survey, Robert J. Schreiter, "The Future of Mission *ad Gentes* in a Global Context", in James H. Kroeger, *The Gift of Mission*, 36-54.

5 Robert Schreiter, in James Kroeger, ed. *The Gift of Mission: Yesterday, Today, Tomorrow*, New York: Orbis Books, 2013, 39.

6 *Secular Age*, Cambridge, Mass.: Harvard University Press, 2007.

position in European societies. If the Reformation had challenged the Church on ecclesiastical grounds, the French Revolution and political liberalism challenged the Church's political standing. In the currents of the age, the Church also mobilized itself on many fronts, responding to the political, economic and social changes. Hosts of new religious orders of men and women were founded to address social issues on local and immediate levels as well as to go out and serve humanity's needs. There were more advances in technologies of travel and communication, compressing space and time dramatically. A large number of young missionaries were mobilized by religious orders, founded exclusively for overseas mission. These missionaries and their mission were stamped with a distinctive nationalist character.

This second wave of globalization has left some indelible marks on mission. The decolonization movement led to the end of colonialism. The mission it more or less enabled was branded as "colonial mission", and an attendant symptom of colonialism, although it did have some spectacular successes, for example, in Africa. In 1900, there were ten million Christians in Africa. Today there are 350 million. The attempt to develop a new theology of mission culminated in the document on mission of Vatican II, *Ad Gentes*. The idea of mission as the continuation of the mission of the Trinitarian God, the essentially missionary character of the Church, the appreciation of the role of the laity in the mission of the Church etc. are positive developments in the light of *Ad Gentes*. But Christianity's success in real numbers is still puzzling. In 1900, 34 percent of world population was Christian, but in 2000, after a century of frenetic missionary activity, it was only 33 percent. There are more Muslims than Catholics in the world today. What does it say about the place of Christianity amid the other great religious traditions of the world and the claim of Christians that Christ is the definitive saviour of all humankind? If we take individual countries like India, we can see this problem even more clearly. When 97% of Indians are finding their salvation without any direct reference to Christ and to Christian mission, that too, after centuries of missionary work, we have to accept the fact of the existence of genuine spiritual worlds other than our own, and find ways to encounter them theologically, spiritually, culturally and practically. This touches upon the very identity and destiny of Christianity in the world today.

From the last quarter of the twentieth century, there began another wave of globalization in which we still find ourselves and whose end is being predicted by some as the Corona pandemic rages on. In fact, the fast spread of the virus has been blamed on globalization. Like the previous waves of globalization, the current one, too, grew out of advances in technologies for travel and communication and the uncontrolled power of the market. This wave of globalization has compressed time and space like never before. Distances are now psychological and social rather than physical. The world is present to us at the click of a button. Peoples are floating free of their original locations through migration. Multiculturalism is ubiquitous and with that constant interaction with multiple cultures. Where are the nations to whom the missionary is to go? They are all over. And where are the missionaries? The second wave of globalization fascinated men and women for mission, but no such fascination for Christ and the Church exists among young people today. This is an issue that touches upon the very survival of Christianity. What could be some of the essential features of Christian mission in our times, a mission that is led by the Spirit of Christ in the service of the Kingdom of God? I shall mention five of them.

2. Mission of the Future

2.1. Witness – Proclamation – Dialogue

Mission of the future will depend on the quality of witness, proclamation and dialogue, in that order. There is an uneasy relationship between these three activities, but all three will be essential components of mission in the future. One of the breakthrough moments of Vatican II was the acknowledgement of the Church's fundamental missionary nature and its willingness to engage the world. Among other things, the Council showed a much more positive appreciation of other religions, which eventually led to the inclusion of interreligious dialogue as a necessary component of mission. This has created the incorrect impression that the Council has diluted the essential dimension of mission to proclaim the Gospel and invite people to become members of the Church. In fact, what the Council has done is widening the horizon of mission by affirming that God's omnipotent grace and presence extended beyond the Church and that the Church needs to recognize and engage these signs of the times. The understanding of mission has shifted from bringing God to the pagans and the world to meeting God already present in human experience, culture, Christian Churches and denominations and all religions. Thus mission is redefined as "proclaiming, serving, and witnessing to God's reign of love, salvation and justice."[7]

So, the mission of the future must comprise witness, proclamation and dialogue – interreligious and secular. "The first means of evangelization is the witness of an authentically Christian life"[8] and direct proclamation of the gospel "is the foundation, summit and centre of evangelization.[9] Witness can be of an individual, a local Christian community, or an institution, or it can be the common witness of Christians of various traditions working together.

7 Roger P. Schroeder, *What is the Mission of the Church? A Guide for Catholics* (Maryknoll: N.Y., Orbis Books, 2008) 3.

8 *Evangelii Nuntiandi*, 41.

9 *Dialogue and Proclamation*, 1991, 10.

But as Pope John Paul II has clearly said, "the Church proposes, she imposes nothing.[10] Proclamation must avoid at all costs undue pressure and unworthy proselytism. The message must be proclaimed, but must be proclaimed in dialogue, in connection with witness, as an invitation rather than an imposition, and in answer to men and women's real questions in their particular contexts. So "proclamation presupposes and requires a dialogue method in order to respond to the requirements of those to be evangelized and to enable them to interiorize the message received."[11] Proclamation needs to provide an answer for the spiritual and human yearnings that people have in today's multiple contexts. At the same time, it should reflect the Gospel as authentically as possible. This is the task of a suitable missiology today.

For this, Stephen Bevans proposes "prophetic dialogue"[12] in that the Christian must witness to and speak the truth of the gospel with honesty, conviction, and faith. Without the cultivation of the spirit of prophecy, it lacks any direction or purpose. Dialogue is prophetic in two senses. It is a denunciation of or speaking against that which is contrary to God's reign, and an annunciation of or speaking forth the message of God's reign, particularly in and through Jesus Christ.[13] Mission as prophetic dialogue is a very apt image for our situation today. It is more than being nice, or learning from others, or even developing relationships and making friends – as essential these may be. Mission is ultimately about sharing the good news of God's reign with the people of this world. This is an act of prophecy, may be through wordless gestures and witness, and may be through powerful spoken and written messages. The quality of life in a Christian community, the quality of its liturgical celebrations, commitment to education, the openness to fellow Christians and other religions, all these can bear prophetic witness to how the Gospel message can give life to women and men in every situation. They are signs of the already present reign of God and give testimony to the merciful, life-giving, and true God revealed by Jesus Christ. Such communities speak forth a message of encouragement and hope and are powerfully counter-cultural in an unjust, individualistic and life-denying society. They communicate the Gospel message in a clear and focused manner, making it relevant and powerful, in ways that engage people's lives and the cultures in which they live. Dialogue

---

10 *Redemptoris Missio*, Encyclical Letter on the Permanent Validity of the Catholic Church's Missionary Mandate, 1990, 44.

11 Marcello Zago, "The New Millennium and the Emerging Religious Encounters," *Missiology* 28 (January 2000) 17.

12 See Stephen Bevans and Roger P. Schroder, *Constants in Context: A Theology of Mission for Today* (Maryknoll, NY: Orbis 2004) 348-95; *Prophetic Dialogue: Reflections of Christian Mission Today* (Maryknoll, NY: Orbis, 2011); Craig Ott, ed., *The Mission of the Church. Five Views in Dialogue*, Grand Rapids, Michigan: Baker Academic, 2016, 3-20.

13 Bevans and Schroeder, *Prophetic Dialogue*, 40-45.

and prophecy are interwoven in the Church's missionary work. Each context determines where the emphasis will be placed as the Church engages in its missionary work.

This dialogue is not only with other religions, but also with those who have no faith or whose faith is limited by a strictly secular outlook. As in the case of interreligious dialogue, which does not mean falling into a "facile syncretism" that blurs all differences and does not allow for the interplay of both dialogue and proclamation,[14] in secular dialogue, too, while we can find many points of agreement and even allow ourselves to be critiqued and inspired by the unbelievers' or agnostics' honesty and commitment to justice, peacemaking and ecology, as Christians we cannot dodge the responsibility of giving cogent reasons for our own belief or witnessing confidently to it.

Does dialogue water down proclamation? Is dialogue a disguise for proclamation? Can they be complementary? If we take one of the authoritative statements of the Church on the topic seriously,[15] there is no need to fear that dialogue harms mission. According to it, proclamation should be confident and faithful on the one hand, and humble and dialogical on the other.[16] "Interreligious dialogue and proclamation, though not on the same level, are both authentic elements of the Church's evangelizing mission...They are intimately related, but not interchangeable; true interreligious dialogue on the part of the Christian supposes the desire to make Jesus Christ better known, recognized and loved; proclaiming Jesus Christ is to be carried out in the gospel spirit of dialogue."[17] Papal pronouncements, like *Redemptoris Missio* and *Evangelii Gaudium*, explicitly support this and say that dialogue is the norm, necessary manner and form of Christian mission, as service or direct proclamation. Dialogue in this sense is more than a practice but a basic attitude, indeed a kind of spirituality that underlies every aspect of mission. The understanding of the Church is that both are complementary. Interreligious dialogue is a necessity, a duty and a benefit but it does not exonerate the Christian community from the proclamation of Christ. There is a distinction in purpose. Dialogue is a search for mutual knowledge and enrichment while proclamation incorporates the idea of a challenge to accept the message. There is also the contextual nature of mission in that some contexts call for proclamation while others call for dialogue and human promotion. So the Church has the right and the duty to undertake both as the situation warrants and permits. In fact, dialogic method

---

14 *Evangelii Gaudium*, 250-1.

15 *Dialogue and Proclamation:* Reflection And Orientations On Interreligious Dialogue And The Proclamation Of The Gospel Of Jesus Christ, by Pontifical Council for Interreligious Dialogue, 1991.

16 Ibid., No. 70

17 Ibid., No. 77.

should be characteristic of all the activities of the Christian community and its leaders. But at the same time there needs to be a constant deepening and strengthening of one's own Christian identity and faith. Theologically we need to hold two basic principles in a balance, that Christ is the face of God and the means of salvation for all and that God is drawing all peoples back to him in ways we do not understand. A focus on the first principle without the second leads to fundamentalism, while an exclusive focus on the second without the first leads to the danger of relativism.

2.2. Mission as Witness in Unity

It is a fact that Christians are divided into countless groups and often work against each other in many parts of the world. Is such a situation viable? The Second Vatican Council had made the establishment of Christian unity one of its priorities and theologians from all Christian Churches have been working to study the nature of differences and find agreements among different Churches. It is right that they continue to do it and see what unites and what divides them. But whether a visible unity will be established in the near future is doubtful. In fact, the emerging secular and post-secular world makes us doubt the viability of the whole project of the ecumenical movement understood in this way. The ecumenical problem may not play any significant role at all in the future. The establishment of ecumenical unity is more a political problem where power and influence play a greater role than the working of the Holy Spirit.[18] But given the existence of various Christian groups, a missionary cooperation is essential. Since the 1980s, there is some convergence around basic issues of mission theology among Catholics, mainline Protestants and Evangelicals.[19] This momentum culminated in the centennial of the "1910 Edinburgh World Missionary Conference", held from June 2 to 6, 2010, at Edinburgh. Although the original Edinburgh 1910 Conference had involved only Protestants, the hundredth anniversary of the meeting inspired mission leaders around the world to reflect upon the meaning of mission for the twenty-first century. It demonstrated the tremendous vitality of the multicultural and multi-ecclesial Christianity in the early twenty first century. There was a longing to witness to Christ in all Churches. As a follow up, on 28 June, 2011, the Pontifical Council for Interreligious Dialogue, the World Council of Churches and the World Evangelical Alliance issued their first common agreement called "Christian Witness in a Multi-Religious World: Recommendations for Conduct." Despite ongoing theological differences, it demonstrated a new willingness to accept

18 Gisbert Geshake, *Kirche Wohin? Ein real-utopischer Blick in die Zukunft*, Freiburg, Basel Wien: Herder, 2020, 13.

19 *You are the Light of the World. Statements on Mission by the World Council of Churches 1980-2005* (Geneva: WCC Publications, 2005); *Redemptoris Missio*, Encyclical Letter on the Permanent Validity of the Catholic Church's Missionary Mandate, 1990.

the validity of each other's faith and give witness to the faith with respect and love for all.

Another initiative was the founding of the Global Christian Forum in 2002, which includes the full range of Christian denominations, communities and traditions worldwide, Catholic Orthodox, Protestant, Pentecostal, Evangelical, and indigenous Churches. The premise of the GCF process is to build a respectful Christian community through listening to each other's experiences of Jesus Christ. The process behind this forum is important because the spirit of mission *ad gentes* is thriving in some new Churches which send out thousands of missionaries worldwide and there is a competitive anarchy that often takes place because of it. Therefore, relationships are paramount and service more than doctrine as the touchstone for Christian cooperation. A shared commitment to witness provides a common ground for bridging differences. Vatican II opened up the possibility of an ecumenical theology and hence an ecumenical missiology. The approaches of different Christian Churches to mission can complement substantially.[20] Here again, it is to be noted that while ecumenical dialogue involves Christians working together, praying together, and sharing their own faith perspectives and spiritualities, we cannot reduce our particular perspective (Catholic, Protestant, Evangelical) to an easy and naive agreement. An authentic dialogue of any sort involves courage and the commitment to prophecy. But the wat forward for Christian mission has to be one of collaboration among all the Christians.

2.3. Mission as Reconciliation and Peacemaking

Missiologists have recognized in the last decade that reconciliation and peacemaking are constitutive parts of the Church's mission in the world today which is marked by unimaginable violence.[21] They were essential components of Jesus' mission too. These words come easily to our mouth but we struggle to follow his mandate to do something tangible to create them. The development of a deep reflection on mission as peacemaking and reconciliation is a great challenge to missiology today. Proclamation of the Good News in this broken and violated world, in other words, to speak of peace and reconciliation, is, on the one hand, naive, but on the other, necessary, and enormously complex. To make the nonviolent Jesus present and visible in a world that is convulsed in violence is a demanding and multidimensional vocation that requires tremendous creativity and persistence. Often it will be dismissed as naive, not

20 For comparison of these views, see Craig Ott, ed., *The Mission of the Church. Five Views in Dialogue*, Grand Rapids, Michigan: Baker Academic, 2016.

21 Marie Dennis, "Mission as Peacemaking", in James H. Kroeger, ed., *The Gift of Mission: Yesterday, Today, Tomorrow*, Maryknoll, New York: Orbis, 2013, 130-138; See Scott Appleby, Jerry Powers and Robert Schreiter, eds., *Peacebuilding: Catholic Theology, Ethics and Praxis*, New York, Orbis, 2010.

up to the task, not politically useful or pertinent. Far too often, the Gospel of peace and reconciliation will be considered dangerous, and those who pursue it will pay a price. But Jesus mission was to bring peace and harmony with God and among humans and Jesus continues this Spirit-filled mission through his disciples.

Mission as peacemaking and reconciliation involves proclamation of the Good News, witnessing to it, and readiness to dialogue and practise genuine inculturation. But the final goal is transformation of the world by engaging the roots of war and the drivers of violent conflict, such as relentless pursuit of natural resources, economic injustice, craving for power and dominance, unbridled greed for money, creating geopolitical or territorial advantage, environmental destruction and climate change, religious, cultural and ideological intolerance, and so on. Transformation of this reality needs the full engagement of the institutional, theological, and spiritual resources of our tradition. The amazing fact is that the Church has rich resources for engaging the mission of peacemaking, peace building and reconciliation – Scripture, our rituals and our sacramental life. Lasting peace in the future is possible only when there is social justice and ecological integrity. It will require that we engage the full spectrum of peace work and recognize the interrelatedness of peace with social and economic justice and respect the integrity of creation. The death of Jesus on the cross was "the ultimate witness for the peacemaking mission of the Church as he took on the horrific violence of his own time and overcame it with the fullness of life and resurrection. To imitate Christ now, to overcome, root out, and heal from the multifaceted and multilayered violence of this world is one of the most urgent challenges for the mission of the Church in the twenty-first century."[22]

2.4. Mission in the Care of Creation

Creation is the context in which mission takes place. Ever since the publication of Pope Francis' famous encyclical, *Laudato Si,* it must be clear to us that humanity has brought to earth immense ecological devastation, causing the breakdown of life support systems, hardship for many peoples, and heartbreaking injustice. It is well established now that we are part of a long evolutionary journey and this fundamental knowledge should influence how we know and understand God, ourselves and also our mission. The long unfolding of the universe from the distant past will go on into the future and creation will continue to bring forth life and beauty in increasingly intricate forms. Therefore, the entire creation must serve as a source of ethical and moral guidance and sustainability of the earth is linked to a life in harmony with nature. More and more people are fighting for the rights of the earth. Humanity should assume

22 Marie Dennis, "Mission as Peacemaking", 138.

personal responsibility for the well being of the planet because at the centre of the universe is the principle of relationality. Not only do all things affect each other but everything is the other. We are part of the natural world, and at this point in our evolutionary journey it is becoming increasingly clear that we are responsible for how our planet will evolve in the future. Therefore, our mission is to the entire earth community. Increasingly, missiologists are recognizing the importance of a strong ecological commitment to the establishment of both justice and regional and world peace. Justice, peace and integrity of creation are intimately linked to one another for without justice there can be no lasting peace, and without peace there can be no justice. All questions of justice are ultimately questions of who decides how the resources of the earth are to be used, and who benefits. But while it is necessary to take a prophetic stance, it is important to recognize that constant dialogue also needs to be practised in these areas. People's real needs must be discerned and listened to so that justice can be authentically established. It becomes more and more apparent that we should assume personal responsibility for the health and well being of the planet.[23] How far is this part of the missiological education and practices of the Church today?

2.5. Mission to the Globalized Post-Corona World

The terrain for preaching the Gospel has been radically transformed by the newest wave of contemporary globalization which consists of the twin phenomena of global economic integration and the emergence of the digitalized knowledge economy. The whole world is increasingly functioning as a single global village, making nations and peoples ever more interdependent and equally vulnerable as the Corona pandemic has just shown. With the virus, the unavoidable process of globalization has apparently reached its peak and now we are shown the global vulnerability of the globalized world. Global economic integration and the emerging knowledge economy mutually reinforce each other to produce epochal shifts in the way we live, work, consume and relate to each other. The changes we are witnessing are as dramatic and transformative as the Industrial Revolution was for the modern era. These shifts present both hurdles and opportunities to mission and evangelization.[24]

The globalized knowledge economy has created even greater obligations for mission and evangelization for at least two reasons. First, mission has a new role, that of correcting some of the harmful values spawned by the market which drives contemporary globalization. The globalized market has

---

23 See, Anne Braudis, "Mission in the Care of creation, in James H. Kroeger, *The Gift of Mission*, 139-143.

24 See, Albino Barrera, OP, "Mission in a Globalized Economy", in James H. Kroeger, *The Gift of Mission*, 157-161.

led to cultural globalization, the globalization of crime, the globalization of politics, and the globalization of mutual vulnerability. The power of the market goes beyond merely economic matters. It has emerged as a powerful social institution. It now shapes the public's ethos, values and habits. No doubt, the market can nurture good habits such as an excellent work ethic, collaborative work and private initiative, but brings with it also extreme individualism, impersonalism, consumerism, materialism, and an egoistic utilitarianism. We find evidence of this in the erosion of traditional values in many societies, once they attain material prosperity. The market has become a competitor for people's hearts and minds. It even appears that secularism is not the most formidable rival to religion but the unfettered marketplace and some of the misplaced values that it creates. Thus mission and evangelization must address some of the aforesaid ill effects of a market-shaped morality. Unfortunately, the task of mission has become much more difficult because a globalized knowledge economy has greatly expanded peoples opportunities. Their time is ever more valuable because of the many other opportunities now open to them through the market and the worldwide web and mission and evangelization have to compete even more for people's time and attention.

Secondly, the globalized market place has produced a large number of poor who have no real access to it. The globalized knowledge economy has brought about better knowledge of the plight of others and a better understanding of the adverse ripple effects of our actions but very little is done to ameliorate their suffering in spite of having the resources for it. Faith and good works hold the key to evangelization today. Charity convinces by the power of its own truth. Mission and evangelization are sterile if they are limited to words alone. They must be backed by action and example. If globalization has created manifold opportunities for close contacts, it also calls for a keener awareness of the negative sides of it and readiness to mitigate them. The development of the poor must be reflected in the manner by which we engage in mission in the 21st century.

The information and communication technologies have expanded our capabilities but they have also unleashed an information overload. The Church faces a fierce fight and an uphill battle to get heard and to stay relevant. Younger generations are travelling exclusively on the e-highway at tremendous speed and if the Church takes the country roads, there will be no meeting points. This means that mission requires imagination, flexibility, and agility in communicating its message. There is need for a healthy and vibrant engagement with the world through this new highway. Mission must not flee from this responsibility. The scope and target of evangelization now are the whole world and all peoples and not merely some far away regions or countries. The information revolution presents mission with the challenge of preaching its message in the midst of a cacophony of competing voices.

But at the same time the Church should keep in mind that reliance on nano-electronics alone will not solve all its problems. In the final analysis, mission is personal and personal contact, example, and friendships still are key to effective evangelization.

Opportunities for both have been offered to the Church in this time of the Covid-19 pandemic. It is perhaps time to appropriate the image that Pope John Paul II used in his Jubilee Year 2000 vision of mission in *Tertio Millennio Ineunte*.[25] He invited the Church to "set out into the deep." What the Pope seems to have had in mind was the Church taking risks in its missionary commitment to seek out the new possibilities, the new *areopagoi*, the new social and cultural spaces where evangelization might take place.

The Corona Pandemic is an opportunity to address fundamental questions about evangelization, to ask questions about God, about the world, about human beings, about nature, about creation and finally about the Church. In the context of the pandemic, mission is also about bringing to people's lives a God who is perhaps far beyond the categories of the Church. Many people, including Christians still have the idea of a vengeful God who is behind this misfortune. The Church could help people to come out of an infantile faith and teach people to live as part of this creation which is itself yearning for redemption[26] and where there is constant death and resurrection, suffering and healing. As for the globalised world, this small but not so harmless virus is a chance to introspect and see how imperfect it is, in spite of the alleged progress in all fields. God has created the world as a world in process, in evolution. Many be it is time for an old world, including the religious, to die and then there will be another world.[27] We must never succumb to the illusion that technological developments, social revolutions and genetic manipulation will succeed in eliminating the questionability of reality, the dialectic of the negative, in breaking the vicious circles of human self-destruction, in taming the power of the void, in facing the chaos and senselessness in the world and creating a paradise on earth, a golden age, an age of freedom even from all suffering itself. Looking at Jesus will help us to remain realistic about suffering which we try to combat with all our means at hand. But even the one who follows Jesus, carrying his cross daily, will not be able to remove all pain and suffering from life but he will be able to endure it and survive it in faith. He will not be crushed by it nor will he sink into despair. If Jesus in the face of abandonment by his friends and even by God was not crushed and defeated, one who trusts in him also will not be crushed or abandoned by him. Faith

25 Apostolic Letter of His Holiness Pope John Paul II at the Close of the Great Jubilee Year 2000, 6 January, 2001.

26 Rom 8:22-23.

27 Is 43:19.

in Jesus gives the hope that suffering does not have the last word. What is definitive and final in life is that there is life without suffering but it is a divine reality and not something that can be ushered in by human creativity.

For the Church, it is an opportunity to realize the dream of Jesus, that true worshippers will worship the Father in spirit and in truth,[28] to rediscover the poor and the meaning of loving one's neighbour as oneself, to practise solidarity and simplicity, all fundamental Christian virtues. The Czech priest, sociologist and theologian, Tomáš Halík, prophetically observed in a recent article[29] that the empty churches that we saw in the past months are a symbol of the emptiness many Christians feel in the Church and the churches would remain empty and closed for ever if the Church does not change.

Now is the time for the Church to be what Pope Francis wants it to be: "a field hospital." With this metaphor, the Pope means that the Church should not be comfortable with its splendid isolation from the world, but should go beyond its borders and help those who are physically, psychologically, socially and spiritually wounded. A good hospital should not only heal, it should diagnose (recognize "the signs of the times"), prevent (immunize societies in which the malicious viruses of fear, hatred, populism and nationalism rage) and help convalesce (heal the trauma of the past through forgiveness).[30] It is a good way of evangelizing in the 21st century.

---

28 Jn 4:23.

29 "Christentum in Zeiten der Krankheit," *Münsteraner Forum für Theologie und Kirche*, 2 April, 2020.

30 Ibid., 1.

10

Inspiration of Sacred Scripture
Testimony of Lukan Writings

Thomas Manjaly

Introduction

The Apostolic Exhortation, *Verbum Domini*, discusses the theme of Inspiration and Truth with an appeal to undertake a deeper study of these key themes (VD 19).[1] We shall look at the relevant excerpts from this Document as they help to understand better the theme under our study.

A key concept for understanding the sacred text as the word of God in human words is certainly that of *inspiration*... Sacred Scripture is "the word of God set down in writing under the inspiration of the Holy Spirit". In this way one recognizes the full importance of the human author who wrote the inspired texts and, at the same time, God himself as the true author.

1 Benedict XVI, *Post-Synodal Apostolic Exhortation, Verbum Domini* (2010). The present author has drawn inspiration from the Document of the Pontifical Biblical Commission, *The Inspiration and Truth of Sacred Scripture: The Word that Comes from God and Speaks of God for the Salvation of the World* (English edition; Collegeville: Liturgical Press, 2014; Indian edition - Bangalore: TPI, 2015). He was a member of the Commission who prepared the Document (2009-2019).

> ...the theme of inspiration is clearly decisive for an adequate approach to the Scriptures and their correct interpretation, which for its part is to be done in the same Spirit in whom the sacred texts were written. Whenever our awareness of its inspiration grows weak, we risk reading Scripture as an object of historical curiosity and not as the work of the Holy Spirit in which we can hear the Lord himself speak and recognize his presence in history.
>
> ...The Synod Fathers also stressed the link between the theme of inspiration and that of the *truth of the Scriptures*. ...Theological reflection has always considered inspiration and truth as two key concepts for an ecclesial hermeneutic of the sacred Scriptures. Nonetheless, one must acknowledge the need today for a fuller and more adequate study of these realities, in order better to respond to the need to interpret the sacred texts in accordance with their nature. Here I would express my fervent hope that research in this field will progress and bear fruit both for biblical science and for the spiritual life of the faithful.

This desire of the Synod and the invitation of Pope emeritus Benedict XVI were taken up by the Pontifical Biblical Commission for its study during 2009-2013. The scope was to see how the sacred Scripture itself attests to the fact of inspiration.

In this essay, we restrict our search only to Lukan Writings. First of all, it is important to keep in mind that the traditional technical terms or expressions - like "inspired by God" (*theopneustos*: 2 Tim 3:16-17) or "moved by the Holy Spirit they spoke from God" (*hypo pneumatos hagiou pheromenoi elalesan apo theou anthropoi:* 2 Pet 1:19-21) - are not found in Lukan Writings, be it regarding the books or in relation to Luke, the author. These are technical expressions around which we have developed the notion of inspiration as divine-human interplay. We must look at how the concept or idea of being influenced by God/Spirit has been communicated, rather than whether the vocabulary of inspiration can be found. We approach the question by looking at indications in some of the texts.[2]

2 The following commentaries and articles have been used extensively in the preparation of this article. D. L. Bock, *Luke* (Baker Commentary – NT; Grand Rapids: Baker, 1994); H. Conzelmann, *The Theology of St Luke* (Philadelphia: Fortress, 1982); J. R. Edwards, *The Gospel according to Luke* (Pillar NT; Grand Rapids & Cambridge (UK): Eerdmans; Nottingham: Apollos, 2015); J.A. Fitzmyer, *The Gospel According to Luke, I,II* (Anchor Bible; New York : Doubleday, 1985); H. Hendrickx, *The Third Gospel for the Third Wor*ld (Multivolume; Collegeville: Liturgical Press, 1996-); L. T. Johnson, *The Gospel of Luke* (Sacra Pagina; Collegeville: Michael Glazier & Liturgical Press, 1991); I. H. Marshall, *The Gospel According to Luke* (Grand Rapids: Eerdmans, 1978); L. Sabourin, L., *The*

1. Luke's Link with Jesus

There is no indication in NT Writings that Luke the author of Luke-Acts was among the disciples of the historical Jesus. Further, there is no reference to any Paul-like experience. So what we present below are indications of indirect contact with Jesus, indications which are sufficient to give credibility to his two-volume work.

1. General Comments

1.1. Luke as Member of the Inspired Community

Inspiration can be looked at from a wider context. We read in *Redemptoris Missio,* "The Spirit's presence and activity affect not only individuals but also society and history, peoples, cultures and religions" (no.28). Can we speak of a 'Spirit-inspired' community? Here we are referring to an 'ecclesial understanding' or a 'social' understanding of inspiration. It means that the intention of God to bring into existence the community of salvation includes His intention to inspire the community to write down its experience of the Lord Jesus Christ. Thus this experience and its communication become constitutive of and normative for the community. The community had a lived experience of the Gospel (Christ-event) before it communicated it in writing (cf. 1 Jn 1:1-4). In that sense, it is the inspired community that speaks through individual authors. Luke considers himself a member of that inspired community when he in the introduction (Lk 1:1-4) implies that he is a member of the group of ministers of the Word, and that he has taken utmost care to verify the facts on the basis of apostolic tradition and wanted to give an account of them as faithfully as possible. This dimension is further emphasized by the social understanding of inspiration where the various stages of the formation of the tradition – from oral to writing - are a divinely guided / Spirit-guided process. By faithfully reporting the proclamation ministry of Peter, Luke indicated his link with Peter who in turn was part of the group gathered in the Upper Room (Acts 1:12-14 and 2:1-14). They were empowered by the Spirit. So he makes it clear that his *source was a Spirit-inspired group* (Acts 1:8). It is the Spirit who guarantees the *kerygma.*

Gospel According to St. Luke. (Bombay: St. Paul's, 1984); E. Schweizer, *The Good News according to Luke* (Atlanta: John Knox, 1984); See also P. Grech, "Further Reflections on Biblical Inspiration and Truth," *Biblical Theology Bulletin*, 42/2 (2012) 81-89; Grisez, G. "The Inspiration and Inerrancy of Scriptures," *Letter and Spirit*, 6 (2010) 181-190; Manjaly, T., "Inspiration and Truth of sacred Scripture," *Mission Today,* XVIII/2 (2016) 100-112.

1.2. Luke's Link with Jesus through the Apostles

The book of Acts presents the proclamation of the Gospel by eyewitnesses and others, more especially by Peter and Paul. Luke's lists of the apostles are identical in the Gospel (Lk 6:4-6) and Acts (Acts 1:13). In this way, he was trying to emphasize the continuity of Jesus tradition through these witnesses (Lk 1:1-4; Acts 6:4) and to show his own role in its transmission and his link with Jesus through the apostles (Acts 1:21-22; 10:34-43).

Paul too, as one called by the Lord had encountered the risen Lord (Acts 9:1-22; 22:5-16; 26:12-18). Paul states clearly that 'his' gospel came through a revelation of Christ (Gal 1:11-12:16; cf. (2 Cor 13:3), and interventions of the Holy Spirit (Acts 9:17; 13:2, 4, 9; 15:28; 16:6-10). Luke's close association with Paul and indirectly with Jesus is also indicated in the 'we' passages (Acts 16:10-18; 20:6-15; 27:1-28:16).

1.3. Luke and the 'Pauline Circle'

As a close associate of Paul, Luke was influenced by Paul's thought. Paul considered that the Scriptures as a whole were inspired by God, and hence are "able to instruct you for salvation through faith in Christ Jesus…" (2 Tim 3:15-16). He was convinced that he was truly proclaiming the Word / Gospel of God (1 Thess 2: 2,8,13; 2 Cor 2:17). He had also attached great authority to the *apostolic* tradition (cf. 1 Cor 11:2, 23; 15:3; 2 Thess 2:15; 3:6). 2 Timothy 3:16-17 expresses the shared idea of the 'Pauline circle' including Luke that the biblical authors were under the power of the Spirit. The Pastoral letters belong to the times of Luke-Acts, whose theological trends they also share.

1.4. A Common Introduction to Luke's Two Volume Writing (Lk 1:1-4; Acts 1:1)

In this common introduction to his two volume-work – the Gospel and Acts - (Lk 1:1-4; cf. Acts 1:1), Luke attempts to make it clear that his sources were those who had been *eyewitnesses* from the beginning (Acts 1:21-22) and who later became *ministers* of the Word (Lk 1:2). This affirms further the *veracity* and *completeness* of his tradition. He indicates his *link* with these eyewitnesses, and places his two volume work as part of the ongoing transmission - both oral and written – of the Jesus-*tradition* (Acts 1:13, 21-22). He was then presenting a written record of the process of re-telling the story of Jesus (Acts 1:5, 8; 13:30-31). The fact that they were Spirit-transformed witnesses (Acts 1:8; 2:1-14), further *guarantees the authenticity of their tradition* (Acts 15:28).

Looking at the transmission of the Jesus-tradition in three stages and the accompanying actions of the Spirit is helpful to understand better the process of inspiration: firstly, Jesus, full of the Spirit (Lk 4:1, 18) proclaimed the Gospel-message; secondly, eyewitnesses and others transmitted it *orally*

(Acts 1:8; 2:1-14) and finally, Luke (and others before him) communicated this tradition *in writing*. Many of those who proclaimed these traditions were directly *commissioned* to do so by the risen Lord (Acts 1:8; cf. Lk 24:48-49). Because of his awareness that he was transmitting this sacred Tradition, Luke tried to ensure its accuracy and certainty (Lk 1:3-4). Inspiration is a process and writing is the last stage (cf. 1 Jn 1:1-4). The entire process takes place under the *power of the Spirit or as divinely-guided.*

2. Indications in the Gospel of Luke

2.1. The Use of paradidomi / paradosis

In Lk 1:1-4 Luke makes four important statements: (a) Many have undertaken to set an orderly account of the events; (b) The tradition was handed down by witnesses and servants of the Word; (c) Luke too decided to write an orderly account after carefully and thoroughly studying everything; (d) ′Purpose: So that he (Theophilus) may know the truth concerning the things about which he had been instructed.

Regarding the content that Luke was communicating he was very conscientious to hand down the apostolic tradition which is expressed by his use the *paradidomi* group of words. This word-group, which was a NT technical term for handing down apostolic tradition - both oral and written - is used by Luke (1:2). The NT authors made use of it when they wanted to guarantee the truthfulness or veracity of the content and its apostolic origin (e.g. Mk 7:13; Acts 6:14; 1 Cor 11:2, 23; 15:3; 2 Thess 2:15; 3:6).

Luke 1:2 affirms the veracity of his tradition by referring to it as coming from *eyewitnesses* (hence, first hand information), who therefore could guarantee its veracity, and from those who were also *ministers of the Word.* The fact that he made all efforts to examine the details carefully (*akribos*) indicates that he intends to exclude any hearsay or unverified accounts (1:3). The fact that they were witnesses from the beginning emphasizes the *completeness of the Gospel tradition*. In fact for Luke, being a witness "from the beginning from the baptism of John until the day when was taken up from us" is a necessary qualification to be an apostle (Acts 1:22). The addition of 'everything' further underlines the comprehensive nature of the testimony even more. The transmitters of the tradition were *competent/reliable* (*hyperetes*) who had ascertained the *veracity and accuracy* of their tradition. This group which gathered in the Upper Room (Acts 1:12-14; 2:1-14), was empowered by the Spirit.

The care that Luke showed to ascertain the accuracy of the source is a further indication of his awareness that he was communicating God's work in Jesus, which for him is the *truth* (*asphaleia*- 1:4). So he could say, "it seemed good to me" to hand down this tradition. This expression is further qualified in

Acts by the addition, "it has seemed good to the Holy Spirit and to us" (Acts 15:28). Moreover *katechein* (1:4) which is used here, occurs in the NT more *in relation to instruction in religious matters* or *sacred tradition* (cf. Acts 18:25; 21:21,24; Rom 2:18; 1 Cor 14:19; Gal 6:6).[3] The use of *logos* is also significant (cf. 1:2; 5:1; 8:12; 8:15) because *logos* stands for the Christ-event. It is in Acts that Luke develops the theme of '*logos*' where it refers to the preaching of the Apostles and its effectiveness (cf. 4:4; 6:4; 8:4; 10:36,44).

Luke was aware that the *apostolic tradition* had its ultimate origin in Jesus. He presents Jesus as referring to and interpreting the OT Scripture as being fulfilled in himself. So it was *not any kind of tradition but the one which had its origin in Jesus* that Luke was communicating. By being a transmitter of this apostolic tradition, he considers that he too has become a minister of the Word even though he was not an eyewitness (1:2).

The apostolic tradition is sacred as it comes from persons who were specifically called to be witnesses to the words and deeds of Jesus (1:2) and who were commissioned to continue his work through their preaching (24:48-49). Their call and mission was to mediate the Word which originated from Jesus. Luke also mentions that he had *carefully investigated and examined the matter* before putting it down, thereby pointing to his active involvement in handing down the apostolic tradition. While remaining faithful to the *apostolic tradition as the Word of God*, he has taken personal responsibility to interpret it. This may be considered the *human* aspect of scriptural authorship.

Luke states that what he wrote is also the result of his own study and followed his own theological patterns. For example, he places the Roman chronology in the beginning of chapters Two and Three. At the same time, he created his own arrangement of the Gospel through the insertion of a Travel Narrative (beginning Lk 9:51). Inspiration here means a *divinely guided movement* with the author's theological vision being transformed by the divine power.

2.2. Communication through Divine Intervention in Luke

Luke, more than other Gospels, makes use of 'angels' as the messengers/intermediaries of God: the angel who announces the birth of John the Baptist to Zachary (1:11-23), the angel who announces the birth of Jesus to Mary (cf. 1:26-38; 2:21), the angel who proclaims the Good news of Jesus birth to the shepherds (2:9-13), the angels who announce the message of peace (2:14), and finally, the two angels (two men in dazzling apparel) who announce the resurrection to the women (24:4, 5-6; compare 24:4 with 24:23). Luke

3 See G. Schneider, "Katecheo," in Horst Balz-Gerhard Schneider (eds.) *Exegetical Dictionary of the New Testament* Vol. 2, 273. The religious aspect of the word becomes clearer in 2 Clement 17:1, though it has still not become a technical term for catechetical instruction.

mentions the divine origin of Jesus (1:35), and affirms his divine sonship at the time of his baptism (3:21-22). The transfiguration episode is another event which shows clearly the transcendent origin of Jesus (9:28-36, especially verse 35). Both 3:22 and 9:35 testify that the affirmation of the identity of Jesus is a divine communication. Jesus, as the risen Lord, gives the Spirit to his community (3:16; 24:49; cf. also Acts 1:5, 8). In this way, Luke makes it clear that what he intends to communicate is not merely human history, but God's continuous intervention in history. This is the content of his gospel.

2.3. The Spirit-inspired Communication/Proclamation

Luke presents several persons who 'speak being inspired by the Spirit.' Mary was 'overshadowed' by the Spirit (1:35) and later she sings the *Magnificat*; Zacharia was 'filled with the Holy Spirit and spoke the prophecy' (1:67); Simeon is presented as one in whom the Holy Spirit was present and utters a prophecy (2:25, 26, 27. John the Baptist spoke as the 'word of God' came to him (3:2,4-6). He had already come under the influence of the Lord (and His Spirit when he was still mother's womb (1:44). Finally, Jesus is presented as one who is born under the power of the Holy Spirit (1:35), on whom the Spirit descends in the form of a dove (3:22), who is filled with the Holy Spirit (4:1) and is with 'the power of the Spirit' (4:14). Jesus began his ministry as one who was anointed by the Spirit (4:18).

Luke indicates that what he communicates in writing is the 'spoken word of God' which existed as 'oral tradition,' and hence has God/Spirit as its real source though the actual communication takes place in human language. It would not be correct to say that the 'spoken word is inspired', but not its written form. The Spirit of the Lord which was at work in the prophets continues to inspire other human beings. This is a further indication of the continuity of God's inspiring action in history. Here one must admit that Luke does not explicitly refer to being under the Spirit as is the case of the Prophets like Jeremiah, Ezekiel or Amos. We must also keep in mind the words of the letter to the Hebrews, "In many and various ways God spoke" (Heb 1:1)

The texts, where the Holy Spirit is mentioned in connection with the communication of the Word, or where prophesying (*propheteuein*) or praising (*eulogein*) is attributed to the Holy Spirit, also attest to the Spirit-inspired content of the Gospel.[4]

4 Certain texts in the infancy narratives, especially the introductions of the canticles - 1:41f; 1:64, 67; 2:25-27 as also introduction to 1:68 or even 10:21- can be looked at from this perspective.

2.4. Promise and Fulfillment

Luke presents Jesus – his life and mission – as the fulfillment of the OT. The following texts are of special significance in this regard: 4:16-30; 22:37; 24:26-27,32, 44-47. Citations from or reference to OT texts clarify and confirm the NT texts that it is the same God who was at work in Israel (OT), is now at work in Jesus. Hence there is continuity between the two covenants. The use of *plerophorein* in relation to *pragmata* in 1:1 is important in that 1:1-4 is an introduction to the entire Lukan writings (cf. 4:16-21; 18:31; 22:37). The *pragmata* are the events of salvation-history. Luke sees that the Christ event is the fulfillment of God's plan. This is what he wants to communicate in the Gospel (1:4). He brings out the aspect of fulfillment clearly in 4:21, "Today this scripture has been fulfilled in your hearing" (4:21; Isa 61:1-2). Isa 61:1-2 is a vision of the mission of the Messiah. But the aspect of fulfillment goes beyond mere material continuity. Luke 22:37 refers to Isa 53:12 – the prophecy concerning the suffering servant - which is being fulfilled in Jesus. Jesus explicitly mentions that the Scripture is speaking of him and thereby places the course of events, namely, his death and resurrection, within God's plan. The words of the prophets find their full meaning beyond their immediate addressees.

In the Emmaus story, Jesus is presented as the one in whom the law (Moses), the prophets and the Scriptures were being fulfilled. Here too Jesus applies the Scriptures to himself. Thus we find that in these texts it is Jesus who acts and this story of promise and fulfillment, through the continuity-discontinuity process, is what Luke wants to present in his Gospel (1:1-4). These texts which deal with 'fulfillment' (cf. 1:1-4; 4:16-21; 24:13-27) are located in key places of the gospel: in the introduction of the Gospel, in the introduction to the ministry of Jesus and at the conclusion of his mission. In 4:16-21 and 24:13-24 Jesus himself interprets and applies the text to his life and mission. We cannot speak of promise except in relation to fulfillment; nor can we speak of fulfillment without promise. This is what Luke was trying to communicate as the apostolic tradition that he had received. He indicates by means of this promise-fulfillment method that *what God began in the history of Israel is now being fulfilled in Jesus Christ.*

2.5. Lukan Understanding of Salvation History

The Promise-fulfillment approach is to be seen in relation to Luke's understanding of Salvation history as a continuity of 3 periods (time of the prophets, time of Jesus, time of the Church). It is the *Spirit* who ensures this continuity. The Spirit who was at work in the Prophets is even more active in the ministry of Jesus and in the preaching of the Apostles. The use of 'midrash' in Lk 1-2 further affirms the authority of the OT and the belief that one and the same God is behind the salvation history events. So, for Luke, the Spirit is still *in-spiring* those who hand down the message of salvation. This may be considered "factual inspiration" or "oral inspiration."

2.6. Old Testament as Inspired Book in Luke

More than the other synoptic Gospels, Luke stresses the *inspiration of the Old Testament* by calling it also the *graphē*. Though reference to *graphē* (4:21; 24:27,32,45) is not more frequent than in Mt-Mk (4/3/4), the use of the phrase verb *graphein* in reference to Scripture especially in the form *gegraptai* is more frequent (10/10/24). He takes Scripture (*he graphē*) as normative, i.e., it has authority (e.g. 2:23-24; 4:8,10,12; 10:25-37; 18:18-25). The *graphē* that he refers to includes the OT which was considered as inspired (see 2 Tim 3:16-17; 2 Pet 1:19-21).

Luke refers to particular books of the OT, instead of referring to the OT in a general way (e.g. 3:4 = book of the words of Isaiah; 4:17 = Isaiah 18:31 [prophets]; 20:42-43 = the book of Psalms). Various aspects of Jesus' life (2:23-24; 4:8) and ministry including his rejection and death (4:24; 11:47-51) are being interpreted by means of the OT texts. This close link between the OT texts and the Jesus-event points to the idea that Jesus' life and ministry were planned by God. It is quite significant that Jesus too applies the OT texts to himself (4:18-19; 18:31-33; 24:26-27,44-47). We must also note that such a use of OT Scriptures in Luke is an indication that he was aware that what he was communicating was in line with the inspired texts of the OT (4:18-19; 18:31; 24:44). LK 24:44 refers to the Law of Moses, the prophets and the book of Psalms, all major sections of the OT which were used in Synagogue worship.

The sacred Scripture unfolds God's plan and acts of salvation in the past, in the present and in the future. This salvific aspect is highlighted by the fact that of the 12 usages of the OT by Luke, 5 are in relation to Jesus' teaching, life and mission in Jerusalem (19:46 = Isa 56:7; 20:17 = Ps 118:22; 20:37 = Ex 3:15; 20:42-43 = Ps 110:1; 22:37 = Isa 53:12) and three more in 24:27,32,44-45. In Acts 17, Luke together with Paul seems to think that in the presentation of the *kerygma to the Gentiles,* quotations of the Greek poets from the religious philosophy of the Stoics (Acts 17:28) play role parallel to that of the Scriptures in the kerygma to the Jews. Using the *much more* argument we can think reasonably conclude that Luke was convinced of the 'inspired nature' of the OT.

Luke presents some of his texts structured as *parallel* to some OT texts: The song of Zachary 1: 67-79 to the song of Miriam at Exodus (Ex 15: 20-21; 15:1-18 – Canticle of Moses); discourse on the plain (6:20-36) to the discourses of Moses (Ex 19-24; 30-32). Together they contain strong exodus motifs - the Christ event as the new exodus and Jesus as the giver of the new Law. The *Magnificat* makes abundant use of Biblical texts to point out that what was foreshadowed in the OT reaches its fulfillment and culmination in the Christ event (Canticle of Hanna in 1 Sam 2).

Another related feature of the Lukan Gospel is *Septuagintism*. He seems to have relied more on LXX in his two-volume writing. This peculiarity shows his desire to situate his work in relation to the "Bible" which he knew, i.e. the LXX. The use of LXX or 'Septuagintism' is quite evident in Luke 1-2, particularly in the '*Magnificat*.'[5] '*Septuagintism*' is more than the use of style or language, but an attempt to present the words and deeds of Jesus as parallel to the salvific deeds of God in the past.[6] In this way Luke wanted to show that his writings were in *continuity* with a *text* which was widely used and was already considered as *inspired*, and hence the authoritative biblical text by Hellenistic Jews. This was accepted as *normative* also by the early Christian community. This *continuity* was understood within the single plan of God. Hence, fulfillment included *continuity* as well.

2.6.1. Canon within the Canon?

The question itself might seem a contradiction, as the whole of Scripture is normative. But here we may take it in the sense of preference, just as an individual may have preference for a particular book in the Bible. Luke was familiar with the tripartite division of the Hebrew Scriptures (*TeNaK*) - the Law of Moses (10 times), the prophets (7 times) and the psalms (7 times).[7] In the OT itself, one may speak of a preference for the *Torah* in so far as the prophets (and to a lesser degree the Wisdom Writings) accepted the normative nature of the *Torah* and were reinterpreting and expanding its teaching. It may be for this reason, though not exclusively, that Luke uses more texts from the Pentateuch. He presents Jesus' life and ministry in terms of fulfillment of the law (*nomos kyriou* – see 2:23-24; 4:8, 10, 12; 19:46). Luke mentions that Jesus refers to the Law, Prophets and Psalms (Lk 24:44; cf. 24:27) and in 24:45 to the entire OT as Scriptures. On the authority of Jesus, Luke endorses the inspired nature of the OT. Further, Luke thinks that the Scripture (*hē graphē*) normatively directs the actions of the people (cf. 2:23-24; 4:8,10,12; 10:25-37;

5 Similar preference for the *Septuagint* is seen in the book of Acts as well (Acts 2:17-21=Joel 3:5.

6 2 Pet 1:19-21 refers to the inspiration of prophetic writings, i.e. prophecy as an action that takes place under the inspiration of the Holy Spirit. In that sense, the prophetic writings have the Spirit as their source. 2 Tim 3:16 extends the inspiring action of God to the entire Scripture.

7 The historical books (Joshua, Judges, 1-2 Samuel and 1-2 Kings considered as former prophets) belong to the prophetic writings in the *TeNaK*.

18:18-25). Though he seems to indicate some preference for the Pentateuch, the evidence is not strong enough to speak of 'a canon within a canon' in Luke.

3. Acts of the Apostles

It is easier to illustrate that the evangelists were aware of being 'inspired' while composing the gospel texts. It is not so easy with regard to other NT books including the Acts. Some of the important indications are: continuity within sacred history, and the aspects of fulfillment and consummation of salvation history. Luke shows that he was an 'inspired' author in the common introduction to his two-volume work (Lk 1:1-4; Acts 1:1), by his link with Jesus, the risen Lord and his Spirit through the Apostles, in the continuity of transmitting the Jesus-tradition, in the interventions of the Holy Spirit, and by presenting the Acts as fulfillment of the Old Testament. [8]

3.1. Continuity of Jesus-Tradition in the Acts of the Apostles

Acts 1:1-11, which is a re-worked summary of the Lucan gospel, highlights the continuity between the Jesus event and its proclamation by the apostles and others, and between the gospel and the Acts. The 'Kingdom' which is the core of the preaching of Jesus (Lk 4:43) and of the disciples (Lk 9:2), is an important theme in the book of Acts as well (Acts 1:3; 8:12; 28:23, 31).

The continuity of Jesus-tradition is noticeable in the discourses and miracles, but particularly in the former

3.1.1. The Speeches /Discourses (Words).

The speeches of Peter (e.g. Acts 1:15-22; 2:14-36; 3:12-26) and Paul (e.g. Acts 13:16-41) are significant summaries of the life and ministry of Jesus. Although these were delivered to particular groups, they are now presented by Luke (cf. Acts 2:40). Many of the listeners of the apostles' preaching and Luke's immediate readers were familiar with the story of Jesus. Yet, he presents all the basic elements of the Jesus-tradition: origin of Jesus as David's offspring (13:22-23) in relation to Nazareth (2:22; 4:10) and his ministry (10:37-39). His passion and death involving the Jews (2:36; 3:13; 4:10-11), the Gentiles (2:23; 4:26-28), Herod (4:27) and Pilate (3:13; 13:28), his death on the tree outside

8 The following sources have been consulted in the preparation of the section on Acts. C. K. Barrett, *Acts*, vols. 1-2 (ICC) Edinburgh: T & T Clark, 1998; H. Conzelmann, *Acts of the Apostles* (Hermeneia) Philadelphia: Fortress, 1997; E. Haenchen, *The Acts of the Apostles*. Philadelphia: Westminster, 1971; M. Hengel, *Acts and History of Earliest Christianity*. Philadelphia: Fortress, 1980; L. T. Johnson, *The Acts of the Apostles* (SP) Collegeville: Liturgical Press, 1992; I. H. Marshall, *The Acts of the Apostles: An introduction and Commentary*. Grand Rapids: Eerdmans, 1980; D. G. Peterson, *The Acts of the Apostles* (Pillar NT) Grand Rapids & Cambridge (UK): Eerdmans; Leicester: Apollos, 2009.

Jerusalem (Acts 10:39), burial (13:29) and resurrection (2:24; 4:10; 13:30) receive special attention in Acts.

The role of God the Father is emphasized in the presentation of the resurrection of Jesus (2:24; 4:10; cf. Acts 1:10-11). The Spirit is given to the witnesses (Acts 2:33; 3:13) to continue Jesus' work (Acts 4:10). The Christological titles used by Luke in the Gospel are resumed in the Acts: 'the Christ' (Acts 2:31; 3:18), 'the Lord' (2:36; 11:20), 'the Son of God' (9:20), 'the Saviour' (5:31; 13:23), etc. These are some indications of similarity of basic contents in Lk-Acts

By re-telling the story of Jesus, Luke indicates that the book of Acts continues the story of Jesus and enables the readers of Acts to experience the salvific effects of the Christ-event. He wants his readers to respond in faith as is the case in Acts 15:7, in which Peter summarizes his speech in 10:34-43 as the 'word of the gospel'. The discourses reveal the *nucleus of the faith-confessions of the early Church* - the passion, death and resurrection of Jesus (Acts 2:23-36; 3:14-26; 13:27-35; cf. 1 Cor 15:3-8). These faith-expressions were considered already as *inspired traditions and canonical* before they were inserted into the book of Acts.

3.1.2. The Miracles (Deeds)

Jesus performed the miracles as signs of the Kingdom (Lk 4:18; cf. Acts 2:22; 10:38) and entrusted this task to the twelve (Lk 9:1). Besides mentioning 'signs and wonders' in a general way (Acts 2:43; 6:8; 8:6,13), the book of Acts mentions specific miracles which were performed by the apostles and others (Peter, Philip and Paul) – healing (3:1-10; 9:32-35; 14:8-10), exorcism (8:7), raising the dead to life (9:36-42), healing and exorcism (5:15-16; 8: 7). They performed these actions in the name of Jesus, and with his power and authority (Acts 3:1-10; 9:32-35). Luke saw these actions as actualization of the 'Kingdom', thus continuing the ministry of Jesus.

Thus, Luke indicates that the book of Acts, like the Lucan gospel, was presenting the Jesus-tradition

3.2. Acts as Record of Communications/Interventions of the Spirit

As in the gospel (e.g. *theophany*: Lk 3:21-22; 9:28-36), and in the book of Acts too, Luke mentions cases of divine communication: at the Ascension of the Lord (Acts 1:10-11) and the conversion of Cornelius (Acts 10-11). Paul's encounter with the risen Lord is presented as a *theophany* (Acts 9:1-22; cf. 13:2).

Further, the book of Acts presents the Spirit as *actively communicating*. This is done by the use of expressions like, "saying" (Acts 8:29; 10:19; 21:11), "predicting" through David (Acts 1:16), "speaking" through Isaiah (Acts

28:25), "testifying' (Acts 20:23), and "teaching" (2:4b) or 'God speaking' (Acts 7:6, 7). These introductory expressions, similar to the prophetic formula, "Thus speaks the Lord...", point to the fact that Luke was conscious that he was transmitting divine communication. Besides, Peter's speech at Pentecost is presented as the immediate consequence of the outpouring of the Spirit (Acts 2:14-36).

The apostles are presented as exercising their ministry in *conjunction with the Spirit* - "It has seemed good to the Holy spirit and to us..." (Acts 15:28; cf. 1:5, 8; 2:4). Through the Spirit, the risen Lord made himself present in the mission of the Church: e.g. beginning of a new mission (9:17; 13:2) or launching of the gentile mission (15:28). The Spirit functioned as the connecting link in the linear movement from the mission of Jesus (Lk 4:1, 14, 18) to that of the Church (Acts 2:1:8; 2:4). Luke, being part of the missionary team, was aware that what he narrated were interventions of the Spirit even though he does not state that he was explicitly 'told' to communicate them in writing.

3.3. Acts as Record of Fulfillment of the OT

By means of OT texts, Luke shows that the work of Jesus and of the apostles was in fulfillment of the OT (Acts 3:22-24; 26:23). Luke interpreted the mission of Jesus in terms of the OT (Lk 4:18-19 = Isa 61:1-2), and he repeated this approach with regard to the apostles (Acts 2:17-21 = Joel 3:1-5; Acts 28:26-27 = Isa 6:9-10), thus placing their work within the one plan of God. Peter refers to David as a prophet (cf. Acts 2:25, 29-31) at the inauguration of his mission, and Paul quotes Isaiah (Acts 28:25-28 = Isa 6:9-10) at the conclusion of his mission, which makes the mission a kind of *inclusion.* This is done to show that the mission of the Church from the beginning to the end, as presented in the Acts, is in fulfillment of the prophetic vision.

Regarding the use of OT texts, Luke is often more specific (Acts 1:20 = Ps 69:26 & 109:8; Acts 2:17-21= Joel 3:1-5; 28:26-27 = Isa 6:9-10). But, there are places where he refers to the prophets in a general way (Acts 3:18; 17:3; 18:28). Of the 37 OT quotations in Acts, most are found in the speeches of Peter, Stephen, and Paul, and addressed to those who were already familiar with them and who, therefore, could see more clearly the link between the Old and New Testaments.

The formulas, which introduce the OT texts, refer to the *Old Testament writings as Scripture*. We find formulas such as, "as it is written...' (Acts 7:42) or "even as it is written..." (Acts 13:33) or "for it is written..." (Acts 1:20; 23:5). Luke presents Peter's speech (Acts 2: 17-21=Joel 3:1-5) as an *interpretation of what God had spoken through the prophet. He affirms that just as the risen Lord opened the mind of his own disciples* (Lk 24:45), he did also with *Lydia* (Acts 16:14) to understand and interpret the Jesus event.

On the one hand, Luke indicates that *OT texts become fully meaningful* only in the context of a 'Spirit-inspired' interpretation of the NT events (Acts 2:17; cf. Lk 24:27). On the other hand, he shows that the *NT events are better understood* in the light of OT texts (Acts 2:17-21 = Joel 3:1-5; Lk 4:18-19 = Isa 61:1-2). Peter does a re-reading / contextual reading of OT text by Peter, - e.g. by changing, "after these things" of Joel 3:1 into "in the last days" (Acts 2:17). This re-reading, which places the mission of the Church within an *eschatological* perspective, is considered as inspired and valid for the fulfillment of the vision of Joel.

3.4. Inspiration beyond Judeo-Christian Scriptures

A point which needs our attention is the question of inspiration in non-biblical scriptures The Document of the Pontifical Biblical Commission refers to the book of Numbers (Num 24) to show how "(inspired) prophecy is not the exclusive prerogative of the people of God" and affirms that "it is fully recognized that the literature of the Old Testament is greatly indebted to Mesopotamian and Egyptian writings, just as the New Testament books draw extensively on the cultural heritage of the Hellenistic world." It recalls how Saint Paul, "in his discourse on the Areopagus, expressed his wholehearted agreement with the intuitions of Greek poets and philosophers (cf. Acts 17:28)."[9]

Luke, who reports Paul's interaction, seems to think that in the presentation of the *kerygma to the Gentiles,* reference to the Greek poets (Acts 17:28) plays a significant role, similar to what OT played in the kerygma to the Jews. We need to look at the possibility of reading Paul's Areopagus speech in this perspective (Acts 17:22-34; cf. 14:15-17). These texts which do not have the same value as OT texts seem to indicate that texts from Greek poets can help to present the *Gospel to Gentiles* who would not understand 'the prophets or the law' (Origen, *In epistulam i ad Corinthios* [*homiliae* 1-44]). The 'Unknown God' referred to in 17:23 is presented as the "God who made the world and all that is in it, the Lord of the heaven and the earth" (17: 24). And again, quoting from the Greek poet (Aratus of Soli in *Phaenomena*) who said, "For we too are his offspring" (17:28), he explained the mystery of salvation (17:31; cf. 1 Thess 1:10).

Paul/Luke looks positively at Greek religious literature as a search for the transcendent, as expressed by one of its writers, "in him we live and move and have our being…" (Acts 17:28). Paul (Luke) was also emphasizing thereby the

9 *The Inspiration and Truth of Sacred Scripture,* no. 148.

unity of God's revelation and its unfolding at various levels and ways (cf. Rom 1:18-23; Heb 1:1-2).

The Lystra incident presents a similar thought (Acts 14:15-17; compare 14: 15 with 1 Thess 1:9; see also Ex 20:11; Ps 146:6). In these texts, the preaching on the one God is expressed by terms used for proclamation of the Gospel (14:15 – *euangelizomai*; 17:23- *katangelo*). The one God is the Father of Jesus Christ (Jan 17:3; 1 Cor 8:6; 12:2; Eph 1:3; 1 Tim 2:5; 6:13). Luke sees that the religious aspirations of the Greeks can find their fulfillment in the plan of the God of the Bible (cf. 2:29; 3:25; 7:48; 15:7,14).

Quite significantly, two documents of the Church refer to Acts 17. *Nostra Aetate* (no. 1), while speaking of the common origin and destiny of humanity, mentions Acts 17:26 along with 14:17. *Ecclesia in Asia* (no. 20), while dealing with how various religious traditions find their fulfillment in Christ, refers to Acts 17:22-31 and 14:13-17.

In the light of the teachings of the Church, and following the principle of analogy, it may be possible to read Acts 17:22-34, 15-17 as hinting at inspiration in non-biblical scriptures as a kind of 'preparation for the Gospel' (*praeparatio evangelica*) and hinting at the presence of the Word "which enlightens all men" (Jn 1:9) in non-biblical scriptures at least in an initial manner. It is possible that Paul was doing a *re-reading* of the stoic poets in the light of the Gospel of Jesus Christ.

While from a biblical point of view, these sources cannot be regarded as channels of God's '*historical*' revelation, can we not recognize in them 'whisperings and enunciations of the Word' or hidden words of God? The NT books proclaim the universal salvation effected through Jesus Christ, but they *do not thereby deny* that God had communicated aspects of that salvation in other writings. Acts 17:23, 28 can serve as a starting point for further study.

How this is to be explained remains still a question. As a preparation for the Gospel, or as the pre-defined pre-history of the OT people of God, and of the Church and the NT, or as a part of the unknown ways of God's inter4ventions in salvation history or as a collection of developing traditions which lead to the inspired Scriptures and are fulfilled by Jesus Christ, other scriptures may be considered as parallel to the OT.

The document provides some insights for the pastoral engagement of the Church in the context of multi-religious communities and opens the way for meaningful dialogue (cf. DV 25; VD 118-119; *Evangelii Gaudium*, 251).[10]

10 The document states, "Such a question is of pressing relevance today for interreligious dialogue...The ***semina Verbi*** (*seeds of the Word*) are scattered throughout the world, and cannot therefore be confined to the text of the Bible alone. The Church has defined what she holds to be inspired, but she has not pronounced negatively on all the rest" (no. 148). It further affirms, "It is the Word of God handed down in the canonical Scriptures, in particular in that part which testifies to the Word made flesh that provides the principle of

Conclusion

As was stated in the introduction, there are no explicit statements by Luke that he was writing under the inspiration of the Spirit or that what he hands down is an 'inspired text.' But there are sufficient indications to show that Luke was aware that he was communicating not just history, but salvation history; not just information about Jesus, but God's saving intervention in Jesus. Salvation history is a Spirit-guided movement and Luke was commissioned to present this work of the Spirit to posterity.

Luke was also conscious that he was using OT texts not just for their own sake, but for the sake of illustrating that these are fulfilled in the person of Jesus. His way of using the Old Testament is a further indication of his awareness of his role in transmitting the message of salvation.

Further, even though Luke did not have any direct link with Jesus, he had a link with the risen Lord through those who either were witnesses to Jesus' life and ministry (Peter), or encountered him as the risen Lord (Paul). This association guaranteed the authenticity of his source and the trustworthiness of his presentation of the Jesus-tradition. As the Spirit-inspired community was brought into existence by the intervention of God, the sacred Scripture, in this case the two volume work of Luke (Luke-Acts), as constitutive of the community, belongs to the founding act of God. Like other authors, Luke too was guided and directed by the Spirit. By putting in writing the existing oral traditions (preaching by Peter and Paul), he was sure that he was faithful to the 'eyewitnesses' and 'earwitnesses' of the Jesus-traditions.

By making use of the principle of analogy to 'inspiration', Luke seems to indicate that the notion of inspiration may be applied to texts beyond the Judeo-Christian Scriptures. They may be considered as inspired in a broad sense ('seminal' inspiration) as preparation for the 'inspired texts of Judeo-Christian sacred. But it does not mean that we can draw a parallel between the OT texts and such texts.[11]

---

discernment of the truth of every other religious attestation, both in the church and in the diverse religious traditions of the various people of the earth. Finally, it is the role of the Spirit to be that principle of truth which sets in motion the course of belief and brings it to completion, in an indefinite openness to the self-manifestation of God in history" (no. 148).

11 The document of the Biblical Commission is however careful to avoid the danger of drawing parallelism between biblical texts and texts of other religions. It affirms what the texts reveal, without going into the details of how the process of inspiration has taken place and without theologizing. Only a few texts are taken up to point out some lines of approach for further study. See T. Manjaly, "Inspiration and Truth of sacred Scripture," 111-112.

11

Imperatives of Discipleship
A Gospel Persepctive*

Thomas Karimundackal, SJ

Introduction

Discipleship is a recurring theme in the whole of New Testament literature especially in the four canonical Gospels - Matthew, Mark, Luke and John. It is quite obvious that anyone who reads the Gospels will immediately notice that almost all the chapters of the Gospels directly or indirectly speak on the cost of discipleship. Discipleship is basically a call or invitation of Jesus for the proclamation of the Kingdom of God (cf. Mk 1:16-20; 2:13f; Lk 9:57-62).[1] Disciples of Jesus are the ones who follow Jesus in every way.[2] Freed

* It is a great pleasure and privilege for me to be able to contribute this article in honour of Prof. Scaria Kuthirakattel an inspiring teacher and an erudite scholar. I am indeed happy to write on a theme that is very dear to Prof. Scaria: discipleship in the Gospels. I am indebted to his inspiring lectures on discipleship and his ways of challenging to follow Jesus as a true disciple.

1 Jesus' call to discipleship is a common theme of the Gospels. All the four Gospels narrate the call of the first disciples of Christ (Mk 1:16-20; Mt 4:18-22: Lk 5:1-11; Jn 1:35-51).

2 In the Gospels and the Acts of the Apostles the term 'disciple' is applied not only to the Twelve Apostles (Mk 3:14), or to those who responded to the message of Jesus (Mt 5:1; Lk 6:17; 19:37), or to those who accompanied him on his journeys (Mk 6:45; Lk 8:2f; 10:1),

from attention to extraneous things of the world they are to share in the ministry of Jesus and adopt his way of life, and bring him known to the world around us. Therefore, it is understood that discipleship is not merely a human choice. Rather, it is a response to the summons of Jesus, "follow me" (Mk 1:17).[3] In the Gospels Jesus puts down the imperatives of discipleship quite clearly. This paper intends to show the imperatives of discipleship as they are illustrated in the Gospel traditions and their call for our wholehearted commitment to the demands of Jesus on discipleship in the present day.

1. Follow Jesus Radically

In the New Testament there are two types of following Jesus: one is by imitation and another by having an intimate relationship of a disciple to Jesus. The former, that is, imitation of Jesus Christ is profoundly developed in the Johannine (cf. Jn 13:15, 34; 15:12 etc.) and Pauline literature (cf. Rom 15:7; Eph 5:2, 25; 1 Cor 11:1; 1 Thess 1:6; Phil 2:5 etc.), and the latter is emphasized in the Synoptic Gospels and Acts of the Apostles.

In the Synoptic Gospels and Acts of the Apostles the relationship between Jesus and the disciples is expressed by the term *akoloutheo*. This particular word appears with three basic meanings:

1. To follow Jesus physically (Mk 10:52; 14:13.54; Mt 9:19.27; 20:34; Lk 22:39). The blind man follows Jesus on the way (Mk 10:52), the disciples follow the man carrying water (Mk 14:13); the disciples follow Jesus in the boat (Mt 8:23), Peter follows Jesus at a distance on the way of Jesus (Mk 14:54; Mt 26:58),[4] the two blind men follow Jesus (Mt 9:27), and the disciples follow Jesus to the Mount of Olives (Lk 22:39).
2. To follow Jesus as a crowd (Mk 2:15; 3:7; 5:24; 10:32; 11:9; Mt 8:1,10; 12:15; Lk 7:9; 23:27). In Mk "the crowd", "many 'or "a multitude" are said to follow Jesus (Mk 2:15.3.7; 5:24; 10:32; 11:9). In 8 texts of Mathew "many," "those who," "great (large) crowd" are said to follow Jesus (Mt 4:25; 8:1.10; 12:15; 14:13; 19:2; 20:29;

---

but also to the Christians (Acts 6:1 .2.7; 9:1 .20.36). In this way the term is used 230 times in the Gospels and 22 times in the Acts of the Apostles, cf. M. L. Held, Disciple, in *the New Catholic Encyclopedia*, 4 (1967), 895.

3 Cf. Julian Charley, *Fifty Key Words of the Bible* (Virginia: John Knox Press, Richmond, 1971), 15-16.

4 "Since the way of Jesus may denote the way of suffering through which the master goes before his followers even following in the case of Peter becomes more than mere physical following." Paul Palatty, Discipleship in the Synoptic Gospels, *Bible Bhashyam*, 4 (1985), 232.

21:9). Luke speaks of "the multitude" or "crowd" following Jesus (7:9; 9:11; 23:27).

3. To follow Jesus as his disciples (Mk 1:18; 6:1; 10:28; 15:41; Mt 8:19, 22; 9:9; 16:24-28, 19:27-28; Lk 8:23; 9:49,59; 18:22).[5] Mark uses *akoloutheo* in a strict sense of discipleship 8 times (cf. Mk 1:18; 2:14 (2); 6:1; 8:34(2); 10:21.28). The first disciples and Levi followed Jesus leaving their job (Mk1:18; 2:14). Jesus asks the rich man to sell his possessions, and give it to the poor, and then to follow him (Mk 10:21), and taught his disciples to deny oneself, taking up one's cross to follow him (Mk 8:34). As a true disciple, Peter speaks for his companions affirming that "we have left everything and followed you" (Mk10:28), and as a reward an eternal life is promised (Mk10:30).

   Mathew also uses *akoloutheo* in a similar sense 11 times (cf. Mt 4:22.40; 8:19.22; 9:9.19; 10:38; 16:24.19:21.27.28). As in Mark the first disciples and Levi follow Jesus leaving everything (Mt 4:20.22; 9:9.19). In Mt 8:19 a scribe wants to follow Jesus wherever he goes. Jesus asks one of the would be followers to follow him by not even considering the burial of his father (Mt 8:22). In Mt10:38 Jesus says that the disciple who does not take his cross and follow him is not worthy of him, and in Mt 16:24 Jesus exhorts his disciples to deny himself and take up his cross and follow him. As in Mk 10:21 Jesus also asks the rich young man to sell everything, give to the poor to follow him (Mt 19:21). Peter is assured of an eternal kingdom for leaving everything and following (Mt 19:27.28).

   Luke also uses *akoloutheo* in a strict sense of discipleship in 9 times (cf. Lk 5:11.27.28; 9:23.57.59.61; 18:22-28). Like Mark and Mathew, Luke notes that the first disciples and Levi leave everything to follow Jesus (Lk 5:11.27.28). The demand of discipleship is put in 4 texts as: denying oneself and taking up one's cross (Lk 8: 23); following him wherever he goes (Lk 9:57); forsaking the burial of the father (Lk 9:59) and other family members (Lk 9:61); selling everything and giving to the poor (Lk18:22). Like in Mt and Mk, eternal life is promised to Peter who said: "we have left our homes and followed you" (Lk18:28-30).

In short, following Jesus in the Synoptics includes: an immediate response (Mk 1:18:20; Mt 4: 20-22), readiness to leave everything (Mk 1:18.20; Mt 4: 20-22; Lk 5:11), forsaking of all the old ties (Lk 9: 59-61; 18: 22); walking

5 Cf. Paul Palatty, Discipleship in the Synoptic Gospels, *Bible Bhashyam* 4 (1985) 11,231-234.

through the way of Jesus, a way of suffering (Mk 8:34; Mt 10: 38) and denying oneself expressed by taking up one's cross (Mk 8:34; Mt 10:38; 16:24; Lk 9: 23).[6]

2. To be with Jesus and to be Commissioned by Jesus on the Mission

Jesus called the disciples (cf. Mt 4:18-22; 9:9-13; 10:1-4; MK 1:16-20; 3:13-19; Lk 5: 2-11; 6:13-16; Jn 1:40-42) for two main reasons: to be with him and to be sent out to proclaim the Kingdom message (Mk 3:14). The former is for their personal sanctification, conversion and salvation (Mk 2:17). The latter is specifically for the salvation of all (Mt 4:18:22) through the missionary activities, i.e., preach the Kingdom of God, heal the sick, raise the dead, cleanse the lepers and cast out demons (Mk 3:15; 6:12-13; Mt 10:7-8; Lk 10:9,11). Having recognized Jesus as the *Messiah*, the disciples were always with Jesus, except during their special mission (Mk 6:13-30), his prayer in seclusion (Mk 1:35; 6:46; 14:32, 35, 39) and at the moment of his arrest (Mk 14:50). Being with Jesus means to imbibe his spirit and values. The disciples are "to spend some time with their master, seeing and hearing him, and learning whatever it was he wished to teach them."[7]

The disciples are authorized by Jesus to discharge their duties in five ways: preach the Kingdom of God, heal the sick, raise the dead, cleanse the lepers and cast out demons (Mt 10:7-8).

1. The disciples are to proclaim the good news: "The Kingdom of heaven is at hand" (Mt 10:7). Jesus proclaimed the Kingdom of God and brought many people to real conversion of heart. These people with changed heart and mind, caused transformation of the world by their new way of thinking and acting which the preaching of Jesus directly influenced. Thus, the disciples are to preach repentance and proclaim the good tidings to the people for the transformation of the world from its chaos and confusion, and also for restoration of the paradise in the eschatological age (cf. Mk 16:14-18; Lk 24:44-49; Acts 1:4-8; Jn 20:19-23).
2. The disciples are to heal the sick. They are not only to heal the physical sickness but also to heal every disease and sickness (Mt 10:1). Thus, Jesus sent them for ministry of healing which consists the healing of the whole person, i.e., the body, mind and soul.

---

6 Ibid., 235.

7 William Hendriksen, *The Gospel of Mark: New Testament Commentary* (Edinburgh: The Banner of Trust, 1975), 123. The Gospel of Mark lays a heavy emphasis on the role of the disciples in the company of Jesus, and in fact "being with Jesus" is the basis of Marcan discipleship, cf. Raymond E. Brown, Joseph A. Fitzmyer, et al., *The New Jerome Biblical Commentary* (Bangalore: Theological Publications in India, 1999), 604.

3. The disciples are to raise the dead. During his public ministry Jesus raised the dead: raised the daughter of the official (Mt 9:18-19.23-25; Mk 5:21-24. 35-43; Lk 8:40-42.49-56), the son of the widow of Nain (Lk 7:11-15) and Lazarus (Jn 11:38-44). In the New Testament raising the dead was exclusively the work of Jesus. So, when he sent them on their mission, he empowered them with the same power to give life to the dead (Mt 10:7-8).
4. The disciples are to cleanse the lepers. Leprosy was considered unclean so the lepers were ostracized from society and forced them to live in isolation (cf. Lev 13:45-46; Num 5:1-4). If a leper got cured from leprosy he had to show himself to a priest. The priest had the authority to certify his cure from leprosy and purify him, and then only reintegrate him into the society (Lev 14: 1-32). However, Jesus cleansed lepers with great compassion (Mt 8:1-4; Mk 1:40-44; Lk 5:12-14; 17: 11-14).
5. The disciples are to cast out demons. Jesus casted out the demons during his ministry (Mk 1:23-28; 3:11; 5:1-20;9:14-19; Mt 8:28-34; 9:32-33; 12:22; 17:14-18; Lk 4:41; 8:26-39; 9:38-42; 11:14 etc.). Now, he gives this authority to his disciples to put an end to the power of demon by establishing the Kingdom of God on earth.

In short, the call for discipleship demands to be with their master through and through and to engage in the ministries that he had exercised in his earthly ministry.

3. To Be a Light of the World and Salt of the Earth

The disciples are to be the light of the world (Mt 5:14-16; Mk 4:21; Lk 8:16; 11:33), which cause people to transform the world. The main purpose of a lit lamp is to dispel the darkness, illumine the objects, help people to see the objects and lead them into action. As true followers of Jesus, the disciples bear the light of truth to the world by their preaching the Gospel and teachings to enlighten the minds as well as hearts of the people. They also bear witness of Jesus by their own good works and virtuous lives.[8] In their ministries the disciples are to be the salt of the earth to preserve the Gospel teachings (Mt 5:13; Mk 9:50; Lk 14:34-35). The purpose of salt is to preserve things from corruption and to season it. As the material salt savours, preserves and seasons the material food, so the disciples are to savour, preserve and season the spiritual food of mankind, i.e., the Gospel teachings.

8 Charles J. Callan, *The Parables of Christ* (New York City: Joseph F. Wager, Inc., 1946), 269.

4. To Make New Disciples

After the resurrection Jesus extends his authority to his disciples to make new disciples for the Kingdom of God (Mt 28:19-20; Mk 16:15). The very purpose of following Jesus is to go and bear fruit – fruit that will last (Jn15:16), and to make others disciples: "Come, follow me,' Jesus said, 'and I will send you out to fish for people. At once they left their nets and followed him" (Mt 4:19-20). The disciples are to make disciples of all nations by baptizing them in the name of the Holy Trinity and teach them to observe the commandments of Jesus (Mt 28:18-19). In disciple-making, the Risen Christ abides in their midst and helps them in their missionary endeavors. For he is the Emmanuel, "God with us" (Mt 28:20; cf. 1:23).

The mission command in Mt 28:18-20 entails two things: first, the new disciples are to be baptized by water, while using the Trinitarian formula "in the name of the Father and of the son and of the Holy Spirit." That is to say, by baptism a new disciple is incorporated into the family of God and of his Church. Thus, the Christian discipleship is a way of life initiated, based on and centred on the Holy Trinity. Secondly, the disciples are to teach them to observe all the teachings of Christ. One of the most important mission activities of Jesus was teaching. He began to teach the commandments of God right from the beginning of his ministry (Mt 4:23; Mk 1:39), continued to teach throughout his earthly life (Mt 5:2; 7:29; 9:35; 11: 1; 13:54; 21:23). The gospel of the Kingdom should be proclaimed throughout the whole world as a testimony to all nations (Mt 24:14).

5. Deny Oneself and Take up One's Cross

The disciples are to deny their very earthly existence, carry their cross daily and fully share the life and mission of Jesus (Lk 9:23-24). He demands from them to share his life and mission by self-denial (Mk 8:34), by hating themselves (Lk 14:25), and by losing their earthly lives for the sake of the Kingdom of God (Mk 8:35; Mt 10:39; Jn 12:25). To deny oneself and take up one's cross means to consent and contribute to one's gain for the Kingdom of God (Lk 9:23-24). The Greek term *aparneomai*, translated in English as "deny" has the meaning to "disown" or "renounce." Used within the context of the imagery of taking up the cross and following Jesus, "denying oneself" conveys the sense of a person disassociating himself from his self-interest to serve a higher purpose (Mt 16:24; Mk 8:34; Lk 9:23). According to Luke one has to carry his or her difficulties throughout the life and live in conformity with the demands of Jesus.

The cross represents true discipleship (cf. Mt 10:38; 16:24-26; Mk 8:34-35; Lk 9:23-24; 14:27). It is a paradox that one has to lose earthly life in order to gain eternal life (Mt 10:39; Lk 9:24; 17:33; Jn 12:25) or die for the sake of the Gospel (Mk 8:35; 10:29). Yet Jesus says, "What benefit is it to anyone to win the whole world and forfeit or lose his very self?" (Lk 9:25). The disciples have to accept the role of the suffering and rejection that Jesus himself had to carry out through His own passion-death and resurrection (Mk 8:34-9:1).[9]

Cross is inevitable to the disciple who faithfully walks in the footprints of Jesus, for the disciple will be treated as his master was treated. The cross was the consequence of the obedience of Jesus to the will of the Father (Jn 4:34; 6:38; 8:29, 55; 10:17-18; 12:27-28; 14:31). While speaking about his "hour" of glorification (i.e., passion, death and resurrection) Jesus says that it is necessary that a grain of wheat falls to the ground and dies in order to bear much fruit (Jn 12:24). In the same way the disciple has to die to self (Jn 12:25), serve Jesus and follow him on the way to the eternal life (Jn 12:26). Further, Jesus warns them that the world will hate them because of him (Jn 15:18). They will be persecuted (Jn 15:20), expelled from the synagogues and killed (Jn 16:1-2) by the opponents. These events will take place because of two main reasons: first a special union of the disciples with Jesus and secondly, the disciples are "not of the world" (Jn 17:14). Therefore, hatred, persecution and eventually death are part and parcel of following of Jesus. The cross is always present for anyone who really follows Jesus.[10]

In short, Jesus demands his disciples to deny themselves, carry their own cross and follow in the footsteps of Him. Indeed, he teaches and demands that discipleship is calling to live without security. Jesus says "Foxes have holes, birds have nets but the son of man has nowhere to lay His head" (Mt 8:20; Lk 9:58). His followers must decide if they can give up everything and follow Him.

6. Leave Everything

One who follows Jesus radically leaves everything behind. *Aphienai* is a very frequent verb in the Synoptics and the Acts of the Apostles to denote this aspect of discipleship (Mt 47 times; Mk 34; Lk 31; Acts 14). It is used about 15 times in Mk "to mean, to leave", "to abandon" (cf. Mk 13:34; 14:50 etc); 10 times to mean "to suffer", "to permit" (Mk 1:34; 5:19; 11:16; 14:6; 15:36 etc) and 8 times to mean to forgive (Mk 11:25(2); 11:26 (2) etc.) and once at Mk 15:37 to mean "utter." This word represents the external leaving behind of "everything," together with the significance of following Jesus in the path of suffering as a disciple. With this nuance, *aphienai* can be a key word for discipleship in the Synoptics. Disciples leave behind their nets (Mk 1:18; Mt

---

9 Cf. Matura Thaddee, *Gospel Radicalism: The Hard Sayings of Jesus* (New York: Orbis Books, 1984), 45-52.

10 John Karuvelil, Discipleship in the Gospel of John, Indian Journal of spirituality, Vol 11/2 (1998), 238.

4:20). The sons of Zebedee leave their father in the boat with the hired servants (Mk 1:20), leave behind their father and the boat (Mt 4:22), and they leave everything and follow (Mk 10:28; Lk 18:28).

7. Renounce Family and Possessions

Discipleship demands to forsake everything, such as the house, father, mother, brothers, sisters, children or lands for the sake of the Gospel (Mk 10:29). Jesus teaches that anyone who wants to follow him and be his disciple must be ready to pay the cost. In the first place, the disciple must freely break up the family relationship (Mt 8:22) and ready to bear up the brunt of family opposition as well as persecution (Mt 10:34-36). As a true disciple he or she is bound to hate his family because it is the specific demand of Jesus that unless a disciple loves Jesus more than his father, mother, wife, children, brother, sister, property and even his very life, cannot be his disciple (Lk 14:26). In fact, the first disciples left their family and fellow workers to be with Jesus (Mk 1:20; Mt 4:22), who later on assured them that they would attain the eternal life and form a new family in heaven (Lk 18:28-30). Secondly, the disciples must give up all their possessions (Lk 14:33),[11] sell them, and give them to the poor as alms (Lk 12:33). In fact, Peter, Andrew, James, John (Mk 1:16-20), and Levi (Mk 2:13-14), voluntarily broke their business ties when Jesus gave them the invitation to follow him. Such prospective disciples are demanded to sell what they own and give to the needy (Mt 10: 17 -22). Even before they set for their missions, Jesus strictly tells them to take neither gold, silver, coppers for their purse, haversack, bread, nor the spare tunics (Mk 6:8-9), because those who receive their message during evangelization, will provide for their needs (Mk 10:10; Lk 10:7). Adhering to the demands and obeying the commands of Jesus, the disciples are promised an abundant reward, i.e., eternal life (Mk 10:29).[12]

The cost of real discipleship is to renounce or give up all relationships and possessions, i.e., all one has: material things, family, one's own life, desires, plans and interests (Lk 14:33). This radical statement does not mean the rejection of all one has, but that all one has must be placed at the service of others (Lk 13:24; Mt 7:14; Jn 16:33).[13] In the immediate context, the disciple leads a poor life, but it is not the detachment or poverty of an ascetic. In joining Jesus, a disciple radically changes his or her lifestyle and trade, not out of scorn for material goods or family but because of different kind of existence that

11 This saying, "renounce all your possessions" (Lk 14:33) is peculiar to Luke and is a part of a grouping on renunciation common to Matthew (10:37-39) and Luke (12:33; 18:22).

12 Cf. John Karuvelil, Discipleship in the Gospel of John, 238.17-18.

13 Donald C. Stamps and J. Wesley Adams, *The Full Life Study Bible New International Version* (Michigan: Zondervan Publishing House, 1992), 1554.

imposes itself.[14] So, in "the well-to-do people among Jesus' friends (Martha and Mary, Lk 10:38; women who provided for him out of their own resources, Lk 8:3; Mk 15:41; Joseph of Arimathea, Mt 27:57) excludes a literal and legalistic interpretation of this demand but does not invalidate it, especially since these few figures are presented in the very act of giving and sharing."[15]

8. Do not Hoard up Riches on Earth

As an itinerant preacher and harbinger of the Kingdom of God Jesus lived with the poor and experienced the struggles of human life. He allows his disciples to have life's material necessities. But he is aware of the dangers of making the accumulation of material things the goal of one's life.[16] Jesus, therefore, tells his disciples not to over accumulate the material things which are fleeting, being subject to loss from moth and thieves (Lk 12:33). The disciples are obliged to be faithful with regard to the proper use of money and wealth (Lk 16:11).

Although Jesus is an itinerant preacher of the Kingdom, he did not worry about the material possession or for the basic necessities of life (Lk 9:58; Mt 6:25-34; Jn 4:31-34). He generously cares for the poor and disadvantaged, oppressed, down-trodden (Lk 4:18-19), Samaritans (Lk 17:11-129; Jn 4:1-42), lepers (Mt 8:2-43; Lk 17: 11-19), widows (Lk 17:11-25; 20:45-47). Jesus and his disciples gave from their money bag to the poor (12:5-6; 13:29). He used harsh words for those who love worldly possessions (Mk 10:17-25; Lk 6:24-25; 12:16-20; 16:13-15.19-31). He expects his disciples to give generously to the poor and needy (Mt 6:1-4). Fulfilling his commands the disciples cared for the poor and gave them money (Mt 19:21; Lk 12:33; 12:`12-14, 16-24; 18:22).[17]

The disciples are, therefore, exhorted to store up treasures in heaven by concentrating upon the righteousness.[18] Jesus demands that all his disciples be wholehearted in the Kingdom of God and set their hearts on the intangible

---

14 Matura, Gospel Radicalism: The Hard Sayings of Jesus, 29.

15 Dom Bernard Orchard and E. F. Sutcliff, ed., et al, *A Catholic Commentary on Holy Scripture* (London: Thomas Nelson and sons Ltd., 1955), 94-95

16 Clair M. Crissey, *Layman's Bible Book Commentary*, 15 (Nashville: Broadman Press, 1981), 43. A common error of Pharisaism and Judaism in general is the undue emphasis upon material wealth as evident of God's approval (Prov 10:15), cf. Donald C. Stamps and J. Wesley Adams, The Full Life Study Bible New international Version, (Michigan: Zondervan Publishing House, 1992), 1562.

17 Charles F. Pfeiffer ed., et al, *The Wycliffe Bible Commentary* (Chicago: Moody Press, 1978), 1041.

18 Cf. Charles F. Pfeiffer, *The Wycliffe Bible Commentary*, 940.

yet real and permanent treasures of heaven, instead of transient materialism. Therefore, he condemns not wealth as such, but enslavement to wealth.[19]

9. Rely on the Providence of God

The disciples who have committed their lives for the service of the Kingdom are not to worry about the material things, instead they should rely on the providence of God. Jesus cautions His disciples against anxiety concerning food and clothing (Mt 6:25-34). He claims that the life in God is more than necessities of life. He reminds them about God's provisions for the birds of the air, far less valuable to God than human beings (Mt 6:25-26). "Jesus is not advocating a shiftless, thriftless, reckless, thoughtless, improvident attitude to life; He is forbidding a care-worn, worried fear which takes all the joy out of life."[20] It is the care of this world, and the deceitfulness of riches, and the pleasures of this life; silently but surely - choke the world, and no fruit is brought to perfection (Mk 4:7). Jesus reminds that anxiety cannot lengthen the life of a person but only shortens (Mt 6:25-34). He illustrates the futility of the clothes by comparing it with the short-lived lilies of the field (Mt 6:28-30). Actually, an unbeliever worries unnecessarily over the food, drinks, clothing and the future provisions of the life. He chides them that they have to rely on God who is aware of all the needs of His children (Mt 6:31-32). Jesus himself has sought the Kingdom of God and His hearers, who have already given their allegiance to Him, must continue seeking the Kingdom by concentrating upon the spiritual values and resting their full confidence in God (Mt 6:33); and God who knows their temporal needs will supply what is necessary for them in their daily lives.[21] This means that the disciples should seek first the Kingdom of God and his righteousness, rather than worrying about the mundane things.

10. Do the Will of God

The mission of Jesus on earth was to do the will of God, his Father (Jn 4:34; 5:36; 6:38; 8:29; 10:18; 14:23; 17:4). Therefore, his disciples must not follow the majority (Mt 7:13-14), nor run after every teacher (Mt 7:15-20), nor be content with mere professions of loyalty or even with the grace of miracle working (Mt 7:21-23). They must do the will of the Father as declared by the Son; otherwise their efforts are wasted (Mt 7: 24-27).[22]

---

19 Cf. Morris, Leon, *The Gospel According to Matthew* (Michigan: Baker Book House,1982) 152-156.

20 Barclay William, *The Gospel of Matthew* (Bangalore: Theological Publication in India 2001) Vol. 1,225.

21 Charles F. Pfeiffer ed., et al, *The Wycliffe Bible Commentary*, 940.

22 Dom Bernard Orchad, ed., A Catholic Commentary on Holy Scripture (London: Thomas Nelson and Sons Ltd., 1955), 865.

Jesus fulfills the will of God so perfectly in his life (Mt 26:39; Mk 14:36; Lk 22:42; Jn 4:34; 5:30; 6:38) that his disciples are compelled to follow his examples (Acts 2:42-47; 5:12-16). In fact, Jesus is fully aware of his Father's will regarding his mission at every moment of his life. He shows his awareness of his mission to Mary and Joseph at the age of twelve (Lk 2:49), during his public ministry (Mk 1:38f; Lk 4:18-21), at the hour of his agony (Lk 22:42; Mt 26:39), arrest (Mk 15:3-5), on the Cross (Lk 23:34.42.46), and after the resurrection (Jn 20:22-23). He goes on preaching about the Kingdom of God in the world (Mk 1:15), transforms it (Mt 4:23-24; Lk 7:21 ff) and finally ushers it in the eschatological age (Lk 19:10; Jn 20:22-23; Acts 2:3-4; Rev 21:1-27). Jesus warns the disciples against the false prophets who will do and say wonderful and impressive things (Mt 7:21 ff; Acts 19:13). Therefore, Jesus demands that all his disciples must seek first the Kingdom of God (Mt 6:33ff; Acts 5:29) as well as do the will of God. What does it mean to do the will of God? It does not mean the mere work of evangelization that consists of empty words and ceremonies (Mt 7:21-22).[23] But it means to live out a true faith (Mt 7:24-25), a certain hope (Lk 23:42-43) and do a perfect charity (Mt 25:35-40; Lk 10:33ff).

11. Have Faith in Jesus

One of the most fundamental marks of true discipleship is to have faith in Jesus (Jn 1:50; 6:69; 14:11; 16:30; 17:8). For the Gospel of John, a disciple of Jesus is the one who believes in Jesus and remains in Him (Jn 8:31-32). The importance of believing in Jesus is seen right from the beginning of the Gospel of John (Jn 1:7.12), which finally reaches its climax when Thomas fully surrenders himself to Jesus in faith (Jn 20:28).[24]

Believing in Jesus basically means to have faith in Jesus. This faith leads one to believe that Jesus is the Christ, the Son of God (Jn 20:31). It is to believe in the very person of Jesus (Jn 4:21; 5:38.46; 6:30; 8:31.45-46; 10:37-38; 14:11), his words (Jn 2:22; 4:50; 5:47), and his works (Jn 10:38). Thus, we can say that the disciples' faith in Jesus should be Christo-centric in character.

John develops disciples' belief in Jesus in three stages:

23 C.H. Spurgeon, *Spurgeon's Popular Exposition of Matthew* (Michigan: Baker Book House, 1981), 45.

24 The term *pisteuein* (to believe) occurs 98 times in John's Gospel and it can be found in all the sections of John's Gospel (Jn 2:11.23; 4:42, 53; 6:68-69; 9:38; 10:42; 11:27; 16:30; 20:28-31) except in the appendix (Jn 21), cf. John Karuvelil, Discipleship in the Gospel of John, 228. See also Mathew Vellanickal, *Studies in the Gospel of John* (Bangalore: Asian Trading Corporation 1982), 114; George Mlakuzhiyil, *The Christo-Centric Literary Structure of the Fourth Gospel* (Roma Editrice Pontifico Biblico 1987), 287.

1. To believe in Jesus by accepting the claims of Jesus (Jn 4:21; 5:24.38.46.47; 8: 31.45-46; 10:25.26.38 and 14:11).
2. To believe in Jesus' by accepting his identity and mission (cf. 6:69; 11:42; 17:8)
3. To believe in Jesus' assurance of eternal life (Jn 3:16.18; 6:9.35.40; 7:5.31.38.48; 8:30; 11:25.26.45.48; 12:11.36. 37.42.44.46; 14:1.12 etc.).

John himself presents people who have gone through these stages of belief in Jesus: the first disciples (Jn 1:41.45.49-50), the royal official (Jn 4:50), the Samaritan woman and the Samaritans (Jn 4:1-42), Peter (6:69), Martha (Jn 11:27), the disciples (Jn16:30), Thomas (Jn 20:28) etc. In short, faith in Jesus "involves an acknowledgement and acceptance that Jesus has been sent into the world by God to reveal the Father, to do his will as the Son and also to acknowledge and accept that in and through Jesus we have eternal life, which in turn demands an active commitment."[25]

12. Bearing Witness to Jesus

One of the most joyful experiences of being a disciple is to share one's experience of Jesus with others, and this is exemplified by "bearing witness" to Jesus. As Jesus has borne witness to his Father (Jn 3:11.32-33; 5:31), the truth (Jn 18:37) and to himself (Jn 3:33; 5:31; 8:13.14.18), Jesus asks his disciples to bear witness to him (Jn 15:26-27).

John the Baptist bears witness to Jesus (Jn 1:7.8.15.32.34; 3:26; 5:33): he was sent by God to bear witness to Jesus (Jn 1:6); he speaks about Jesus to the people (Jn 1:15.29-34), to the people who came from Jerusalem (Jn 1:19-28), and to his own disciples (Jn 1:3: 3:25-30). Andrew testifies his brother Simon that he met Jesus, the Messiah (Jn 1:41). Philip testifies to Nathanael that he has found "the one Moses wrote about in the Law, and about whom the prophets also wrote—Jesus of Nazareth, the son of Joseph" (Jn 1:45). The whole town of Samaritans believed in Jesus because of the testimony of the Samaritan woman (Jn 4:39-42). The crowds bear witness to Jesus (Jn 12:17). The disciple whom Jesus loved, bears witness to him (Jn 19:35; 21:24). The believer must bear witness to Jesus as he has born witness to the Father (Jn 3:11.32-33; 5:31).

Having met with Jesus, Martha informs Mary that the Master is calling her (Jn 11:28). After her encounter with the Risen Lord, Mary Magdalene hurries back and bears witness to Jesus' resurrection to the disciples: "I have seen the Lord" (Jn 20:18). Another concrete example of a true witness is the man born blind who got sight from Jesus (Jn 9:1-14). He was healed both of his physical and spiritual blindness and so he believed in Jesus. His personal

25 John Karuvelil, Discipleship in the Gospel of John, 231.

encounter with Jesus gave him faith and courage to witness Jesus even before the Pharisees who expelled him from the synagogue.[26]

In short, having experienced Jesus, disciples bear witness to Jesus to others. Bearing witness of Jesus is the responsibility of every believer. Every believer is a disciple (cf. Jn 9:27-28) and every disciple is necessarily a witness. [27] In other words, no one can bear witness to Jesus unless he/she has a personal experience of Jesus. And no one can keep quiet after having an experience of Jesus, but has to share with others and bring them to Jesus.

13. Abide, Love and Serve

Abiding in Jesus's words is another characteristic of true discipleship. Jesus says: "If you abide in my word, you are my disciples indeed. And you shall know the truth, and the truth shall make you free" (Jn 8:31-32). Thus, abiding in Jesus' words becomes an imperative for knowing the truth that makes the disciples free. Disciples' abiding presence in Jesus is characterized by three imperatives: first of all abiding in his word (Jn 8:31; 15:7) and obeying his commandments (Jn 14:15; 15:10); secondly to heed and keep the Father's word (Jn14:24); and thirdly to abide in his love (Jn 15:9-10). This mutual abiding presence is illustrated in the imagery of the wine and the branches (Jn 15:1-8). Just as the branches of wine cannot bear fruit by themselves, the disciples of Jesus cannot bear fruits without him.

To be a true disciple of Jesus is to abide in his love (Jn 15:9-10). Love becomes the imperative of recognizing someone as Jesus' disciple: "A new commandment I give to you, that you love one another; as I have loved you, that you also love one another. By this all will know that you are my disciples, if you have love for one another" (Jn 13:34-35). The only one commandment that Jesus gave to his disciples is to "love one another" (Jn 13:34; 15:12.17). Moreover, Jesus makes love as a criterion of discipleship: "If you will love me you will keep my commandments" (Jn 14:15). The emphasis of love is so much that it is repeated four times in just ten verses in Jn 14:15-24.[28]

Reciprocal love of the disciples is to be based on the love that Jesus has for them: "Love one another as I have loved you" (Jn 13:34; 15:12). The love of Jesus for his disciples is similar to the love of the Father for Jesus (Jn l5:9). Therefore, disciples' love for one another should be patterned after Father's love towards Jesus. Just as, Jesus manifested his love towards the Father by doing his will (Jn 4:34; 14:31; 15:10), the disciples should also manifest their love towards Jesus by keeping his commandments (Jn 14:21.23).

26 Ibid., 238-41

27 Cf. John Kurichianil, Bearing witness to Jesus, *Bible Bhashyam*, XX/3 (1994), September, 200.

28 George Mlakuzhiyil, *The Christo-centric Literary Structure of the Fourth Gospel*, 285.

Jesus manifests his love for disciples by loving them to the end (Jn 13:1), even to the extent of laying down his life for others (Jn 10:17-18; 15:13), and this becomes an imperative for his followers. He shows his love to the disciples by washing their feet (Jn 33: 1-20). Here, Jesus teaches the disciples that love is concretized only in the service of one another, in other words, the greatest needs to be the servant of all. Jesus says: "I have set you an example that you also should do as I have done to you" (Jn13:15). Jesus loved his disciples as his own and called them his friends and partner of his mission (Jn 15:14-15). He loves them and gives examples to them, so that they love one another (Jn 13:34). The type of love that Jesus expects his disciples to practice is "a selfless, self-sacrificing and another-oriented love".[29]

The disciple who abides in Jesus and loves Jesus will be also ready to serve him (Jn 12:26). Jesus has categorically exhorted them that the greatest among them should be their servant (Mt 23:11; Mk 9:35). Whoever wants to be first must be their slave, just as the Son of Man did not come to be served, but to serve, and to give his life as a ransom for many (Mt 20:27-28; Mk 10:45). The rulers of the gentiles lord it over them, and their great men exercise authority over them. But it should not be the "way" among the disciples but whoever wishes to become great among them shall be their servant, and whoever wishes to be first among them shall be slave of all (Mark 10:42-44).

14. Manifesting Worthy Fruits

The disciples are expected to produce worthy fruits of repentance and faith. John the Baptist, while preaching the baptism of repentance for forgiveness of their sins, demanded that all must produce fruits to match repentance (Lk 3:3-18).[30] In order to produce worthy fruits of repentance first they must be baptized with the water as a sign of repentance (Lk 3:3-14). Secondly, there should be a selfless concern for one's disadvantaged brothers and sisters (Lk 3:10-11; 19:8). Thirdly, they must live a righteous life (Lk 3:13; 5:7.10.32; 18:13-14). Fourthly, they must be just and humane (Lk 3:14; 7:5-8; 23:47; Acts 10:1-2). Fifthly, they must be baptized with the Holy Spirit and fire (Lk 3:21-22) that will be brought by Jesus Christ (Jn 14:26; Acts 1:5; 2:1-4; 11:16).[31]

The disciples are expected to manifest the integrity of life in their perfect Christian way of life. The disciples hold the fivefold ministries (Eph 4:11)- apostle (1 Cor 3:10; I Cor 12:12), prophet (1 Cor 14:29), evangelist (Acts 8:6-7), pastor and teacher. So, for the evangelization of the world they must manifest in their lives the fruits of the Holy Spirit that is love, joy, peace, patience, kindness, goodness, truthfulness, gentleness and self-control (Gal

29 John Karuvelil, Discipleship in the Gospel of John, 241-44.

30 Barclay, *The Gospel of Luke*, 32-35.

31 Raymond E. Brown, Joseph A. Fitzmer, et al, The New Jerome Biblical Commentary, 686.

5:22). They should also witness the gifts of wisdom (Mt 22:17-22), knowledge (Jn 4:18), faith (Acts 27:21-25), healing (Acts 3:6-7), miracles (Acts 13:11), prophecy (Acts 21:9), discerning of Spirits (Acts 8:20), tongues (1 Cor 14:4-5; Acts 10:45-46), interpretation of tongues (l Cor 14:13). They should manifest that they are gifted for the functions of prophecy (1 Cor 14:3; Acts 21:9), ministry or service (1 Cor 12:28, Acts 6:2-3), teaching (Acts 18:24-25), exhortation (Heb 3:13, Acts 2:40), giving (Acts 4:36- 37), and gift of mercy (Acts 9:36) etc.

Conclusion

Jesus calls us to his discipleship and to share in his mission and bring him known to the world around us, and the demands of Jesus on discipleship are straight, clear and immediate. It requires a committed response, readiness to leave everything, detachment to forsake family ties, ability to walk through the way of Jesus, a way of suffering, and denying oneself by taking up one's cross. They are called to be with him and to be sent out to proclaim the Kingdom message. Consequently they become light of the world and salt of the earth. Founded themselves in the teachings of their master, accepting his identity and mission, they bear witness to their master by producing worthy fruits in their life. Abiding in his words and love, and emptying themselves as a servant, they reach out to the needy and marginalized and to those who need to experience God's mercy. Relying on the providence of God, they communicate God's providential love to everyone in the cosmos. By seeking and doing the will of their Lord, they fulfill the mission of their master, and live out the true faith in hope and perfect charity. In short, as Douglas rightly says, "it involved personal allegiance to him, expressed in following him and giving him an exclusive loyalty (Mk 8:34-38; Lk 14:26-33). At least in some cases it meant literal abandonment of home, business ties and possessions (Mk 10:21, 28), but in every case readiness to put the claims of Jesus first, whatever the cost, was demanded. Such an attitude went beyond the normal pupil - teacher relationship and gave the word 'disciple' a new sense."[32]

32 J.D. Douglas, *New Bible Dictionary Om Books* (Secundarabad: Om Books, 1997), 285.

Ministering the LOGOS

12

The Pedagogy of Jesus
A Relevant Model for Effective Teaching

Jacob Parappally, MSFS

Introduction

Teaching was an important part of the prophetic ministry of Jesus. We may be surprised to know that of the 90 times Jesus was addressed directly, 60 times he was addressed as teacher. Some consider him, *the teacher* and not just nay teacher. Others consider him, *the master teacher*. Though it is not easy to know the style of his teaching from the Gospels we have enough testimony from the Gospel narratives the content of Jesus' teaching and the pedagogical methods he employed in communicating it. Though both the Synoptic Gospels and the Gospel of John present Jesus as a teacher, we find the role of Jesus as an ethical or moral teacher prominently in the Gospel according to Matthew. What we know about Jesus as a teacher as different from all other teachers of his time is that he taught with authority unlike the scribes of Jesus' time who were considered to have certain authority due to their knowledge of the Scripture as well as their scholarship concerning matters of theology. In comparison with the Jewish teachers Jesus was acclaimed by the people as one with authority. Both Mark and Matthew refer to the authority of Jesus a teacher. "And they went into Capernaum; and immediately on the Sabbath he entered the synagogue and taught. And they were astonished at his teaching, for he taught them as one who had authority, and not as the scribes (Mk 1:21-22; cf. Mt 7:29). Both the authority of his person and his teaching made such an impact on the lives of the people who listened to him that they were transformed to have a new vision about themselves, God, others and the world. Jesus was a unique teacher. His words were effective and so his teaching was transformative.

We do not have any systematic presentation of the pedagogical methods Jesus followed in communicating his transformative message. Even the content of his teaching presented in the Gospels is an interpretation of it in the light of the resurrection experience as well as according to the need of the of the community for which they were originally composed and edited. Therefore, the primary concern of the Gospel narratives is to present the person of Jesus Christ as the one whom the disciples encountered in history as "a prophet mighty in deed and word before God and all the people" (Lk 24:19). He taught his disciples as well as the people who came to listen to him and to get healed of their sicknesses. So it is certain that he taught.

We can search in the Gospels for the pedagogy he employed in his teaching to get an insight into his way of teaching that may help us to evolve our own pedagogy in communicating the message of the Gospel effectively. According to George Soares Prabhu, "No systematic 'discourse' of Jesus on his educational theory has come down to us. And even the occasional sayings of his that might throw light on his pedagogy are available to us only in the loose collections of the sayings of Jesus that we find in the Gospels; and these have been strung together thematically with little reference to the original circumstances in which they uttered."[1]

The teaching of Jesus was not according to the traditions of the scribal schools which trained the student to become trained interpreters of the Law. Even though Jesus taught mainly in the villages both the content of his teaching and the pedagogical methods he followed in communicating his message were unique as his person. So also the message and the objective of his teaching were unique. In this paper an attempt is made only to explain mainly the various pedagogical methods he followed and it can be shown that his ways of teaching was effective in transforming the lives of those who listened to his teaching. However, we would also explain briefly the relationship of Jesus with the disciples and the people who listened to his teaching, the content of his teaching and the objective of his teaching before we see the methods he employed in his teaching.

1 George M. Soaraest Prabhu, *A Bibilical Theology for India: Collected Writings of George M .Soares Prabhu,* ed. Scaria Kuthirakkattel SVD (Pune: Jnana-Deepa Vidyapeth, 1999), 141-142.

1. Relationship of Jesus with Whom He Taught

The Gospels narrate to us that Jesus had a personal relationship with his disciples and a very empathetic relationship with the crowd that came to listen to his teaching. At the time Jesus and even in our times those who want to learn anything formally seek admission from an institution where he or she wants learn or approach any teacher seeking permission to be a student. Jesus did not wait for the disciples to come to him. In the Synoptic Gospels we find that unlike the rabbis of his time Jesus went out and called the disciples to himself (Mt 4:18-22; Mk 1:16-34; Lk 5:1-11). Mark clearly expresses the purpose of calling the twelve. "And he [Jesus] went up on the mountain, and called to him those whom he desired; and they came to him. And he appointed twelve, to be with him, and to be sent out to preach and have authority to cast out demons" (Mk 3:13-15). He called the disciples *to be with* him so that by their personal relationship with Jesus they were empowered with the authority to preach and heal. Jesus' authority or *exousia* originates from his intimate relationship with his Father whom he called *Abba.* The disciples' authority must come from their intimate union with Jesus.

In Jesus' style of formation the attitude of servant-hood is the quality of the master. It involves a patient waiting with confident optimism that the disciples' 'little faith' will be transformed into self-sacrificing love. Jesus had tremendous respect for his disciples as well as trust in them. Even when he was disappointed at their lack of understanding his teaching he did not abandon his ministry of teaching. He did not force them to accept his teaching. He offered them his insights into the mystery of human life in relation to God and the world as he experienced it from his *Abba.* He did not impose his vision on them but invited them to share his vision. He taught them to see the entire reality of God, humans and the world differently. It was a different vision of reality because he was not a rabbi like other teachers of the Jewish religion. His centre of life was not the traditions that enslaved but God who liberated. His was not a religion of temple, rituals and laws but a religion of love, justice, equality, reconciliation and communion. It was a radically new vision. One needs a conversion of mind and heart, ways of thinking and relating in order to enter into that vision of Jesus. Being a wise teacher he does not provide a blue-print for his disciples to execute, but opens the minds of his disciples to a vision that they can commit themselves to and actualize creatively and uniquely in their own way but always remaining faithful to him, the Master.

Within the group of the Twelve, three belonged to the inner circle of disciples. They were Peter, James and John who were alone the witnesses of certain important events during Jesus' public ministry. They were present at the transfiguration of Jesus (Mk 9:2-3); they witnessed the raising of Jairus' daughter (Lk 8:49-56) and they accompanied Jesus to the Garden of

Gethsemane (Mt 26:36-38). In all probability, Jesus had a closer relationship with these three disciples. They were expected to know more about his person and his message.

Besides the Twelve Jesus had other disciples whom he taught. Luke mentions 70 other disciples of Jesus whom he sent two by two into towns and villages. "After this the Lord appointed seventy others, and sent them on ahead of him, two by two, into every town and place where he himself was about to come" (Lk 10:1). They were given special instructions how they should prepare themselves for the journey and how they should conduct themselves during their ministry of preaching and healing (Lk 10:2-11). Then there were also other people whom Jesus taught. They are often mentioned in the Gospels as "the crowd". They were the masses who flocked to him and listened to his teaching. They were the ones marginalized and considered outcasts by the Pharisees and the Scribes.

> Rabbinic disdain for the masses is evidenced also in the failure of the rabbis to mount any sort of outreach program to them. Perhaps the school of the patriarch was a real "academy," a perpetual institution with a corporate identity and a hierarchical structure, but the schools of other rabbis were nothing more than disciple circles. A single master was surrounded at all times by a handful of apprentices who attended their master like servants in order to learn from his every action... Needless to say, a limited number of masters teaching a limited number of disciples in a limited number of disciple circles was not the vehicle for mass education. Furthermore, there is no indication that the tannaim [teachers] ever attempted to propagate their teachings among the masses On the contrary, Judah the Patriarch, in whose time the rabbinic establishment entered the cities and broadened its social base, decreed that Torah was not to be taught in the marketplace. Like the thighs of a woman, Torah was to be kept covered in public. Presumably he was afraid of casting the pearls before swine.[2]

Jesus was a different type of rabbi. He had compassion for the crowd who came to listen to him. He treated everyone who came to him as a human person. He did not exclude anyone. He did not insist on having only a particular group to teach or that he would teach only at a particular place or at a particular time. He taught anywhere he found people who were willing to listen to him at anywhere and at any time. Matthew narrates: "And he went about all Galilee, teaching in their synagogues and preaching the gospel of the kingdom and

2 Cohen SJD, "The Place of Rabbi in Jewish Society of the Second Century", ed. L.I. Levine (New York: Jewish Theological Seminary of America, 1992), 162

healing every disease and every infirmity among the people" (Mt 4:23). We find him teaching on the mountains (Mt 5:1-12, 15:29-30) and on the seashore, "He went out again beside the sea; and all the crowd gathered about him, and he taught them" (Mk 2:13). We find Jesus teaching at the temple (Lk 19:47), in the cornfields (Mk 2:23-28; Mt 12:1-8) and even at a chief Pharisees house (Lk 14:1). No place or institution defined his teaching. His mission defined his teaching. He taught with authority, he taught everyone who was willing to listen to him and he taught everywhere he found someone to listen to him. The people were amazed at his teaching. "And when Jesus had finished these parables, he went away from there,[54] and coming to his own country he taught them in their synagogue, so that they were astonished, and said, "Where did this man get this wisdom and these mighty works?" (Mt 13:53-54). From the various narratives of the Gospels we get some indications of the pedagogical methods he employed to communicate his wisdom.

2. The Pedagogical Methods of Jesus the Teacher

When we look at the entire teaching of Jesus as narrated in the Gospels we can find that Jesus had some clear objectives for his teaching. He was not sharing some information about God's relation with humans or about the Kingdom of God or about judgment and final destiny of humans. As any good and wise teacher Jesus wanted the disciples and all his listeners be transformed by his teaching. The heart of his education was the education of the heart[3]. The disciples needed to have a close personal relationship with him. The crowd that came to listen to his teaching experienced him as the one who recognized, accepted, respected and loved them. He had table-fellowship or commensality with them. The accusation against Jesus was that he was eating with outcasts and sinners. "And the scribes of the Pharisees, when they saw that he was eating with sinners and tax collectors, said to his disciples, "Why does he eat with tax collectors and sinners?" (Mk 2:16). His teaching was effective because he cultivated a personal relationship with those who came to listen to him. Without a loving and respectful relationship with his or her students no teacher can be effective in communicating that knowledge which transforms the lives of the students. Information about anything can be communicated without any relationship with the students but formation is possible only through a personal relationship with the students. Jesus' teaching about "the way of God" (Mt 22:16) could not have been communicated without his personal relationship with his disciples and the crowd that came to listen to him.

Though no 'systematic theology' of education has down to us from Jesus, it is clear from the Gospel narratives that various methods of effective communication were used by Jesus when he taught his disciples and the crowd.

---

3 The purpose of education according to Servant of God Fr Peter Mermier (1790 -1862).

If we appreciate Jesus' method of teaching with the theories of educational models since the second part of 20th century like Bloom's taxonomy[4] we will be surprised to find that 20 centuries ago Jesus used the methods of education in his teaching to communicate his message effectively. According to Bloom's taxonomy, at the cognitive level students must be taken from knowledge to comprehension followed by application and analysis, evaluation and finally synthesis. In the revised version of Bloom's taxonomy the same ideas are expanded: remembering, understanding, applying, analyzing, evaluating and creating. For example: we can see the different questions of Jesus raised when teaching at all the six levels:

- *Knowledge/Remembering*: Jesus asks a question to the Pharisees and Herodians: "Whose likeness and inscription is this?" (Mk 12:17).
- *Comprehension/ Understanding*: "What man of you, if his son asks him for bread, will give him a stone?" (Mt 7:9).
- *Application/Applying*: "But if God so clothes the grass which is alive in the field today and tomorrow is thrown into the oven, how much more will he clothe you?" (Lk 12:28).
- *Analysis/Analyzing:* "How can you say to your brother, `Let me take the speck out of your eye,' when there is the log in your own eye?" (Mt 7:4).
- *Synthesis/Evaluating:* "Who do you say that I am" (Mt 16:15; Mk 8:29).
- *Evaluation / Creating:* "What does it profit a man, to gain the whole world and forfeit his life?" (Mk 8:36).

Many of the pedagogical methods of Bloom's taxonomy both the earlier one and the revised one can be found in Jesus' way teaching through parables. Probably to emphasize this Matthew narrates: "All this Jesus said to the crowds in parables; indeed he said nothing to them without a parable" (Mt 13:34). Mark says, "And he taught them many things in parables" (Mk 4:2), and further he says, "With many such parables he spoke the word to them, as they were able to hear it; he did not speak to them without a parable, but privately to his own disciples he explained everything" (Mk 4:33-34). Certainly Jesus used other methods of teaching the disciples and the crowd. Probably, Mark is reminding the reader that there is a 'parabolic' character to all the public teaching of Jesus. All what Jesus said and did and his own person had a parabolic character in the sense that it was the disclosure of the secret of the Kingdom of God. This

4 The models of educational learning devised by Benjamin Bloom and a team of educators from 1949-1953. It came to be known as Bloom's taxonomy. It classified educational learning objectives in cognitive, affective and sensory domains. The cognitive level learning is the primary focus of traditional education. The revised Bloom's taxonomy published in 2001 is an elaboration of the original classification.

disclosure comes not by the use of power but by his lowliness and suffering.[5] Jesus used parables in teaching to enter into dialogue with those who listened to him in order to lead them to critical thinking and positive response. All who were open to his teaching were transformed. Those observers of his teaching remained unaffected by his teaching and some of them became hostile to him and tried to eliminate him. Teaching as a profession by giving specific and thematic information to the students may be harmless. But teaching as a vocation to transform the students to become better humans can be dangerous! Think of Socrates and Jesus!

The use of parables or stories in teaching is very effective in communication of a message as it evokes thinking in the mind of the students. "The parables of Jesus are dialogical. They do not convey information, offer prescriptions, or give lessons to a passive and receptive listener. Instead, by telling a 'shocking' story, they provoke and tease the listener into a radically new insight into his own situation, which the parable has put before him in story form" [6] The parable which prophet Nathan tells David in 2 Samuel 12:1-7) is the best example of it. David was shocked by the story when it was brought to his awareness that he was the wrong-doer of the parable. Then he accepted that he had done wrong and repented over it. Jesus told parables to evoke such responses. His parables are not moral stories like Aesop's fables or *panchatantra* tales. Jesus' parables have no closure or ending. If at all we find some ending of the story, it is added by the final redactors of the New Testament. When Jesus spoke in parables, the listener was expected to supply the lesson as it applies to him or her. This response of the listener is integral to Jesus' parables. It involves, dialogue, personal reflection, critical thinking, ability to relate the insights of the parable with the actual life and the life-situation of the listener and the readiness to correct and re-orient one's life according to the demands of the message of God communicated to the listener. Certainly, one is free to accept or reject it. Only one who is willing to change his or her ways of life responding to the insights of the parable completes the story.

In Jesus teaching both through the parables and other ways of communicating about the way of God we can find following pedagogical strategies. He used questioning, analysis and reasoning, illustrations, demonstrations with tangible objects, hyperboles, comparisons, contrasts and analogies, teaching by enacting,, using historical references, using news items

---

5 George M. Soaraest Prabhu, *A Bibilical Theology for India: Collected Writings of George M.Soares Prabhu,* ed. Scaria Kuthirakkattel SVD (Pune: Jnana-Deepa Vidyapeth, 1999), 150.

6 Ibid., 150

and referring to context, participatory and praxis-oriented teaching, repetitions etc. [7]

2.1. Questioning

Posing a question by a teacher makes the students think as they are expected to answer the question. For various reasons Jesus asked questions to his disciples, to the crowd and to the Scribes and the Pharisees. Sometimes it was to clarify concepts and de-construct their ideas about God, religion, human beings and the world and to challenge them to construct a liberating vision about what matters important in one's life. Jesus asks the question, "Does not each of you on the Sabbath untie his ox or his ass from the manger, and lead it away to water it? [16] And ought not this woman, a daughter of Abraham whom Satan bound for eighteen years, be loosed from this bond on the Sabbath day?" (Lk 13:15-16) or "Have you not read what David did, when he was hungry, and those who were with him: how he entered the house of God and ate the bread of the Presence, which it was not lawful for him to eat nor for those who were with him, but only for the priests? Or have you not read in the law how on the Sabbath the priests in the temple profane the Sabbath, and are guiltless?" (Mt 12:3-5). Such questions require the listener to deconstruct some of the ideas about religion which he or she had accepted without reasoning or questioning. Sometimes the questions are asked to correct their erroneous thinking. For example: "Do you not say, 'There are yet four months, then comes the harvest'? I tell you, lift up your eyes, and see how the fields are already white for harvest" (Jn 4:35).

Sometimes questions are asked to make the disciple to call to their mind and understand an important event that had happened in Jesus' public ministry so that they remain open to receive new insights. For example, Jesus' question to disciples when they informed him that they had no bread with them: "Do you not yet perceive? Do you not remember the five loaves of the five thousand, and how many baskets you gathered? Or the seven loaves of the four thousand, and how many baskets you gathered?" (Mt 16:9-10). Jesus' questions open up a new perception and a new understanding about Jesus the questioner, the self-understanding of the questioned and the matter which the question raises. Jesus raises questions in order to empower the listener with a new and transforming perception and vision and not to belittle those who listened to him. From these examples it is clear that questions are one of the powerful methods of teaching. More than century ago, one of the educationist Charles DeGarmo said, "To question well is to teach well". Further he says: "In the skillful use of the question more than anything else lies the fine art of

7 Some of these methods are mentioned in https://www.slideshare.net/debbiealam/jesus-the-teacherlessons-from-the-master-teacher?next_slideshow=1

teaching; for in such use we have the guide to clear vivid ideas, the quick spur to imagination, the stimulus to thought, the incentive to action."[8] Besides these, Jesus used to ask questions skillfully to the disciples and his other listeners that they might discover the truth that sets them free.

Perhaps, the most important question that Jesus asked his disciples was: "Who do you say that I am" (Mt 16:16; Mk 8:29). It is not a question at the cognitive level. It is also a question at the affective level. It involves not only the head but also the heart. It involves the entire person. The answer to that question involves the identity of Jesus as well as the identity of the person who answers that question. It is a disclosure from 'above'. One must accept it with total self-surrender. Otherwise, one would get drowned in the stormy water of confusion and Jesus would ask yet another question, "Why did you doubt?" (Mt 14:31). One's surrender to the disclosure from above leads one to the truth about God, his self-manifestation in Jesus Christ, about oneself and the world. Jesus' questions subvert the dehumanizing myths about God and the world and one's understanding about oneself. Jesus' questions open up new horizons for humans for their self-discovery and a critical understanding of the existing society and its enslaving power structures including religion and evoke convictions to challenge them.

2.2. Analysis and Reasoning

During his teaching Jesus invited his listeners to use their intellectual capacity for analyzing and reasoning. They were not supposed to accept anything including his teaching blindly. He was aware that the religious leaders of his times enslaved the people by instilling in them the fear of a punishing God. The cause of the poverty and misery of the people as well as their physical, psychological, social and spiritual sicknesses were attributed to their sins and the consequent punishment of God. Thus they were told to believe that they were under the power of the Satan or the evil spirits. For example: Jesus asks the crowd, "If Satan casts out Satan, he is divided against himself; how then will his kingdom stand? … But if it is by the Spirit of God that I cast out demons, then the kingdom of God has come upon you. Or how can one enter a strong man's house and plunder his goods, unless he first binds the strong man?" (Mt 12:26-29). Jesus does not want a blind acceptance of his teaching. The listeners are encouraged to use their capacity for analyzing and reasoning.

2.3. Illustrations

An effective teacher employs illustrations or examples from familiar things and events in his or her life to make clear to the students abstract ideas or spiritual truths. Jesus explains the truth about the Kingdom of God, the ways

8 Charles DeGarmo, Interest and Education (New York: McMillan Publ., 1911), p. 179

of God and human responses and so on with examples taken from the nature and from the events from the ordinary lives of the people of his times. Some of the examples of such illustrations in his teaching are: "Enter by the narrow gate; for the gate is wide and the way is easy, that leads to destruction, and those who enter by it are many. For the gate is narrow and the way is hard, that leads to life, and those who find it are few. "Beware of false prophets, who come to you in sheep's clothing but inwardly are ravenous wolves. You will know them by their fruits. Are grapes gathered from thorns, or figs from thistles?" (Mt 7:13-16). How many examples are given in these three verses! The Gospels are replete with such illustrations: the blind leading the blind (Mt 15:14), the thief breaking into the house unexpectedly (Mt 24:23) etc.

2.4. Comparisons, Contrasts and Analogies

To communicate an idea with clarity and to emphasize the point a teacher may use comparisons and contrasts. Jesus used such comparisons and contrasts very effectively in teaching his disciples and the crowd. In the first discourse of the Gospel of Matthew known as the Sermon on the Mount Jesus contrasts his teaching with the understanding and practices of the Old Testament times (Mt 5:21-48). "You have heard that it was said to the men of old, `You shall not kill; and whoever kills shall be liable to judgment.' But I say to you that everyone who is angry with his brother shall be liable to judgment; whoever insults his brother shall be liable to the council, and whoever says, `You fool!' shall be liable to the hell of fire"(Mt 5:21-22). In the Synoptic Gospels there are many parables which use comparisons and contrasts; the speck and the log (Mt 7:1-5); new cloth on old garment (Mt 9:16-17; Mk 2:21-22); the divided kingdom (Mt 12:24-30; Mk 3:23-27); the weeds among the wheat (Mt 13:24-30); the unforgiving servant (Mt 18:23-35); the two sons (Mt 21:25-32); the faithful servant and the wicked servant (Mt 24:45-51; Mk 13:34-37); the ten virgins (Mt 25:1-13); rich man and Lazarus (Lk 16:19-31), the Pharisee and the tax collector (18:9-14). The comparisons and contrasts are very vivid in these parables. There are many such comparisons and contrasts in the various sayings of Jesus as narrated in the Gospels. Jesus used also similes, metaphors which are developed into analogies to clarify the themes of importance which Jesus wanted to teach his disciples and the crowd. Jesus says, "But to what shall I compare this generation? It is like children sitting in the market places and calling to their playmates, `We piped to you, and you did not dance; we wailed, and you did not mourn"(Mt 11:16-17). Jesus' observation about the life of the Pharisees and Scribes is expressed using metaphors and analogies. You blind Pharisee! first cleanse the inside of the cup and of the plate, that the outside also may be clean. "Woe to you, scribes and Pharisees, hypocrites! For you are like whitewashed tombs, which outwardly appear beautiful, but within they are full of dead men's bones and all uncleanness" (Mt 23:26-27). The ability of a teacher to use of imageries to emphasize what he/teaches makes the students remember vividly the content of what is taught.

2.5. Hyperboles

Hyperbole is an exaggerated statement or a claim that is not meant to be understood literally. Jesus used hyperboles in order to emphasize and to bring to the understanding of his listeners that some of their inherited beliefs were absolutely wrong. At the time of Jesus the poor believed that their poverty was a curse of God or a punishment of God and richness was a sign of God's favour. To remove from the minds of his listeners such a false notion of God whom Jesus experienced as a loving, infinitely generous and unconditionally forgiving God, he taught the listeners that it was easy for a camel to go through the eye of a needle than a rich man to enter heaven or his condemnation of the Pharisees who used to take care of unimportant details of law and neglect the most important of them. Jesus says: "You blind guides, straining out a gnat and swallowing a camel!" (Mt 23:24). He reminds those who judge others for their small failures and do not see their grave faults using a hyperbole: "Why do you see the speck that is in your brother's eye, but do not notice the log that is in your own eye? (Mt 7:3). The power of hyperbole in communication is such that it immediately challenges the listener with the seriousness of the matter that is communicated. Jesus used it effectively in his teaching.

2.6. Demonstrations with Tangible Objects

Demonstrations used during teaching can make the students understand the matter that is taught with better clarity. It is easy for them to remember the theme of discussion when they associate with the object that is used by the teacher to explain the matter. Sometimes Jesus used objects or pointed to persons in order to explain the truth about the Kingdom of God or to defend his teaching before others who try to discredit him. When some Pharisees and Herodians came to Jesus and asked him: "Is it right to pay taxes to Caesar or not? Jesus told them: "Show me the money for the tax." And they brought him a coin. And Jesus said to them, "Whose likeness and inscription is this? They said, "Caesar's." Then he said to them, "Render therefore to Caesar the things that are Caesar's, and to God the things that are God's" (Mt 22: 19-21). To teach his disciples an important value they should have in their lives he gives the example of a child. "And he sat down and called the twelve; and he said to them, "If anyone would be first, he must be last of all and servant of all." And he took a child, and put him in the midst of them; and taking him in his arms, he said to them, "Whoever receives one such child in my name receives me; and whoever receives me, receives not me but him who sent me" (Mk 9:35-

37). To teach the disciples that God cares about them more than all creatures, he asks them: "Look at the birds of the air: they neither sow nor reap nor gather into barns, and yet your heavenly Father feeds them. Are you not of more value than they?" (Mt 6:26). An efficient and effective teacher uses all the means at his/her disposal to demonstrate to the students the deeper meaning of what he/ she teaches.

2.7. Teaching by Enacting

Jesus taught only with his words but also with his actions. In the Last Supper with his disciples he washed their feet and he taught his disciples the importance of servant-leadership. "When he had washed their feet, and taken his garments, and resumed his place, he said to them, "Do you know what I have done to you? [13] You call me Teacher and Lord; and you are right, for so I am. If I then, your Lord and Teacher, have washed your feet, you also ought to wash one another's feet. For I have given you an example, that you also should do as I have done to you" (Jn 13:12-15). Every effective teacher uses his/her ability to act while teaching. To get the attention of the students he/ she employs different gestures, facial expressions, tone of the voice etc. The narrations about the way Jesus teaches the truth about himself and his message to the Samaritan woman (Jn 4:7-27) or how the risen Jesus teaches the entire law and the prophets to the disciples going to Emmaus (Lk 24:15-32) give us an indication about his effective use of acting while teaching.

2.8. Historical and References

To highlight a point and to emphasize its importance a teacher can effectively put into service the historical narration of any event of the past or what is happening in the present context of the teacher and the students. Jesus reminds the disciples and the crowd the historical events of the past as well as the current events that would become history. When the Pharisees accused the disciples of Jesus breaking the Sabbath by plucking grains, Jesus reminded them of a historical event in teaching about the lawful breaking of the Sabbath. "Have you not read what David did, when he was hungry, and those who were with him: how he entered the house of God and ate the bread of the Presence, which it was not lawful for him to eat nor for those who were with him, but only for the priests? Or have you not read in the law how on the Sabbath the priests in the temple profane the Sabbath, and are guiltless? I tell you, something greater than the temple is here" (Mt 12:3-6). On another occasion Jesus reminded them of Moses and what he wrote (Jn 5:46-47) and about prophet Zachariah who was killed between the sanctuary and the altar (Mt 23:35). A saying which is attributed to philosopher George Santayana (1863-1952) and having various version of it, is: "Those who cannot remember the past is condemned to repeat it". Referring to historical events is very helpful in teaching even when the subject taught is not history!

2.9. Use of News Items and Referring to Context

Jesus teaches also by using the current events of his context. "There were some present at that very time who told him of the Galileans whose blood Pilate had mingled with their sacrifices. And he answered them, "Do you think that these Galileans were worse sinners than all the other Galileans, because they suffered thus? I tell you, No; but unless you repent you will all likewise perish" (Lk 13:1-3). Only one who is alert to the happenings of the present and is able to critically look at them can use such knowledge in his/her teaching and challenge the students to be critical in their assessment of them.

2.10. Participatory and Praxis-Oriented Teaching

The participation of the students in teaching makes them understand the deeper dimensions of what they are taught. The present-day education includes such participation of the students by giving them opportunities to practice what they learn. Jesus used such a participatory and praxis-oriented teaching method by sending the disciples to teach in the towns and villages where Jesus had planned to go later to teach them the way of God and the mysteries of the kingdom of God. Luke narrates that "the Lord appointed seventy others, and sent them on ahead of him, two by two, into every town and place where he himself was about to come" (Lk 10:1). Before sending his disciples to teach Jesus instructs them about the content of their teaching as well as informs them about the place of their stay during their ministry of teaching and healing and also the code of conduct they should follow. Every practice has a theory behind it. But every theory without the application of it in practical life remains abstract and life-less.

2.11. Use of Repetitions

Every teacher knows that important matters cannot be taught with a single exposure of the same. It has to be repeated. But repeating a matter, however important it may be, it can be monotonous. The ability of the teacher to repeat the matter in a variety of ways makes the students to appreciate it and commit it to their memory. One of the most important themes of Jesus' teaching was the mystery of the Kingdom of God or the Kingdom of Heaven. Jesus never got tired of repeating it in his teaching. But he did it by explaining it in a variety of ways and through various parables. And he answered them, "To you it has been given to know the secrets of the kingdom of heaven, but to them it has not been given. This is why I speak to them in parables, because seeing they do not see, and hearing they do not hear, nor do they understand" (Mt

13:11). Jesus tells a number of parables and in a variety of ways he explains the Kingdom of Heaven or the Kingdom of God repeatedly. In the same chapter 13 of Matthew we find the narration about the Kingdom of Heaven one after another. It is like the mustard seed (13:31-32) the leaven in the dough (13:33), the hidden treasure (13:44), the pearl of great price (13:45-46), the dragnet (13:47-50), the household treasures (13:52). With each repetition a deeper dimension of the teaching on the Kingdom of Heaven is communicated. An effective teacher repeats the important points of his/her teaching in order to communicate to the students that these concepts or messages are important not only for the enhancement of their knowledge but also for their life depending on the subject-matter that is taught.

Conclusion

The Gospels present Jesus as an authentic and effective teacher who used highly efficient and impactful pedagogical methods to teach his disciples and all who came to listen to him. As it is said, "the medium is the message," his very person was his teaching. Never before him or after him there lived a teacher who lived his teaching. In other words, there was no dichotomy between his life and what he taught. Jesus did not teach abstract notions about God but how to experience God and relate with God. Knowing God was to experience God and organize one's life accordingly in loving relationship with others and with reverence for all what God had created. Though Jesus did not follow any system of education available at his time, in his own teaching as narrated in the Gospels we can find a method of teaching that was highly effective to transform the minds of those who listened to him with openness of heart and mind. His way of teaching was dialogical, participative, inclusive and critical. He was not depositing in the minds of his disciples and those who listened to him some thoughts about God, the destiny of humans and the entire creation but he asked questions and evoked thinking and demanded their participation in his kingdom-project. He taught with authority hitherto unknown to his predecessors. His personal relationship with those whom he taught transformed their hearts and eventually they became teachers and preachers of him and his message. What we discover as the pedagogical methods of Jesus are relevant for any teacher who is committed to transform persons and the society through his or her teaching!

13

Jesus, the Synagogue Teacher
A Narrative Portrait of Jesus' Teaching in Mark 1:21-28

Naveen Rebello, SVD

Introduction

Prof. Scaria K. J. SVD, in whose honour I make this contribution, has been a passionate "teacher" of the NT, imparting the message of Jesus convincingly like the evangelist Mark, for over three decades. Innumerable personal interactions, scholarly discussions and challenging conversations on varied scriptural themes and pastoral issues related to the art of homiletics have enlightened and offered insights into his systematic and methodical teaching and well-researched writings that can be summed up in three points: a) he is an erudite NT scholar and exegete with a commendable breadth of expertise and equally a passionate professor, having a unique ability to interpret the biblical texts with clarity; b) a firm teacher and faithful priest, combining keen pastoral sensitivity towards the manifold Indian realities with a praxis-oriented, dialogical, critical and liberative pedagogy, exemplified by Jesus; c) a formator of missionaries, he has endeavored to enkindle the desire to love and live the Divine Word as the "center" of one's missionary life. This volume that celebrates Scaria's distinguished and stellar career, who can eponymously be called the "Mark" of JDV is truly an enduring and memorable tribute that acknowledges the indelible "mark" that he has left behind in the NT scholarship.

In the Canonical Gospels, "teaching" is a key component of Jesus' messianic ministry. In the Gospel of Matthew, the extensive Galilean ministry is signaled by the oft-repeated transitional summary reports: "and he went throughout all Galilee, *teaching* (διδάσκων) in their synagogues, and *preaching* (κηρύσσων) the good news of the Kingdom, and *healing* (θεραπεύων) every disease and every sickness among the people" (Mt 4:23; cf. 9:35; 11:1). The Gospel of Mark describes the teaching activity of Jesus in and around the Sea of Galilee involving large crowds (Mk 2:13; 4:1; 6:34), while the Gospel of Luke recounts many instances of Jesus' teaching in the synagogues (Lk 4:15.31; 6:6; 13:10) as well as in the Temple (Lk 19:47; 20:1; 21:37).[1] The Gospel of John, in the words of Nicodemus, a Pharisee and a teacher of Israel, acknowledges Jesus as a unique "Rabbi" (*teacher*), whose origin is from God (Jn 3:2) and who performs the "signs" (σημεῖα) thus, offering a revealing Christological affirmation.[2] Acknowledging Jesus as a "teacher" par-excellence of the reign of God, this article intends to focus on some of the salient features of his unique and liberative "teaching" or "pedagogy" by analyzing the Marcan pericope of 1:21-28, where the verb διδάσκω (= *to teach* or *instruct*) occurs twice (1:21-22) and the noun διδαχή (= *teaching* or *instruction*) also occurs twice (1:22. 27), the first instance of Jesus' teaching activity in the Second Gospel.[3]

1. Mark 1:21-28 – Preliminary Remarks

Mk 1:21-28 focuses on the *teaching* and *exorcism* of Jesus in the synagogue of Capernaum. In terms of its literary context, these dual activities follow the proclamation of the reign of God and the need for repentance (1:14-15), and the call of first four disciples (1:16-20). Subsequently, the evangelist presents a series of messianic activities that demonstrate the coming of the reign of God beginning with teaching and exorcism in the synagogue (1:21-28); the healing of Peter's mother-in-law and a summary of healings (1:29-34); preaching in

1 For the Synoptic presentation of Jesus' teaching, see, George M. Soares-Prabhu, "Jesus the Teacher: The Liberative Pedagogy of Jesus of Nazareth", in *A Biblical Theology for India: Collected Writings of George M. Soares-Prabhu, S.J.,* Vol. 2 (ed. Scaria Kuthirakkattel) (Pune: JDV, 1999) 141-155. However, Soares-Prabhu overlooks the Johannine portrait of Jesus, the teacher by assessing the Fourth Gospel in terms of its *theological* value in contrast to the *historical* value of the Synoptic traditions.

2 In the Gospel of John, besides Nicodemus, the first disciples of Jesus (1:39); Nathanael (1:49); disciples (4:31; 9:2: 11:8) and crowds (6:25) address him as *Rabbi*, while Mary Magdalene (20:16) addresses the risen Lord as *Rabbouni* (actually *Aramaic* form of address).

3 The fact that out of the seventeen instances of διδάσκειν, fifteen instances (except 6:30 and 7:7) have Jesus as the *subject* and the attribution of all five instances of διδαχή to him shows that the teaching is a *characteristic activity* of Jesus in the Gospel of Mark.

Galilee (1:35-39); cleansing of a leper (1:40-45); and healing of a paralyzed man (2:1-12).

In Mk 1:21-28, Jesus is the protagonist, who plays an active role in the development of the plot and always remains in the foreground. Immediately after their arrival in Capernaum (v.21), his four new companions, called to be the collaborators of the kingdom ministry (1:16-20) disappear from the scene, only to reappear in verse 29. Though the reader can assume their presence at the synagogue as witnesses to his teaching and exorcism, the narrator nevertheless sets the disciples aside and prefers to focus on Jesus' character, whose *divine* identity is recognized by an unexpected character, namely, the man with an unclean spirit and as *authoritative teacher* by the onlookers.

In terms of the literary structure of the pericope, the narrator's triple use of the adverb εὐθύς (vv.21.23.28) with structuring function facilitates the narrative flow and the internal cohesion. Its first appearance in verse 21 introduces the settings of the story (*space-time*); the second occurrence in verse 23 introduces the encounter between Jesus and the man with an unclean spirit and finally, its third usage in verse 28 rounds off the pericope, extending the fame of Jesus from the synagogue of Capernaum to the surrounding region of Galilee. His departure from the synagogue in verse 29 ends the pericope and paves the way for a new episode. In light of the triple use of adverb εὐθύς, the narrative structure of 1:21-28 can be delineated into three parts: a) the introductory frame that contains spatio-temporal settings with emphasis on Jesus' teaching (vv.21-22); b) the center of the pericope with focus on exorcism and teaching authority (vv.23-27); and c) the concluding frame that deals with his growing fame (v.28).

The above pericope is mostly studied by the Marcan scholars as Jesus' first exorcism account with a "programmatic" character in the Second Gospel. However, for our study, I would like to focus on some of the essential "teaching" elements articulated in the text by the Marcan narrator.[4]

2. Place and Time of Teaching

The introductory frame introduces the *spatio-temporal* settings: "where" and "when" of Jesus' teaching (vv.21-22). The first geographical name that finds

4 For a detailed discussion on Mk 1:21-28, see, Scaria Kuthirakkattel, *The Beginning of Jesus' Ministry According to Mark's Gospel (1,14-3,6): A Redaction Critical Study* (AnBib 123; Rome: EPIB, 1990) 116-141; E. K. Broadhead, *Teaching with Authority: Miracles and Christology in the Gospel of Mark* (JSNTSS 74; Sheffield: JSOT Press, 1992) 56-62; R. J. Dillon, "'As one Having Authority' (Mark 1:22): The Controversial Distinction of Jesus' Teaching," *CBQ* 57 (1995): 92-113; J. C. Iwe, *Jesus in the Synagogue of Capernaum: The Pericope and Its Programmatic Character for the Gospel of Mark: An Exegetico-Theological Study of Mark 1:21-28* (TGST 57; Rome: EPUG, 1999); Andreas Hauw, *The Function of Exorcism Stories in Mark's Gospel* (Eugene, OR: Wipf & Stock, 2019) 59-90.

a mention is *Capernaum* ("village of Nahum"), a fishing village located on the northwest side of the shore of the Sea of Galilee, about two and a half miles from the source of the Jordan river.[5] Unlike Matthew, who elaborates on Jesus's withdrawal to Galilee and subsequent coming to Capernaum with the fulfillment of Isaiah's prophecy (cf. Isa 8:23–9:1//Mt 4:12-16), Mark prefers to present Capernaum in a modest way as the starting point of his public ministry, to where he would return after his itinerant tours in Galilee (cf. Mk 2:1; 9:33). That made Capernaum the center of Jesus' Galilean ministry. Soares-Prabhu rightly observes Jesus' preference to teach in the villages (κώμη) rather than the cities (πόλις) of Palestine, a fact that demonstrates his "non-elitist pedagogy", making him feel at home in the rural countryside (χώρα, ἀγρός, μέρος, ὅριον) than in the hellenized urban settlements.[6] In Synoptics, apart from Jerusalem (after his entry into the Davidic City), he does not appear to teach in major towns and cities of Galilee or Judea (like Sepphoris, Tiberias) but instead moves around obscure hamlets like Nazareth (Mt 2:23; Mk 1:9); or remote fishing villages like Bethsaida (Mk 6:45; 8:22; Lk 9:10) or small rural townships like Capernaum, which seem to be his headquarters during his public ministry in Galilee (Mt 9:1; Mk 1:21; 2:1; 9:33; Lk 10:15).[7] The choice of such locale like Capernaum also confirms the beneficiaries of his didactic activity, especially the poor, sinners and outcast.

The second spatial setting that the reader comes across in the story is the *synagogue*, the place of teaching, instruction and the study of the Law. The Greek term συναγωγή refers to a gathering of people or assembling of the people. As an *architectural* structure, the public *synagogue* is an important Jewish religious institution, to where like other Jewish people, Jesus often goes (*enters* [εἰσελθῶν; v.21] and *departs* [ἐξελθόντες; v.29) and participates in the religious assembly.[8] But eventually in the Marcan narrative, the *synagogue* becomes the locus of antagonism and hostility, resulting in the rejection of Jesus (3:1-6; 6:1-6a); a place of aristocracy and ostentatious display (12:39) and of persecution (13:9). Consequently, he begins to teach primarily in

5 For details see, John R. Donahue and Daniel J. Harrington, *The Gospel of Mark* (SP 2; Collegeville, MN: Liturgical Press, 2002) 78.

6 Cf. Soares-Prabhu, "Jesus the Teacher," 143-144.

7 Ibid., 143.

8 The public *synagogue* where Jesus exercised his public ministry was the administrative center of town and villages in Galilee and Judaea, where the decisions were made about all "local" things. It was home to archives and juridical proceedings and also where Torah was read and discussed publicly on Sabbaths, as in antiquity there was no distinction between secular and religious. For an extensive discussion on the origin and function of *synagogue* see A. Runesson, *The Origins of the Synagogue: A Socio-Historical Study* (CBNT 37; Stockholm: Almqvist & Wiksell Int., 2001).

houses, where he would give private instruction the disciples (7:17; 9:28.33-50; 10:10-12).[9]

The temporal setting of "Sabbath" (sacred time)[10] is closely linked to the *synagogue* (religious place) where the pious and law-abiding Jews would take part in the prayers officiated on Saturday. The highpoint of this *synagogue service* was the reading from scripture (Torah and the Prophets), followed by a sermon or brief commentary or exposition on the text read aloud, besides prayers and blessings.[11] Any adult male Jew at the invitation of the head or the official of the synagogue (cf. Acts 13:14-16; Paul at the synagogue of Antioch on Sabbath) could preach the sermon. In the present text, though verses 21-22 do not mention any explicit invitation from the part of synagogue official, Jesus' authoritative teaching to the gathered there should be understood in the context of the prevalent Jewish religious traditions that valued sacred time and religious place. The qualitative distinction in observing the Sabbath by Jesus and by his contemporaries becomes a deeply contentious issue on several occasions (cf. 2:23-28; 3:1-6; 6:1-6a) in the Second Gospel.

From the narrative point of view, the spatio-temporal settings (v.21) prepare immediately and anticipate keenly a possible *contrast* between two types of teaching that of an "outsider" (itinerant Jesus) and of the "insiders" (official scribes), in the following verse.

3. Teaching, Preaching and Healing – Core of the Messianic Ministry

The didactic activity (*words*) and the liberative ministry of exorcism (*deeds*) of Jesus go hand in hand in Mk 1:21-28.[12] If vv.21-22 (*introductory frame*) focus on his teaching then vv.23-27 (*center*) narrate the exorcism story of a hostile encounter between Jesus (*kingdom of God*) and the unclean spirit (*kingdom of Satan*). The close relationship between these two activities resurfaces in the onlookers' reaction in v.27 (διδαχὴ καινὴ κατ' ἐξουσίαν – τοῖς πνεύμασιν τοῖς ἀκαθάρτοις). Going by the narrative sequence, the exorcism takes place

9 Cf. Donahue and Harrington, *The Gospel of Mark*, 79.

10 Resseguie understands "Sabbath" as a *religious setting* like Passover, Tabernacles, etc. which occasion healings as well as conflicts between Jesus and the authorities. Cf. James L. Resseguie, *Narrative Criticism of the New Testament: An Introduction* (Grand Rapids, MI: Baker Academic, 2005) 113-14. The religious settings like that of "Sabbath" are important in plot and characterization as they intensify the differing perspectives of *protagonist* and *antagonist*.

11 Cf. Kuthirakkattel, *The Beginning of Jesus' Ministry*, 127.

12 The exorcism in Mk 1:21-28, according to Culpepper, follows the general pattern of a miracle story, comprising: a) setting (vv.21-22); b) illness, problem, or challenge (vv.23-24); c) Jesus' word or act (v.25); d) miraculous act (v.26); and e) response of the witnesses, confirming the miracle (vv.27-28). Cf. R. A. Culpepper, *Mark* (SHBC; Macon, GA: Smyth & Helwys Publishing, 2007) 55.

in the context of Jesus' teaching in the synagogue (v.21) and his teaching authority mentioned prior to the event (v.22) is re-emphasized soon after the event (v.27). Further, the following events of the healing of Simon's mother-in-law and other sick and the possessed (vv.29-34) continue to complement the message of the fulfillment of time (καιρός) and manifest the arrival of the definitive moment of salvation that he *proclaimed* in 1:14-15 as well as the liberative ministry that he *initiated* in 1:21-28.

As corollary, these three activities *teaching, preaching* and *healing* (that includes exorcism) are to be seen as forming a constellation of Jesus' messianic ministry. Among them, the meaning of "preaching" (κηρύσσιεν) and "teaching" (διδάσκειν) has often been disputed although both the terms are interrelated in the context of his ministry. Ambrozic argues that *teaching* is for insiders while preaching is for *outsiders*.[13] Others scholars like Broadhead and Marcus, Jesus' teaching is simultaneously preaching.[14] However, Soares-Prabhu offers a valuable and insightful distinction between both the acts. According to him, 'preaching' is primarily the *proclamation* or *announcing* of the good news of the reign of God (i.e., God's definitive offer of salvation as already present in Jesus), while 'teaching' is the *ethical and religious instruction*, rooted in one's personal conversion (μετάνοια), by having accepted the good news of the divine rule. In other words, Jesus *preaches* the "good news of the reign of God" (Mt 4:23; Mk 1:14-15), while he *teaches* the "way of God" (τὴν ὁδὸν τοῦ θεοῦ) i.e., spelling out the proper *human response* to the proclamation of the reign of God (Mt 22:16; Mk 12:14).[15] Though the above distinction clarifies the nature of both activities, they are nevertheless *complementary* or *reciprocal ways* by which Jesus endeavors to make present the *reign of God*. In short, both 'teaching' and 'preaching' as well as 'healing' are Jesus' threefold liberative way of communicating the presence of God by means of *words* and *deeds*.

4. Teaching – a Regular Pedagogical Activity

The story of the *teaching* and *exorcism* in the synagogue (1:21-28) is part of a *typical* day of Jesus' public ministry in Capernaum (1:21-34) followed by another day of messianic ministry across Galilee (1:35-45). The so-called "programmatic day of Capernaum" (vv.21-34) offers an overview of the common activities of Jesus, namely, teaching (1:22.27); exorcism (1:23-

13 Cf. Aloysius M. Ambrozic, "New Teaching with Power (Mk 1:27)," in *Word and Spirit* (ed. J. Plevnik) (Ontario: Regis College, 1975): 143-49.

14 Cf. Joel Marcus, *Mark 1–8: A New Translation with Introduction and Commentary* (AB 27; New York: Doubleday, 2000) 187; Broadhead, *Teaching with Authority*, 69.

15 Cf. Soares-Prabhu, "Jesus the Teacher," 142-43.

27.32.34), and healing (1:29-31.32.34).[16] Although the arrangement of these typical activities may have some theological or thematic motives but there is no reason to doubt that they could have taken place on a single day or every day.[17] This programmatic character suggests that "teaching" could have been his regular public activity. Some of the instances of his "teaching" during the Galilean ministry (Mk 1:14–8:26) are:

1:21-22	–	Jesus teaching (ἐδίδασκεν; διδάσκων) at the synagogue in Capernaum
2:13	–	Jesus teaching (ἐδίδασκεν) beside the Sea of Galilee
4:1-2	–	Jesus teaching (διδάσκειν; ἐδίδασκεν) besides the Sea of Galilee in parables
6:2	–	Jesus teaching (διδάσκειν) in the synagogue at Nazareth
6:6	–	Jesus teaching (διδάσκων) in the villages (of Galilee)
6:34	–	Jesus teaching (διδάσκειν) on the shores of the Sea of Galilee

Mark clearly emphasizes that Jesus' didactic activity would be *regular* in nature and *programmatic* in character in the entire Gospel by choosing to mention "teaching" (*he entered the synagogue and taught* [ἐδίδασκεν]; v.21b) as one of the first and foremost acts of his public ministry and that too on a typical "day in Capernaum". In fact, "teaching" is the central issue in the introductory verses (vv. 21-22) of the episode. The verb ἐδίδασκεν is an *ingressive* or *inceptive* imperfect and can be translated as "he began teaching" underscoring the *beginning* of his teaching activity. It reinforces that the public synagogue in Capernaum was a communitarian place of teaching where Jesus began to carry out his "teaching" along with expelling the unclean spirit, thus, demonstrating his power as an authoritative teacher.

5. Teaching with Authority (ἐξουσία)

Following the spatio-temporal framework, Marcan narrator presents Jesus as an authoritative teacher, whose teaching is characterized by unique efficacy that leaves the Sabbath congregation amazed: *they were astonished at his teaching, for he taught them as one having authority and not as the scribes*; v.22). The focal point of this verse is his teaching *authority* (ἐξουσία) that impacts the onlookers. From the syntactic point of view, the accusative ἐξουσίαν precedes the participle ἔχων of which it is the object complement (as *having* authority).

16 Cf. Donahue and Harrington, *The Gospel of Mark*, 82-86.

17 Cf. Mark Strauss, *Mark: Zondervan Exegetical on the New Testament* (Grand Rapids, MI: Zondervan, 2014) 87; see, Brendan Byrne, *A Costly Freedom: A Theological Reading of Mark's Gospel* (Collegeville, MN: Liturgical Press, 2008) 44-51 considers a single but a long "day at Capernaum" from verse 21 to verse 45 (1:21-45); also, Culpepper, *Mark*, 54-63.

Since ἐξουσία is the object of the verb ἔχω, it can be surmised according to E. Raponi that the authority which belongs to the person of Jesus as teacher is a *personal* quality that is communicated then to his action of teaching.[18] In other words, Jesus' teaching authority is somewhat intrinsic, manifested externally through words.

In fact, ἐξουσία of Jesus is a major motif in the Gospel of Mark.[19] Several authors have debated and discussed the meaning of ἐξουσία in the individual texts as well as the overall narrative of the Second Gospel. For example, Daube identifies the ἐξουσία of Jesus with the Hebrew רשׁת referring to the official authority of an ordained rabbi in Judaism, licensed to teach the authoritative doctrine but distinct from inferior or elementary teachers of Jewish law such as the γραμματεῖς. The people of Galilee were amazed because Jesus taught like as if he were an ordained rabbi, a sight quite rare and uncommon in those times.[20] Cranfield suggests that the ἐξουσία of Jesus that corresponds to the Hebrew רשׁת is the authority of an OT prophet, sent with direct commission from God.[21]

Going beyond these two suggested opinions, Soares-Prabhu prefers to look at Jesus' authority as "charismatic" authority (his own personal *charisma*) which is both *personal* as well as *prophetic* in nature. It is "personal", because it is derived from his '*abba* experience', a profound personal experience of God as unconditional love at the time of his baptism (cf. 1:9-11) that becomes the basis of his life and mission. It is also "prophetic" because such authority is the result of the possession of the 'Spirit' that he receives at his baptism (also announced by John that Jesus would be baptizing with the *Holy Spirit*; cf. 1:8) similar to those of the OT prophets, who were authorized as divine messengers during their call experience.[22] In other words, Jesus' *personal* and *prophetic* authority is of *divine* and *supernatural* in origin (cf. 1:1). It, however, becomes a contentious issue in 11:27-33 where the legitimacy of his teaching is questioned by the Jewish leaders (the chief priests, scribes and the elders) in terms of its origin ("by what authority [ἐξουσίᾳ] do you do these things or who gave you the authority [ἐξουσίαν] to do them?"; v.28). His refutation of their charges in light of the *prophetic authority* of John the Baptist makes the reader recognize his *divine authority*, which he received at the moment of baptism—a moment of prophetic calling—in the hands of John, even though the opponents

18 Cf. Eleonora Raponi, *Il significato dell'aggettivo ΚΑΙΝΟΣ in Mc 1,27: Una lettura esegetica e teologica* (Rome: Angelicum University Press, 2016) 89-90.

19 Broadhead, *Teaching with Authority*, 56-62.

20 Cf. David Daube, "ἐξουσία in Mark 1.22 and 27," *JTS* 39 (1938): 45-59.

21 Cf. C. E. B. Cranfield, *The Gospel According to St. Mark* (CGTC; Cambridge: University Press, 1959) 74.

22 Cf. Soares-Prabhu, "Jesus the Teacher," 145-149.

feign ignorance (11:31-33). In this regard Soares-Prabhu comments: "For by referring to the baptism of John, Jesus is really asking official Judaism whether it is prepared to recognize extra-institutional, prophetic authority, such as is claimed by John (Mk 11:32) and by himself; and he is probably pointing to his baptism by John as the moment of his prophetic calling."[23] The source of his *divine* authority is further established by his claim in 2:10 that as the Son of Man, he has the authority to forgive sins, which is the exclusive prerogative of God (cf. 2:7).

In light of the above discussion, we recognize that in the Gospel of Mark, Jesus' authority (ἐξουσία) is of *divine* origin as he is the *Messiah* and the *Son of God* (cf. 1:1) and *charismatic* in nature with *personal* and *prophetic* dimensions. He derives it from his foundational *abba experience* at the moment of his baptism, when the Spirit descends upon him and the heavenly voice solemnly declares his divine sonship (cf. 1:9-11).

6. Jesus' Teaching versus Scribal Teaching

In Mk 1:22, the narrator contrasts the teaching of Jesus with that of the 'scribes' (γραμματεῖς).[24] It is for the first time the *collective* group (*note* οἱ) of γραμματεῖς is introduced in the Gospel. Since vv.21-22 are the narrator's comments, the text does not suggest conclusively that the scribes were present while Jesus was teaching in the synagogue, as there is no direct interaction between both. In fact, they arrive on the narrative stage for the first time only in 2:6, where they question interiorly about his authority to forgive sins. In the global context of the Gospel, the scribes are characterized as one of the principal adversaries of Jesus during his public ministry: in Galilee (cf. 2:1-12.15-17; 3:22-30; 7:1); in Jerusalem (11:27-33) and in the Passion Narrative (14:1.43.53; 15:1.31), besides being implicated in passion predictions (8:31; 10:33). Here in 1:22, the clear comparison between Jesus and the scribes points to two important details: firstly, it suggests implicitly that the scribes exercise considerable teaching authority recognized by people in general while secondly, it evidently intensifies the opposition between the nature of their teaching.

Most likely, the γραμματεῖς did exercise recognizable authority in the Jewish society because they served as legal experts, enjoying an elevated status by virtue of their knowledge of the law. Being learned teachers, "their specialized and even esoteric knowledge of the Torah and of the oral traditions, both legal (*halakhah*) and religious (*haggadah*), which had grown up around

23 Ibid., 147.

24 In ancient societies, the scribes (or the modern day "secretary") performed a wide variety of tasks from composing documents to holding official administrative positions. Cf. Donahue and Harrington, *The Gospel of Mark*, 79-80.

it... acquired through long years of assiduous discipleship in the scribal schools, and institutionally recognized by an 'ordination' – (*semikah*) which licensed made them 'ordained scholars' (*hekamim*), equipped the scribes"[25] to assume positions of competence in political, administrative, and religious matters. Moreover, along with the "chief priests" who belonged to the entourage of the high priest and the "elders" of people (*the heads of leading aristocratic families*), they made up the official council known as the *Sanhedrin* (cf.15:1). In Mark, the scribes are characterized as those who *interpret* the scriptures (cf. 9:11; 12:35) thus performing the function of a teacher. Given this privileged status in the society, deeply and strongly theocratic in nature, the scribes wielded enormous influence over people in matters of scripture, doctrines and law and their accurate and strict observance.

Precisely, therefore, the scribal teaching is presented as a "counter-model" to that of Jesus in v.22. Although the *tertium comparationis* is *teaching* here as Dillon claims rather than *authority*[26] the reader however does not miss the essential element of *authority* closely linked to *teaching*. The scribal authority was an *institutional* or *traditional* authority with emphasis on "legality" at the core of their teaching (cf. 2:6-7). By contrast, Jesus' authority is *charismatic* in nature, defined by *personal* and *prophetic* dimensions and so, it represents an *extra-institutional* or *non-traditional* authority, grounded in the message of the reign of God. Without having to draw from the formal teachings of ancient well-known rabbi or teacher, it is independent of any institution or tradition. Moreover, Jesus taught with authority unlike the scribes, because his teaching was of *divine* origin and had the *reign of God* as its focal point while the scribal teaching was of *human* origin. This critical distinction is unambiguously illustrated with the prophetic words of Isaiah, "...teaching human precepts as doctrines. You abandon the commandment of God and hold to human tradition" (cf. 7:6-8). In brief, from the beginning of the Gospel, starting with v.22, Mark offers a perceptible opposition and antithesis between Jesus and the scribes in terms of their teaching explicitly and their authority implicitly and thus, prepares the readers for their recurring conflicts in the rest of the Gospel.

7. Newness (καινός) – the Defining Quality of Jesus' Teaching

The reaction of the onlookers, after listening to Jesus' teaching and witnessing to the subduing of the unclean spirit is articulated in a question ("what is this?"); an exclamation ("A new [kind of)] teaching—with authority!")[27] and a

25 Soares-Prabhu, "Jesus the Teacher," 146.

26 Cf. Dillon, "As one Having Authority (Mark 1:22)," 103.

27 The textual apparatus of NA[28] presents variant readings of people's reaction, especially confusion with regard to joining κατ' ἐξουσίαν to the preceding διδαχὴ καινὴ or to the

statement ("He commands even the unclean spirits, and they obey him") that reaches a crescendo in the scene. Firstly, the question born out of amazement, "what is this" (τί ἐστιν τοῦτο;) indicates the *scope of the event*, but it can also have a *Christological* function, pointing to his *teaching authority* directly and to his *identity* indirectly. Guelich suggests that the question "what is this?" should be understood in light of the disciples' question "who then is this?" (τίς ἄρα οὗτος ἐστιν; 4:41) that concerns Jesus' identity after stilling the storm.[28] Within the episode itself, the Marcan irony is at display, since the unclean spirit knows who Jesus *is* ("the Holy One of God"; v.24), while the people do not know who he is (v.27).[29]

In fact, people recognize that Jesus' teaching is something *unique* and *qualitatively* different from what they have seen or known before. In v.27, καινός is a key word that defines the *quality* or the *substance* of Jesus' teaching as *new* (διδαχὴ καινή). The Greek term καινός (unlike νέος [= new] concerns 'time') denotes different meanings, like new, fresh, novel, something not used before, unknown, strange, remarkable, or something in contrast to old.[30] This suggests that the adjective καινός used here indicates *qualitative newness* and not *temporal* one.[31] The "newness" of Jesus' teaching in v.27 is conspicuous in the fact that his authoritative didactic activity (vv.21-22) is accompanied by an equally commanding act of exorcism (vv.23-26) that brings the reign of Satan to an end. In other words, the spoken words complemented by performative deeds truly manifest the concreteness of the reign of God, announcing God's definitive offer of salvation to people. In fact, the use of καινός in 2:21 (new piece of garment) and 2:22 (new wine), while emphasizing the incompatibility of the old and the new clearly suggests that the time of salvation has arrived in the person and mission of Jesus whose teaching of the reign of God requires new attitudes from people's part. In short, as Scaria has rightly observed it, the teaching of Jesus as the "διδαχὴ καινή connotes a teaching that is revelatory and Messianic, final and definitive."[32]

---

following verse ἐπιτάσσει (*he commands*). According to Metzger, in view of v.22, the punctuation suggested by the first option and found in ℵ B L 33 is to be preferred. Cf. Bruce M. Metzger, *A Textual Commentary on the Greek New Testament*. 2nd ed. (Stuttgart: UBS, 1994) 64.

28 Cf. Robert A. Guelich, *Mark 1–8:26* (WBC 34A; Waco, TX: Word Books, 1989) 58.

29 Cf. Marcus, *Mark 1–8*, 189; Hauw, *The Function of Exorcism Stories*, 69.

30 Cf. "καινός," *BDAG*, 496-497.

31 Cf. Camille Focant, *The Gospel According to Mark: A Commentary* (trans. L. Keylock) (Eugene, OR: Pickwick, 2012) 67.

32 Kuthirakkattel, *The Beginning of Jesus' Ministry*, 139.

8. Regin of God as the Content of Teaching

In fact, in vv. 21-22.27 there is no indication about the content of Jesus' teaching. This should not imply that the evangelist wants to focus only on Jesus' deeds (*exorcism*) rather than his words (*teaching*). However, the reader can easily infer the object of his teaching from what has already preceded, namely, the proclamation of the reign of God and the need for repentance or conversion (1:14-15) with which he has inaugurated the messianic ministry. Further, as we have seen above, all three components of public ministry (*teaching, preaching,* and *healing*) are complementary in nature, whose singular purpose and object is to make present the reign of God in the lives of people, as shown in 1:16–8:26. So, given this "programmatic" nature of this inaugural announcement and the complementarity of words and deeds, the content of his teaching is essentially the *reign of God* although it is not mentioned here. Though it remains relatively obscure in 1:21-28, it is however conspicuous in 4:1-34 where Jesus teaches by means of parables about the *reign of God* (cf. 4:2; διδάσκω and διδαχή).[33] In fact, the parables of Jesus manifest his dialogical and critical pedagogy of God's reign, "continually subverting the world of his listeners: inverting their expectations, upsetting their accepted attitudes and values."[34] Therefore, the core of Jesus' didactic project is nothing but the *reign of God* that is carried out effectively by the one who is bestowed with the divine authority (cf. 1:11).[35] As regards the teaching content, Scaria attributes the possible reason for its absence in these verses (also in the first part of the Gospel) to the Marcan "secrecy motif", a major theological preoccupation of the evangelist who attempts to conceal the identity of Jesus in the first part while such veil of secrecy is eventually lifted in the second part of the Gospel.[36] However, it is to be noted that although Mk uses the "teaching" of Jesus as a deliberate, systematic, and progressive Christological motif, the above argument does not hold true because his teaching in parables in 4:1-34 (that occurs in the first part of the Gospel) clearly shows the *reign of God* as the fundamental content of his didactic activity.

9. Jesus' Teaching and People's Response

The teaching of Jesus evokes reactions of *wonder* or *astonishment* or *amazement* or *awe* in his audience. The two key terms that are employed to express the onlookers' response at the synagogue are: ἐκπλήσσειν (*amaze*) and θαμβεῖν

33 For a brief study on Jesus, the teacher of Parables in Mark, see, Donald H. Juel, *The Gospel of Mark* (IBT; Nashville, TN: Abingdon Press, 1999) 119-137.

34 Soares-Prabhu, "Jesus the Teacher," 151.

35 Similar assertion by Hauw, *The Function of Exorcism Stories*, 64: "God's royal dominion is the content of the good news that Jesus teaches."

36 Cf. Kuthirakkattel, *The Beginning of Jesus' Ministry*, 127.

(*astonish, shock, wonder,* or *amaze*).[37] In fact, *wonder* or *amazement* is typically a Marcan literary motif.[38] For example, the verb ἐκπλήσσειν frequently occurs as people's reaction to Jesus' words (cf. 6:2; 10:26: 11:8) or his deeds (cf. 7:37) and the emotive verb θαμβεῖν is used only in the Second Gospel (cf. 1:27; 10:24.32) where the onlookers and disciples are astonished at his teaching. In v.22 the verb ἐκπλήσσειν is a response to Jesus' authoritative teaching (as implied by the use of causal γάρ), which is clearly differentiated from that of the scribes. As Scaria observes that its use indicates, "man's reaction of astonishment at Jesus' revelatory teaching and it possibly connotes the first step towards faith."[39] In v.27, θαμβεῖν with an all-embracing subject ἅπαντες is another fitting response that recognizes the authoritative teaching evident in the act of exorcism. In short, both ἐκπλήσσειν and θαμβεῖν are immediate and appropriate human responses to Jesus' authoritative words and deeds that usher in the reign of God, in and through the events that are liberative in nature.

10. From Synagogue Teacher to Itinerant Preacher

Jesus was a wandering or itinerant teacher.[40] His teaching and preaching tours throughout the region of Galilee along with his companions reinforce that his didactic activity took place beyond the four walls of a physical-material structure. In Mk 1, Jesus moves from Nazareth to the Jordan (v.9), remains in the desert forty days (v.13) and goes to Galilee (v.14). In the present text in v.21, his arrival into the town of Capernaum (εἰσπορεύονται) and entry into the synagogue (εἰσελθῶν) marks a spatial movement from the shores of the Sea of Galilee, where he called his first disciples (vv.16-20) to a seashore village that was home to a structure of religious importance. His departure (ἐξελθόντες) from the synagogue in v.29 to carry out further acts of ministry in Capernaum suggests that he was an itinerant teacher and preacher, constantly moving about with the people. Unlike the religious cum architectural setting in v.21 (cf. 6:2), he also teaches the crowds beside the sea (παρὰ τὴν θάασσαν; 2:13; 4:1; 6:34); and in the region of Judea and beyond the Jordan (10:1).

37 Besides ἐκπλησσω and θαμβέω, the other two verbs that are used for "amazement" in the NT Greek are θαυμάζω and ἐξίστημι along with their cognates.

38 Cf. Timothy Dwyer, "The Motif of Wonder in the Gospel of Mark", *JSNT* 57 (1995): 49-59; Id., *The Motif of Wonder in the Gospel of Mark* ((JSNTSS 128; Sheffield: Sheffield Academic Press, 1996) 92-195; William R. Telford, "Maze and Amazement in Mark's Gospel," *The Way* 41 (2001): 339-348.

39 Kuthirakkattel, *The Beginning of Jesus' Ministry*, 128.

40 D. Dormeyer, "Jesus as Wandering Prophetic Wisdom Teacher," *HTS* 49 (1993): 101-17 explores the three qualities attributed to Jesus as the wandering wisdom teacher: *prophecy*, *miracle working* and *wandering*, and concludes that *wandering* was the major action of the pre-Paschal Jesus in Mark (also in NT) in a physical as well as a metaphorical-theological way.

The itinerant nature of his *didactic* and *kerygmatic* project can be inferred from 1:38, when he responds to Simon and his associates who pursue him: "Let us go on to the neighboring towns that I may preach (κηρύσσιεν) there also, for that is why I came out." The narrative detail that he was sought by people (ζητεῖν) when he was in a lonely place (ἔρημον τόπον; v.35) evidently suggests that he was a much sought-after travelling teacher without a stable or permanent dwelling, whose teaching ministry in the open-air space and in structures that belonged to the community (like synagogue or temple) was not confined to a single geographical or architectural setting. In the first part of the Gospel, he would later undertake two journeys to the land of the Gentiles (5:1-20; 7:24-28) before moving to Jericho (10:1-52; v.46) in the second part, a journey that ultimately ends in Jerusalem (11:1–16:8), where he would teach in the temple (11:17; 12:14.35; 14:49).

Conclusion

In the Gospel of Mark, Jesus begins his messianic ministry as a "synagogue teacher" in Capernaum in 1:21-28. His pedagogical activity (διδάσκειν and διδαχή) as an educational project of the "reign of God" is communicated through teaching and preaching (*words*) and accompanied by healing (*deeds*). It possesses both *authority* (ἐξουσία) and *newness* (καινός) and announces God's definitive offer of salvation as present reality. Profoundly *charismatic* in nature, with *personal* and *prophetic* qualities, Jesus' synagogue teaching is *essentially* and *qualitatively* different from the so-called institutional, hereditary and traditional teaching of the scribes, whose scholarship was meticulously grounded on the legality of scriptural and religious matters. In the broader context of the Marcan narrative, Jesus' first teaching stint at Capernaum becomes "programmatic" in character as it serves as a gateway to the eventual itinerary teaching mission in Galilee, advancing the reign of God.

Relating the LOGOS

14

The Logos as the Basis of Biblical Universalism

Jacob Kavunkal, SVD

Introduction

Since Fr. Scaria is a veteran Scripture scholar, with an illustrious academic history, in this paper I wish to examine a biblical theme that has immense relevance to an Indian reading of the Bible, especially in the context of the plurality of religions. Of all the themes of Christian theology, expressing universalism, that of the *Logos* is second only to the God of creation (Gen 1:1). The fourth evangelist begins his gospel with "the great hymn to the universe," opening with the words: "In the beginning was the Word," that is revealed, first in his role in creation, along with universal revelation (Jn 1:3-4), and then, in his incarnation in Jesus (Jn 1:14). For this all-comprehensive universalism John makes use of the term *Logos*, that has its roots both in the Jewish thought and in the Greek Philosophy.

1. *Dabar* in the Old Testament

In the Bible, the link between Jesus Christ and the universal connectedness and relationship is the incarnation of the divine word (*dabar*). The Old Testament makes use of two words as intermediary between God and creation: wisdom (*hokma*) and word (*dabar*). "The worlds were made by the word of God"

(Ps 33:6). However, the word wisdom is made use of more frequently in the context of this creation.

Recent biblical studies have given new insights into the centrality of wisdom in the ancient Hebrew tradition. Biblical scholarship has shown the importance of the figure of personified wisdom, particularly in the books of Job, Proverbs, Sirach and the Wisdom of Solomon. Wisdom is always closely associated with God's work of creation. Wisdom is connected with the whole of creation; it is present with God at creation as a skilled co-worker (Prov 8:30; Wis 7:22; 8:6). It pervades and penetrates all things (Wis 7:24), renews all things (Wis 7:27). Wisdom "reaches mightily from one end of the earth to the other and orders all things well" (Wis 8:1).

Wisdom is presented at most times in the image of a woman, lady Wisdom, whose primary mode is relational (Job 2:8; Prov 1:8-9; Sir 1:9-10; 4:11-19; Wis 6:11-12). Her connections extend to every part of reality. No aspect of reality is closed off from her. She exists as it were in a tapestry of connected threads, patterned into an intricate whole of which she is the centre.

In the book of Job, the figure of personified wisdom occupies a central role. Chapter 28 is a hymn to Wisdom, with the theme "where shall wisdom be found" (28:12,20). Similarly, in the first nine chapters of Proverbs we find a series of poems in which Lady Wisdom looms large (1:20-33; 3:13-24; 4:5-9; 8:1-9:5). God "begot" or "created" Wisdom as the first born (8:22). In the book of Sirach Wisdom proclaims that she has come forth from God, born from God's mouth as the Word of God. She speaks of her role in creation, of her exploration of the universe and of her sway over all nations. She comes to the earth like mist, as the breath of God covers the waters (24:3-7). God has placed her in every human being as the eye (*olam*) (Sir 17:8).

The book of Wisdom describes Wisdom as God's power and as an emanation of the glory of God (7:25), living with God (8:3) and associated with all God's works (8:4). Roland Murphy summarizes Wisdom as "a divine communication: God's communication, extension of self, to human beings. And that is no small insight the biblical literature bequeaths to us."[1]

2. *Logos* in Greek Philosophy

Heraclitus (c 535-475 BCE), was the first to make use of the concept of the Logos in Greek Philosophy. For Heraclitus, *logos* was the principle that ensured continuity in a world that was in the process of constant flux. It is the ground, word, speech, account, and reason. Heraclitus used it as a technical term, as the principle of order and perception. Already here we see how the

1 Murphy, Roland, "Wisdom Literature and Biblical Theology," *Biblical Theology Bulletin* 24 (1994), 7

logos was a principle of relation, the principle that related the two moments of the reality in flux: the present and the past as well as the present and the future.

When we come to the Platonic world, we are told that the Platonic ideas were located in the *logos* that acted in the physical world, on behalf of God. Justin the martyr who spoke of the *logos spermaticoi* (seeds of the Word) has said that Plato, in fact, lifted the idea of the *logos* from the *Tora*![2]

The Stoic Philosophers identified *logos* with the all-pervading divine animating principle of the universe. It is the divine principle implicit in the cosmos giving its order and meaning. Similar related ideas we come across in Indian, Egyptian and Persian Philosophical systems. The Indian scriptures, the *Vedas,* are believed to be the articulations of the Sages' experience of the eternally resounding *Vak,* the divine revelation.

3. Jesus the *Logos*

However, it is in Christian thought that we come across the full flowering of the principle of *logos,* to explain the mystery of the Christ-event, integrating the Old Testament and Greek philosophy.

The Jewish philosopher Philo of Alexandria (ca 20 BCE – CE 50) adopted the Greek term *logos* into Jewish philosophy describing it as the intermediary between God and the cosmos, as the agent of creation and as the agent through which humans understood God. No doubt, Philo was influenced by the *hokma/dabar* in the Old Testament.

Evangelist John writing towards the end of first century CE, continuing the early church's search to understand deeper the person of Jesus Christ, takes the then prevailing cultural term *logos* and presents Jesus as the Incarnation of the eternal *logos* that existed from the beginning, i.e., the beginningless beginning, in contrast to the Old Testament description of the *hokma/dabar* that was God's first creation. John tells us how the *logos* was God and with the God, showing the universal connectedness and relationship of Jesus as the Incarnation of the biblical *hokma/dabar.*

The ancient Christian hymns such as Phil 2:6-11; Col 1:15-20, and Hebrews 1:3-4, identify Jesus with the biblical Wisdom. These hymns could have been sung well before the writing of the books in which they figure. Hence, we could conclude that the identification of Jesus with divine wisdom could have occurred in the early post-Easter community. St. Paul speaks of Christ as the wisdom of God (1Cor 1:24). He is the pre-existent wisdom present from before all ages and in creation.

Scripture scholar Edward D Miller has pointed out how in John 1:1-5 we have four strophes, each making an assertion about Logos' relation to something, and in each strophe to something different. Thus, the first strophe

2 Justin, The Martyr, *First Apology,* 59-60

is about Logos in his personal relation to God, the second is about his creative relation to the world, strophe three expresses the Logos in his incarnate relation to humans, and strophe four turns our attention to the Logos' victorious relation to evil.[3]

Through the prologue John makes history a theological category due to the salvific presence of the Word. Nowhere in the New Testament do we find the empirical historical reality so permeated by the divine as we do in John due to the presence of the *Logos*. Incarnation is in relation to and in continuity with the other three states of God's saving activity in *Logos*. The pre-creation, creation, Incarnation and the present glorious state are the four stages of the activity of the *Logos*.

The opening verses of the Johannine prologue, verses 1-4, presents us with an amazing and all-embracing universality, openness without boundary, hospitality without reservation, dialogue without discrimination, acceptance without conditions.

Due to this all-pervading activity of the *Logos* graphically narrated in the prologue, St. Augustine in his *City of God* approvingly quotes a Platonic philosopher who is reported to have said that the first five verses of the prologue must be written in gold and displayed in the most prominent places in every church (X, 29).

The prologue of John uses the language of the *logos* rather than that of the *hokma/Sophia* – wisdom. Yet what is said in terms of *logos* is very much dependent on what is said of wisdom in the Old Testament. Raymond Brown is of the opinion that John substituted *Sophia* with *logos* because the latter is masculine while the former is feminine.[4]

In the prologue, as well as in the early Christological hymns, we find a theological connection between God's action in creation and Jesus Christ. Everything in creation bears the mark of the Word, the divine reaching out to the world. God had God's salvific plan close to God from the beginning. All history and every single thing that happened took place through the mediation of the *Logos*. The world is the realm of the revealing Word. The Word that became flesh in Jesus of Nazareth is already with God in whom the entire divine mystery of salvation is already hidden. The whole creation stands bathed in the light of salvation through the Word.

There is a theological flow in the Johannine presentation of the *Logos* from his pre-existence to creation, accompanying it by bestowing it life and light, to the Incarnation of the same in Jesus of Nazareth with his ministry, until he is raised to the glory that he had from all eternity (Jn 17:5). The Word was from the beginning, *en arche,* outside the limits of space and time, neither

---

3 Miller, Edward, *Salvation History in the Prologue of John* (Leiden: Brill, 1989), 91

4 Brown, Raymond, *The Gospel According to John,* (New York: Garden City, 1966), cxxiv

of which existed then. The use of the past imperfect *en,* indicates how God's Word was not an after-thought, but was from the beginning. That is to say the illumination, the revealing the light-giving work of the Word did not start just with Christianity or any other religion, but it is coeternal with God. It is the common patrimony of all religions. No wonder, most world religions have a theology of the Word expressed in different ways.

The Word pre-exists the story of humankind, though in relationship with the God (*pros ton theon*). Here John makes a distinction between the Absolute Mystery of God (the *apara Braman,* in terms of Indian Philosophy) and the Word, *logos,* (the *Vak).* The Word is spoken from the intimacy of God, it is revelatory. The main function of the Incarnate Word too is revelatory (Jn 12:45 & 14:6). The history of humanity can be weaved through from the pre-existence of the Word, to the life and light brought to every human person by the same Word through creation, and the Word that becomes Flesh in Jesus of Nazareth. What is specific to the Christian community is the Incarnation with the ministry, where the Incarnate Word invites all "to come and see" (Jn 1:39), to follow him and thus reveal God who is with us, Emmanuel (Mt 1:23).

Logos is God's presence and self-expression. God communicates God's self through God's Word. The traditionally prevalent way to understand the Incarnation is in the context of sin. This is only one school. Here Jesus Christ is seen as the unique Saviour. The alternative is to see Incarnation flowing from God's free love expressed through God's Word through creation and Incarnation, as a continuous process. Incarnation is not dependent on a fall, it was part of God's plan, the free self-communication of divine love.

The interesting fact is that according to the Hellenistic mind there could not be a greater contradiction than associating the *logos* with *sarx* (flesh). Yet, that precisely is what John does in the prologue: *o logos sarx egeneto* (the Word became flesh), making that affirmation the most influential New Testament affirmation in the history of Christian teachings. *Sarx* points to what is most ordinary in human beings, their frailty. John's affirmation underlines the sharpness of the antitheses and the depth of the synthesis of *logos* and *sarx*. God's Word has entered completely into our human existence.

4. Incarnation and the World

In the light of what we have seen, it is obvious that Christian theology cannot subscribe without qualification to the various anthropological theories regarding the origin or explanation of religions, including the many primal religions. Anthropologists tend to describe the origin of religions, especially those of the primal religions in terms of pre-animatism, animism, magic, totemism, and others.

The biblical realism goes beyond them and affirms that any genuine religious expression is the result of the 'illumining' activity of the Word through whom God created the universe (Jn 1:4 & 9). That Word is the source of their religious relationship with God, even when there have been tendencies of deviation and corruption in the form of witchcraft, sorcery, divination, idolatry and others.

The *logos* that was from the beginning with God, becomes flesh, as a succession of events in history. The key point is his relationship with God. As W. Ross Blackburn has shown, the beginning of mission is divine self-manifestation. Commenting on the book of Exodus, Ross Blackburn writes: "[T]he Lord's missionary commitment to make himself known to the nations is the central theological concern of Exodus."[5] The same is true of the Incarnation of the *logos* as well.

Incarnation is the visible and concrete presentation of the Word who is operative in the world from "the beginning," enabling us to "see and touch his glory." The whole ministry of Jesus was the manifestation of the true divine nature in human form. In Jesus we encounter the divine in the fullest form as far as humans are concerned. The picture that emerges from the earthly ministry of Jesus in the gospels is that he was intensely conscious of God as his intimate *abba* and that he was anointed and sent to inaugurate the divine reign.

His food is to do the will of the Father (Jn 4:34), to remain in the Father as the branch and the vine (Jn 15:1-8 & 17:20-23). He can do nothing on his own, but only what he sees the Father is doing (5:19). The term Father, the only absolute, occurs 120 times in John in contrast to the 64 times in the Synoptics. All this effects a perfect transparency between the Father and the Word so that the Word can manifest the Father (Jn 1: 18).

He is the *hokma,* divine wisdom, the divine plan for creation. God is revealed in the concreteness of this person. In him we have the experience of God in history. God's attributes are to be experienced not apriori, but in human history through the Word made flesh. "We have heard it; we have seen it with our own eyes; felt it with our own hands and of this we tell, about the word of life" (1Jn 1:1).

Jesus, the Word incarnate, is a reader of the signs of the times. The Jewish society and the religion of the times stood in need of a transformation from legalism and ritualism as well as priestly careerism. Jesus begins his mission with his experience of the divine grip on him through the anointing of the divine Spirit at the time of his baptism by John in the Jordan. His miracles were not so much to prove his divinity as much to show how God is already

5 Blackburn, W. Ross, *The God Who Makes Himself Known: The Missionary Heart of the Book of Exodus,* Downers Grove: Intervarsity Press,2012), 15.

at work to transform the society. They were the signs of the setting in of the divine reign in and through him.

In the process of the doctrinal developments that came in the course of Greek inculturation the church lost sight of this biblical realism. For the Hellenistic mind Christ (Messiah) was only a proper name. For the Greeks a messiah who came to manifest the God of Abraham, Isaac, Jacob and others operating in history was not as important as the understanding of the person, substance and nature of Jesus Christ.

The historical Jesus with his ministry of "the deeds of light" (Jn 3: 18-21), becomes peripheral. What was important was the correct academic expression of faith, in line with Greek philosophy that was accustomed to a God of Plato, Aristotle, Socrates, Plotinus and others for whom God was the unmoved mover, uninvolved in the material world. However, the focus of the prologue is the advent of the pre-existent *logos* into the world at a certain moment of time and the rest of the gospel is the narration of the activity of the Incarnate *logos*.

We need to return to the biblical understanding of Jesus Christ that the fourth evangelist has spelt out providing absolute universalism and openness, while realizing the significance of the Incarnation, to manifest God in the concrete (Jn 1:18; 12: 45 and 14:9) through his ministry. While Jn 1:1-5 describes the work of the pre-existent *logos,* Jn 1:14 onwards is the narration of the work of the Incarnate *Logos.* The synoptic gospels in particular describe this ministry in terms of the divine reign which John presents as the deeds of light, passing from the deeds of evil. In both ways it is a process of historical transformation of the world while preserving the openness to the religions and cultures of the world.

The parabolic nature of Jesus' life, ministry, death and resurrection, is the revelation of Gods compassionate love. World history is a love story, a narrative of God's love for the world, always permeated by God's creative and enlightening Word. No one is outside of this story, this narrative. In this narrative there are different points or milestones of events and persons, even if they cannot be equated, nor equally significant: creation, exodus, covenant, Incarnation, Zorashter, Buddha, Socrates, Mohammed Sri Sankaracharia, Vivekananda, Mahatma Gandi, and many others, all of whom and which are integral or related to the *logos.*

In the fullness of time the *logos* pitches his tent among humans by becoming flesh disclosing how humans are to approach God and neighbour within the spectre of relationality. The community of his disciples is the visible sacrament of this love story, to concretize what happened in Incarnation, always aware that the mystery of the *logos* is Universal. That mystery belongs to all religions and they all belong to that mystery.

In Christian terminology, in the words of Jac Dupuis, "the divine Word is the universal agent of all historical divine self-manifestation, even before his incarnation in Jesus Christ that his historical incarnation transpires in view of its meta historical and universal operative presence as the resurrected Lord."[6] The universality of this mystery cannot be localized exclusively in a point of time in history. This vision and this mission have to contour Christian service today as a step in the creation of the divine household: Word-inspired to inspire the world.

5. Christ the Saviour

The first thing that we come across in the gospels is that Jesus is not working to change God's attitude to people, to win back divine friendship, rather, he tries to change people's mind to each other and to God. In fact, some of the parables like that of the Vineyard (Mk 12: 1-12) clearly state that the passion and death of Jesus was due to the disbelief of the people, though by raising him from the dead, God made him the cornerstone of the Kingdom. For Jesus the main issue was a religious faith permeated by selfishness and fear, due to ignorance, suffering from a sense of distance from the divine. In this context he calls for repentance. It is a question of the change of mind, of attitude. "It is about changing (converting) people's thoughts and images about God and how they see themselves in relationship with God", observes Michael Morwood.[7]

The Paschal Mystery comes in the context of, as a consequence of the Ministry of the Lord, that could be described as the "stone rejected by the builders," and make it the "corner stone" of Christian service. Through his ministry, according to the gospels, Jesus is busy in the realization of the divine reign.

6. Relating to Other Religions

One of the striking features of creation is the plurality that permeates it. An example of this plurality is the mind-boggling variety of life that fills the earth. In so far as the whole creation is the work of God through the Word who enlightens everyone coming into the world (Jn 1:1-4,9), every religion too is permeated by the Word. Religious pluralism is an enrichment and a source of creative catholicity. The gospels do not present Jesus as a representative of any particular religion. His passion was God's reign, as we have explained. True, he formed a community and commissioned this community to continue his mission of witnessing to the good news. No doubt eventually this community

6 Dupuis, Jac, *Jesus Christ at the Encounter of World Religions,* (New York: Orbis Books, 1993), 243.

7 M. Morwood, *Tomorrow's Catholic: Understanding God & Jesus in the New Millennium,* (Melbourne: Spectrum Publications, 1997), 81.

became a new religion. This transformation in its identity from the "way of the Nazarene" to the Christian religion, should not lead to the conclusion that its mission is to displace other religions, rather it is relating to other religions.

Vatican II opened a new chapter in the church's mission by exhorting Christians to "acknowledge, preserve and promote the values of other religions" (NA 2) and also to enter into dialogue with the followers of other religions.

The Word becoming flesh entered into the world of human meaning in a four-fold way: cognitive, i.e., the Word enters human experience as an objective datum demanding a surrender to the reality of the revealing God; constitutive, i.e., affecting the experience of human identity, forming our identity in the light of divine meaning; communicative, i.e., giving the shared possession of the deeply meaningful, and effective, i.e., enabling Christians to transform the world in new ways. The experience of the Word becoming flesh inspires the Christian to a world-shaping praxis.

"What are you looking for" (Jn 1:37), the first words of the Word incarnate is addressed to every Christian, as to every disciple. "Rabbi, where are you staying?" (Jn 1:38), the counter question reveals the disciple's search as well as the readiness to learn from, to be anchored in the Word. The Word's reply, "come and see" (1: 39), is the invitation to stay with him, to be with him (Mk 3:14). It is the beginning of the journey of discipleship, which will culminate in the apostolic sending (Jn 20:21). Even when the disciple comes to the Word, he/she is aware how his/her turning to the Word is through the Word's initiative as shown in 1:42. The Word bestows a new identity to those who listen to the Word and follow him: "you shall be called Cephas, Peter" (1:42).

The Johannine Gospel presents a whole series of words and deeds to introduce the disciple into the mystery of the Word, into the mystery of the Kingdom. In the language of the Synoptics, to outsiders it is given only in parables (MK 4:11). The very first act of the Word incarnate in the Johannine gospel is an act of transforming the water meant for Jewish purification, into a new and perfect wine, manifesting his glory which, in turn, leads the disciple to have faith in him (2:11). He teaches the disciple as to how discipleship demands entering a new relationship of life, like a newborn child, through the generative activity of God, the source of the new life (3:3). All this prepares the disciple to "do whatever he tells you" (2:5) and thus come to the light (3:21). The Father's love for the world is the energizing factor of disciple's mission (3:16), even as the Incarnate Word's food is to do the will of the Father and complete his work (4:34). The Word that became flesh is concerned about the flesh of the world, the world of suffering, the blind, the lame, and the paralysed (5:4). He is the Lord of the Sabbath (5:10-13) for he is working even on the Sabbath as his Father is working (5:17). He is the new Moses, the true revelation in contrast to the Thora that Moses gave (6:30-33). The disciple realizes that though his sayings are hard, there is no one else that we can turn to as he has the words of eternal life (6:68-69).

The Word incarnate is the true living water, rather than the water used in the libation rite on the day of the Jewish feast of the tabernacle (7:37-38). He is the true light and not the light with which the temple was illumined for the feast of the tabernacle (8:12). He is the light, God's self-revelation, given for the light of the world, rather than the law (8:58). He is not one more servant of God, but God, who can pronounce the great "I AM" (8:58), for what God was, the Word was (1:1).

Like the blind man (9:1-38), the disciple is to be led to faith in the Incarnate Word so that he/she can confess: "Lord, I believe!" (9:38), and worship him. As the conversion of the blind man is a process of a slow journey, so too, the disciple gradually grows to the maturity of faith. This in turn, like the blind man, leads the disciple to a new presence of the other, to new relationships, to a new identity, oriented in accord with the light he/she has received from the Word. He is the true shepherd (10:1f) who gathers all into one flock of God's children (11:52). Mutual knowledge and self-surrendering love are characteristic to this new relationship (10:14-15).

The Word Incarnate gave the supreme example of service in washing the feet of the disciples (13:4f). The vertical God-ward movement is expressed in the horizontal plane by service to one another. The upward exodus to God is enshrined in the outward exodus to neighbour in service.

Conclusion

The biblical understanding of the ***Logos*** reminds the church that its call is to serve human beings by manifesting the love of God made present in God's Word Incarnate, Jesus Christ (*Redemptoris Missio* 2). "God so loved the world that he gave his only Son so that whoever believes in him should have eternal life" (Jn 3:16). Mission, above all, is a love-affair. Though the world is God's work through God's Word in the Spirit, Incarnation takes place to make this love more concrete and tangible. Hence, the Johannine letter describes mission as a proclamation to share the experience that the disciple had in the Word incarnate (1Jn 1: 1-4). Christian service today is primarily a matter of inspiring the world by making God's love and compassion present. This implies that the Christians overcome all prejudices about the world and its peoples as they are Word-permeated-created and enlightened by the Word.

15

Protagonist, Place and Proximate "Other"
Jesus Vis-à-Vis Jerusalem in the Gospel of Mark*

Dominic S. Irudayaraj, SJ

Introduction

In Jerusalem, it seems, Jesus has few friends.[1]

The significance of Jerusalem in the Bible can hardly be overstated.[2] Mark's gospel[3] is no exception. Within this shortest canonical gospel of

---

* It is a delight to dedicate this paper as a small gesture of gratitude to our passionate, personable New Testament Professor, Rev. Scaria Kuthirakattel SVD. And I gratefully acknowledge Prof. Henry Pattarumadathil SJ for his helpful comments on an earlier draft of this chapter.

1 R. T. France, *The Gospel of Mark: A Commentary on the Greek Text*, NIGTC (Grand Rapids, MI: Wm. B. Eerdmans, 2002), 168.

2 For a helpful overview of Jerusalem's significance, see Antti Laato, "Understanding the Spiritual Meaning of Jerusalem: A Religious Historical and Theological Overview," in *Understanding the Spiritual Meaning of Jerusalem in Three Abrahamic Religions*, ed. Antti Laato, Studies on the Children of Abraham 6 (Leiden: Brill, 2019), 3–40.

3 While the title "The Gospel according to Mark" may be the most appropriate, for the purpose of brevity, this chapter uses "Marcan gospel," "Gospel of Mark" and "The Second Gospel." On these terms, see Douglas R. A. Hare, *Mark*, Westminster Bible Companion (Louisville, KY: Westminster John Knox, 1996), 4–5.

16 chapters,[4] the cherished city Jerusalem appears a notable number of 11 times. Already in the prologue (1:2–13)[5]—where John the Baptist, the precursor to the protagonist is introduced to the audience[6]/reader—Jerusalem makes its maiden appearance, as crowds converge at the Jordan river (1:5). The city's second occurrence unfolds, in a curiously comparable fashion, when greater multitudes come to someone mightier than John (3:7). Attraction, however, does not seem to be the only reason for the arrivals from the holy city. The third Jerusalem entry, for instance, depicts the scribes coming down from Jerusalem (3:22), only to accuse Jesus of demonic possession. Similar tone seems to characterize the next instance, where fierce contestations break out between Jesus on the one hand, the Pharisees and some scribes from Jerusalem on the other hand (7:1). Later, as Jesus' march to and ministry in Jerusalem are outlined, a tone of intensity marks the narrative and, as though matching that tone, the Jerusalem occurrences grow in number: Jesus' determination to go up to Jerusalem (10:32), his third passion prediction (10:33), approaching the holy city (11:1), his first day's evening act of looking around the temple (11:11), his second day's prophetic act of driving out the sellers and buyers (11:15), all of which leading to confrontations with the chief priests, the scribes and the elders at the Jerusalem temple (11:27), resulting in his condemnation and death. The final occurrence of Jerusalem is presented in the context of the women disciples who have come up with Jesus from Galilee to Jerusalem (15:41) and are now witnesses to his death, burial and the empty tomb.

Even a cursory look at these Jerusalem occurrences in Mark makes it obvious that no single, much less a coherent, picture of the holy city emerges from the Second Gospel. Yet, considerable Marcan scholarly ink has been spent in making such inquiries. Some, for example, ask: in the evangelist's view, does Jerusalem fare positively or negatively? Others pose the question slightly differently: given the gospel's two primary geographical foci—Galilee and Jerusalem—is the Marcan view predominantly positive of Jesus' birth and growth place (Galilee) as opposed to the city of his final days and passion (Jerusalem)?[7] Either way of posing the question, however, may bespeak an

---

4 The multiple endings of the Marcan gospel is still a hotly debated issue. As such, the present work limits the survey to Mark 16:8.

5 On the literary structure, including the prologue, see France, *The Gospel of Mark*, 11.

6 Hare notes how "the book [of Mark] can be read in its entirety in about an hour" and so avers, "it seems likely that Mark was designed to be read aloud, probably to an audience." Hare, *Mark*, 2.

7 Senior states, "Galilee … has basically a positive value in Mark while Jerusalem has a mainly negative one." Donald Senior, *The Passion of Jesus in the Gospel of Mark*, The Passion Series 2 (Collegeville, MN: Liturgical Press, 1984), 34–35. On Galilee vs. Jerusalem, see David C. I. Joy, *Mark and Its Subalterns: A Hermeneutical Paradigm for a Postcolonial Context* (London: Routledge, 2014), 67–70.

underlying assumption: that the gospel contents could be arranged along a clearly demarked binaries. But other scholarly voices helpfully note that given the diversity of the content and the tonality of the evangelist with respect to Jerusalem, it is a near impossibility to domesticate the gospel to any neatly drawn binaries. Riches' critique of Freyne's work[8] presents an illustrative instance: "the important themes of rejection/acceptance, openness/closedness, disclosure/concealment, new/old apply unevenly to the pair of terms Galilee/ Jerusalem."[9]

Some scholarly voices therefore have pertinently called for a nuanced reading of Marcan views of Jerusalem.[10] Liminality[11] marks Marcan telling of Jesus's gospel. The same can also be noted in and around the Jerusalem portrayals. Sharing in such a nuanced disposition, the present chapter attempts to weave together the various Jerusalem occurrences to probe if these may tell a story.[12] And it is pursued in a style that is imitative of some of the Marcan literary styles such as anticipation, recalling, and building upon theme(s).[13] At each Jerusalem occurrence, some pertinent details of the pericopes are presented, all with an aim to underscore how identities of the protagonist and place are constructed and negotiated. For the said purpose, a Social Identity-

8 Seán Freyne, *Galilee, Jesus and the Gospels: Literary Approaches and Historical Investigations* (Philadelphia, PA: Fortress Press, 1988).

9 John K. Riches, *Conflicting Mythologies: Identity Formation in the Gospels of Mark and Matthew*, Scholars' Editions in Biblical Studies (Edinburgh, UK: T&T Clark, 2000), 129. For a similar critical view of Malbon by Bruegge, see John Vonder Bruegge, *Mapping Galilee in Josephus, Luke, and John: Critical Geography and the Construction of an Ancient Space*, Ancient Judaism and Early Christianity 93 (Leiden: Brill, 2016), 97–98. Cf. Elizabeth S. Malbon, "Galilee and Jerusalem: History and Literature in Marcan Interpretation," *CBQ* 44.2 (April 1982): 242–55. See also a critical review of Walker's work in Barry S. Crawford, review of *Jesus and the Holy City: New Testament Perspectives on Jerusalem*, by Peter W. L. Walker, *CBQ* 60.4 (1998): 779.

10 "Although a contrast between Jerusalem and Galilee exists, the divergent descriptions are not so dramatic as to demand a different theology of Galilee and Jerusalem." Dean B. Deppe, *The Theological Intentions of Mark's Literary Devices: Markan Intercalations, Frames, Allusionary Repetitions, Narrative Surprises, and Three Types of Mirroring* (Eugene, OR: Wipf and Stock, 2015), 308.

11 "[T]he figure of Jesus in Mark … is a figure of deep ambivalence: a striking mixture of defiance and defeat, loss and endurance." Leif E. Vaage, "Violence as Religious Experience in the Gospel of Mark," in *Experientia, Volume 2: Linking Text and Experience*, ed. Colleen Shantz and Rodney Werline (Atlanta, GA: SBL, 2012), 134. On the reasons for such liminality, see Simon Samuel, *A Postcolonial Reading of Mark's Story of Jesus*, LNTS 340 (London: T&T Clark, 2007), 33.

12 Cf. David M. Rhoads and Donald Michie, *Mark as Story: An Introduction to the Narrative of a Gospel* (Minneapolis, MN: Fortress Press, 1982).

13 Cf. prolepsis (cf. 10:32 → 15:41), sandwiched stories (cf. 5:21-43; 11:12-25; 14:53-72), etc.

cued heuristic term, proximate "other" is availed. We begin, therefore, with a brief elucidation of the said term.

1. Proximate "Other"

On the expansive horizon of biblical hermeneutics, methodological plurality and interpretive diversity have ushered in an enviable array of hues to the meaning-making process. Though a much recent entry, social scientific studies have brought in their own shares of reading ancient texts under fresh light.[14] Within the broad umbrella of social scientific studies, Social Identity Approach (henceforth, SIA) has proved to be particularly fruitful for identity-adumbrating readings of ancient texts.[15] Taking a definite cue from SIA and drawing on the notion of Jonathan Z. Smith,[16] I have elsewhere outlined proximate "other" and availed the same to read Isaiah and Qumran texts.[17] A slightly revised schema of the same is presented here, which helps highlight some identity-affirming aspects in the Jerusalem-dotting Marcan pericopes.

1.1. A Conceptual Schema

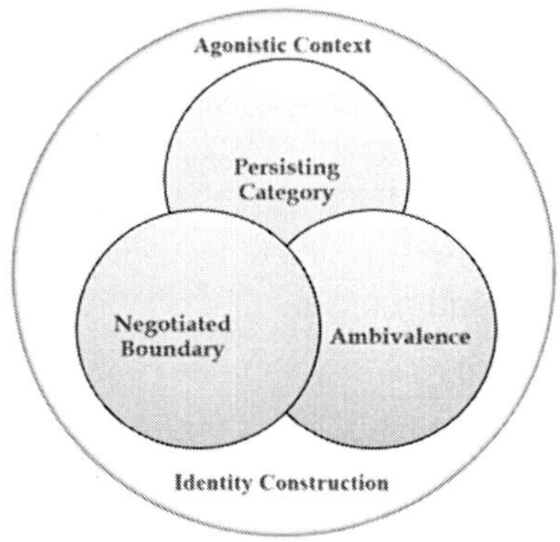

Proximate "other" comprises of three key aspects: *persisting category, negotiated boundary*, and *ambivalence*. These aspects aid in noting, especially in contexts of inter-group interactions, (1) the "other" who is proximate rarely leaves the discursive arena of an ingroup, thus making it a *persisting category*; (2) despite repeated efforts at painting a formidable boundary between oneself/in-group and the "other"/out-group, a closer scrutiny would reveal that the boundary is not so much of a dividing

14 See Richard L. Rohrbaugh, *The Social Sciences and New Testament Interpretation* (Peabody, MA: Hendrickson, 2004).

15 See J. Brian Tucker and Coleman A. Baker, *T&T Clark Handbook to Social Identity in the New Testament* (New York: Bloomsbury, 2014). See also Rafael Rodrígues, "Mark," in *T&T Clark Social Identity Commentary on the New Testament*, ed. J. Brian Tucker and Aaron Kuecker (London: Bloomsbury T&T Clark, 2018), 69–102.

16 Jonathan Z. Smith, *Relating Religion: Essays in the Study of Religion* (Chicago: University of Chicago Press, 2004).

17 Dominic S. Irudayaraj, *Violence, Otherness and Identity in Isaiah 63:1-6: The Trampling One Coming from Edom*, LHBOTS 633 (London: Bloomsbury T&T Clark, 2017), 36–89. Dominic S. Irudayaraj, "Jerusalem, the Proximate 'Other': Constructing Identity and Negotiating Boundary in Pesher Micah (1Q14)," *Sapientia Logos* 9, no. 1 & 2 (2017): 61–84.

barrier as a locus of intense interactions (so, *negotiated boundary*); and (3) on account of such intense interactions, the discursive context turns into a consistently contested arena, contributing to an *agonistic context.* The same agonistic contestations are often borne out in ambivalences that attend inter-group interactions. All the same, the ambivalences may bespeak an ingroup's earnest desire to *construct* one's own *identity*.[18]

1.2. Mark: Agonistic (Con)Text

What grants ground to employ the said term for the Marcan gospel? Any response necessitates at least a brief note on the context of the gospel. Much scholarly speculation surrounds the questions of authorship, audience, and date of the second gospel. While some situate "the historical moment of Mark" in "the revolt of 66-70 C.E,"[19] others view the gospel as a Rome-centered counter-propaganda.[20] There is hardly any consensus.[21] Although the exact Marcan *context* is far from forthcoming, the *text* exhibits certain notable features. The literary witness of the gospel attests to an agonistic (con) text.[22] A fair amount of pericopies are filled with contestations and conflicts,[23] all leading to the climactic confrontation at the Temple and the ensuing crucifixion.[24] On this, the observations by Donahue and Harrington are apt: "The shadow of the cross, opposition from powerful leaders, divisions among Jesus' followers, persecutions, and betrayals" are the themes that stand out in the gospel.[25] In sum, while the exact historical context is far from clear, the repeated contestations and confrontations (so, *agonistic text*) grants sufficient ground for our recourse to the term, proximate "other."

---

18 See Irudayaraj, *Violence, Otherness and Identity in Isaiah 63*, 56–57.

19 Ched Myers, *Binding the Strong Man: A Political Reading of Mark's Story of Jesus* (Maryknoll, NY: Orbis Books, 1988), 65–69.

20 See Adam Winn, *The Purpose of Mark's Gospel: An Early Christian Response to Roman Imperial Propaganda*, WUNT 2 245 (Tübingen: Mohr Siebeck, 2008).

21 The old consensus of "the origin of Mark's gospel at Rome before 70 C.E. no longer holds" as proposals of Galilean origin, sectarian source, and southern Syria roots have come to demand their share of scholarly attention. See John R. Donahue and Daniel J. Harrington, *The Gospel of Mark*, Sacra Pagina (Collegeville, MN: Liturgical Press, 2002), 41–47.

22 The construct *(con)text* is an attempt to capture (i) the lack of contextual clarity (hence, "con" within parentheses) and therefore (ii) the turn to the notable literary features of the "text."

23 Cf. Richard A. Horsley, *Hearing the Whole Story: The Politics of Plot in Mark's Gospel* (Louisville, KY: Westminster John Knox, 2001), 18.

24 Mark is often described as a passion narrative with a long introduction. Ben Witherington III, *The Gospel of Mark: A Socio-Rhetorical Commentary* (Grand Rapids, MI: Wm. B. Eerdmans, 2001), 5.

25 Donahue and Harrington, *The Gospel of Mark*, 43.

1.3. Jerusalem: The Persisting Category

Marcan scholarship frequently conceives of the gospel outline in three place-based parts: (i) Jesus' ministry in and around Galilee (1:1–8:21); (ii) Jesus and his disciples, on the way to Jerusalem (8:22–10:52); (iii) Jesus' final days in Jerusalem (11:1–16:8). As the titles indicate, Jerusalem's twin appearance already points to its prominence.[26]

True, the focus of the gospel is not so much on the city[27] as on the protagonist, Jesus Christ.[28] The very opening statement of the gospel makes the same more than obvious (cf. 1:1). Further, the name "Jesus" appears an impressive number of 96 times. Plotting these occurrences on a map point to the ever-present person of Jesus (cf. the orange line, on the graph). This hardly surprises.

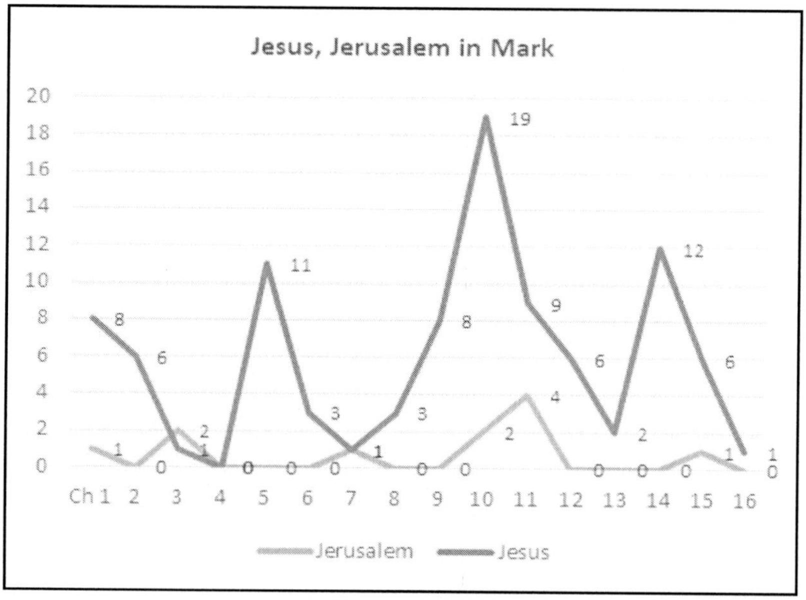

All the same, if one attempts a parallel plotting of Jerusalem (cf. blue line), a couple of intriguing details stand out: (i) Jesus' determination to go to Jerusalem occurs only in chapter 10. All the same, by the time a reader reaches this point, Jerusalem has already been encountered more than once. These earlier Jerusalem entries bespeak the *persisting category* that this cherished

26 For a critique of this division, see France, *The Gospel of Mark*, 12.

27 "[T]here is little in the text that gives any theological reflection on what these events signify for the city itself." Peter W. L. Walker, *Jesus and the Holy City: New Testament Perspectives on Jerusalem* (Grand Rapids, MI: Wm. B. Eerdmans, 1996), 13.

28 Cf. Daniel Johansson, "The Identity of Jesus in the Gospel of Mark: Past and Present Proposals," *CurBR* 9.3 (June 1, 2011): 364–93.

city is; (ii) there is a comparable ebb and flow in the number of entries (of both Jesus and Jerusalem), especially from chapter 10 onwards. It is as though the prospects of both the protagonist and the place are interlinked. It is with such an interlinking sensitivity, the proposed identity-adumbrating Jerusalem texts are woven together here![29]

2. Jerusalem Symphony

2.1. The First Convergence

> *And [people from] the whole Judean countryside and all [the people] of Jerusalem were going out to him, and were baptized by him in the river Jordan, confessing their sins* (1:5).[30]

The first occurrence of Jerusalem features in the context of a voice in the wilderness. At the prophetic call of the precursor, people from both the countryside and the city (Jerusalem) go out (ἐξεπορεύετο) to him. A chiasm[31] captures the enormity of the convergence:

A - Whole (πᾶσα)
    B - Judean countryside (ἡ Ἰουδαία χώρα)
    B' - Jerusalemites (οἱ Ἱεροσολυμῖται)
A' - All (πάντες)

Not only is the gathering enormous[32] but may also be repetitive, as the imperfect tense might indicate.[33] In short, a large populace regularly converged to hear the baptizer. Further, people's movement is expressed by the verb ἐκπορεύομαι. In Mark's gospel, when this verb occurs, together with the end point of the movement, it connotes a sense of rejection (cf. 1:5; 6:11; 7:15, 19, 20, 21, 23; 10:17; 10:46; 11:19; 13:1).[34] In the given context, as such, the verb can indicate people's resolve to "reject" their sins. All the same, the immediately following instance of ἐκπορεύομαι (6:11) can be suggestive of something more here.

---

29 In fact, the term "text" is derived from the Latin *texere* ("weave") which suggests that "every text is an interwoven tapestry." See Donahue and Harrington, *The Gospel of Mark*, 16.

30 Unless stated otherwise, the Greek NT texts are taken from the BibleWorks, v.9 database (BGT) and the English translations are from NRSV.

31 Donahue and Harrington, *The Gospel of Mark*, 62.

32 On John's wide appeal with attendant population estimates, see Eckhard J. Schnabel, *Mark*, TNTC (Downers Grove, IL: InterVarsity Press, 2017), 42 n.10.

33 Marvin R. Vincent, *Word Studies in the New Testament*, vol. 1 (Peabody, MA: Hendrickson, 1887; repr. 1985), 162.

34 Cf. Thayer §1699

In the context of the mission of the Twelve (6:6b-13), Jesus instructs that when a place does not welcome the evangelizing apostles, they are to leave the place (ἐκπορεύομαι), shaking of the dust as a testimony against them (6:11). If these two adjacent occurrences of ἐκπορεύομαι are juxtaposed (1:5 || 6:11), a nuance might be forthcoming. The Jerusalemites' movement to hear the baptizer is indicative of their *positive* disposition. In the light of the general use of the verb within the gospel, the move away "from" Jerusalem may already be *suggestive* of the negative shades[35] with which the city will feature in the subsequent occurrences. Thus, though subtle, Marcan *ambivalence* towards the cherished city can already be heard here.

Interestingly, the enormous convergence of the populace does not so much climax on the identity of the baptizer as on someone else's. It is about the coming one (Ἔρχεται)—one, stronger than John. This sets the stage for the next occurrence of Jerusalem.

2.2. The Second, Sweeping Convergence

> *hearing all that he [Jesus] was doing, they came to him in great numbers from Judea, Jerusalem, Idumea, beyond the Jordan, and the region around Tyre and Sidon* (3:8).

The mightier one comes with authoritative words (cf. 1:22, 27) and astounding deeds (cf. 2:12). The summary of the same is presented in 3:7-12 where Jerusalem features a second time. The geographic sweep is at once arresting. Hare traces the places counter-clockwise on the Palestine map of Jesus' time: the place names begin with Jesus' home territory, Galilee (3:7), moves southward to Judea and Jerusalem, expands southeastward to include Idumea, moves eastward to add "beyond the Jordan" (cf. Perea) and ends with Tyre and Sidon (north of Galilee). The contrast is at once obvious. Jesus "outshines his forerunner."[36]

In such an expansive list, Jerusalem however makes an odd entry. All other places refer to regions: Galilee, Judea, Idumea, and beyond the Jordan. Even in the case of two cities, Tyre and Sidon, the description "the region around" points to areas beyond the purview of the cities. In such a "regional" list, Jerusalem as a city stands apart. This could point to not only the city's significance (so, *persisting category* and enhancing Jesus' *identity*) but also anticipates, indirectly though, the critical gaze under which the city will be singled out.

---

35 *Contra* the dominant Jerusalem-centered nationalist ideology that promotes triumphal pilgrimage to Zion, the subversive crowds "flee to the margins, for purposes of repentance." France, *The Gospel of Mark*, 68. Here, France draws from Myers, *Binding the Strong Man*, 125–26.

36 Hare, *Mark*, 45.

2.3. The Third Coming with a Divergent Motive

> *And the scribes who came down from Jerusalem said, "He has Beelzebul, and by the ruler of the demons he casts out demons"* (3:22).

Jesus' determination to go up to Jerusalem is far from coming (Mark 10). Yet, his popularity has already drawn the attention of the city populace. If the previous two instances of Jerusalem bespeak a predominantly positive disposition of Jerusalem to the ministries of both the precursor and the coming one, the present one brings the latter in sharp contestation with those coming down from Jerusalem. The directional description in this and the immediately preceding instances is expressed by a same preposition: ἀπὸ. However, the intentions can hardly be more contrastive! If attraction fueled the people from the surrounding regions to come, accusation motivates the scribal delegation from the city.[37] The exorcising power of the wonder worker is the scribes' point of attack. Jesus is summarily accused of being possessed, and that too by Beelzebul, the prince/ruler of the demons. The *contestation* is hard to miss!

The response of Jesus takes a parable form. The use of parables is obviously in keeping with the teaching style of the itinerant preacher. All the same, the present instance might point to more than what meets the eyes. On this, Schnabel's comment is helpful: "Jesus asserts in 4:11-12 that he uses explicit speech for 'insiders' and parables for 'outsiders,' of which the Jerusalem scribes who accuse him of being empowered by Satan [*sic*] are extreme representatives."[38] If Schnabel's reading can be granted, then in the fierce contestation of the current pericope, the response of Jesus can be seen as an instance of "othering," which is commensurate with his opponents' attempts at undermining him. Stated differently, while Jesus' geographically sweeping popularity declare the identity of the Son of God in all its arresting proportion, the accusation of the opponents aims to make deep dents on the expansive contours of that identity. And there is more! Their charge threatens to associate the identity of Jesus ("Son of God") with the quintessential power, opposed to God. In response, Jesus' use of parable not only points to the mere illogicality of their accusation but also seems to "other" the accusing voices from the city. As such, *agonistic contestation* in the context of *identity construction* and *negotiation* can be heard in this pericope.

37 For a conjecture on why Jerusalem must have been interested in a Galilean preacher, see France, *The Gospel of Mark*, 168.

38 Schnabel, *Mark*, 93.

2.4. Tradition/al Challenge-and-Riposte

> *Now when the Pharisees and some of the scribes who had come from Jerusalem gathered around him* (7:1).

As in the previous Jerusalem occurrence (cf. 3:22), the arrival of a city delegation marks the current instance of Jerusalem (cf. 7:1). France sees here "an equally bitter confrontation."[39] Nonetheless, there is a subtle difference. Whereas in the previous pericope, the accusation against Jesus is in the third person ("*He* has Beelzebul"), now the delegation engages the preacher head on: "Why are not *your* disciples…?" (7:5). In short, the accusation dares to enter Jesus' space. Also the group has grown larger with the addition of the Pharisees to the scribes.

The accusers take up the ablution tradition as their tool. In response, Jesus draws their attention to the Scripture in order to shift the spotlight on weightier things (caring for one's parents). He quotes from the prophet Isaiah with a view to lay bare his opponent's religious hypocrisy.

As in the previous contestation, the reference to the use of parable (cf. 7:17-18) continues to add to the "othering" whose objects are the accusers. Further, in the post-confrontation conversation with his disciples, Jesus characterizes the opponents as those "without understanding" (v.18). This is particularly intriguing, given the fact that together with the Scriptures, the Pharisees "gave some authority to the living tradition passed along by their teachers (Josephus, *Ant.* 13.297–298; 18.12–15)."[40]

Situating this contestation in the First Century Palestinian socio-cultural context can help underscore a key dynamic. In those cultures, where honor and shame played key roles, an exchange or a "question and response" is often a means of gaining/losing honor and/or assigning/avoiding shame. In an act of questioning, for example, the questioner dares to enter into the social space of the one questioned and thus threaten to undermine the latter's honor. The respondent counteracts by one's answer in order to claim back one's honor that is at stake.[41] Against this cultural backdrop, the present pericope may indicate: the opponents' accusing question (Jesus' failure in making his disciples follow the ablution norms) would amount to their attempt to enter Jesus' social space and question his identity as a teacher. By his response, which points to

---

39 France, *The Gospel of Mark*, 168.

40 Steve Mason and Thomas A. Robinson, eds., "The Origin of the Gospel (Mark)," in *Early Christian Reader: Christian Texts from the First and Second Centuries in Contemporary English Translations Including the New Revised Standard Version of the New Testament* (Atlanta, GA: SBL, 2013), 297.

41 Bruce J. Malina, *The New Testament World: Insights from Cultural Anthropology*, Rev. ed. (Louisville, KY: Westminster John Knox, 1993), 35, 40 (passim).

weightier things as well as the authoritative source (Scripture), Jesus appears to not only claim back his social space but also assert his identity as a teacher!

2.5. A Determinate Move[42]

> *They were on the road, going up to Jerusalem, and Jesus was walking ahead of them; they were amazed, and those who followed were afraid. He took the twelve aside again and began to tell them what was to happen to him, saying, "See, we are going up to Jerusalem, and the Son of Man will be handed over to the chief priests and the scribes, and they will condemn him to death; then they will hand him over to the Gentiles* (10:32-33).

Earlier, attraction and accusation motivated the people and the opponents from Jerusalem. Now, the very object of attraction and accusation—Jesus—decides go up to that city. If mixed motivations brought his audience and interlocutors to Jesus, here and in an interesting correlation, two seemingly diverse reactions mark the responses to Jesus' determination. Some were amazed[43] and others were afraid.

The directional details stand out here. While the accusing delegation is shown to be "coming down" (καταβαίνω) from Jerusalem, Jesus is portrayed as "going up" (ἀναβαίνω) to the city. Of course, the reversal in the movements befits the Palestinian topography since from Galilee to the temple mount, one typically "goes up." There seems to be, however more at play here. Telford helps highlight the same:

> Scribes come down (3:22 *katabantes*) from Jerusalem to confront Jesus (3:22; 7:1), and Jesus and his followers go up (10:32, *anabainontes*; 10:33, *anabainomen*; 15:41, *synanabasai*) to Jerusalem.... Jesus and the scribes move in opposite directions, not only spatially but also theologically. Jesus seeks to break down and break open the exclusive categories of the sacred and the profane that the scribes, and the entire religious establishment, seek to maintain.[44]

---

42 On Jesus' decisive act and single visit, see M. Eugene Boring, *Mark: A Commentary*, NTL (Louisville, KY: Westminster John Knox, 2006), 311. See also John Wilkinson, *Jerusalem as Jesus Knew It: Archaeology as Evidence* (London: Thames and Hudson, 1978), 92. And also, Paula Fredriksen, *When Christians Were Jews: The First Generation* (New Haven, CT: Yale University Press, 2018), 14–16.

43 On the disciples' reaction, see Mark J. Keown, *Jesus in a World of Colliding Empires: Mark's Jesus from the Perspective of Power and Expectations*, vol. 2: Mark 8:30–16:8 and Implications (Eugene, OR: Wipf & Stock, 2018), 69.

44 W. R. Telford, *Writing on the Gospel of Mark*, Guides to Advanced Biblical Research 1 (Leiden: Brill, 2019), 129–30.

Through such a theological mismatch, Mark outlines the *identity* of the Son of God in contradistinction to the traditional expectations.

Further, in contrast to the earlier passion predictions (cf. 8:31; 9:31), the present one comes is more details, with an explicit mentioning of Jerusalem. The explicit mention reiterates the importance of the city. However, in an ironic twist, that would turn out to be the very place of rejection. It is borne out in the city's reaction to Jesus: some receive him with joyful shouts while others conspire to get rid of him. In such narrative juxtaposition of diverse themes, Marcan *ambivalence* towards the city is hard to miss!

2.6. Approaching and Observing

> *When they were approaching Jerusalem, at Bethphage and Bethany, near the Mount of Olives, he sent two of his disciples ... Then he entered Jerusalem and went into the temple; and when he had looked around at everything, as it was already late, he went out to Bethany with the twelve* (11:1, 11).

As Jesus approaches Jerusalem, the moment of reckoning appears to be at hand. As though to underscore its import, the narrative slows down with more details[45] of places[46] and times.[47] Again, much scholarly debate surrounds the significance of Jesus' Jerusalem entry. Is it a prophetic act[48] or a messianic manifestation[49] or a royal procession[50] or a combination of these?[51]

While a definite answer can hardly be confidently adduced, the details that relate to king/ship are pertinent for the present discussion. Three such details are worth underscoring: the mode of entry, the manner in which the animal is pressed into service, and the type of animal used. As Hare notes, (i) "Because it was customary for pilgrims to walk into the holy city, this

---

45 "Mark devotes over a third of his book to this last week." Hare, *Mark*, 137. See also Boring, *Mark*, 312.

46 On how the topographical notations grow clearer and denser, see Robert Gundry, *Mark: A Commentary on His Apology for the Cross* (Grand Rapids, MI: Wm. B. Eerdmans, 1993), 1039. As cited in Witherington III, *The Gospel of Mark*, 25 n.80.

47 From general designations of time (1:9; 8:1; 2:1; 9:1; also 1:32, 35; 4:35; 6:47) to time in terms of days (11:11-12, 19; 14:1, 12, 17; 15:1, 42; 16:2) and of hours (cf. 15:1, 25, 33, 34), see Donahue and Harrington, *The Gospel of Mark*, 17–18. See also Boring, *Mark*, 312.

48 Cf. Isa 20:1-6; Jer 13:1-11; 28:1-17; 32:1-15; Ezek 2:1-3:3; Hos 1:2-2:1. See Donahue and Harrington, *The Gospel of Mark*, 324.

49 Cf. Pesch, Moloney, Evans and France, as cited in Winn, *The Purpose of Mark's Gospel*, 123 n.98.

50 See Myers, *Binding the Strong Man*, 290. See also Gregg S. Morrison, *The Turning Point in the Gospel of Mark: A Study in Markan Christology* (Eugene, OR: Pickwick, 2014), 182.

51 See Winn, *The Purpose of Mark's Gospel*, 123.

choice [to ride a colt] sets him [Jesus] apart."[52] Also, (ii) "Because a king has the right to impress a privately owned animal into his service as need arises, the statement 'The Lord needs it' suggests that Jesus is asserting a royal prerogative."[53] Further, (iii) the requirement that the animal has not been ridden has royal significance.[54]

While these details help augment the royal allusions in Jerusalem entry, there are other features that add a different shade to the Marcan portrait of Jesus' entry. Typically, kings in Israel were anointed at the temple. In Jesus' case, as Focant perceptively notes, "it will not be in the temple of Jerusalem, but instead in a house in Bethany, that too on the eve before his crucifixion, the Messiah will receive a paradoxical anointing."[55] The paradox already sets the tone for other such instances. Jipp, for example, suggests "Mark interprets Jesus's crucifixion against the background of Israel's Messiah language and texts so as to reinterpret that language—to present Jesus as one who is indeed king, but whose kingship is revealed through suffering and death."[56] Myers too concludes, "Jesus is hailed as bringer of the very Davidic kingdom he will in fact repudiate."[57] These paradoxes help situate Jesus' reaction to the crowds' joyful acclamation. While the traditional view expected a marching king, who makes a triumphal entry, to take possession of the temple, Mark presents Jesus as looking around the temple and quietly leaving for Bethany![58]

In sum, the pericope presents Jesus' identity as more than a mere pilgrim, in fact, aligning along royal/messianic terms. While the former points to the salience of his identity, the latter (particularly, the paradoxes) keep the kingly claims under circumspection. Together, these attest to the *negotiated boundary* of the coming one's *identity*. A similar dynamic can be deciphered with regard to the city. On the one hand, as the end point of the triumphal entry, the city's

52 Hare, *Mark*, 138.

53 Hare, 138.

54 "A later rabbinic document, which may reflect first century custom, claims that no other person may ride on the king's horse." Hare, 138.

55 Camille Focant, *The Gospel According to Mark: A Commentary*, trans. Leslie R. Keylock (Eugene, OR: Pickwick, 2012), 449.

56 See Joshua W. Jipp, "Messiah Language and Gospel Writing," in *Writing the Gospels: A Dialogue with Francis Watson*, ed. Joel Willitts and Catherine S. Hamilton, LNTS 606 (London: Bloomsbury T&T Clark, 2019), 126–44. As summarized in Catherine S. Hamilton, "Introduction: Francis Watson's Gospel Writing and the Fourfold Gospel: Engaging a 'New Paradigm,'" in *Writing the Gospels: A Dialogue with Francis Watson*, ed. Joel Willitts and Catherine S. Hamilton, LNTS 606 (London: Bloomsbury T&T Clark, 2019), 12.

57 Myers, *Binding the Strong Man*, 291.

58 For a comparison with Zechariah 14 and Greco-Roman entry processions, see Paul B. Duff, "The March of the Divine Warrior and the Advent of the Greco-Roman King: Mark's Account of Jesus' Entry into Jerusalem," *JBL* 111.1 (1992): 70.

importance seems to correlate with the traditional expectations. However, Jesus' act of leaving the city quietly tempers such expectations greatly. In other words, it points to the *negotiated boundary* of the city's *identity* as well.

2.7. Confrontation at the Central Locus

> *Then they came to Jerusalem. And he entered the temple and began to drive out those who were selling and those who were buying in the temple, and he overturned the tables of the money changers and the seats of those who sold doves; ... Again they came to Jerusalem. As he was walking in the temple, the chief priests, the scribes, and the elders came to him* (11:15, 27).

Earlier, when Jerusalem delegation came to Jesus' turf, it attempted to turn the tables by (i) questioning Jesus' authority and (ii) more damagingly, assigning Jesus' exorcising power to the prince of demons (3:22). In short, their effort was to define Jesus' identity along the lines of the power that is opposed to God! Now, Jesus comes to the opponents' arena—in fact, to their central locus and begins to literally turn the tables.[59] Again, there is more than what meets the eyes. As Boring observes, "In this section [11:1-13:4], Jesus is constantly in the temple; he speaks and acts with authority as though it is his possession."[60] Such a display of authority, particularly when faced with the most dangerous group,[61] meaningfully correlates with Jesus identity as "the stronger one." Further, his quoting of the Isaian words ("My house…") alludes to Jesus' claim on the temple.

With Jesus' powerful display of authority as well as the allusive claim to the temple, Mark leaves us with an unmistakable *identity* of the son of God, especially in the very holy city of Jerusalem. What more is left to be said? The final occurrence of the city, therefore, beckons.

2.8. The Serving Accompaniment and Discipleship Par Excellence

> *These used to follow him and provided for him when he was in Galilee; and there were many other women who had come up with him to Jerusalem* (15:41).

If the Jerusalem entries have thus far been along the lines of Jesus vis-à-vis the city, the final entry sheds much light on another key theme of the gospel: discipleship. Donave teases out a lexical inventory from this single

---

59 On the nature of this act, see Hare, *Mark*, 144.

60 Boring, *Mark*, 313.

61 "[T]he council that will condemn Jesus to death consists of chief priests, scribes, and elders (14:53–64)." Hare, *Mark*, 147. For a brief exposé of each, see Hare, 100–101.

verse in order to show how these accompanying women constitute the ideal disciples:

1. The reference to Galilee (Γαλιλαία, 1:9, 14, 28, 39; 3:7; 6:21; 9:30; 14:28) recalls a multitude from Galilee that followed Jesus (3:7).
2. Follow (ἀκολουθέω) with Jesus as goal in Marcan rendition points to a positive evaluation of the agent.
3. Serve (διακονέω) aligns the women directly and positively with God's messengers (1:13), Simon's mother-in-law (1:31), and the Son of Man (10:45b), and the disciple who would be first (9:35) or great (10:43) by being a servant (διάκονος).
4. Into Jerusalem (εἰς Ἱεροσόλυμα) has most recently occurred in contexts of the positive evaluation of Jesus' disciples (11:1, 15, 27; *contra* 10:32, 33).[62]

To these we might add,

5. Their action of "coming up" shares in their teacher's determinate move to the city as well as all that the move entailed.

If previous Jerusalem occurrences can be appreciated for the *negotiated boundaries* of the *identities* of the protagonist and the place,[63] the present instance extends the same to the *identity* of an ideal disciple. In other words, the shaping of the identities of both the master and his disciples can be meaningfully teased out from this–one other–pericope where Jerusalem features, attesting yet again to its *persisting category* around which *identity construction* can be meaningfully appropriated.

Conclusion

This work commenced with a recognition of Jerusalem's significance in the second Gospel. All the same, given the scholarly divide on how this cherished city fares in the purview of the evangelist, it was proposed that an option beyond an oft-availed binary (positive or negative) might have its value. To this end, a Social Identity-cued heuristic term—proximate "other"—was suggested. While the noted contestation in Marcan (con)text granted the scope for applying the said category, the aspects of the same term then

62 Paul L. Danove, *The Rhetoric of Characterization of God, Jesus and Jesus' Disciples in the Gospel of Mark*, JSNTSup 290 (London: T & T Clark International, 2005), 128–29. For a similar discussion, see Susan Miller, *Women in Mark's Gospel*, Journal for the Study of New Testament Supplement Series 259 (London: T & T Clark International, 2004), 193.

63 On how Mark's view on the city and Temple "integrally connected with the claims and identity of the Jesus," see Walker, *Jesus and the Holy City*, 22–23; 22 n.69. See also Kenneth E. Bailey, "The Fall of Jerusalem and Mark's Account of the Cross," *The Expository Times* 102, no. 4 (1991 1990): 104. As cited in Walker, *Jesus and the Holy City*, 23 n.74.

helped underscore how in a protagonist-focused text, the place (Jerusalem) features as a *persisting category*. In its various occurrences, there are details that bespeak the *negotiated boundary* of both Jesus and Jerusalem. In other words, Jerusalem seems to be an ever *proximate* and yet repeatedly *othered* trope. As such, the present work has proposed that in our interpretive efforts, rather than attempting a quick resolution of Marcan *ambivalences* towards Jerusalem to one of the binaries, there is value in the very ambivalence itself. After all, as Social Identity theorists have repeatedly reiterated, ambivalences aid in appropriating *identity-constructing* features of a discourse. In sum, in the various occurrences of Jerusalem's drawing close to Jesus as well as its daring attempts to distance him, the city appears to approach the teacher as its proximate "other." In turn, Marcan depiction of Jesus in similar dynamics of drawing close to the city as well as distancing it, Jerusalem turns out to be Jesus' proximate "other"!

16

Theological and Hermeneutical Significance of the 'Temple' in Mark

Wilson D'souza, OFM Cap

Introduction

There are two categories of people in our world. The first category is known as temple- friendly and the second category is temple-critical. These are the two extreme positions in the world; the former being hyper-conservatives and who do not wish to hear anything negative (even are reluctant to change) while the latter being super-progressive who are always ready with arms-up to find fault with the worshiping places and their working. In this context, this article will help to find out the Marcan position of the temple along with Scaria who spent his entire life teaching the gospel of Mark. Today in the midst of Covid 19, where the places of worship like temples, churches and mosques are closed, we need to ponder to find out what type of worship places we need today?

1. Temple of Jerusalem

When we talk about the temple, the first thing that comes to our mind is the Jerusalem temple. So, at the outset, a brief summary of Jerusalem temple regarding its origin, construction, re-construction and final destruction by the Romans is presented.[1]

No temple has played as significant a role in the history of its people as the temple of Jerusalem. It was the principal or the only place of worship of Israel. It was a great symbol of Jewish identity and unity. From its construction to re-construction as well as to its dedication, it had a religio-political influence. It was constructed by Solomon (1Kgs 5-9), destroyed by the Babylonian in 586-587 BCE, then it was re-build by Zerubbabel in 520 BCE (Ezra 3-6). It was Antiochus Epiphanes IV in 169-167 BCE who desecrated it (Dan 9-11). In 164 BCE Judas Maccabeus re-dedicated it (1Macc 4:36-39). This re-dedication is celebrated by the Jews as the feast of Hanukkah, the Jewish Diwali or Feast of Lights. Herod the Great renovated the temple in 23 or 20 BCE and finally in 70 CE the Romans completely destroyed it.

As such, the temple was called in Near Ancient East as a dwelling place of deity and therefore as the house of God or God's palace. However, the biblical Yahweh was not a God of place but of people. He was not static but dynamic, not confined to one place but all pervading. He was a jealous God and claimed exclusive loyalty. He was a God of ethical command not to be manipulated by rituals, demands right conduct. It was only after building the temple by Solomon that Yahweh's presence is described to the place (1Kgs 8:13). However, He was never completely at home with shrine but in the heavens (Gen 24:7, Deut 26:15, Ps 2:4). The temple became a highly localized centre of Jewish piety. It became the "House of God" (1Chron 6:48, 2 Chron 3:3, Ezra 3:8 and Neh 8:6, 16). The transcendence of Yahweh, the one God (Deut 6:5) is strongly maintained in Israel even after the installation of Yahweh in the temple. The idea of temple kept on changing and became revolutionized from tribal religion to legitimizing of the monarchy. During the monarchy, especially in the time of the divided kingdom, the Jerusalem temple suffered and was finally destroyed by the Babylonians. The prophets forth rightly condemned the temple and its cult. What the people expected was ethical religion with passionate concern for the poor and demands of social righteousness.[2]

After their return from exile, the temple was reconstructed. Thus there was a shift from religio-political influence to its being the centre for holy community that took place. It was not the sole shrine of the kings and Judaism of that time but the unifying centre of the people. It was a holy place. Indeed the reform of Hezekiah and Josiah (2 Kgs 18, 23) attempted to purify the

1 George Soares Prabhu, "The Temple of Jerusalem: Its Religious and Political Role in the History of Israel", *Jeevadhara,* Vol. 23, No. 134, (1993), 130-152- cf. 130-132. We find description of the temple in three biblical sources: in the book of Kings (1Kgs 6:7), the Chronicles (2Chron 2:1-5:14), and the prophet Ezekiel (40-43).

2 *Ibid,* 144.

Jerusalem cult element. As a great integral institution of its religion, the temple offered the Jews the symbol of identity. But although it had an integral role, it was powerless to prevent the inflation of cult and the hardening of purity rules. Thus it indicated a decline of religion.[3] It is against this decline that Jesus protested when he reminded his hearers of Israel's prophetic tradition that Mercy is preferable to the Sacrifice (Mt 9:13) and when putting this into practice. He freely violated purity regulations by eating with tax-collectors and sinners (Lk 15:1-2).

2. Temple in the Structural Composition of Mark

2.1. The Remote Structure of Mark

Many scholars propose a structure that is primarily and fundamentally based on geographical criteria. Jesus' ministry begins at Galilee and culminates at Jerusalem. When we look at geographical structure it is: Introduction 1:1-13, followed by Galilean ministry 1:14-9:50, then Jesus' journey from Galilee to Jerusalem 10:1-52, and finally Jesus' ministry and death in Jerusalem 11:1-16:8. Some other scholars make 8:27-30, as centre and thereafter give us another structure: 1:1-13, introduction, 1:14- 8:26, the ministry in Galilee, 8:31-10:52, the way of the passion, 11:1:13-37, ministry in Jerusalem, 14:1-16:8, passion and resurrection. Apart from geographical structure there is a concentric and dramatic structure to the gospel of Mark.

A: 'desert' (1:1-13)
B: Galilee (1:16-8:26)
C: the way (8:27-10:52)
B': Jerusalem (11:1-15:39)
A': the tomb (15:42- 16:8).

The other structure is considered as a drama or tragedy based on complication, crisis and denouement.

Prologue 1:1-13
Narration 1:14-6:13
Argumentation 6:14-10:52
Dramatic denouement 11:1-15:47
Epilogue 16:1-8

From the above description, one thing is clear that scholarly world considered short ending of the gospel and felt that long ending 16:9-20, is a later addition.[4]

---

3 *Ibid,* 152.

4 The NRSV of the Holy Bible tells that some of the most ancient authorities bring the book to a close at the end of verse 8 while authority concludes the book with the shorter ending. In most authorities verses 9-20 follow immediately after verse 8, though in some of these

The above structures were studied by Scaria for his doctoral thesis. When the scholarly world has geographical, topographical, concentric and dramatic structure, Scaria wishes to have theological structure based on progressive revelation of the mystery of Jesus' messiahship. He divides the Mark's plan in two-fold way.

1. The progressive revelation of the mystery of Jesus' messiahship (1:14-8:26) and
2. The mystery of the suffering messiah (8:31-16:8).[5]

Thus Mark 1:1-13, is the prologue, 8:27-30, is the centre and 16:9-20, is an epilogue.

2.2. Immediate Structure of Mark

From the remote structure one thing is clear that the scholarly world agrees that 11:1-13:37, is the ministry of Jesus at Jerusalem. If we consider 1:14-8:26, as the first part dealing with messianic secret then the second part 8:31-15:47, could be called the mystery and mission of the son of man, 1:1-13, as the prologue, 8:27-30, as the centre and 16:1-20, as an epilogue.

In part II there are various responses to the person of Jesus from disciples, Jewish authority, crowd and Gentiles. 8:31-10:52, we have major three predictions of Jesus (8:31-33, 9:30-32, 10:32-34). These three predictions follow the call of disciples to authentic discipleship (8:34-38, 9:33-37, 10:35-45). This section deals on the way to Jerusalem, the place of final confrontation and revelation. The section is ended with the symbolic and significant story of the healing of blind Bartimaeus (10:46-52). This is not a mere physical healing but a healing that teaches symbolically what discipleship is: Bartimaeus prayed to Jesus, he came to him, received eye-sight, left his old identity and life and followed Jesus on the way.[6]

The central passage of our consideration is 11:1-13:37. It deals with the ministry of Jesus at Jerusalem. The whole section is centred on the temple of Jerusalem. Jesus' ministry in Jerusalem could be summed up as the entry, temple actions and encounters leading to eschatological discourse.

A. Messianic entry into Jerusalem11:1-11

Judgement in symbolic action11:12-26

a) Cursing of the fig tree (11:12-14)

authorities the passage is marked as being doubtful. Second observation is that there are number of variations and critical apparatus in the text of 9-20.

5 Scaria Kuthirakkattel, The Beginning of Jesus' Ministry According to Mark's Gospel (1:14-3:6) A Redaction Critical Study, *AnaBib 123,* Rome: Editrice Pontificio Istituto Biblico, 1990, 29, 37-39, 45.

6 Jose Maniparampil, Synoptic Gospels, Bangalore: Claretian Publications, 2004, 172-73.

b) Cleansing the temple (11:15-19)
c) Withering away of the fig tree (11:20-26) the so called cleansing of the temple is sandwiched between the cursing and the withering of the fig tree.

B. Two cycles of controversies

a) Chief priests, scribes and elders (11:27-12:12)
b) Pharisees and Herodians (12:13-34)
c) Jesus' teaching in the temple (12:35-44)

C. Judgement in prophetic word (13:1-37)

a) Prophecy of the destruction of the temple (13:1-23)
b) Coming of the glorious son of man (13:24-31)
c) Warning to the disciples to be watchful (13:32-37).[7]

Scaria has structured the second part of the Gospel in a way that emphasizes three key facets.

1. Mystery of Jesus' passion and death three predictions (8-10),
2. The plot of Jewish authorities (11-13) and the role of the disciples (14:1-42),
3. This is dramatically fulfilled in the arrest, condemnation and crucifixion of Jesus.[8]

Part II: The revelation of the mystery of the suffering son of man (8:27-16:8) is further worked by Scaria as follows:

a. The way of the son of man and discipleship (8:27-10:52)
b. Revelation in Jerusalem and the definitive break with the Jews (11:1-13:37)
c. The fulfilment and culmination of the mystery: Passion, death and resurrection of the son of man (14:1-16:8).

2.3. The Prediction of the Destruction of the Temple

Scaria presents his article on the theme of the temple and highlights Marcan narration in the ministry of Jesus at Jerusalem. He highlights the theme of continuation of Jesus' self-revelation. Jesus predicts the destruction of man-made temple while at the same time highlights the emergence of the God-made

---

7 *Ibid,* 175. Cf. Bas Van Lersel, Reading Mark, Collegeville, Minnesota: The Liturgical Press, 1988, 143.

8 Scaria Kuthirakkattel, The Beginning of Jesus' Ministry According to Mark's Gospel (1:14-3:6) A Redaction Critical Study, 43. Pheme Perkins, New Testament Introduction, Mumbai, Bandra: St. Paul's, 2002, 259- 268. The author describes Jesus as suffering Messiah, the powerful Saviour and Suffering Son of Man.

sanctuary.[9] The ministry of Jesus in chapters 11-13, of Mark is not centred on the city of Jerusalem rather on the temple of Jerusalem. However, the immediate context of 11:1-13:37 is studied from 'spatio-temporal categories'.[10] The spatial demarcations are indicated in three successive steps:

a. Jesus' journey to Jerusalem and His entry into the city and temple,
b. His activities in the temple and,
c. His exit from the city and temple.

While temporal designation is shown on three successive days. This scheme reveals a steady progress in Jesus' ministry in the temple. We have three days ministry. First day He has a searching look at everything but no word or deed (Mk 11:1-11), on the second day has His authoritative deed followed by teachings (11:12-19) and third day is engaged exclusively in dialogues often controversial, in which the nature of his person and mission is clearly revealed (11:20-27, 11:27b-12:44 and 13:1-37).[11] A system of purities centred around the temple and its cult began to supersede a system of ethical demands on which persons are judged righteous because of their right relationship of justice towards each other (Jer 7:4-7, Hos 6:6, Mich 6:6-8, Isa 58:1-12).

Chapter 12 is showing Jesus' own initiative and later we have total reversal plan of the Sanhedrin. One begins to wonder: why such a change exists in the strategy of people and Jewish authority? (Mk 14:2) Mark, the evangelist is introducing the passion narrative. Again, the answer to the question is found in Mark 13, where Jesus predicts the destruction of the temple. In 13:1, Jesus is already out of the temple, disciples marvel at temple (13:2-4) and finally we have an eschatological or farewell discourse (13:5-37). Jesus speaks of the destruction of the temple but does not name its agent. Jesus' sitting on the Mount of Olives (13:2) indicates his Messianic authority (Zech 14:4, Mk 4:1, 12:36, and 14:62). However, he sat opposite of the temple, why? This denotes not merely spatial distance but a theological one. There is a contrast between the temple and Jesus in and through whom the messianic era has been ushered in.[12] The aim of 11:1-13:37, was to show who Jesus' opponents were and what issues got him into trouble with the Jerusalem authorities. Mark 13 is an eschatological discourse. The evangelist sought to cool down eschatological

---

9 Scaria Kuthirakkattel, "The Man-made Temple and the God-made Sanctuary: Some Aspects of the New Testament Theology of the Temple", *Jeevadhara*, Vol. 23, No. 134, (1993), 153-170. 153.

10 Scaria Kuthirakkattel, The Beginning of Jesus' Ministry According to Mark's Gospel (1:14-3:6) A Redaction Critical Study, 45, 53-54.

11 *Ibid,* 53-56. Cf. Raymond E. Brown, An Introduction to the New Testament, Bangalore: TPI, 2014, 142.

12 Scaria Kuthirakkattel, "The Man-made Temple and the God-made Sanctuary: Some Aspects of the New Testament Theology of the Temple", 159-160.

fears and to inculcate patient endurance. He warns about the necessity of persecution and suffering, while encouraging the community to face whatever horrors the future may bring in the firm conviction that the climax of human history is the coming of the Son of Man and the kingdom of God.

2.3.1. The Destruction of the Temple

The gospel of Mark has been described as a passion narrative. Jesus knows beforehand what awaits him. All throughout, He behaves as the suffering servant and shows himself to be the king of the Jews. Despite of the mocking and blindness of his opponents, the disciples, however, reach the bottom of their descent in Judas' betrayal and Peter's denial. Section 14:1-2 deals with the plot. It is a natural outcome of Jesus' confrontation in Jerusalem. The plot to kill Jesus is affirmed by anointing which is the symbolic death of Jesus (14:3-8). Thus 14:9-15:39, is the narration of the passion and death of Jesus the Messiah and 15:40-47 we have burial of Jesus, where the temple personified in his person. In this section 14:9-16:8, we have preparation for the passion, for anointing again prepared to deny, betray and flight of the disciples and finally we have passion proper with arrest of Jesus, Jewish trial, followed by Roman trial and finally crucifixion, death, burial, and resurrection.

Mark 14:58, during his trials, the words of Jesus on the temple were repeated by the authority. And finally, Jesus gave a loud cry and breathed his last. The curtain of the temple was torn in two from top to bottom (15:37-38). The splitting of the temple veil is closely connected with Jesus' death. It was not veil from holy of holies but from the whole sanctuary. This shows that Jesus' anti-temple stance in 11:15-17, continued in 13:2 adduced as evidence against him in 14:58, used as a taunt in 15:29-30 and reaches its pinnacle in his death in 15:37-38.[13]

Again the splitting of the temple veil signifies the abrogation of the temple-centred relationship with God and all that the temple stood for. There is a connection between baptism and death of Jesus. At the baptism, we have rending of the heavens (Mk 1:10) and the voice from heaven declares that Jesus is the Son of God (Mk 1:11). Similarly, at Jesus' death, there was rending of the temple curtain and confession of the Centurion: truly this man was God's Son (15:38-39) to support the same[14]. These similarities in these two events show the true identity and mission of Jesus as a Son of God and suffering servant (Ps 2:7, 2 Sam 7:14, Isa 42:1). The Son of God is common and frequent title in Mark (1:11, 3:11, 5:7, 9:7 and 15:39). The confession of Centurion that Jesus is God's Son comes from seeing the death of Jesus (15:39). The mystery of the

13 *Ibid,* 161.

14 Scaria Kuthirakkattel, The Beginning of Jesus' Ministry According to Mark's Gospel (1:14-3:6): A Redaction Critical Study, 20.

suffering messiahship is fully realized in Jesus' death. The passion, crucifixion and death are not an end to Jesus' life. Chapter 16 narrates to us the resurrection of Jesus. The man-made temple will be destroyed but the temple built by the Risen Lord and His Spirit can never be destroyed.

2.3.2. The Old Testament Background

The triumphal entry of Jesus into Jerusalem (Mk 11:1-11) highlights his messiahship. It has its background in the OT (Zech 9:9, 14:4) and he is shown as the Son of David in the NT (Mk 11:10) that resounds messianic title from the Psalm (118:25-26). The authority of John the Baptist is that of Elijah (Mk 9:11-13, 11:27-32), the expected precursor of the Messiah and Jesus' authority is obviously messianic. The cursing of the fig tree and its withering away has another significant sign (Mk 11:12-14, 19:26). Again there are number of prophetic texts (Jer 8:13, Hos 9:10, 16-17, Joel 1:7 and Mich 7:1-6). The fig tree symbolizes Israel. The Evangelist highlights the unproductivity of Israel as the barren of salvation and the consequent rejection of Israel by God.[15]

Mark 11:15-18 contains the narration of Jesus' cleansing of the temple followed by his teaching. This is not a new pattern rather Mark has used in 1:21-28 and 2:1-12 words and deeds go hand in hand. They reveal the messiahship of Jesus. In fact, Jesus' teaching in Mark as a whole is messianic.[16] It has allusions in the prophetic literature (Isa 56:7, Jer 7:11). The temple will be replaced with an eschatological sanctuary where all nations will authentically relate themselves to God and to one another. The messiahship and his messianic mission were not acceptable to Scribes, Pharisees and High priests. Thus, they wanted to kill him (Mk 11:18, 12:12, 14:2, 43-50, 55-65). His death was theologically motivated. When leaders of the temple wanted to execute him, people were appreciative of him (11:18, 12:12) on the contrary.

3. Theology of Temple in Mark

The cursing of the fig tree (11:12-14) and its withering (11:20-26) comes under Marcan sandwich. Mark understood the cursing and its fulfilment as an act of power done by Jesus. The symbolic story focuses on Israel's lack of readiness to accept Jesus. It is a prophetic action and message is presented symbolically (Jer 19:1-2, 10-11, Ezk 12:1-7). The cleansing of the temple is seen as a mere cleansing of offensive practices but Jesus was the cause of the violent reaction of the Jerusalem authorities against Jesus and their determination to do away

15 Scaria Kuthirakkattel, "The Man-made Temple and the God-made Sanctuary: Some Aspects of the New Testament Theology of the Temple", 156. Henry Wansbrough, The Lion and the Bull: the Gospel of Mark and Luke, London, Darton: Longman and Todd Ltd, 1996, 34.

16 Scaria Kuthirakkattel, The Beginning of Jesus' Ministry According to Mark's Gospel (1:14-3:6): A Redaction Critical Study, 127.

with him (11:15-19). The temple and its rites were the glory of Jerusalem.[17] It was a symbolic act of destruction to build new temple. It was a renewal of the hope of Israel (Ezk 40-44). The main idea is of Jesus' self-revelation. We have his identity as God's promised messiah. This self-revelation took place through his words and deeds in the temple.

Jesus' triumphal entry into Jerusalem (Mk 11:1-11) looks fairly harmless today but for Jewish contemporaries of Jesus' time, it is full of mysterious allusions (Gen 49:10-11, Zech 9:9).[18] In Jacob's blessings, Judah is promised the sceptre, the ruler's staff that belongs to the obedient people. Prophet Zechariah gives prophetic words for the understanding of the figure of Jesus who is meek and humble of heart (Zech 9:9, Mt 11:27-30). The theme of the kingdom and its promises is ever-present. He claims the right of kings: A king of peace and simplicity, a king of the poor and reigns over a kingdom embracing the whole world. The OT promises are fulfilled in his person. Jesus does not build his kingdom on violence, nor on instigating a military revolt against Rome. His power is of another kind: it is in God's poverty, God's peace that he identifies the only power that can redeem. The Hosanna proclamation has come from the pilgrim liturgy of the OT (Ps 118:26, Mk 11:9-10). It is messianic homage to Jesus that was played out on his entry into the city by people of Jerusalem, disciples and the crowds.

The episode of the cleansing of the temple is related in all four gospels (Mt 21:12f, Mk 11:15-18, Lk 19:45f and John 2:14-17). The cleansing of the temple has been interpreted on three principles by Joseph Ratzinger.[19] First, it was considered that cleansing of the temple constituted an attack, not on the temple as such, but only on its misuse. The temple and business did not correspond to the purpose for which the temple was built. He was attacking the existing practice that had been set up by the temple aristocracy. He was not violating the law and prophets rather implementing it. Jesus was lost in the temple and Mary and Joseph were searching for him. Why were you searching for me? Did you not know that I must be in my Father's house? (Lk 2:48-49). Later the temple authority merely asked Jesus by what authority he acted in this way. Thus, the action was against the religious authority of the time who failed to know the importance of the house of the Lord.

The second principle of interpretation is political and revolutionary. Jesus was neither a reformer nor an agitator. The act of dedicating the temple was done by Maccabee brothers who went against Hellenist (1Mac 2:22-26).

17 *Ibid,* 55. Cf. Henry Wansbrough, The Lion and the Bull: the Gospels of Mark and Luke, 64.

18 Pope Benedict XVI, Jesus of Nazareth, Holy Week: from the Entrance into Jerusalem to the Resurrection, Part 2, San Francisco: Ignatius Press, 2011, 3-5. Scaria Kuthirakkattel, "The Role of Prophetic Theologizing in Jesus' Dharma", *Jnanadeepa Pune Journal for Religious Study,* Vol. 18, No. 2, (2015), 77-96, 87-89.

19 *Ibid,* 11-23.

It was done out of zeal as well as violence for the freedom. His zeal for the kingdom of God took quite a different form. The king of peace arriving on donkey presented the slain shepherd, who saves by his death. Jesus located his ministry as the suffering servant, offers up his life for the multitude and thus brings salvation (Isa 52:13-53:12).

My house shall be called the house of prayer... but you have made it a den of robbers (Isa 56:7, Jer 7:11, Mk 11:17). The temple was to be a house of prayer for all people who would bring their wealth for the service of the temple and the glory of the temple of Zerubbabel exceeded the glory of the temple of Solomon (Hag 2:6-9). To this temple would come Yahweh and the angel of the covenant (Mal 3:1). Here we have another stream of thought where temple was disappearing in the messianic fulfillment. In Ezekiel the temple became sacred, the source of a stream of living water that fertilized the desert of Judah and sweetened the water of the Dead Sea (47:1ff, Zech 14:8).[20] Isaiah presented a universalistic vision in which all people would come together in the house of God to worship the Lord as the one God. The fundamental purpose of cleansing the temple was to remove whatever obstacles might have been there to the common recognition and worship of God and thereby to opening up a space for common worship.

The third principle of interpretation is Jesus himself. The cleansing of the temple in John took place during Jesus' first Passover in John's account (2:13-25), while Synoptics had one Passover in the last days of Jesus' ministry. The universality of Isaiah's prophecy is taken up by John when Greeks came to see Jesus (12:20-21). Having received the message from Philip and Andrew, Jesus said 'the hour has come for the son of man to be glorified... unless a grain of wheat falls into the earth and dies, it remains alone, but if it dies, it bears much fruit' (12:23-24). Jesus' glorification was possible only in His passion. Jesus as a true God was found by the Greeks on the cross.

Jeremiah is an impassioned advocate of the unity of worship and life in the context of divine Justice. He prophesied that "You have made my house into a den of robbers" (7:11). Prophet argues that God would protect his temple but does not do it for it has become a den of robbers. Jesus' words and actions constituted a warning that could be understood together with his reference to the destruction of the temple. Both Jeremiah and Jesus were not responsible for the destruction of the temple but their passion indicates who and what would truly destroy the temple.

Destroy this temple and in three days I will raise it up (Jn 2:19) demonstrate his authority for acting as he did in the cleansing of the temple. The cross and resurrection gave him authority as the one who would usher true worship. The

20 John L. McKenzie, "Temple", In *Dictionary of the Bible,* London- Dublin: Geoffrey Chapman, 1966, 872-878, 876.

rejection and crucifixion of Jesus means the end of the temple. Thus, a new form of worship is being introduced, in a temple not built by human hands (Mk 14:58). This temple is his body, the risen one, who gathers the peoples and unites them in the sacrament of his body and blood. He himself is the new temple of humanity.[21] Jesus here affirms that he himself becomes the cultic centre, the place where God is present in his dwelling; as such he is greater than the temple (Mt 12:6). "It is not on mountain or temple but worship in spirit and truth" (Jn 4:23).

It is zeal for the house of God leads Jesus to the passion and cross (Jn 2:17). The zeal that would serve God through violence has been transformed into the zeal of the cross. It is zeal of self-giving love. Instead of cattle-trading and money changing, Jesus tells us that the purpose of the temple and its priest would bring healing (Mt 21:14). Jesus the true temple brings his healing and goodness. This is in reality a true cleansing of the temple. He does not come to destroy as a destroyer. He reveals God as the one who loves and showcases his power as the power of love. Mark announces the coming of the new temple and that temple is Jesus himself.

Conclusion

The situation of our time is not different from the situation in the time of Jesus. What we see is lot more of religiosity and less of spirituality in the world today. Jesus was not against the temple that he cleansed, rather whatever was practiced in the temple and the behavior that was manifested outside. What we see is the priority given to the building of the temple that is man-made, and God-made sanctuary called human beings is destroyed in the name of God and temple. What we need today is to pull ourselves out of other-worldly orientation to a sense of history, and go through the process of modernization and secularization. Jesus, while cleansing the temple felt a need of liberating the temple from within. It suffered from political revolutions, conflicts, the religious movements against domination, injustice and oppression.

As Indians, we highlight not so much centripetal aspect of our relationship with God and temple, rather centrifugal, where we meet the needs of the other by reaching to the peripheries. It is an authentic emancipatory praxis seen from the *anubhava,* a deep experience of being, truth, beauty, life and freedom. Jesus saw in the Jewish society and its religiosity a lack of *anubhava* as well as practice of *adharma* based on poverty, oppression and exploitation. He, the new, living temple, which needs to be worshiped in spirit and truth, promoted the *dharma* of righteousness. He says no religious practices are possible without a spirit of detachment, renunciation, emptiness, and silence.

21 Pope Benedict XVI, Jesus of Nazareth, Holy Week: from the Entrance into Jerusalem to the Resurrection, Part 2, 21-22.

The temple of the Mark and its practices within stood for contradiction against which this prophecy made by Jesus saying, 'destroy this man-made temple and I will build God-made Sanctuary', first by his resurrection and secondly, everyone who believes in him becoming the temple of the Holy Spirit.

Let me conclude with the words of Rabindranath Tagore in his great poem in Gitanjali. He writes: "Leave this chanting and singing and telling of beads! Whom dost thou worship in this lonely corner of a temple with doors shut? Open thine eyes and see thy God is not before thee! He is there where the tiller is tilling the hard ground and where the path-maker is breaking stones. He is with them in sun and in shower, and his garment is covered with dust. Put off thy holy mantle and even like him come down on the dusty soil" (Poem XI).

The poem from Gatanjali resembles the teaching of prophet Isaiah. He says, "When you come to appear before me, who requires of you this trampling of my court… when you spread forth your hands, I will hide my eyes from you; even though you make many prayers, I will not listen… wash yourselves; make yourselves clean; seek justice, correct oppression, defend the fatherless, plead for the widow (1:12-16). What we need is a new kind of temple with new orientation, new commitment above all the temple and its worship should help us to transform ourselves, our world and solidarity with the least and last of the society. Yes, divine is not confined to any limited space and place but present everywhere in the entire universe, his presence is all pervading (Mt 18:20, 28:20). The divine is not to be sought and meditated upon only in the temple of one's inner self or in the temples of stones, but to be encountered and contemplated within history through liberative involvement. Jesus is that temple, to whom all human and man-made temples are subservient.

17

The Marriage of Zion
The Exegetical Implications of Isaiah 62:1-5*

Saji Joseph Kizhakkayil

Introduction

Isa 62:1-5 corresponds thematically to Rev 21:1-22:5, portraying the intimate relationship of God to the renewed heavenly Jerusalem, portrayed through a Bridal/marital imagery. This article exegetically studies this OT text of the marital imagery, explaining the concept of Jerusalem as the people of God.[1] While elucidating the meaning of the text, it also clarifies the apparent logical incongruence in some verses (e.g., your sons shall marry you, cf. 62:5) through the text-critical and exegetical interpretation of the text.

---

* I am honored to present this article in honor of my first teacher in biblical exegesis, Dr. Scaria Kuthirakkattel SVD, for a Festschrift on the occasion of his 80th Birthday. This article on Isa 62:1-5 is a complementary writing for an earlier article of mine, published on the New Jerusalem (Rev 21:1-22:5), in another Festschrift in 2014, cf. Saji Joseph Kizhakkayil, "New Jerusalem as Bride of God, Holy of Holies and as Paradise: A threefold affirmation of God's intimacy with his people (Rev 21:1-22:5)," in Dominik Markl, Claudia Paganini, et.al (eds.), *Gottes Wort im Menschenwort: festschrift für Georg Fischer SJ zum 60. Geburtstag*, ÖBS 43, Peter Lang, Frankfurt am Main, 2014, 249-270., 249-270.

1 The conjugal imagery describing the relationship of YHWH to his people and to the city of Jerusalem is an oft recurring motif in the Old Testament. Cf. Isa 54:5-7; 62:1; Ezek 16:1, 8.

This small exegetical study[2] contains three main parts: (1) The translation, delimitation and structural analysis of Isa 62:1-5, (2) an inter-textual analysis of the text, and (3) an exegetical interpretation of it. The exegetical interpretation will be done only as much to explain the central meaning of the text. The article is concluded by drawing up the spiritual implication of the text.

1. Translation and Text Critics of Isaiah 62:1-5

The passage (Isa 62:1-5) is attempted to translate as closely as possible to the Hebrew text, dividing the verses into phrases, to help us to refer back to the text during its interpretation. Concurrently we also look into the most important text-critical problems relevant to our interpretation of the text. The less relevant text-critical problems are ignored due to the limited scope of this paper.[3]

למען צִיון לא אחשה	1 a	For the sake of Zion, I will not be silent
ולמען ירושלם לא אשקוט	b	and for the sake of Jerusalem, I will not rest
עד־יצא כנגה צדקה	c	till her righteousness goes forth like the daylight
וישועתה כלפיד יבער	d	and her salvation like a torch burns
וראו גוים צדקך	2 a	and the nations will see your Righteousness
וכל־מלכים כבודך	b	and all the kings your glory
וקרא לך שם חדש	c	and (to) you will be designated a new name,
אשר פי יהוה יקבנו	d	that the mouth of the Lord will carve.
והיית עטרת תפארת ביד־יהוה	3 a	and you will be a glorious crown in the hand of YHWH
(וצנוף) [וצניף] מלוכה בכף־אלהיך	b	and a royal turban[4] in the hand of your Lord.
לא־יאמר לך עוד עזובה	4 a	No long will you be called "*'azuvah"* (forsaken)
ולארצך לא־יאמר עוד שממה	b	and never again will be (to) your land said "*shamama*" (barren)
כי לך יקרא חפצי־בה	c	But (to) you will be said "*heptzi-vah*" (my delight in her)
ולארצך בעולה	d	and (to) your land "*Baula"* (married)
כי־חפץ יהוה בך	e	for the Lord will delight in you

2 Due to the limited scope of the article, this study is limited to a small unit of the chapter. It was surely preferable to include the rest of the chapter (v7-12) in the exegetical interpretation.

3 For a detailed discussion of text critical problems, see Watts, *Isaiah 34-66* (Word Biblical Commentary 25: Dallas, Texas: Word Books, Publisher, 1987), 879; and John N Oswalt, *The Book of Isaiah: Chapters 40-66* (Eerdmans, Grand Rapids, Michigan, Cambridge: 1998). 576-77.

4 *Ketib* and 1QIsa[a] have וצנוף (qal inf. abs. – 'to wrap') *Qere* suggestion by *Massorets* is: וצניף a – 'a turban' (noun).

וארצך תבעל	f	and your land will be married.
כי־יבעל בחור בתולה	5 a	for as a young man marries[5] a virgin
יבעלוך בניך	b	so will your sons marry you.[6]
ומשוש חתן על־כלה	c	and (as) the exaltation of a bridegroom over the bride,
ישיש עליך אלהיך	d	will your Lord exalt over you.

1.1. Delimitation of the Text

The Masoretic Text (MT) presents Isa 61:10-62:9 as a single unit[7] delimited by two *Setumot.* In this bigger unit, Isa 62:1-5 could be taken as a small subunit[8] on the basis of other literary parameters. The reasons are: Thematically, Isa 61:1-11 speaks of the Mission of the servant of YHWH. Isa 62:1 brings in a new turn with a new proclamation by the speaker. Further, in v2 the speaker begins to address directly Jerusalem in the second person (notably, in the second person feminine), which proceeds till the end of v5, the unit has a single theme – the new status of Jerusalem. The subunit ends in v5, because from v6, the style of the metaphoric speech, the Scene, as well as the direction of the speech changes. Just as in v1, v6 begins with another proclamation by the speaker, which then proceeds with a different discourse. Hence, we can presuppose a new subunit with v6, although it begins with the same motif (of not keeping silent, cf. חשה) as in v1.

5 MT has: כי־יבעל (verb qal imp. 3rd mas. Sing – "for he marries/ will marry"); and 1QIsa[a] has כיא כבעול (verb qal Participle – "for as one marries"). *Targum* ("for as one dwels with") and *LXX* ("for as one lives with"), support 1QIsa[a]. Cf. Watts, *Isaiah 34-66*, 879 (note 5a). I, however, see *Targum* and *LXX* as explanatory, as it could also be in the case of 1QIsa[a]. Hence, I prefer the hard and shorter reading of MT.

6 Instead of יִבְעָלֵךְ בֹּנֵךְ BHS suggests: יִבְעָלוּךְ בָּנָיִךְ. Here BHS is trying to clarify an incongruity of the text, which amounts to an interpretation of the text and not faithfulness to the authenticity of the text. The metaphoric, poetic and multivalent character of the Hebrew words is thus overlooked. All the more, this suggestion has no textual support at all. Hence, the suggestion does not merit a serious consideration. For a text critical suggestion for translation, see, De Ward, *A Handbook on Isaiah,* Harold P. Scanlin *(ed.), Vol. 1. (Eisenbrauns, New York: 1997)*, 208.

7 For an acquaintance with the general structure of Isa 56-66, see, Ulrich Berges, *Das Buch Jesaja* (HBS 16. Herder, Freiburg, Basel, Wien: 1998), 420 &483; and for the structure of Ch. 61-62, see, J. Alec Motyer, *The Prophesy of Isaiah: An Introduction and Commentary* (Inter Varsity Press, Downers Grove, Illinois:1993), 504.

8 Contrary to this position, many authors hold 62:1-7 as a single unit, Childs Brevards S., *Isaiah* (John Knox Press, Louisville, London: 2001*,* 509-10; Watts, *Isaiah 34-66*, 878-79; Ulrich Berges, *Das Buch*, 455.

1.2 The Structure, Movement and the other Literary Features

This subunit is a poetic text, rich with similes and metaphoric language marked by well-balanced strophes and parallelisms. The parallelisms in the strophes are depicted below.

למען צִיון לא אחשה // ולמען ירושלם לא אשקוט
עד־יצא כנגה צדקה // וישועתה כלפיד יבער
וראו גוים צדקך // וכל־מלכים כבודך
וקרא לך שם חדש // אשר פי יהוה יקבנו
והיית עטרת תפארת ביד־יהוה // (וצנוף) [וצניף] מלוכה בכף־אלהיך
לא־יאמר לך עוד עזובה // ולארצך לא־יאמר עוד שממה

כי לך יקרא חפצי־בה // ולארצך בעולה
כי־חפץ יהוה בך // וארצך תבעל
כי־יבעל בחור בתולה // יבעלוך בניך
ומשוש חתן על־כלה // ישיש עליך אלהיך

In v1, one sees evidently the intensification of the motif of not keeping silent and a progression of it in the use of the verbs חשה (v1a) and שקט (v1b) successively. Concurrently, noticeable is the focus on Jerusalem brought in by the juxtaposition of Jerusalem and Zion. This is followed by the personality description of Jerusalem with the royal/divine and conjugal terminologies that dominate the unit. The general movement within the unit could be construed as follows:

(**Speaker's urge to actualize Jerusalem's salvation**)
Speaker pitches for Jerusalem's Salvation
Till her uprightness brightens and her salvation dawns

↓

(**Consequence of Jerusalem's impending salvation**)
People will see her righteousness and Kings her Glory
And Jerusalem gets a new status
(Jerusalem – called by a new name, given by the mouth of YHWH
Jerusalem – Crown of beauty and kingly turban in her Lord's Hand
Jerusalem – called no more "abandoned", her land no more "devastation
Jerusalem – called "my delight in her", and her land "married")

↓

(**Reason for her new status – she is the bride of YHWH**)
Because the Lord has delight in her and that her land is married

↓

(**Evidence of her new status**)

As a young man marries a bride, so will Jerusalem's 'sons' 'marry' her
And as a bridegroom rejoices over the bride, her Lord will rejoice over her

Among the other notable literary finesse include the alliteration in v5a[9]; the pun on words with חפצי־בה, עזובה, בעולה, and שׁממה in v4;[10] the use of the verb חשׁה as a transition technique (cf. v1a and v6b); etc.

Further, the text has very positive, picturesque scenes – especially, negative scenes are avoided. The verses in the text are connected with terms that progressively lead one verse to the other literarily: for example, v1-2 has צדק as the connecting word; v2-3 has יהוה, v2-4 has קרא, יהוה and v4-5 has בעל, etc.

2. Inter-textual Analysis

A very important textual feature in this unit is its inter-textual relationship of this subunit with other biblical texts. Isaiah 62:1-5 has inter-textual parallels in the books of Psalms and in the book of Jeremiah. The closest parallel is seen in Ps 83.

Is 62:1ab	למען צִיון לא אחשה ולמען ירושלם לא אשׁקוט
Ps 83:2	אלהים אל־דמי־לך אל־תחרשׁ ואל־תשׁקט אל

Concurrently, the other half of Ps 83:2 has a parallel again in Isa 62:6c:

Ps 83:2	אלהים אל־דמי־לך אל־תחרשׁ ואל־תשׁקט אל
Is 62:6c	המזכרים את־יהוה אל־דמי לכם

Ps 83:2 is thus parallel both to Isa 62:1 and to Isa 62:6c. Ps 83, the last of the *Asaph* Psalms could be argued to be prior to the post exilic redaction of Isaiah on the basis of the use of the word אלהים in the Psalm (v2) and on the basis of the names of the kingdoms – Edom, Ishmaelites, Moab, the Hagarenes, Gebal, Ammon, Amalek, Philistia Tyre, Asshur – cited in Ps 83:6-8. Hence, the question arises: Is the last redactor of Isaiah borrowing from Ps 83:2? It is unlikely, because YHWH as the subject of the verbs שׁקט and חשׁה are more familiar in Isaiah than in the other books of the OT.[11] Moreover, the prophetic collections *N^e^viim* predate the *K^e^tuviim*. Hence, Ps 83:2 is likely to be dependent on Isa 62:1 and Isa 62:6. Isa 62:2-5 has further literary and thematic parallels in the book of Jeremiah.

Is 62:5	ומשׂושׂ חתן על־כלה ישׂישׂ עליך אלהיך
Jer 7:34	והשׁבתי מערי יהודה ומחצות ירושלם קול שׂשׂון וקול שׂמחה קול חתן וקול כלה

---

9 The Hebrew words in this section of the verse begin in ב or יב

10 See for details the interpretation of the verses below.

11 See, the interpretation of the text below.

Here, Isaiah seems to rework on Jeramiah's prophesy, effectively revising them.[12] Thus, the prophecy of Isaiah signifies a changed situation by the end of the exile, in which the Jeremiah's exilic prophesy on the situation of Jerusalem stands something of the past. Hence, the text presupposes a situation that begins with the end of the exile and the strong expectation of the renewed glory of the city of Jerusalem.

3. Interpretation Isa 62:1-5

In Isa 62:1 two verbs – שקט and חשה – are used in a synonymous manner. חשה appears 16 times in OT and connotes hesitation or inactivity at the face of an opportunity.[13] Out of these 16 occurrences, six are in Isaiah and it mainly refers to YHWH's inactivity in relation to a need of the people,[14] or to his silence. Hence, associated with the adverbial particle of negation לא (v1a&b), these verbs (שקט and חשה) bring in just the opposite nuance - an affirmation of the intention by the speaker.

Normally the words חשה and שקט have YHWH as the subject in Isaiah (cf. 18:4; 42:14; 57:11; 64:11; 65:6). From the inter-textual perspective too, in Ps 83, the word has YHWH as the subject. This led some authors to think that the speaker here is YHWH.[15] However, in this instance, the subject of the verbs cannot be YHWH, because the speech leads to the reference to YHWH in the third person (cf. v2d, 3ab, 4d and 5c). Moreover, the same speaker in v6 exhorts 'the reminders of YHWH' not to give him peace/rest until he establishes Jerusalem as per his promise (cf. YHWH's promise to Jerusalem in 60:18). Is it the prophet himself or some other speaker, who is trying to oblige YHWH to fulfill the promise he made earlier (cf. 58:8, 60:1-22)? What we can say here is: (i) The identity of the speaker is not clearly distinguishable here,[16] and (ii) the speaker is using these words, to expresses his resoluteness for the cause of Jerusalem's redemption. He is surely not YHWH. He may be the

---

12 For a detailed discussion on Jeremiah's reception in Isaiah, see Baruch Halpern, "The New Names of Isaiah 62:4: Jeremiah's Reception in the Restoration and the Politics of "Third Isaiah," in *Journal of Biblical Literature,* Vol. 117, No. 4 (1998): 623-643.

13 Cf. John N. Oswalt, *hvx*, in *New International Dictionary of Old Testament Theology and Exegesis,* Vol.2. (Zondervan, Grand Rapids, Michigan: 1997), 311.311.

14 This nuance is evident in the following citations Is 65:6; see also, Isa 42:14; 57:11; Ps 28:1

15 Cf. Delitzsch, *Der Prophet Jesaja* (Wentworth Press: Manchester 2018) 626-27.

16 There are different opinion as to who is the speaker: 1. YHWH (Delitzsch, *Jesaja* 626-27); 2. Messenger of Joy (Freudenbote – Beuken, IIIA, 225-26 as mentioned by Ulrich Bergs, *Das Buch*, 456); 3. Teitto-Isaiah (Duhm, *Jesaja*, 458; Westermann Claus. Das Buch Jesaja Kapital 40-66. ATD 19. Vandwnhoeck & Ruprecht, Göttingen, Zürich: 1986, 297-98); 4. The prophet-servant (Childs, *Isaiah*, 511-12); 5. The anointed one (Motyer, *The prophesy*, 504-05); etc. For short discussions on the topic, see, Ulrich Bergs, *Das Buch*, 456; Watts, *Isaiah 34-66*, 880; John N Oswalt, *The Book*, 578; Brevard S. Childs, Isaiah, 510; etc.

prophet himself, or the servant of YHWH, who speaks in the previous subunit, or generally speaking, he could be named 'a herald' of hope.

Both Zion and Jerusalem are used in Parallel like the verbs שקט and חשה. Without entering into the exegetical nuances of these names for the sake of brevity, the notable fact is the personification of these two, signified by the feminine ending of the two verbs (צדקה and ישועתה). This signification is metaphorically and poetically essential to portray the city as queen mothers and as the bride of YHWH (cf.v4cd) in the following verses.

The tireless effort of the herald is directed towards the shining forth of the righteousness (צדק) in the city. The motifs of shining forth of Zion in righteousness (צדק), her glory, the redemption (ישועה) of Jerusalem, as well as the people and kings flowing to Jerusalem are already introduced in Isa 2:1-5.[17] In the transformation of this personified city, the first change expected is its shining forth in Righteousness. Implicitly, her salvation (ישועה) is presented parallel and as the second aspect of her transformation. Hence the salvation of the city follows as the consequence of her being righteous. Moreover, Jerusalem's new glorious status as YHWH's bride will declare her righteousness to the peoples of the world and her glory to the kings (v2ab). Or as Motyer[18] puts it – what the Lord does for Zion attracts the attention of the whole world - she is a light in their darkness. Thus, one could even metaphorically interpret that righteousness (צדק) and salvation (ישועה) are the adornments of this woman (Jerusalem) as the bride of YHWH, which attracts people and kings of the world to Zion.[19]

The new name (שם חדש) indicates YHWH's exerting power and ownership over Jerusalem. It also can signify a new identity of a person renamed. Thus, from the context of the text, i.e., of the visualized new status of Jerusalem (glorious crown, royal turban) and of the YHWH's ownership (cf. the conjugal imagery – Husband) of Jerusalem, both the nuances of renaming are evident here. This motive presents also a contrast to the fallen, devastated (שממה – cf. 1:7; 6:11; 17:9; 64:9) Jerusalem, who is called a prostitute in Isa 1:26. Now, she - the glorious crown (עטרת תפארת) and the royal turban (צניף מלוכה) - [20] is in the hand of the Lord. When associated with Isa 54 and 60, this could signify that YHWH is her builder (cf. 54:5-6).[21] He is also her bride groom (cf. 60:14-15).

17 See also, 49:7; 52:15; 60:3, 10-11, 16.

18 J. Alec Motyer, *The Prophesy*, 506.

19 This motif is common even in the New Testament writings, like the Pauline letters and especially, of the book of Revelation (cf. 21:3, 10-21), which directly takes over motifs from the book of Isaiah.

20 Proverbs 12:4 speaks of a good wife as the crown of the husband.

21 For your Maker is your husband, the Lord Almighty is his name … Cf. Edward Joung, *The Book of Isaiah: The English Text with Introduction, Exposition and Notes. Vol 3* (William

The motif of the promise of a new name in v2 finds further progression in v4 and Jerusalem is renamed here. The naming of Jerusalem in these verses has antecedents in Hos 1:4f, where the naming of the children of the prophet corresponds to a socio-religious and political situation of Israel.[22] The prophet's marriage with a prostitute, and in turn, their juxtaposition to YHWH and Jerusalem respectively, can also be seen in comparative terms in the context of our text. The two antonymous names of Jerusalem: *'Azuvah* (עזובה – abandoned cf. 54:1-6 and 60:15) and *Heptzi-vah* (חפצי־בה- my delight in her) are names of two queen mothers of Israel. *'Azuvah* is mother of Jehoshaphat (1Kgs 22:42) & *heptzi-vah* mother of Manasse (2Kgs 21:1). The word *'Azuvah* signifies the abandonment of a woman by her husband (cf. Isa 54:6; 60:15; 1Kings 22:42) and *Heptzi-vah* represents just the opposite motif. Jerusalem is seen here belonging to the royal heritage in both the cases. She is Queen – in both the cases of her abandonment and in the status of God's delight in her. Baruch Halpern[23] brings in an excellent interpretation, when he juxtaposes the queen mothers of Israel and the kingdom of Israel, in which the queen mother personifies the Land. On the other hand, the land as YHWH's consort/bride is a familiar motif in the prophetic books (cf. Hos 2:1ff). Thus, by reading together the above factors and the royal and conjugal motives applied to Jerusalem in this text, it emerges that the author here employs a play on words (pun – but again a juxtaposition) projecting Jerusalem's visualized Royal Status[24] (cf. royal turban, glorious crown & names of the queen-mothers) and her status as the bride of YHWH (cf. 54:1-6). The implied meaning is that Jerusalem will no more remain devastated (שׁממה) or be an abandoned (עזובה) city. In contrast, she will be owned or inhibited (בעל) and she will be a delight (חפצי־בה) to YHWH and to the world.

In v5 the author continues with the play with the two words בעל and בנים to project two sets of meanings – 'to marry' vs. 'to possess' and 'sons' vs. 'inhabitants' respectively. Seeing the incongruity of sons' marrying "mother" some of the authors[25] as well as the BHS, as we have already seen

B. Eerdmans, Grand Rapids, Michigan, Cambridge: 1972), 469.

22 See the names יזרעאל (Hos 1:4), and לא רחמה (Hos 1:6).

23 For a convincing interpretation for the use of דנא עזובה חפצי־בה in Isa 62:4, see, Baruch Halpern, "New Names ...", 636-643.

24 I think Watts, *Isaiah 34-66*, 878, overlooks many thematic elements, and literary indications like inter-textuality of themes and motifs, when he interprets צדק as 'legitimacy'. Though the term צדק can mean legitimacy, vindication, etc., it is better to translate the word into righteousness. Watts interprets the royal terminologies of the unit presuming that it signifies the royal ambitions of the speaker in the unit.

25 Lowth, *Isaiah*, 618-19, as mentioned by De Ward, *A Handbook*, 208.

it in Text-critical analysis, suggest a change of "Sons" with "Builder".[26] This suggestion is however, unwarranted, as the prophetic author seems to be intentionally using the very words as it stands today. Moreover YHWH being the Bridegroom of Jerusalem cancels out any nuance of 'sons' (בנים) 'marrying' (בעל) her. Hence the second set of nuances, i.e., the 'inhabitants' (בנים) of Jerusalem 'possessing'(בעל) or occupying her (in contrast to her being devastated and abandoned) need to be applied here. The interpretative translations of *Targum* ("for as one dwels with") and *LXX* ("for as one lives with")[27] vindicate this nuance. Moreover, this sort of play on words is very characteristic of the author of Isaiah.

Conclusion

Seen from the exegetical perspective, the passage is the portrayal of the urge and pining of the speaker to see the salvation of Jerusalem actualized concretely. The text brings a strong hope for the people at the end of the exile through an ideal representation of the earthly kingdom of God symbolized by Zion and Jerusalem. Thus, the text begins with an enthusiastic proclamation: "For Zion's sake I will not be silent, and for Jerusalem's sake I will not rest until her righteousness breaks out like light and her salvation burns like a torch."

Subsequently, the herald of Zion shares a very soothing message in a pictorial presentation of a Marriage bond! The people of Israel were very familiar with how close, moving, warm, overwhelming, and joyful the coming together of a newly married couple was. The prophet uses this image of marriage to describe God's relationship to his people.

In conclusion, the text says: (i) YHWH delights in his beloved people - He comes to dwell among them. (ii) He wants to make his people a bright light (example) and a guide for the whole world; (iii) for this YHWH demands from his people a commitment, and their untiring will to Justice and righteousness, so that salvation of the world becomes a reality through a people wedded to YHWH and to his righteousness.

Thereby the herald comforts the people in need in a very effective, touching and pictorial way, and encourages them to await the coming salvation. This exegetical study equips one to understand its spiritual implication.

The speaker of the text proclaims Good news to Jerusalem. But the so called 'good news' of the herald is not mere pleasing words to the ears of the hearer. The proclamation stresses on establishing righteousness as a way of life. Hence, every prophetical message is a challenge to the society to establish justice as a way of life, which will initiate the sparks of salvation.

---

26 See note 7 of this paper.

27 See note 6 of this paper.

Further, the text hints that the salvation of the people is consequent to the dawning of righteousness. Hence, according to the herald, the righteousness of the city, or the return of righteousness to the people is the reason for salvation (cf. Isa 30:15; 32:17). This means, the arrival of the rule of God happens simultaneously, when the people turn righteous.

Concluding Article

18

Intercultural Challenges for Exegetes in India

Francis X D'Sa, SJ

Introduction

Fr. Scaria Kuthirakkattel SVD, a serious scholar of the Gospel of Mark has been all along, a fully committed JDV faculty member. George M. Soares-Prabhu SJ and he created a fresh wave of interest in the Scripture in general and in the New Testament in particular. Personally, he has been an inspiration to me from the beginning, besides being a true and trusted friend. Scaria, as he was popularly known among us, is not a populist and does not play to the gallery. Like John the Baptist, he is a rock, not a reed and like Mark, the focus of his life, he discovers great significance in small details. He has the features of a prophet with the difference that no one would ever think of stoning him.

I am glad that on his 80th birthday JDV honours him with a well-deserved Festschrift. To make the cup full, the Indian tradition bestows on the celebrant of the 80th birthday an altogether different gift: *sahasra-candra-darśanam* (A life that has had the darśana of a thousand moons!). Modesty is Scaria's ferial vestment and his work programme will not be overly perturbed by these titles. We who honour and admire him will do so on a deeper level when we walk his path of silent and unwavering commitment. On this occasion, I offer this piece to Scaria, a scholar and critical writer, which I have written both in the sweat of my brow and with the conviction of my heart in appreciation of his commitment.

The following is a plea to Biblical Scholars (Scaria's profession) and to Indologists (my profession) whom I address together as Exegetes, because of the similarity of the formal object though not the material object, to exercize a hermeneutic of suspicion about the world from which we practise our vocation, and become more aware of the world[view] of Gandhi's India, as Soares-Prabhu would have admonished us to do, a quarter of century after his departure from our midst.

1. The Mīmāṃsā's *Apauruṣeya Śabda*

For Gandhi's India (Soares-Prabhu's phrase), history was not the problem, as our modernists are trying to convince us, but our mythical Kurukṣetras and Ayodhyas and their accompanying myths and pseudo-myths that oppress or liberate—all of which are operating on/in the background of our community consciousness. As R. Panikkar would have put it, we experience *temporality*, not history. For one thing, history is an ideological expression of the myth of the western worldview. Review our early literature in whatever Indian language you like and there you will discover the soul of India pulsating. For another, it is from this context that our discussion in the following text of India's *Śabara-Bhāṣya* of the Mīmāṃsā tradition takes off in what follows.

> The words of the *Sūtras* are, so far as possible, to be understood in that same sense which they are known to convey in common parlance; it is not right to assume meanings for them on the basis of elliptical and other devices, —or to attribute to them any special technical signification. It is only in this way that all that would have to be done would be to explain the Vedic texts directly (with the help of the *Sūtras*); otherwise (if we did not take the words of the *Sūtras* in their ordinary sense), it would be necessary for us to explain the extra-ordinary (technical) meanings of the words of the *Sūtras* themselves, and the texts of the Vedas. This would involve a great exertion.[1]

The point of the quotation is this. It stresses the importance of *everyday language*, the language that everyone understands over against technical terminology. The *vedavākyāni* are symbolic language which those who have grown up in that world understand. The great Ganganath Jha who has translated very many difficult texts rightly translates *vedavākyāni* as Vedic texts and not as Vedic sentences because in common parlance the phrase refers to the Vedic

1 Ganganath Jha, *Śabara-Bhāṣya*. Translated into English. Vol. I (Oriental Institute, Baroda, 1973), 1.

texts. Unfortunately, the otherwise normally meticulous Austrian Indologist-Buddhologist Scholar Erich Frauwallner misses the mark when he translates the phrase literally as die vedischen Sätze[2]. On the other hand, Jha seems to have overlooked the argument about everyday language when his translation brings in words like elliptical and other devices which are not part of everyday language.

It is important to remember that everyday language does not refer to just any words. Panikkar has drawn our attention to the fact that in everyday language we implicitly make a distinction between words and terms. Words are worlds which distinguish themselves from terms like H_20 which have strict borders.[3]

The Śabara-Bhāṣya asserts something similar. In the Śabara-Bhāṣya quotation, the discerning reader must have noticed that the compound *vedavākyāni* –vedic texts– keeps on recurring without comment. The compound *vedavākyāni* is not explained; it stands by itself as self-explanatory. And indeed, for the Vedic Indian it was self-explanatory. To understand this, we need to take a detour and in order to reach the threshold of the Mīmāṃsā mystery of *apauruṣeya śabda* with which the Vedic Indian was familiar but not the later generations. From earliest times, the Mīmāṃsā tradition, as handed down by the Jaiminisūtras and the Śabara-Bhāṣya (=commentary on the Jaiminisūtras), the phrase *apauruṣeya śabda* has been employed and consistently understood as language that is untouched, untainted, uncaused, uncreated by any Puruṣa, (Apuruṣa, from there *apauruṣeya*).[4]

The *apauruṣeya śabda* was a foundational *belief* of the adherents of the Mīmāṃsā tradition resting on the *experience* of everyday language. The other traditions unable to make sense of this originary inspiration consistently

2 Eric Frauwallner, *Materialien zur ältesten Erkenntnislehre der Karmamīmāmsā* (Wien: Hermann Böhlaus Nachf./Graz-Wien-Köln, 1968, 11): Die Bedeutungen, in welchen die Wörter im täglichen Leben gebräuchlich sind, dieselben Bedeutungen haben sie, sofern es möglich ist, auch in den Sūtren; das ist festzuhalten. Es ist weder auf Grund von Ergänzungen usw. eine Bedeutung derselben anzunehmen noch terminologisch festzuhalten. Denn auf diese Weise werden nur die vedischen Sätze durch die (Sūtren) erklärt. Andernfalls müssten die vedischen Sätze erklärt werden, und die Bedeutungen der eigenen Wörter erklärt werden. Und dadurch würde sich so große Mühseligkeit der Arbeit ergeben.

3 See R. Panikkar's "Words and Terms" in: M.M. Olivetti (Ed.), *Esistenza, Mito, Ermeneutica* (Rome:1980), 117-133.

4 *The Vedic Experience*, 14: "In short, the fact that the Vedas have no author and thus no anterior authority, the fact they possess only the value contained in the actual existential act of really hearing them, imparts them a universality that makes them peculiarly relevant today. They dispose us to listen and then we hear what we hear, trusting that it is also what was to be heard."

ridiculed it.[5] Now, in what does the experience of everyday language consist? This tradition speaks of the *apauruṣeya śabda*, of *vedavākyāni* and *vedavākyam*.

The later stages of the Mīmāṃsā tradition seemed to have lost the stress on the *experience* of everyday language.[6] Instead of reflecting deeply on the depth-dimension of everyday language they took to analyzing and explaining the external structures of language, its syllables, words and word-meaning, sentences and sentence-meaning, etc. The shift in discussion had started. From the level of *experiencing* they had descended to *explaining*. Historically, that was the beginning of their downfall.

Neither the later Mīmāṃsā teachers nor the scholars from the opposition had a deeper understanding of the basic core of the Mīmāṃsā but spent their time squabbling about petty details. The scholars I visited to get some enlightenment on Mīmāṃsā made it abundantly clear that they are as much at sea as I was, proving that the Mīmāṃsā tradition was long dead. Most of them were not even interested in the subject and were surprised at my interest.

Then unexpectedly I came across an article by an Australian friend of mine, Gerhard Hall, wherein a footnote had the following to say: "Panikkar says that he derives his notion of 'primordial language' from the *apauruṣeya* insight of the Vedas. The claim here is that there is no (human) authorship. The language of the Vedas is, in this understanding, an 'ultimate language.' There is no need for authors or other interpreters."[7] Following this clue, I discovered that

5 When I was researching for my book on the Mīmāṃsā, one of my friends who was a well-known Sanskrit Professor in a Pune college said he would take me to a famous Pandit in Deccan College who was conversant with all the Darśanas. He could hopefully be of help to me and that he would accompany me. Together we went to Deccan College where my friend introduced me to the Pandit who received us in the library where a number of people were working. For starters, I asked him whether he could help me with the question of *apauruṣeya śabda*. Hardly had I had uttered the words, the Pandit launched a tirade against the Mīmāṃsā fools. When I dared to interrupt him to remind him that the Mīmāṃsā had written such wonderful things, he turned to my friend to say, this fellow is not as stupid as he appears! At that moment, I realized that he had not grasped the uniqueness of the Mīmāṃsā contribution and that I was wasting my time with this wise Pandit. In my *Śabdaprāmāṇyam in Śabara and Kumārila*. Towards a Study of the Mīmāṃsā Experience of Language (Vienna: De Nobili Research Library Vol. VII, University of Vienna, 1980) in Ch. II. I have quoted in the footnotes serious authors who say what they think of the Mīmāṃsā. It speaks volumes of their Mīmāṃsā scholarship. They have not distinguished the contribution of the wholly originary inspiration of the early Mīmāṃsā, namely, of the Jaiminisūtras and the Śabara-Bhāṣya who spoke of *apauruṣeya śabda*, and concentrated, so to say, on the scholastic development of the Mīmāṃsā—in much the same way that one would entirely overlook the original teaching of Jesus and exclusively concentrate on later doctrinal Christianity!

6 It has to do with *experience*, not with *doctrine*.

7 Gerhard Hall, "Raimon Panikkar's Intercultural and Interreligious Hermeneutics", in Clemens Mendonca/Bernd Jochen Hilberath (Eds.), *Religion and Culture. A Multicultural*

later Hall had done his PhD on Panikkar's hermeneutics.[8] This pithy reference was for me only the tip of the iceberg. This will not mean much to people who are not at home in the subject. This justifies my beginning *ab ovo*. My task is to point out the originality of the Mīmāṃsā contribution, and Panikkar's brilliant retrieval of the *apauruṣeya* insight in our age with an equally well worked out application of his hermeneutics of a text in his monumental work *The Vedic Experience.* This well rounded out effort of Panikkar's might appear frighteningly complicated but is not so as we shall proceed step by step. In all this, I shall make use of Panikkar's words as far as possible so that his thinking dominates the entire effort. There is method in his madness, as will be evident from the following.

2. *Diatopical Hermeneutics*

The Vedic world was an altogether different world from ours. Seeing its remarkable relevance, Panikkar's ambition is to interpret *The Vedic Experience* for our times. He discusses diverse hermeneutical approaches required for different hermeneutical problems in his "What is Comparative Philosophy Comparing?"[9]

> Diatopical hermeneutics is the required method of interpretation when the distance to overcome, needed for any understanding, is not just a distance within one single culture (morphological hermeneutics), or a temporal one (diachronic hermeneutics), or rather the distance between two (or more) cultures, which have independently developed in different spaces (*topoi*) their own methods of philosophizing and ways of reaching intelligibility along with their proper categories.

A little later Panikkar adds:

> Diatopical hermeneutics has to proceed without necessarily assuming these myths [of other cultures] as a priori condition of intelligibility.[10]

Discussion. Festschrift in Honour of Francis X. D'Sa SJ. (Pune: Institute for the Study of Religion, 2011), 100-115, here 109 fn.45.

8 Gerhard Hall, Raimon Panikkar's Hermeneutics of Religious Pluralism, PhD dissertation, Catholic University of America (Ann Arbor: UMI, 1994).

9 Raimon Panikkar, "What is Comparative Philosophy Comparing?" In G. J. Larson/E. Deutsch (Eds.) *Interpreting Across Religious Boundaries* (Princeton: University Press, 1988), 130.

10 Raimon Panikkar, "What is Comparative Philosophy Comparing?" 131.

> Taking a hint from Vedic wisdom as developed mainly in Mīmāṃsā, I would like to propose the *apauruṣeya* insight as a main principle of diatopical hermeneutics. The *apauruṣeya* insight says that the Vedas have no author not because there is no scribe or poet who uttered those words for the "first time", but because they are primordial language containing primordial words, and thus, with no need for some author behind them to explain what they mean. If this were not the case the author should again explain the meaning through another language, and so on ad infinitum. The Vedas stand for primordial symbols by means of which we know what is existentially important and by means of which we come to know also other things. The sense of a symbol is in the symbol itself. If we were to need another symbol to explain its sense, this second "thing" would be the real symbol. *Apauruṣeya* stands for primordial language in order to communicate what it means.
>
> The human being is an *animal loquens*, but we do not speak language. We speak a language, and other people speak other languages which we do not know. The primordial language is hidden in our respective languages not as a language, of course but as language. In the effort of communicating with one another—at the beginning without proper understanding, then slowly by dispelling false imaginations and misconceptions—we forge a common language, we reach a mutual comprehension, we cross the boundaries. This is what I call dialogical philosophy. It is not the imposition of one philosophy or one mode of understanding, but the forging of a common universe of discourse taking place not once for all, but in the very encounter.[11]

Panikkar's phenomenological description shows how we gradually notice the new relations of everyday symbols in our everyday language.

And lastly:

> We do not assume here any hermeneutical circle. We create that circle through the existential encounter. We do not start a dialectical dialogue, which accepts a priori some rule before the dialogue takes place. The theory here cannot be severed from the praxis.
>
> Diatopical hermeneutics is not just theory. The rules here do not precede the understanding nor the theory the praxis. At the same time, the praxis implies the theories of the meeting partners.

11 Raimon Panikkar, "What is Comparative Philosophy Comparing?" 132.

> Both are present and required … Diatopical hermeneutics are not universal. They function, generally speaking, between two different *topoi*, not between many. They bring one culture, language, or religion, making it understandable. Diatopical hermeneutics is an art as much as a science, a praxis as much as a theory. It is a creative encounter, and there is no blueprint for creativity.[12]

The justification for this chain of quotations is that, as far as I am aware, this is the only place where Panikkar explains at length his *Apauruṣeya* insight. It is indispensable to follow the path of his insight. This is important not only for the Veda and the Mīmāṃsā but for all intercultural dialogue. His diatopical hermeneutics reveals what we always do without knowing that we are doing it. This is how we also come to know persons and learn new languages.

3. *The Vedic Experience*

At this stage, we need to see now how Panikkar goes about putting this into practice. In *The Vedic Experience*[13] Panikkar reveals the hermeneutics of his enterprise which is germane to our professions.[14] He writes:

> The aim of this anthology is to make available to modern Man the riches of the elders and thus to globalize human experience. If there is one thing that characterizes and even distinguishes the Vedic experience, it is its sacrificial character, its overall feature of orthopraxis.
>
> The Vedic experience does not move on a merely theoretical level; it does not carry a doctrinal message, but a universal form of human celebration. Modern Man is inclined today to accept the idea that he is not saved by reason alone or liberated by willpower alone. He seeks an active participation in the overwhelming dynamism of the universe, in which his involvement is possible only if it is actively passive. *And this could be said to be the core of the experience of Vedic Man: that he is called upon to perform the sacrifice that makes the world and even the Gods subsist.*[15] My highlighting

---

12 Raimon Panikkar, "What is Comparative Philosophy Comparing?" 133.

13 It is striking that Panikkar speaks of Vedic *Experience*, Vedic *Epiphany*, Vedic *Revelation* (my highlighting). The point is that relevance does derive from repeating but from experiencing.

14 Panikkar writes: "In hardly any other culture in the world has the fountainhead been paid more lip service but received less real attention." R. Panikkar, *The Vedic Experience. Mantramañjarī. An Anthology of the Vedas for Modern Man and Contemporary Celebration* (Pondicherry: All India Books, 1977), 14.

15 R. Panikkar, *The Vedic Experience*, 27.

Panikkar explicitly comments on the title of this *Opus* and, among other things, says:

> But the intention of this *mantramañjarī* is not 'translation'[16] but representation; that is, its goal is an existential reenactment. It does not desire to turn the symphony into a poem, but to play the music again, even though the instruments are not the same and the skill of the original composer is missing We do not want to put the music into words or to translate the words into dance. *Our aim is to speak the words, to play the music, to perform the dance, to utter the prayers, to sing the songs, to wonder, love, doubt, suffer, hope, and believe along with those documents of human history which we call the Vedas.* Even if the instruments are poor and the key is not the same, we may still perceive the original, not by a 'translation' but by a reenactment that allows us both to hear the '*sruti*' directly and perhaps even to transmit its vibrations, just as it was heard long ago by the ancients and as we continue to hear it insofar as our ears are open to those same vibrations.[17]

The goal of our commitment is not "to turn the symphony into a poem" but "to play the music again", "even if the instruments are poor and the key is not the same, we may still perceive the original", *mutatis mutandis*. Furthermore, trained as we are in the western methods of historical research, we are in danger of missing the bus of speaking relevantly to Gandhi's India, as Soares-Prabhu wanted us to in his impassioned contribution "Commitment and Conversion".[18]

4. The Texture of a Text: Panikkar's Hermeneutics of a Text[19]

Panikkar formulates his thesis in five Sūtras (threads):

1. A text is a word, crystallized in matter, space, time and Man. This first sūtra (thread) links text with Man.

---

16 Panikkar had sent me without comment a review in a Chennai paper by the internationally known Prof. Raghavan, the Chair of Sanskrit Studies at Madras University with the sarcastic title "A Padre translates Vedic Texts" or some such wording. It doesn't appear that Prof. Raghavan had read this Introduction of *The Vedic Experience* before writing the review.

17 *The Vedic Experience*, p.27. The highlighting is mine.

18 George M. Soares-Prabhu, "Conversion and Commitment: A Biblical Hermeneutic for India Today", in *Theology of Liberation. An Indian Biblical Perspective*. Collected Writings of George M. Soares-Prabhu, S.J. vol.4, ed. Francis X. D'Sa (Pune: Jnana-Deepa Vidyapeeth, 2001), 24-52.

19 Panikkar's "The Texture of a Text: In Response to Paul Ricoeur", *Point of Contact*, New York (1978), II 1, 51-64.

2. A text says. This second sūtra links text with word.
3. A text says what it means. This third sūtra links text with meaning.
4. A text means whatever meaning can be extracted from it. This fourth sūtra links text with present human life.
5. The meaning of a text emerges from an ever-elusive horizon. This sūtra links text with *mythos*.

Man is the starting-point of the discussion because Man, poet and artist, is engaged in the work of *poēsis*, [=making, that is, making sense of the world] preeminently with the help of word. Panikkar goes a step further and states "A text is a word which also crystallizes in Man qua Man. The word becomes 'inworded' in Man. Man himself is a kind of document: he bears within him, like a living library, a fantastic amount of crystallized language, not only in his memory, but also in the circumstances of his historical existence. Historical Man has a been impressed by the words of his predecessors. Cultural Man is himself a written document, a living text. He learns how to express himself out of the impression he has received."[20]

In the second sūtra there is a distinction made between "Man speaks but a text says."[21] For a text to be a text there has to be a special relationship between the reader and the document. There has to be an intelligent or spiritual being who reacts to and reads the document. "A text is a text only insofar as this inner relation between the document and the reader is maintained. A text is culture and history in a very special way. Only Man is a speaking being, but a text is also a saying reality…A text—in this integral sense I am taking it—is a real embodiment of Man's spirit: it transcends human individuality without ceasing to be human."[22]

The third sūtra links saying with meaning. Panikkar introduces here the distinction between speaking and a written text. In the context of oral word the speaker can restrict the meaning but not so when the text is written. A written text is polysemous because there is no speaker to restrict its meaning. Panikkar perceives three basic meanings of a text:

1. The text says what its author wanted it to mean. A text sticks to what the author intended.
2. A text is inserted in a context on which it depends. The meaning of a text depends both on the context of the author and on the context of the text. Panikkar calls the first (*Lebenswelt*) the *circumstance* and the context of the text (*Umwelt*) its *situation*.

20 Panikkar's "The Texture of a Text: In Response to Paul Ricoeur", 57.

21 Panikkar's "The Texture of a Text: In Response to Paul Ricoeur", 57.

22 Panikkar's "The Texture of a Text: In Response to Paul Ricoeur", 58.

3. The situation of the text is distinct from its circumstance. Both are part of the context. With that Panikkar distinguishes three elements: (i) the *document* (the text) and its context which is made up of (ii) the *circumstance* of the author and (iii) the *situation* of the text. The document contains the author's intended work and also what the situation of the text offers from the constant changes that various historical elements offer. So, it is not surprising that some of the later situations reject the positions of earlier situations. Thus, down the ages a stream of disparate interpretations arises.[23]

But we need another element to make a text, which Panikkar calls the *texture* of the text. "This set of relations formed between the text and the reader is what I have called the texture of the text, i.e., the loom composed of the interrelation between the written document and reading people. The reading community forms the tradition of the text. And this tradition is enriched or enlarged by the hermeneutical effort of the readers."[24]

Fourth sūtra: Here we see the linking of the document with present human life. We question the text and in turn the text questions us. In this wrestling with the text, Panikkar asserts, "a text has whatever meaning can be extracted from it. Now, this *can* is not arbitrary. Some meanings simply cannot be extracted from a given text...Yet there are creative moments when the proper questioning of a text yields a meaning which until then was not present in the text. Creative hermeneutics is already considered a proper phase of hermeneutics."[25]

Panikkar illustrates this with the insightful example of the translator who "makes the original intelligible precisely because he makes the text meaningful within another set of references. He creates a new texture between the document and the new readers that enables them to understand the text. A good translation has to be close to the original, but if the distance were zero it would destroy the translation."[26] Panikkar makes it clear that each translation brings in new shades of meaning—not found in the original—which enrich the text by enlarging its texture.[27]

"The meaning of a text, then, is revealed through a double movement on the part of reader, testing and contesting the text: a passive movement of contemplation, understanding, assimilation, and an active dynamism of action, working, struggling with the text. We *do* something with a text and thereby the text triggers, as it were, concealed potentialities, leads to action, becomes a

23 Panikkar's "The Texture of a Text: In Response to Paul Ricoeur", 59-60.

24 Panikkar's "The Texture of a Text: In Response to Paul Ricoeur", 60.

25 Panikkar's "The Texture of a Text: In Response to Paul Ricoeur", 60.

26 Panikkar's "The Texture of a Text: In Response to Paul Ricoeur", 61.

27 Panikkar's "The Texture of a Text: In Response to Paul Ricoeur", 61.

work—a *leitourgia*, an act of the people."[28] "In other words, the text serves to orient the reader. Now, the Orient—where the sun of intelligibility dawns—is always just beyond the horizon."[29]

Fifth sūtra: The meaning of a text emerges from an ever-elusive horizon. This sūtra links text with *mythos*.

Interestingly, Panikkar distinguishes between reading or decoding a document, and interpreting a text. Interpreting means 'converting the given text into a texture in which we are involved'.[30] Further: "We read a text only when we 'co-read' the context so as to form our texture."[31] More importantly, "... the final step for the intelligibility of any text dawns only over an unquestioned horizon. This horizon is ever changing, ever elusive and, in a way, ever moving with the winds of the spirit. It constitutes the mythos of any given culture."[32]

In this context Panikkar makes the significant comment: "The context is the proper mythos.[33] But each time we become conscious of some context, we convert this later into part of the given 'text' and somebody else (perhaps ourselves at a later stage) will discover the proper context of our horizon. There is a constant movement between mythos and logos."[34] We cannot control this double movement. It is the privilege of the original thinker, the creative artist or the stroke of genius to modify that dynamism of horizons.[35]

Panikkar makes it clear that polysemy does not mean a chaotic anarchy of meanings. He locates three basic meanings of a text.

First: The text says what its author wanted it to mean.

Second: A text says more than what its author intended. The meaning of a text depends on the context of its maker and of the text itself. Panikkar calls the context (*Lebenswelt*) of its maker the *circumstance* and the context of the text itself its *situation*. Whereas the first stresses the world of the writer, the second refers to the successive interpretations over the course of time.

Here Panikkar distinguishes between reading and interpreting. Reading has primarily to do with decoding the signs but interpreting is understanding a text. "We interpret a text by putting it over against a context and extracting its meaning. We do not read a context; otherwise, by definition, it would become

28 Panikkar's "The Texture of a Text: In Response to Paul Ricoeur", 61.

29 Panikkar's "The Texture of a Text: In Response to Paul Ricoeur", 61.

30 Panikkar's "The Texture of a Text: In Response to Paul Ricoeur", 61.

31 Panikkar's "The Texture of a Text: In Response to Paul Ricoeur", 61.

32 Panikkar's "The Texture of a Text: In Response to Paul Ricoeur", 61.

33 For a longer discussion of *mythos* and *logos*, see Panikkar's *Myth, Faith and Hermeneutics* (New York (Paulist Press: 1985); Bangalore (Asian Trading Corporation 1983).

34 Panikkar's "The Texture of a Text: In Response to Paul Ricoeur", 62.

35 Panikkar's "The Texture of a Text: In Response to Paul Ricoeur", 61.

a text. Now, we interpret a text when the situation and the circumstance allow us to understand the text by placing it in an intelligible field and thus converting the document into a living text."[36] One who does not know the language of the text will be unable to interpret it. It is not enough to decode. On the other hand, there are readers in course of time who disagree with the author because of their particular circumstance; in spite of being bound to tradition has a degree of freedom to express their disagreement and become part of the interpreting community. (Third) Here Panikkar adds a cryptic comment: "A text, as crystallized words, has the character of a sacrament: It works *ex opere operato*."[37] My guess is that Panikkar is referring to the following. In the sacramental enactment, the conscious will of the celebrant (*ex opere operantis*) is not essential for the validity of the action. The celebrant has responsibility to perform the action and the action has its own dynamism, as it were. Now the text has its own dynamism. The dynamism here refers to its participation in the hermeneutical circle that emerges as soon as the understanding process begins. The text evokes questions and the readers' answers are conditioned by their respective contexts.

The process is like a texture. "Only when the interpretation encompasses both the given text and the world of the reader, so that both share the same universe, only then does the document become a living text with an impact on the reader, an influence which leads to assimilation or reflection: only then have we a real text in from of us. This set of relations formed between the text and the reader is what I have called the texture of the text, i.e. the loom composed of the interrelation between the written document and the reading people. The reading community forms the tradition of the text. And this tradition is enriched or enlarged by the hermeneutical effort of the readers."[38]

With this background, we begin to understand the effort put in by Panikkar in *The Vedic Experience* to bring us "*…to speak the words, to play the music, to perform the dance, to utter the prayers, to sing the songs…*"

5. The Myth of History

For this section, the best is Panikkar's own summary in his *The Cosmotheandric Experience*[39] at the beginning of Part Two: The End of History. The Threefold Structure of Human Time-Consciousness, p.82:

> Man is a temporal being. His experience of time has three focal points: the past, the future and the present. The predominance of

36 Panikkar's "The Texture of a Text: In Response to Paul Ricoeur", 59.

37 Panikkar's "The Texture of a Text: In Response to Paul Ricoeur", 60.

38 Panikkar's "The Texture of a Text: In Response to Paul Ricoeur", 60.

39 Raimon Panikkar, *The Cosmotheandric Experience* (Maryknoll, NY: Orbis Books, 1993), 82.

> the one or another of these foci makes up the three kairological moments to which I have alluded. The development of all three time-experiences accounts for the maturity of the human being—phylogenetically and ontogenetically. When the past is the paradigm though which we experience time, we have the nonhistorical moment (memory and faith are central); when it is the future, historical consciousness prevails (the will and hope are predominant); and when past and present are lived terms of the present, we share in the transhistorical experience of reality (the intellect and love become fundamental)
>
> These three moments in human consciousness correspond to three periods of human existence on Earth—in the indicated sense of the word *period*. We could even date these periods.
>
> Until the invention of writing, Man could not project all his creations into the future; the past had the most powerful grip on him. Tradition was paramount. Time comes from a Beginning. *Mythos*.
>
> With the invention of writing, human specialization becomes possible. Progress is a sacred word. Time marches forward. The future belongs to God and God to the future. *History*.
>
> When Man split the atom, the seemingly indestructible elements on which the entire world rested showed their vulnerability. The human technological miracle has itself been fissioned. The atoms of all sorts (spiritual and intellectual as well) are no longer indestructible). The past is broken, and the future collapses. The present is the only time left. And it is this experience that opens the door to the predominance of the *Mystical*.

Panikkar concludes his chapter on Transhistorical Consciousness with these words:

> My essay here has been to render plausible the thesis that *the exclusive dominance of the myth of history, on the one hand, and historical consciousness, on the other, are both coming to an end.* Man is embarking upon a new venture, about which we know only that we shall act the more freely the more we allow the internal dynamism of our deepest being to express itself, without projecting beforehand what we are to do and to be. We are creatively participating in the very existence of the cosmotheandric reality.[40]
> My highlighting.

40 Raimon Panikkar, *The Cosmotheandric Experience*, 131.

Conclusion: The Purpose of this Plea

I have picked out relevant quotations from Panikkar's hermeneutics and *The Vedic Experience* to achieve the same aim as Panikkar "*...to speak the words, to play the music, to perform the dance, to utter the prayers, to sing the songs...*"

To do this Panikkar had first to accomplish the following:

Having clearly articulated his aim, he had to work out all the possible themes that could be worked out from the texts, order them and comment upon them. One of the earliest chapters I read from the *The Vedic Experience* was Sacrifice (Yajña) with its solemn introductory quotation (This sacrifice is the navel of the world. RV I, 164,35[124].) I cannot ever forget the deep impression it made upon me. Reading the commentaries, I begin to understand what the task implies: "*...to speak the words, to play the music, to perform the dance, to utter the prayers, to sing the songs...*" It was my entry-point to the heart of Hindu spirituality and my life-long study of the Bhagavad-Gītā. [Just for curiosity's sake I add: My delight in the Gītā made me produce a *Word-Index to the Gītā* and *Word-Index to Śaṅkara's Gītā-Bhāṣya*.]

I have relied on Panikkar because I have studied him and found that he has worked consistently and critically; above all, he has sought to be holistic. There has been steady growth in his ideas. The advantage with his work is that it is really interreligious and intercultural and in no way sectarian.

But there may be other giants whom others may have discovered, studied and who have contributed similarly. India is such a vast country that one tends to ignore or is ignorant of the many contributions in the vernacular. As Panikkar put it when introducing his book *The Cosmotheandric Experience* "Colligite Fragmenta – For an Integration of Reality!" We all face a similar challenge, where integration of reality is concerned.

Why have I explained this *per longum et latum*?

There is a suggestion that I wish to make. Can we Indian Exegetes, especially the young generation, do something homologous with our *Indian Biblical Experience*? This is not a task for a single person but for different persons of different generations engaged in hermeneutics, Indology (not just Sanskrit but the different traditions of the poet-saints in the different languages of our country), and most especially, biblical studies, systematic theology, pastoral theology, history, etc., etc.? A younger group could over a weekend reflect and work out a tentative coordinating scheme that suggests how various inputs could, like mosaic stones, contribute towards an *Indian Biblical Experience*...It could be an on-going programme or something in that direction.

Biographical Sketch and Publications of Prof. Dr. Scaria Kuthirakkattel, SVD

Prof. Dr. Scaria Kuthirakkattel, SVD was born on 29th January 1940 at Kurumulloor, a village near Ettumanoor, Kerala, to the very religious parents Joseph and Elizabeth. He joined the Society of the Divine Word (SVD) in 1959 and underwent the initial stages of formation at Indore, M. P. He did his philosophical and theological studies at Jnana-Deepa Vidyapeeth, Pune. After the ordination (1971) and a short period of pastoral ministry at Bandra, Mumbai, he was sent to Pontifical Biblical Institute, Rome for licentiate in Sacred Scripture. After completing licentiate he returned to Pune in 1976 to teach at Jnana-Deepa Vidyapeeth, Pune. Having taught 5 years at Jnana-Deepa Vidyapeeth, he returned to Rome to do his doctorate in Biblical Theology at the Gregorian University, Rome, and his thesis was published by the Pontifical Biblical Institute (Analecta Biblica, 123). Since then he had been a regular staff of the Faculty of Theology at Jnana-Deepa Vidyapeeth and held the office like the Head of the Department (Sacred Scripture) and Dean of the Faculty of Theology etc. He taught Scripture 35 years at Jnana-Deepa Vidyapeeth and various other theological centres. He taught courses like the Gospel according to Mark, Theology of the New Testament, Introduction to the New Testament, The Passion and the Resurrection Narratives etc.

Publications

Book

The Beginning of Jesus' Ministry According to Mark's Gospel (1:4 to 3:6): A Redaction Critical Study (Analectca Bilblica 123: Rome, Pontifical Biblical Institute, 1990).

Books Edited

A Biblical Theology for India: Collected Writings of George M. Soares-Prabhu, SJ, Vol. 2 (Jnana-Deepa Vidyapeeth Theology Series, 1999).

Biblical Spirituality of Liberative Action: Collected Writings of George M. Soares-Prabhu, SJ, Vol. 3 (Jnana-Deepa Vidyapeeth Theology Series, 2003).

Articles

"Eucharistic Celebration in the Early Church", in *Bible Bhashyam*, March 1978, 49-64.

"Social Justice in the Old Testament", in *Bible Bhashyam*, 1978, 163-192.

"Law and Freedom in St. Paul", in *Bible Bhashyam*, September 1980, 265-288.

"Jesus' Prayer", in *Bible Bhashyam*, 1981, 160-185.

"Christian Prayer", in *Bible Bhashyam*, September 1981, 201-224.

"The Man-made Temple and the God-made Sanctuary: Key Aspects of the New Testament Theology on Temple", *Jeevadhara*, 23 (1993), 153-170.

"Christ, The Self-Emptying High Priest", in: *The Dharma of Jesus: Interdisciplinary Essays in Memory of George Soares-Prabhu, S.J.,* (ed. Francis X. D'Sa), Pune: Institute for the Study of Religion and Anand: Gujarat Sahilya Prakash, 1977, 102-177.

"Meaning and Function of Jn 2:1-11", in *Bible Bhashyam*, June 1998, 79-102.

"Johannine Perspective of Sacraments", in *Bible Bhashyam*, September 1998, 149-171.

"Symbols and Sacraments in the Fourth Gospel", in *The World as Sacrament*, (ed. Francis X. D'sa *et al*), Pune: Jnana-Deepa Vidyapeeth, 1998, 73-128.

"The Radicality of Jesus' Priesthood", in *Bible Bhashyam*, June 1999, 85-103; September 1999, 200-243.

"Formation of Christian Leaders: A New Testament Perspective", *Jnanadeepa*, 3(2000), 63-79.

"Fundamentalism: Biblical Perspectives", *Jnanadeepa*, 6(2000), 24-47.

"One Jesus and Manifold Expression of His Mission", in: *Led by the Spirit: Mission, Formation and Spirituality*, (ed. Mohan Doss SVD), DWS, ISPCK, Delhi: Cambridge Press, p. 3-33.

"George M. Soares-Prabhu, S. J.: An Exegetic and a Theologian", *Vidyajyoti*, 73 (2009), 759-771, 816-826.

"Revelation and Faith in Marcan Perspective", *Jeevadhara*, 2013, 114-123.

"Poverty in Palestine during Jesus' Time, Poverty in India in Our Time", *Journal of Indian Theology*, May-August, 7 (2014), 7-29.

"Experience and Context: The Basis of Jesus' Dharma", *Jnanadeepa*, 2(2015), 57-76.

"The Role of Prophetic Theologizing in Jesus' Dharma", Jnanadeepa, 2(2015), 77-96.

"Jesus Community: Marcan Perspective" (*forthcoming in VJTR*).

"Reconciliation: Insights from Pauline Letters" (forthcoming in *VJTR*).

"Who is on Trial? A Critical Reading of John 18:28-19:16a" (forthcoming in *VJTR*).

Divine Disclosure and Human Response: Johannine View" (forthcoming in *Journal of Indian Theology*).

Contributors

Bryan Lobo, SJ: Bryan Lobo is the current Dean of the Faculty of Missiology at the Gregorian University in Rome. After doing his doctorate in theology, Fr. Lobo taught in the Faculties of Theology and Missiology at the Gregorian University. He is also visiting professor at the Dharmaram College in Bangalore and St. Pius X College in Goregaon Mumbai. He has co-edited two books: Enlightenment and Tantra: Hindus and Christians in Dialogue; Maximum Ilud. La missione tra storia e attualità. He has various articles to his credit published in different journals and periodicals. Fr. Lobo's research interests are Christian theology, Theology of religions and Theology of mission in a pluralistic world. E-Mail: bryanlobo@jesuits.net

C. Sunil Ranjar, SJ: Sunil Ranjar is a Jesuit priest belonging to the Karnataka province. He is a Lecturer of New Testament Greek and exegesis at the Pontifical Biblical Institute in Rome and is a visiting Faculty at the Regional Theological Centre of the Jesuits in Bangalore and Ryshivana, Indian Institute of Christian Spirituality, Mangalore. E-Mail: cliffysj@gmail.com.

Dominic S. Irudayaraj, SJ: Dominic S. Irudayaraj, a Jesuit of Andhra Province, teaches biblical exegesis at Pontificio Istituto Biblico, Rome. He is also a visiting Professor at Hekima College, Nairobi, Kenya, and a Research Associate at University of Pretoria, South Africa. In addition to Masters' Degrees in Information Technology (M.S.) and Theology (Th.M), Irudayaraj holds Licentiate (S.T.L.) and Doctoral (S.T.D.) Degrees in Theology from Jesuit School of Theology of Santa Clara University, USA and a Licentiate Degree in Sacred Scripture (S.S.L.) from Pontificio Istituto Biblico. His recent publications include *Violence, Otherness, and Identity in Isaiah 63:1–6: The Trampling One Coming from Edom*, LHBOTS 633 (London: Bloomsbury T&T Clark, 2017) and "Micah" in *New Jerome Biblical Commentary*, 2nd rev.

ed., edited by John J. Collins, Gina Hens-Piazza, Barbara Reid, and Donald Senior (London: Bloomsbury, 2020). E-Mail: irudayaraj@biblico.it

Errol Fernandes, SJ: Errol Fernandes is a Jesuit of the Bombay Province. He is the Vice-Principal (Commerce) of St. Xavier's College, Mumbai and lecturer in Accountancy. He is also a Visiting Lecturer in Scripture at St. Pius X Seminary, Goregaon, Mumbai and JDV, Pune. He has given numerous retreats to the laity, seminarians, priests and religious. He has also conducted six "Net Retreats" for laity and religious from all parts of the world. He has his own blog http://errolsj.blogspot.com/ on which he posts every day and also his own YouTube Channel https://www.youtube.com/channel/UCejo1B53RYH9X2a9RtAsYtA?view_as=subscriber on which he uploads reflections on the daily readings. E-Mail: errolsj@jesuits.net

Francis X. D'Sa SJ: Francis X. D'Sa is emeritus Professor of Systematic Theology and Indian Religions, and Director, Institute for the Study of Religions, Pune. Since 1975 he is the visiting Professor in Innsbruck, Guestprofessorships at the Univ. Frankfurt (Theologie Interkulturell), Uni. Salzburg (Theologie Interkulturell), University of Fribourg (Switzerland), etc. He was also the Endowment professor for Missionswissenschaft und Dialog der Religionen at the University of Würzburg, Germany from 2003 to 2008. He was awarded Honorary Doctorate in Philosophy from the University of Frankfurt/M, Germany (2007) and Theology from the University of Tubingen, German (2016). His publications in English and German include Intercultural Theology and Hermeneutics. E-Mail: francis.x.dsa@gmail.com

Henry Pattarumadathil, SJ: Henry Pattarumadathil is a Jesuit priest belonging to the Kerala Province, and teaches New Testament Greek and exegesis at the Pontifical Biblical Institute, Rome, and currently serves as the Dean of the Biblical Faculty at the Pontifical Biblical Institute, Rome. He was the Director and Superior of the Regional Theology Centre, Sameeksha, Kalady and Province Coordinator for formation. E-Mail: henrypattar@gmail.com

Isaac Padinjarekuttu: Isaac Padinjarekuttu is a priest of the Diocese of Kohima, Nagaland. He did his theological studies at Jnana-Deepa Vidyapeeth, Pune and obtained a doctorate in theology from the Philosophisch-Theologische Hochschule Sankt Georgen, Frankfurt am Main, Germany. From 1994 to 2016 he was Professor of Church History at Jnana-Deepa Vidyapeeth, Pune, where he was also Dean of the Faculty of Theology. From 2006 to 2011 he was Principal of St. Joseph's College (Autonomous) Jakhama, Nagaland and from 2012 he is Professor of Church History at Oriens Theological College, Shillong. He has authored/edited ten books and published more than hundred articles on various theological topics. E-Mail: padinjarekuttu@gmail.com

Jacob Kavunkal, SVD: Jacob Kavunkal retired from Jnana-Deepa Vidyapeeth, Pune, in 2008 as Reader and Director of Post Graduate studies. Later he was Associate Professor and Head of the Department of Theology and Mission at the Yarra Theological Union/University of Divinity, Melbourne. As a Vising Professor he has taught in the Philippines, United States, Myanmar and Sri Lanka. His latest book is *Extensio Dei- Mission as Divine Reaching Out*. E-Mail: jkavunkalsvd@gmail.com

Jacob Parappally, MSFS: Prof. Dr. Jacob Parappally holds a doctorate in Theology from the University of Freiburg, Germany. He was teaching systematic theology at Jnana-Deepa Vidyapeeth (JDV) Pune for 14 years where he served as the dean of the Faculty of Theology. He is a visiting professor of many theological faculties in India and abroad. He was the rector of Tejas Vidya Peetha, Institute of Mission-Oriented and Contextual Theology, Bangalore and was the President of the Indian Theological Association (2005-2011). He is the author of *Emerging Trends in Indian Christology, The Meaning of Jesus Christ: An Introduction to Christology, A Way of the Cross for Today* and the editor or co-editor of another 10 books. He translated the second book on Jesus Christ by Pope Benedict to Malayalam. He published more than 200 theological articles. He is the chief-editor of the *Journal of Indian Theology*. E-Mail: Jacob.Para@gmail.com

Naveen Rebello, SVD: Naveen Rebello is a Divine Word Missionary belonging to the SVD India Mumbai Province. He holds a Licentiate in Scripture (S.S.L) from the Pontifical Biblical Institute, Rome. Currently, he is a doctoral student at the same institute in Rome, specializing in the Synoptic Gospels. From 2016-2018, he was a member of the Department of Scripture at Jnana-Deepa Vidyapeeth (JDV), Pune. He has taught various courses in the OT, NT and classical languages at JDV and other Theology and Philosophy Institutes and Regional Seminaries in India. E-mail: naveensvd@gmail.com

Paul Rolphy Pinto, SJ: Paul Rolphy Pinto is a Jesuit belonging to the Gujarat Province of the Society of Jesus. Currently he is teaching in the Institute of Spirituality of the Gregorian University, Rome. His areas of interest are themes concerning Ignatian spirituality and inter-religious spirituality. He also engages in retreat direction and spiritual accompaniment. E-Mail: pinto@unigre.it

Saji Joseph Kizhakkayil: Saji Joseph Kizhakkayil is a priest of the Diocese of Bhadravati. He taught Theology in the RTCs of Vidya Jyoti, Delhi (Varanasi and Patna) and philosophy (research methodology) in VJG, Varanasi. He holds a Doctorate in the Old Testament from the University of Innsbruck. From March 2011 he worked as the assistant parish priest at different parishes in Germany and in Austria. At present he is a parish priest in the diocese of

Innsbruck, Austria, as well as, the Curate of the local Fire brigade and of the Schützenkompanie (Civil-defense Company). He writes Biblical articles in German magazines. E-Mail: kizhakkayilsaji@gmail.com

Simon Thomas, SJ: Simon Thomas is a Jesuit priest from the Gujarat Province of the Society of Jesus. He did his ecclesiastical studies in Satya Nilayam, Chennai, Gujarat Vidya Deep, Vadodara, and Jnana Deepa Vidyapith, Pune, before getting ordained in 2012. He worked for three years in a tribal parish in South Gujarat. Later he did his licentiate in Sacred Scripture from Pontifical Biblical Institute, Rome in 2019. Currently, he is serving as Assistant Parish Priest in Isunath Mandir, Zankhvav, in South Gujarat. E-Mail: simon.thomas@jesuits.net

Thomas Manjaly: Thomas Manjaly is a priest of the Archdiocese of Shillong. He has been teaching New Testament at Oriens Theological College, Shillong and in other Theological Institutes in India for over three decades. He has presented papers and written extensively on various biblical themes, particularly on mission, evangelization and ministry. He served as a member of the Pontifical Biblical Commission for two terms (2009-2019). He was also a special invitee as theological expert for the XIII Ordinary Assembly of the Synod of Bishops on "New Evangelization for the Transmission of the Christian Faith" (7-28 October 2012). Email: tmanjalyotc@gmail.com

Thomas Karimundackal, SJ: Thomas Karimundackal teaches Old Testament at the Faculty of Theology, Jnana-Deepa Vidyapeeth, Pune, and currently serves as the Head of the Department of Scripture Studies, and coordinator of the Masters Programme in Biblical Studies at JDV. He has presented several research papers in many national and international conferences, and published many books, and articles in national and international Journals as well as in edited books. He is also a visiting faculty in many seminaries and colleges in India and abroad. E-mail: tomksj@gmail.com

Thomas Malipurathu, SVD: Thomas Malipurathu is emeritus Professor of Sacred Scripture at JDV, Pune. He has a licentiate in Sacred Scripture from the Pontifical Biblical Institute in Rome and a doctorate in Biblical Theology from the Pontifical Gregorian University. He is presently an associate staff of Ishvani Kendra, Institute of Missiology and Communications, Pune, where he was also its director (1996-2002), and continues to teach biblical subjects at JDV and other theological centers. E-Mail: malipurathu@gmail.com

Wilson D'souza, OFM Cap.: Wilson D'souza is a Capuchin Friar belonging to St. Bonaventure Province of Maharashtra. He has done his licentiate from St. Peter's Bangalore and doctorate from Angelicum, St. Thomas University,

Rome. He is a visiting faculty at JDV, Pune and other theological institutes in India. Presently, he is one of the counsellors in the Province of Maharashtra and vice-rector at La-Verna Theologate, Pune. He gives retreat, seminar to the various religious congregations and teaches Bible and does mission preaching to the Laity. E-mail: wilsondoz@yahoo.com